Sayyids and Sharifs in Muslim Societies

The global Muslim population includes a large number of lineal descendants and relatives of the Prophet Muḥammad. These kinsfolk, most often known as "*sayyid*s" or "*sharīf*s," form a distinct social category in many Muslim societies, and their status can afford them special treatment in legal matters and in the political sphere.

This book brings together an international group of renowned scholars to provide a comprehensive examination of the place of the kinsfolk of Muḥammad in Muslim societies, throughout history and in a number of different local manifestations. The chapters cover:

- how the status and privileges of *sayyid*s and *sharīf*s have been discussed by religious scholars;
- how the prophetic descent of *sayyid*s and *sharīf*s has functioned as a symbolic capital in different settings;
- the lives of actual *sayyid*s and *sharīf*s in different times and places.

Providing a thorough analysis of *sayyid*s and *sharīf*s from the ninth century to the present day, and from the Iberian Peninsula to the Indonesian Archipelago, this book will be of great interest to scholars of Islamic, Middle East and Asian studies.

MORIMOTO Kazuo is an Associate Professor of Islamic and Iranian History at the Institute for Advanced Studies on Asia, University of Tokyo.

New horizons in Islamic studies (second series)
Founding editor: Professor SATO Tsugitaka
Series editor: Professor YUKAWA Takeshi

This second series of "New horizons in Islamic studies" presents the abundant results of the National Institutes for the Humanities (NIHU) program for Islamic Area Studies (IAS) carried out in Japan from 2006 to date. This program emphasizes multidisciplinary research on the dynamism of Muslim societies, in both Islamic and non-Islamic areas around the world. By taking a historical approach and adopting regional comparison methods in the study of current issues, the program seeks to build a framework of empirical knowledge on Islam and Islamic Civilization.

Islamic Area Studies is a network comprised of five research centers, at Waseda University, the University of Tokyo, Sophia University, Kyoto University, and the Toyo Bunko (Oriental Library). As of 2008, this network has been brought into the fold of a Ministry of Education, Culture, Sports, Science and Technology (MEXT) program, with the Organization for Islamic Area Studies at Waseda University serving as its central office. As research centers recognized by the MEXT, we aim to promote the development of joint research institutions in the human and social sciences, thereby further developing fruitful joint research achievements.

This publication of the results of our IAS joint research has and will have been made possible through the collaborative efforts of the five IAS centers, and with the financial assistance of the NIHU and the MEXT.

The Moral Economy of the Madrasa
Islam and education today
Edited by SAKURAI Keiko and Fariba Adelkhah

Asiatic Russia
Imperial power in regional and international contexts
Edited by UYAMA Tomohiko

Sayyids and Sharifs in Muslim Societies
The living links to the Prophet
Edited by MORIMOTO Kazuo

Previously published in the New horizons in Islamic studies series

Persian Documents
Social history of Iran and Turan in the fifteenth to nineteenth centuries
Edited by KONDO Nobuaki

Islamic Area Studies with Geographical Information Systems
Edited by OKABE Atsuyuki

Muslim Societies
Historical and comparative aspects
Edited by SATO Tsugitaka

Intellectuals in the Modern Islamic World
Transmission, transformation and communication
Edited by Stéphane Dudoignon, KOMATSU Hisao and KOSUGI Yasushi

Popular Movements and Democratization in the Islamic World
Edited by KISAICHI Masatoshi

Sayyids and Sharifs in Muslim Societies

The living links to the Prophet

Edited by
MORIMOTO Kazuo

Routledge
Taylor & Francis Group
LONDON AND NEW YORK

First published 2012
by Routledge
2 Park Square, Milton Park, Abingdon, Oxon OX14 4RN

Simultaneously published in the USA and Canada
by Routledge
270 Madison Ave, New York, NY 10016

Routledge is an imprint of the Taylor & Francis Group, an Informa business

British Library Cataloguing in Publication Data
A catalogue record for this book is available from the British Library

Library of Congress Cataloging in Publication Data
Sayyids and sharifs in Muslim societies: the living links to the Prophet/edited by Kazuo Morimoto.
p. cm. – (New horizons in Islamic studies (second series))
Includes bibliographical references and index.
1. Muhammad, Prophet, d. 632 – Family. 2. Muhammad, Prophet, d. 632 – Genealogy. 3. Religion and social status – Islamic countries. I. Morimoto, Kazuo, 1970–
BP76.8.S394 2011
297.6′4—dc23 2011040538

ISBN 978–0–415–51917–5 (hbk)
ISBN 978–0–203–12315–7 (ebk)

Typeset in Times New Roman
by Florence Production Ltd, Stoodleigh, Devon

Printed and bound in the United States of America by Publishers Graphics, LLC on sustainably sourced paper.

Contents

List of illustrations vii
List of contributors ix
Acknowledgments and Notes xii

Introduction 1
MORIMOTO KAZUO

PART I
Arguing *sayyid*s and *sharīf*s **13**

1 **How to behave toward *sayyid*s and *sharīf*s: a trans-sectarian tradition of dream accounts** 15
MORIMOTO KAZUO

2 **Qur'ānic commentary on the verse of *khums* (al-Anfāl VIII:41)** 37
ROY PARVIZ MOTTAHEDEH

3 **Debate on the status of *sayyid/sharīf*s in the modern era: the ʿAlawī–Irshādī dispute and Islamic reformists in the Middle East** 49
YAMAGUCHI MOTOKI

PART II
***Sayyid*s and *sharīf*s in the Middle East** **73**

4 **Genealogy, marriage, and the drawing of boundaries among the ʿAlids (eighth–twelfth centuries)** 75
TERESA BERNHEIMER

5 A historical atlas on the ʿAlids: a proposal and a few samples 92
BIANCAMARIA SCARCIA AMORETTI

6 The reflection of Islamic tradition on Ottoman social structure: the *sayyids* and *sharīfs* 123
RÜYA KILIÇ

7 The *ashrāf* and the *naqīb al-ashrāf* in Ottoman Egypt and Syria: a comparative analysis 139
MICHAEL WINTER

PART III
***Sayyids* and *sharīfs* beyond the Middle East** **159**

8 *Shurafā* in the last years of al-Andalus and in the Morisco period: *laylat al-mawlid* and genealogies of the Prophet Muḥammad 161
MERCEDES GARCÍA-ARENAL

9 The role of the *masharifu* on the Swahili coast in the nineteenth and twentieth centuries 185
VALERIE J. HOFFMAN

10 *Dihqāns* and sacred families in Central Asia 198
ASHIRBEK MUMINOV

11 Sacred descent and Sufi legitimation in a genealogical text from eighteenth-century Central Asia: the Sharaf Atāʾī tradition in Khwārazm 210
DEVIN DEWEESE

12 Trends of ashrāfization in India 231
ARTHUR F. BUEHLER

13 The *sayyids* as commodities: the Islamic periodical *alKisah* and the *sayyid* community in Indonesia 247
ARAI KAZUHIRO

Index 267

Illustrations

Figures

0.1 Muḥammad's close relatives (simplified) 10
10.1 *Qayrāq* I (Q-050), dated 553/1158–9 201
10.2 *Qayrāq* II (Q-067), dated 560/1165 202
10.3 *Qayrāq* III (Q-126), dated 607/1210 203
11.1 Descendants of Sharaf Ata (simplified) 224
13.1 Cover of *alKisah*, no. 2, year six (cover portrait is Ḥabīb ʿUmar) 254
13.2 *Sayyid*s' portraits in the editorial office of *alKisah* 257

Maps

5.1a Historical events involving the Ḥasanīs (based on al-Bukhārī, *Sirr al-silsila*, tenth century) 95
5.1b Persecutions of the Ḥasanīs (based on al-Bukhārī, *Sirr al-silsila*, tenth century) 96
5.1c Presence of Ḥasanī individuals (based on al-Bukhārī, *Sirr al-silsila*, tenth century) 97
5.1d Locations of Ḥasanīs' descendants (based on al-Bukhārī, *Sirr al-silsila*, tenth century) 98
5.2 Possible birthplaces of Ḥasanīs' concubines (based on al-Bukhārī, *Sirr al-silsila*, tenth century) 99
5.3a Locations of Ismāʿīl b. Jaʿfar's descendants (based on al-Bukhārī, *Sirr al-silsila*, tenth century) 101
5.3b Locations of Ismāʿīl b. Jaʿfar's descendants (based on al-ʿUmarī, *al-Majdī*, eleventh century) 102
5.4a Ḥasanīs' migrations to Qum (based on Qumī, *Tārīkh-i Qum*, tenth century) 105
5.4b Ḥasanīs' migrations from Qum (based on Qumī, *Tārīkh-i Qum*, tenth century) 106
5.4c Locations of the descendants of the Ḥasanīs in Qum (based on Qumī, *Tārīkh-i Qum*, tenth century) 107

5.5a Ḥusaynīs’ migrations to Qum (based on Qumī, *Tārīkh-i Qum*, tenth century) 108
5.5b Ḥusaynīs’ migrations from Qum (based on Qumī, *Tārīkh-i Qum*, tenth century) 109
5.5c Locations of the descendants of the Ḥusaynīs in Qum (based on Qumī, *Tārīkh-i Qum*, tenth century) 110

Tables

1.1 Sectarian derivations of the edifying stories recorded in four Shiʿite sources (seventeenth–twentieth centuries) 20
1.2 Sunnite sources of the stories presented in the four Shiʿite sources (seventeenth–twentieth centuries) 23
1.3 Overlapping of the stories among the Sunnite story collections 25
5.1 The symbols and shadings used in the maps 113
6.1 The list of *naqīb*s in the Ottoman Empire 126

Contributors

Arai Kazuhiro is an Associate Professor at Keio University, Tokyo. He earned his Ph.D. from the University of Michigan in 2004 for "Arabs who Traversed the Indian Ocean: The History of the al-ʿAttas Family in Hadramawt and Southeast Asia, c.1650–c.1960." He has been conducting research on the people of Ḥaḍramawt in the Indian Ocean since the mid 1990s. His main research sites are Indonesia and Ḥaḍramawt. His recent interest is the commodification of Islam and the *sayyid*s in Southeast Asia, especially in Indonesia.

Teresa Bernheimer is a Lecturer in the History of the Near and Middle East in the Early Islamic Period at the School of Oriental and African Studies, University of London. She earned her Ph.D. from the University of Oxford in 2006 for "A Social History of the ʿAlid Family from the Eighth to the Eleventh Century" (currently under revision for publication). Her research focuses on the origins and socio-historical development of religious and social elites in the central and Eastern Islamic lands, and she is coeditor of a volume on Iran from Late Antiquity to Early Islam, entitled *Late Antiquity: Eastern Perspectives* (2011).

Arthur F. Buehler is a Senior Lecturer in the Religious Studies Programme of Victoria University, Wellington, New Zealand. He received his Ph.D. from Harvard University in 1993, specializing in Sufism in South Asia. His first book, *Sufi Heirs of the Prophet* was followed by a set of indexes for Aḥmad Sirhindī's *Maktūbāt*, *Fahāris-i taḥlīlī-yi hashtgāna-yi Maktūbāt-i Aḥmad-i Sirhindī* in 2001. A selected translation of Sirhindī's letters is forthcoming in 2012. He is a senior editor of the *Journal of the History of Sufism.*

Devin DeWeese is a Professor in the Department of Central Eurasian Studies at Indiana University; he earned his Ph.D. at Indiana University in 1985. He is the author of *Islamization and Native Religion in the Golden Horde: Baba Tükles and Conversion to Islam in Historical and Epic Tradition* (1994) and of numerous articles on the religious history of Islamic Central and Inner Asia; recent publications focus on problems of Islamization, on the social and political roles of Sufi communities, and on Sufi literature in Persian and Chaghatay Turkic.

Mercedes García-Arenal is a Research Professor at the Centro de Humanidades y Ciencias Sociales, CSIC, Madrid. She is a historian of the Muslim West, with special focus on religious and cultural history. Her book *Messianism and Puritanical Reform: Mahdīs of the Muslim West* (2006) dealt with *shurafā*, Sufism, and messianic figures. She has worked also on religious minorities in the Iberian Peninsula, Muslim and Jewish converts to Christianity, Jews in al-Andalus and Morocco. Her latest books are: *Ahmad al-Mansur: The Beginnings of Modern Morocco* (2009) and, together with Fernando R. Mediano, *Un Oriente español: Los moriscos y el Sacromonte en tiempos de Contrarreforma* (2010).

Valerie J. Hoffman is a Professor of Religion and Director of the Center for South Asian and Middle Eastern Studies at the University of Illinois at Urbana-Champaign. She earned her Ph.D. in Arabic and Islamic Studies from the University of Chicago in 1986 with a dissertation on the religious lives of Muslim women in contemporary Egypt. Her writings include *Sufism, Mystics and Saints in Modern Egypt* (1995), *The Essentials of Ibadi Islam* (2011) and numerous articles on Islamic gender ideology, Sufism, Ibadism, Islam in East Africa and contemporary Islamic thought.

Rüya Kılıç is an Associate Professor of History at the University of Hacettepe. She earned her Ph.D. from the University of Hacettepe in 2000 for her dissertation, *The Sayyids and Sharifs in the Ottoman Empire* (in Turkish; published in 2005). Her areas of interest are Ottoman thought and Sufism. Her current research focuses on the Islamic tradition in late Ottoman and early Republican Turkey. She published *The Transmitters of Islamic Tradition from the Ottoman Empire to the Turkish Republic* (in Turkish; 2009) in this area.

Morimoto Kazuo is an Associate Professor of Islamic and Iranian History at the Institute for Advanced Studies on Asia, University of Tokyo. He earned his Ph.D. from the University of Tokyo in 2004 for his dissertation "*Sayyid*s, Genealogists, *Naqīb*s: A Study of the Genealogical Literature on *Sayyid/Sharīf*s from the Late Tenth–Early Fifteenth Centuries" (in Japanese). His publications in English include "The Prophet's Family as the Perennial Source of Saintly Scholars: Al-Samhudi on *ʿIlm* and *Nasab*" (forthcoming), "The Earliest ʿAlid Genealogy for the Safavids" (2010) and "Toward the Formation of Sayyido-Sharifology" (2004).

Roy Parviz Mottahedeh is the Gurney Professor of History at Harvard University, where he obtained his AB and Ph.D. in History. He has received an honorary doctorate from Lund University in Sweden and has been awarded MacArthur and Guggenheim Fellowships. He is the author of three books, *Loyalty and Leadership in an Early Islamic Society* (1980), *The Mantle of the Prophet: Religion and Politics in Iran* (1985) and *Lessons in Islamic Jurisprudence* (2003). He is also the author of numerous articles on topics ranging from the ʿAbbasids to the Shiʿites of contemporary Iraq.

Ashirbek Muminov is a Deputy-Director of the Institute of Oriental Studies, Ministry of Education and Science, Republic of Kazakhstan (Almaty). He earned his Ph.D. from the Department of Near East, Institute of Oriental Studies, St Petersburg, Russia in 1991 for "Maḥmūd ibn Sulaymān al-Kafawī (Sixteenth Century) on the History of Ḥanafī School in Central Asia." Since 1992 he has been conducting research on the sacred places and the genealogies of *sayyid*s and *khwāja*s in Central Asia. He is currently preparing two books for publication: *Islamization and Sacred Lineages in Central Asia: The Legacy of Isḥāq Bāb in Narrative and Genealogical Traditions* (in two volumes; in cooperation with D. DeWeese) and *Genealogical Tree of Mukhtar Auezov* (in Russian).

Biancamaria Scarcia Amoretti is a Professor Emeritus at Rome University "La Sapienza." She began her training at the Istituto Orientale of Naples. Most of her scientific productions are dedicated to the spread of Shiʿism, as in the historical overview presented in *Sciiti nel mondo* (1994), with a particular focus on Iran. From there, she became deeply involved in the history of the *Ahl al-Bayt* and its role in the history of the Muslim world. In 1998 she organized the first international colloquium, held in Rome, on *The Role of the* Sâdât/Ašrâf *in Muslim History and Civilization* (Proceedings in *Oriente Moderno* n.s. 18/2 [1999]). Most of her recent publications are dedicated to this subject.

Michael Winter is a Professor Emeritus of the History of the Middle East at Tel Aviv University. He earned his Ph.D. in Islamic Studies at UCLA (1972). His research includes social, cultural and religious themes (such as *ʿulamāʾ*, Sufis, *qāḍī*s, and *ashrāf*) in Egypt and Syria under the Mamluks and the Ottomans, based on the Turkish archives and Arabic and Turkish chronicles and biographies. He has published *Society and Religion in Early Ottoman Egypt: Studies in the Writings of ʿAbd al-Wahhāb al-Shaʿrānī* (1982; paperback, 2007), and *Egyptian Society under Ottoman Rule, 1517–1798* (1992; Arabic translation, 2001). He has co-edited four books, and published numerous scholarly articles.

Yamaguchi Motoki is a Ph.D. Candidate at the Graduate School of Letters, Keio University (Tokyo). His principal research interest is Islamic reformist movements in modern Indonesia, especially those in the local Arab communities. He is currently conducting his doctoral research on the activities of *al-Irshād*, a reformist association established by the Arabs in Indonesia in the early twentieth century. Special light will be shed on the thought and role of its founder, Aḥmad b. Muḥammad al-Sūrkatī. His publications include "Methodological Approach to the Study of ʿAlawī–Irshādī Dispute" (in Japanese, 2006).

Acknowledgments

This volume originates from the international conference "The Role and Position of Sayyid/Sharīfs in Muslim Societies," held on 22–23 September 2009 at the Institute of Oriental Culture (now the Institute for Advanced Studies on Asia), at the University of Tokyo.

I would like to thank, first and foremost, the members of my "task force," Ms Tsuji Asuka (aka *wazīra*), Mr Isahaya Yoichi (*buna-dār*), Mr Mizukami Ryo (*ghulām-bāshī*) and Dr David Durand-Guédy (*sulṭān-i sābiq*), without whose dedication the conference could never have materialized. I would also like to express my sincere gratitude to the members of the organizing committee and panel chairs, Professors Akahori Masayuki, Hamada Masami, Kisaichi Masatoshi, Nigo Toshiharu, Sato Kentaro, Takahashi Kei, Tonaga Yasushi and Yukawa Takeshi. On the financial side, the conference was made possible only through the generous support of the Japan Society for the Promotion of Science (grant-in-aid International Scientific Meetings in Japan); NIHU Program IAS Center General Office at Waseda University; the IAS Center at Sophia University; the IAS Center at Kyoto University; and the University of Tokyo's Institute of Oriental Culture. I would like to thank all these bodies and institutions for the trust they put in me and in my conference.

This volume is published in the series "New horizons in Islamic studies." I would like to dedicate it to the memory of the former editor of the series, my undergraduate and graduate mentor, the late Professor Sato Tsugitaka.

Morimoto Kazuo
Tokyo, July 2011

Notes on the text

1 All the dates given alone are Common Era, unless otherwise noted. When dates are also given in the Islamic calendar (*Hijrī*), the *Hijrī* date is placed first, followed by a slash and the corresponding date in the Common Era. The same system is used for giving dates in the Solar *Hijrī* calendar used in Iran, but with the addition of "AHS" to those dates, as in 1385 AHS/2006–7.

2 Following the style adopted in this series, personal names in Japanese are given in their original order of family name first. Exceptions are the authors' names that are presented in the conventional Western order in publications in European languages, which are reproduced here as they appear in the referenced publication.

Introduction

Morimoto Kazuo

The world today is home to a great number of putative lineal descendants – and collateral relatives – of Muḥammad, the Prophet of Islam. Let us begin by sharing three recent episodes involving some of these kinsfolk of the Prophet.

Episode I: The film *Close-Up* (1990) by the renowned Iranian film director Abbas Kiarostami is an intricate cross between documentary and fiction, featuring a man apprehended for falsely presenting himself as Mohsen Makhmalbaf, a leading figure of Iranian cinema. The film re-enacts the interaction between the cinema-loving "conman" and his "victims," the Āhankhāh family, as well as the trial of the case before a judge. Just as the trial is approaching its conclusion, an interesting incident takes place in the film. The defendant's mother, clad in a black chador, suddenly steps forward and begins to plead with the judge that he should consider the prophetic descent of her son when handing out his sentence. It is true that this incident may not have taken place in reality. However, Kiarostami must certainly have thought that the scene would not appear unrealistic to his audience.

Episode II: Three days after Saddam Hussain was captured by the American troops in a burrow near Takrit, the "Syndic of *Sharīfs*" (*Naqīb al-Ashrāf*) of Iraq, named al-Sharīf al-Aʿrajī, held a press conference. The *naqīb* announced that the investigation by the "Committee of Genealogies" (*Lajnat al-Ansāb*) confirmed that the prophetic descent claimed by the deposed president was utterly false. Saddam, he said, had forced genealogists to approve and sign his baseless genealogy. Further, the *naqīb* stated, Saddam had had a plan to establish the "*Niqābat al-Ashrāf*" (Syndicate of *Sharīfs*) and to become the *naqīb* himself; a plan that was thwarted by the passive resistance of the *sharīfs* themselves. Al-Sharīf al-Aʿrajī was representing the new *niqāba* that was established after the collapse of Saddam's regime, and which held its first meeting two days earlier with the theme, "For the Construction of New Iraq."[1]

Episode III: In March 2010, a new action planned by the Saudi lawyer Faisal Yamani attracted the attention of the press. After getting the Danish newspaper *Politiken* to apologize for having offended Muslims by reprinting the well-known cartoons featuring the Prophet, he sent a "pre-action" letter to the ten other newspapers that had refused to apologize, and announced that he was planning to file a libel case against them with a London court. Yamani had been representing eight associations of the Prophet's descendants from eight countries (Egypt, Libya, Qatar, Jordan, Saudi Arabia, Lebanon, Palestine and Australia) through these processes. Yamani was seeking to sue the newspapers on the ground that the reprinting of the cartoons amounted to defamation against the approximately 95,000 direct descendants of the Prophet that he was representing.[2]

As shown by these episodes, the Prophet's kinsfolk, who are most frequently called by the honorific titles "*sayyid*" (pl. *sāda*, *sādāt*) or "*sharīf*" (pl. *ashrāf*, *shurafā'*), have formed and still form a distinct social category in many Muslim societies. Their lineage may be adduced when an exceptional legal treatment is sought for them. It also constitutes symbolic capital to which a political leader seeking to enhance general perception of his or her qualifications may resort. Moreover, these people, in a good number of cases, possess enough cohesion to form organizations beyond their immediate families in order to promote their shared interests. Reliable statistics showing the number of the Prophet's kinsfolk, spread all through the Muslim world and far beyond it, are not available. Even a conservative estimate, however, would suggest that the number of kinsfolk is in the tens of millions.[3]

The idea that the Prophet's kinsfolk must be differentiated from the rest of the population and be given special treatment in one way or another has been shared by many, if not most, interpretations of Islam. It might appear quite natural to many readers when, for example, the Twelver Shiʿite scholar al-Shaykh al-Ṣadūq Ibn Bābūyah (d. 381/991) writes:

> Our belief concerning the ʿAlids [the descendants of the Prophet's paternal cousin ʿAlī b. Abī Ṭālib, who form the core of the Prophet's kinsfolk; see below] is that they are the Family of the Apostle of God (*Āl Rasūl Allāh*) and that loving them is obligatory (*mawaddatuhum wājiba*).[4]

Those readers may point out (somewhat rhetorically) that Shiʿites, after all, consider the leadership of the Umma (Muslim community) to be the birthright of the Prophet's family. What then is the opinion of the Ḥanbalite scholar Ibn Taymiyya (d. 728/1328) in his *Minhāj al-sunna al-nabawiyya*, a refutation against nothing other than Twelver Shiʿism? This paragon of the traditionalist Sunnism also writes:

> There is no doubt in that Muḥammad's Family (*Āl Muḥammad*) has a right on the Umma that no other people share with them and that they are entitled to an added love and affection to which no other branches of the Quraysh are entitled.[5]

Certainly, the opinions of various Muslim religious scholars, including al-Ṣadūq and Ibn Taymiyya, can be markedly different when it comes to more concrete questions, such as who exactly constitute the Prophet's kinsfolk, what the special treatments are that they are entitled to, or why they must be treated differently from the rest of the people. However, the base line that the Umma considers the Prophet's kinsfolk to constitute a special category within the community and that a particular respect or regard should be offered to them has evidently been shared rather widely by various interpretations of Islam through the centuries.

* * *

It is with these people, *sayyid*s and *sharīf*s, that the present volume, *Sayyids and Sharifs in Muslim Societies: The Living Links to the Prophet*, is concerned. This volume originates from the international conference "The Role and Position of Sayyid/Sharīfs in Muslim Societies," held on 22–23 September 2009 at the University of Tokyo. Needless to say, both the conference and the volume represent the conviction that our present knowledge about *sayyid*s and *sharīf*s is still insufficient and that more scholarly attention should be paid to them. Let me, however, elaborate a little further on the context that brought the conference and the volume into being.

It has long been a rather well-known fact not only among those living in Muslim societies in various regions but also among those who have observed and tried to understand those societies, that *sayyid*s and *sharīf*s – or *ḥabīb*s, *salip*s or *mīr*s, to use just a few examples of the more localized honorific titles used to refer to the Prophet's kinsfolk in certain regions – constitute a ubiquitous component of those societies and are commonly held in special regard. Sixteenth-century Europeans who read Nicolas de Nicolay's (1517–1583) descriptions of the contemporary Ottoman society, for example, could not only obtain basic knowledge about the *emīr*s (another title for the Prophet's kinsfolk) but also enjoy a beautiful woodprint illustration of an *emīr* wearing a green turban, the most prevalent marker of prophetic descent, both then and now.[6]

Because of this general recognition, it is not so difficult to find sporadic references to *sayyid*s and *sharīf*s in historical or anthropological studies pertaining to Muslim societies, for example. We even find systematic accumulations of knowledge concerning the *sayyid*s or *sharīf*s of the societies where they are recognized as having played an especially conspicuous role. Morocco, Ḥaḍramawt and the Ḥaḍramī diaspora in the Indian Ocean world are the cases in point. Missing until recently, however, was a serious attempt to establish a coherent understanding of *sayyid*s and *sharīf*s as a whole through a synthesis of different local manifestations. The approach prevalent in the relevant literature has treated the special status of *sayyid*s and *sharīf*s as though it was a well-understood, and accepted fact, and has presented respective findings in the locales studied as evidence of distinctive manifestations of this well-known phenomenon across the Muslim world. Without an overarching framework to enable the comparison and synthesis of those different local cases, there was only a dim possibility that this "fact," which had been accepted without being seriously examined, would be constructively challenged and substantiated.[7]

The first serious attempt to overcome this situation was marked by the international colloquium "The Role of the *Sâdât/Ašrâf* in Muslim History and Civilization," held in 1998 by Biancamaria Scarcia Amoretti of Rome University. This colloquium put together the studies on relevant cases "from Morocco to Indonesia" for the first time, and indicated that beyond a successful synthesis of seemingly disparate cases might emerge new, coherent knowledge on *sayyid*s and *sharīf*s. The periods covered by the conference also ranged widely from the ninth to the twentieth century, and scholars of history, anthropology and even history of science presented their findings. Furthermore, the presenters included *sayyid*s and *sharīf*s themselves, who furnished the colloquium with "insiders' views." The proceedings of this colloquium were published as a special issue of *Oriente Moderno* the next year.[8]

The Tokyo conference in 2009 was conceived exactly as the "second round," about a decade after, of the Rome colloquium. My interest in *sayyid*s and *sharīf*s had begun well before the Rome colloquium, when I started studying the discipline of *sayyid/sharīf* genealogies with special reference to its role in the control of the prophetic descent.[9] For this reason – as well as for the very personal reason that the colloquium was indeed the first international gathering in which I presented a paper – I came to feel a strong attachment to the Rome colloquium. I began to hold keen interest in whether the nascent "sayyido-sharifology" (my own neologism), the possibility of which was demonstrated by the Rome colloquium, would steadily be continued and developed; I even began to nurture some sense of responsibility for this myself.

With the vague idea of holding a second conference in Tokyo, I published in 2004 an article on the state of the field, titled "Toward the Formation of Sayyido-Sharifology: Questioning Accepted Fact."[10] The article pointed out the absence of a proper framework of research pertaining to *sayyid*s and *sharīf*s, and made some proposals as to how this might be formulated and established. For example, in pointing out the necessity to synthesize the findings concerning different times and places, it suggested that the affinity between popular Sufism and prophetic descent (many Sufi saints are believed to have been *sayyid*s or *sharīf*s) or the *naqīb*-centered social cohesion might serve as an initial point of comparison. This "academic manifesto" also indicated the desirability of research on Muslim discourses about the Prophet's kinsfolk, for the *sayyid*s and *sharīf*s in the realm of discourse may also serve as a useful point of reference to locate different local manifestations in the realm of reality. In order to convince the readers of the significance of studying *sayyid*s and *sharīf*s, the article urged them to recognize that the ubiquitous presence of the Prophet's kinsfolk indicated the favorable attitudes different Muslim societies had shown toward them. Thus, it was argued, to understand those people better would also help understand their respective societies better. At the same time, the article also pointed out that prophetic descent had often been closely associated with other important notions, such as political legitimacy, sainthood, or moral integrity. It would follow then that the elucidation of the particular characteristics accorded to that descent would also contribute to a further clarification of those notions that might appear unrelated at the first glance.

Fortunately, the possibility of holding the conference became more and more real, and the initial contacts with prospective presenters began in 2007. In my invitation, I asked future presenters to take the mentioned state-of-the-field article into account when deciding their topics. At the same time, I proposed simple thematic axes for the conference, namely, "A. Muslim discourses about the household of Muḥammad or *sayyid/sharīf*s (both for and against); B. Historical experiences and historiography of *sayyid/sharīf*s in different Muslim societies; and C. Anthropological and sociological approaches to *sayyid/sharīf*s today."[11] It was of course noted that the topics combining these, especially studies falling under themes B. or C., but also A., would also be welcomed.

This is the story of how the conference came to be held. It goes without saying, however, that the organizer has only a limited capacity to set the tone of an academic conference. The actual contents and directions are always decided by a complex series of "chemical reactions" between the organizer's intentions and the different sets of knowledge and interests represented by the various participants. The Tokyo conference was of course not an exception. The present volume, thus, represents a re-enactment of the chemistry that unfolded in Tokyo for two days between my intentions – as outlined above – and the reactions toward them, both from the podium and the floor.

* * *

The present volume comprises thirteen chapters in three parts. Part one, "Arguing *Sayyid*s and *Sharīf*s," consists of three chapters focusing mainly on the question of how the status and privileges of the Prophet's kinsfolk have been discussed by Muslim religious scholars. In the first chapter, I take up the topic of edifying stories comprising dream accounts, often found in books on the merits of the Prophet's kinsfolk. Those stories, armed with the vividness of dream accounts and the general belief in Islamic cultures to the veracity of dreams, instruct the audience as to how they should behave toward *sayyid*s and *sharīf*s. In this chapter, in addition to clarifying the morals advanced by those stories, I uncover the fact that the overwhelming majority of the stories presented by Shiʿite authors do actually originate from earlier Sunnite works.

Chapter Two by Roy Parviz Mottahedeh discusses *khums* (one fifth), the most well-known economic privilege of *sayyid*s and *sharīf*s. It is the Āya 4 of Sūra VIII in the Qurʾān that offers the ground to the claim that a part of *khums* must be handed out to the Prophet's relatives. Not all Muslims, however, interpret the verse that way. Mottahedeh's extensive survey of Qurʾān exegeses by authors of different strands through the centuries elucidates how divergently this particular verse has been understood. This study broadens at once our knowledge of the opinions concerning the distribution of *khums*, which until now had mostly been confined to the developments among Twelver Shiʿites.

The subject of Yamaguchi Motoki's chapter is the ʿAlawī–Irshādī dispute, a rather well-known dispute in the early twentieth century that involved the Ḥaḍramī *sayyid*s of Southeast Asia. Unlike the existing literature on the subject, Yamaguchi sheds light on the Umma-wide dimensions of the dispute. He focuses on the reconciliation efforts made by Shakīb Arslān and Muḥammad Rashīd Riḍā in the early 1930s, and reconstructs what the two Islamic reformists said concerning the privileges of the Prophet's kinsfolk. Detailed explanation of the reactions the antagonizing camps gave to their interventions is also offered. This study captures an important moment in the transformation of the discourses about *sayyid*s and *sharīf*s in the modern era when Islamic reformism came to exert strong influence.

Parts two and three of the volume comprise the chapters that mainly discuss actual *sayyid*s and *sharīf*s in different times and places. The first two chapters of part two, "*Sayyid*s and *Sharīf*s in the Middle East," deal with the early process through which the Prophet's kinsfolk turned into a ubiquitous social category found throughout the region (and beyond). The subject of Teresa Bernheimer's chapter is the ʿAlid marriage strategy from about the eighth to the twelfth century. Bernheimer points out that the exogamous marriages of the ʿAlids in the earlier centuries mirror the political relations among the Arab ruling elites. This, however, is no longer true with the centuries after the ninth, when the ʿAlids' marriage partners in the ever rarer cases of exogamy came to hail from new types of elites that were no longer limited to the Arabs. As the significance of being Arab waned, the ʿAlids came to differentiate themselves increasingly in terms of their distinctive descent. Bernheimer also notes that the exclusivist marriage strategy by the ʿAlids was by no means sanctioned as part of Islamic law by contemporaneous jurisprudents, including those of Twelver Shiʿism.

Chapter Five by Biancamaria Scarcia Amoretti presents a blueprint of an ambitious joint research project. To what extent is it useful to visualize in map format various pieces of information, such as the records of migrations, pertaining to the history of the ʿAlids? Scarcia Amoretti presents thirteen sample maps based on the sources from the tenth to the eleventh century, and demonstrates the potentials of her "Historical Atlas of the ʿAlids" project. Even the basic pilot maps enable her to make fresh observations concerning the history and migrations of the ʿAlids in the first centuries of Islam. It is a pity that this volume cannot present the full strength of the maps, which are to be produced and circulated as digital GIS data.

Both Chapters Six and Seven discuss the *sayyid*s and *sharīf*s under Ottoman rule. Rüya Kılıç's chapter presents the situation of Istanbul and Anatolia in the sixteenth and seventeenth centuries on the basis of rich archival materials, especially the registers of the *naqīb al-ashrāf*s of the Empire.[12] Kılıç's wide-ranging topics include prosopographical examination on *naqīb*s, contemporaneous ideas concerning the descent from the father's and mother's side as well as the related question of the distinction between the two honorific titles "*sayyid*" and "*sharīf*" and the stances taken by different actors in society with regard to the privileges of the Prophet's kinsfolk. Further, Kılıç discusses how we can understand the status of *sayyid*s and *sharīf*s in the context of the well-known division of the Ottoman society into the *ʿaskerī* and *reʿāyā* classes.

Depicted in Chapter Seven by Michael Winter are the *sayyid*s and *sharīf*s in Egypt and Syrian cities. Winter pays full attention to the specific contexts in respective locales and avoids generalizations. For example, he makes it clear that the formation of a political faction of *ashrāf* under the leadership of the *naqīb*, a well-known development in Aleppo, did not happen in the other places that he discusses. Even in the two cases in Egypt and Jerusalem where a *naqīb* emerged as a major political leader, their wards did not constitute their power base. The institution of the *niqāba* could indeed take different features in accordance with local contexts even within the two neighboring regions ruled by the same dynasty.

Part three, "*Sayyid*s and *Sharīf*s beyond the Middle East," comprises six chapters. Mercedes García-Arenal's chapter takes on a seemingly unapproachable topic, that is, *sayyid*s and *sharīf*s in al-Andalus under the later Nasrids and in the Morisco society under Christian rule. Direct evidence of the activities of *sayyid*s and *sharīf*s in these societies is almost non-existent. Thus, the main strategy that García-Arenal takes is to identify the parallel to the attested symptoms of the rise of "*charifisme*" in contemporary Morocco. Through her analysis of the various types of sources in Arabic, *Aljamia* (Spanish written in Arabic script) and Spanish, details about the roles played by *sayyid*s and *sharīf*s emerge from behind the stories of such phenomena as the rise of Sufism and *zāwiya*s, the spread of *mawlid* celebration, and the prevalence of reverence of the Prophet.

Chapter Nine by Valerie J. Hoffman vividly illustrates the situation on the modern Swahili coast. *Masharifu* (plural of *sharif* in Swahili) in the region, most of whom are Ḥaḍramī in origin, had (until the nineteenth century) enjoyed undisputed respect and reverence as holy people like in many other Muslim societies. Hoffman, however, observes that we can no longer regard the *masharifu* as a dominant social class today. Hoffman describes the process through which the dominance of the *masharifu* has been gradually undermined since the second half of the nineteenth century. The impacts of Islamic reformism and African nationalism, the two big waves that washed the Muslim societies on the Swahili coast, are discussed in detail in her chapter.

Chapters Ten and Eleven explore cases from Central Asia. Ashirbek Muminov in Chapter Ten focuses on the title "*dihqān*," used in the pre-Mongol period. Based primarily on the examination of epitaphs from Samarqand, Muminov reaches the conclusion that the title denoted a sort of noble and sacred descent claimed by some *ʿulamāʾ*. He links the use of this title to the groups of contemporary *ʿulamāʾ* who promoted the status of the Persian language vis-à-vis Arabic. Thus, according to Muminov, the *dihqān*s were those Persophone *ʿulamāʾ* who wanted to bolster their status by a noble descent deriving from the pre-Islamic period. Muminov also observes that it was the influx of a new type of religious leader prompted by the Mongol rule and their use of *sayyid* descent that terminated the use of "*dihqān*."

Devin DeWeese's chapter offers a thorough analysis of a genealogical account from the early eighteenth century which represents the strategy of a family closely linked to Khwārazm. The family claims descent from a Yasavī saint named Sharaf Ata, presented as a descendant of Abū Bakr from the father's side and of Ḥusayn b. ʿAlī from the mother's side. This analysis allows DeWeese to identify different characteristics of the period in terms of the claims to sacred descent. One such finding is that the descent from the first three Rightly-Guided Caliphs was already considered to be as valuable as the ʿAlid descent, as was the case in later centuries.

Chapter Twelve by Arthur F. Buehler investigates the situation in South Asia. As is well known, a prevalent system of social stratification among South Asian Muslims has divided them into *ashrāf*, that is, foreign-born Muslims and their descendants, and *ajlāf*, Muslims of indigenous provenance. *Sayyid*s, the Prophet's kinsfolk, have topped the four sub-categories of the *ashrāf* in this system. Buehler explains this system of social stratification and traces the historical trajectory of the *ashrāf* strata with a view to clarifying the position of *sayyid*s. He also tackles the difficult theoretical question of how we can go beyond a binary mode of explanation, that is, one that resorts to such dichotomies as either "Islamic or indigenous/native" or "greater tradition versus minor tradition," to better understand the *ashrāf–ajlāf* social stratification.

Finally, our journey in pursuit of *sayyid*s and *sharīf*s terminates in twenty-first century Indonesia. Arai Kazuhiro's analysis of the Islamic magazine *alKisah* elucidates the position of Ḥaḍramī *sayyid*s in the commodification process of religion that is (also) under way in Indonesia. *AlKisah* is characterized by its promotion of *sayyid*s as religious leaders. Arai, however, makes it clear that the magazine does not represent any collective efforts for self-promotion by the *sayyid* community. The characteristic contents of the magazine were merely an outcome of the discovery of a niche in the market. The uninterrupted publication of *alKisah*, therefore, should be taken as demonstrating the sizable demand for the *sayyid*s' religious leadership within the Muslim society of contemporary Indonesia.

* * *

The periods covered by the chapters of this volume range over more than a millennium from around the ninth century to the present day. The regions discussed are spread from the Iberian Peninsula to the Indonesian Archipelago. Naturally, the political, social and religious environments surrounding *sayyid*s and *sharīf*s vary significantly from one chapter to another. No chapter, however, ends up with merely presenting particular case studies. Instead, all the chapters of the volume seek to give an answer to the broader question of who the *sayyid*s and *sharīf*s are and what it has meant to be related to the Prophet. It is hoped that the readers will agree with my contention that this shared approach has realized a degree of coherence desirable for an edited volume such as this.

It is not my intention to elaborate here on what I think the achievements of this volume are. Instead, I would like to invite the readers to contribute their own judgments to the ongoing development of the sayyido-sharifology. Some brief comments, however, appear to be in order before closing this introduction.

As already mentioned, the elucidation of Muslim discourses about the kinsfolk of the Prophet was one of the three thematic axes of the conference. I would claim that this volume significantly advances our knowledge in this area. Not only the chapters in part one, which focuses on discourses, but also chapters in the other two parts will present new findings and useful insights. It is especially gratifying that the volume contains examinations of the discourses that are not necessarily favorable to, or openly against, the special status of *sayyid*s and *sharīf*s. Islamic reformism in modern times appears repeatedly through the volume as a proponent of such discourses. The volume also serves as a corrective to the persistent preconception even among some scholars that the attitudes favorable to *sayyid*s and *sharīf*s must always be linked to Shiʿism. All in all, the contributions to this volume demonstrate that the attitudes favorable to *sayyid*s and *sharīf*s have been a phenomenon widely attested in what we may call "intercessional Islam."[13]

The warning implicit in the stances taken by the authors of some chapters might also be counted among the achievements of the volume. The two chapters by the scholars on Central Asia make it clear that in the historical studies on the region it is rather the wider concept of the "sacred families," of which the Prophet's kinsfolk is only a part, that is attracting the scholars' interest. It is indeed necessary not to focus too much on *sayyid*s and *sharīf*s but to widely consider the attitudes of different types of Islam and Muslims toward the concept of descent, whether sacred or not. Such an attitude would also widen the interface through which the studies on *sayyid*s and *sharīf*s are to contribute to Islamic studies as a whole.

Of course, many things still remain unclear in studies on *sayyid*s and *sharīf*s, and our way to coherent knowledge consistently connecting the cases in different times and places remains a very long one. This volume, therefore, poses just as many questions as it provides answers for. For example, Bernheimer points out that the Islamic jurists until about the eleventh century did not sanction the exclusivist marital strategy of the ʿAlids in terms of Islamic law; the Shiʿite jurist al-Sharīf al-Murtaḍā (d. 436/1044) even characterized it explicitly as part of the customs. However, as Yamaguchi's chapter shows, the Ḥaḍramī *sayyid*s in Southeast Asia at the outset of the twentieth century clearly regarded their strategy as one required by the religion. For Yamaguchi, this was an important component of a conservative interpretation of Islam that Islamic reformism challenged. How can we combine the two findings? Does this mean that the special status and treatment of *sayyid*s and *sharīf*s came to be incorporated into the dogmas and legal stipulations of Islam more deeply and extensively during the centuries in between? While I find this scenario rather plausible in this particular question, I have to say that it is beyond the scope of this volume to pursue such questions or ideas that arise when combining the findings in different chapters. It is hoped that they serve the readers as food for thought, useful for the further advancement of our knowledge on *sayyid*s and *sharīf*s.

* * *

Some notes on how the terms "*sayyid*" and "*sharīf*" are used in the different chapters: (1) It is the consensus of all the contributors that the ʿAlids (the descendants of ʿAlī b. Abī Ṭālib), or the Ḥasanids and the Ḥusaynids (the descendants of the two sons between ʿAlī and Fāṭima) for that matter, have constituted the most important part, in terms of significance and, most probably, of number, of the "*sayyid*s" and "*sharīf*s"; (2) The border separating the "*sayyid*s" and "*sharīf*s" from the rest of the people, however, has fluctuated in accordance with the interpretations and customs in different times and places. The Hāshimids and the Ṭālibids are the two other groupings that have often been used. It is left with each contributor to decide, in accordance with the situation in the society under study and the contributor's own approach, how they define the fringes of the *sayyid/sharīf* category; (3) It depends on the customs in different settings if "*sayyid*" and "*sharīf*" denote the same thing or two different sets of people. Clarifying this is an essential question within sayyido-sharifology.

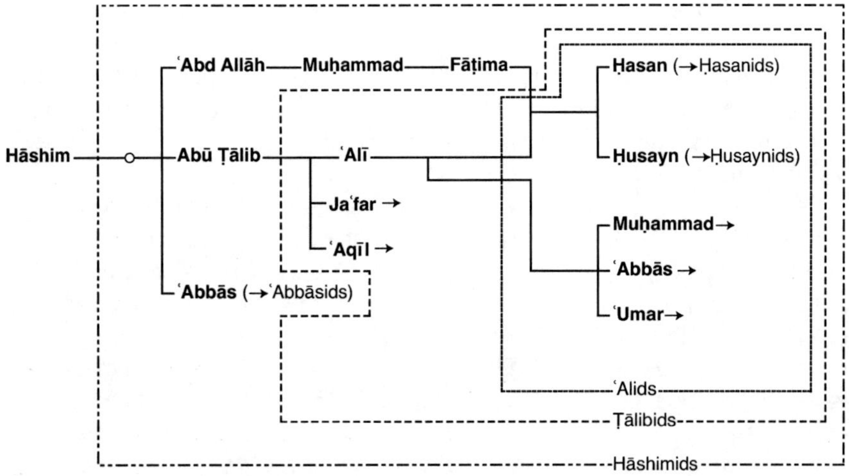

Figure 0.1 Muḥammad's close relatives (simplified)

Notes

1 "'Niqābat al-ashrāf' fī al-ʿIrāq tuʿlinu ibṭāl nasab al-raʾīs al-makhlūʿ," *al-Sharq al-awsaṭ* 9151 (24 Shawwāl 1424/18 December 2003). www.aawsat.com/details.asp?section=1&article=208227&issueno=9151 (accessed 19 April 2011).

2 Richard Kerbaj, "Islamic Cartoon Row is Latest Case of Libel Tourism," *The Sunday Times*, 21 March 2010. www.timesonline.co.uk/tol/news/uk/article 7069734.ece (accessed 19 April 2011); "al-Muḥāmī Fayṣal al-Yamānī yaʿtazimu mulāḥaqat 15 ṣaḥīfa Danmārkiyya nasharat al-rusūm al-musīʾa li-l-Rasūl," najran9.com, 1 March 2010. www.najran9.com/news-action-show-id-6978.htm (accessed 19 April 2011); Lars Eriksen, "Danish Newspaper Apologises in Muhammad Cartoons Row," guardian.co.uk, 26 February 2010. www.guardian.co.uk/world/2010/feb/26/danish-cartoons-muhammad-politiken-apology (accessed 19 April 2011). Yamani's plan, however, has not been actualized as of July 2011. I thank Solicitor Mark Stephens for this update.

3 Ibrāhīm al-Zanjānī al-Mūsawī, in his *Nihāyat al-falsafa al-Islāmiyya* (Beirut: Muʾassasat al-Balāgh, 1407/1987), 109–110, presents his estimate of about thirty million direct descendants (the Ḥasanids and the Ḥusaynids). It is also reported that an estimate commissioned by Abdülhamid II (r. 1293–1327/1876–1909) gave the result of nineteen million direct descendants (*al-dhurriyya al-nabawiyya*) (Jaʿfar al-Shaykh Bāqir Āl Maḥbūbah, *Māḍī al-Najaf wa-ḥāḍiruhā*, 3 vols, 2nd ed. [Beirut: Dār al-Aḍwāʾ, 1406/1986], I:283, n. 1, citing *al-Murshid*, year one). Note also the remark, albeit not undisputed, in 2007 by the then *naqīb al-ashrāf* of Egypt that the *ashrāf* in that country were "close to five to six millions." *Egypt Today*, June 2007. www.egypttoday.com/article.aspx?ArticleID=7407 (accessed 10 June 2009).

4 Al-Ṣadūq, *al-Iʿtiqādāt fī al-dīn al-Imāmiyya*, ed. by Ghulām-Riḍā al-Māzandarānī (Qum: Editor, 1412/1992), 85. Cf. Ash-Shaykh aṣ-Ṣadūq, *A Shīʿite Creed*, trans. by A. A. Fyzee, rev. ed. 1982, 3rd ed. (Tehran: World Organization for Islamic Services, 1999), 99.

5 Ibn Taymiyya, *Minhāj al-sunna al-nabawiyya*, ed. by Muḥammad Rashād Sālim, 9 vols ([Riyadh]: Jāmiʿat al-Imām Muḥammad b. Saʿūd al-Islāmiyya, 1406/1986), IV:599.

6 I consulted Nicolas de Nicolay, *Les navigations peregrinations et voyages, faicts en la Turquie* (Antwerp: Guillaume Silvius, imprimeur du roy, 1576), 196–198, in a black-and-white reproduction. The illustration on p. 198 appears to be colored in the original. Even if it is not, the rather lengthy treatment of the *emīr*s' green turbans preceding the illustration will certainly let the readers recognize the turban in the illustration as such. The parallel (same?) illustration in the copy of the Italian translation of the work kept at Harvard University (*Le navigationi et viaggi nella Turchia*, trans. by Francesco Florid a Lilla [Antwerp: Appresso Guiglielmo Siluio stampatore Regio, 1577]) is beautifully colored. A color digital image of the illustration is accessible at http://ids.lib.harvard.edu/ids/view/14355238?buttons=y (accessed 21 July 2011). I thank Mercedes García-Arenal for bringing this illustration to my attention.

7 See my "Toward the Formation of Sayyido-Sharifology: Questioning Accepted Fact," *The Journal of Sophia Asian Studies* 22 (2004): 87–103. http://ci.nii.ac.jp/naid/110004497103 (accessed 22 July 2011).

8 Biancamaria Scarcia Amoretti and Lora Bottini eds, "The Role of the *Sâdât/Ašrâf* in Muslim History and Civilization. Proceedings of the International Colloquium (Rome 2–4/3/1998)," special issue, *Oriente Moderno* n.s. 18/2 (1999).

9 My contribution to the Rome colloquium was titled "The Formation and Development of the Science of Talibid Genealogies in the 10th and 11th Century Middle East" (Scarcia Amoretti and Bottini, eds, "The Role of the *Sâdât/Ašrâf*," 541–570).

10 See n. 7 above. The Japanese version: Morimoto Kazuo, "Saiido-Sharīfu Kenkyū no Genjō to Tenbō," in Akahori Masayuki, Tōnaga Yasushi and Horikawa Tōru eds, *Isurāmu no Shinpishugi to Seijashinkō* (Tokyo: University of Tokyo Press, 2005), 229–254. Both versions were published in the context of a joint research

project on Sufism and saint veneration in Islam lead by Akahori Masayuki and Tonaga Yasushi, which recognized the research on *sayyid*s and *sharīf*s as one of its important subjects.

11 This is how I presented the three axes in the invitation I sent out to prospective presenters.

12 The position of a *naqīb al-ashrāf* in most Muslim polities, including the Ottoman Empire, was historically an official one. In that sense, it was a part of the state apparatus. However, not many countries keep state-appointed *naqīb*s today, and the title has come to be widely used by the representatives of voluntary associations of *sayyid*s and *sharīf*s, such as al-Sharīf al-Aʿrajī of Iraq mentioned above.

13 I owe this expression to Roy P. Mottahedeh's remark at the concluding panel of the conference.

Part I

Arguing *sayyid*s and *sharīf*s

1 How to behave toward *sayyid*s and *sharīf*s

A trans-sectarian tradition of dream accounts

Morimoto Kazuo

Introduction

The final chapter of *Faḍāʾil al-ashrāf* [The Merits of *Sharīf*s], published in 1970 by Twelver Shiʿite religious scholar (*ʿālim*) ʿAbd al-Razzāq Kammūna al-Ḥusaynī al-Najafī (d. 1390/1970), is entitled "Incidents Which Occurred to Those Who Supported the Family of the Apostle" (*Waqāʾiʿ li-ashkhāṣ awṣalū Āl al-Rasūl*).[1] The title does not reflect the chapter's contents precisely. Ten of the thirty stories presented in the chapter merely offer uneventful accounts of the deeds of historical figures who "behaved appropriately towards the Ṭālibids" (*ʿamila al-maʿrūf maʿa Āl Abī Ṭālib*).[2] Even the genuine "incidents" recounted by Kammūna include those that befell the people who had not behaved properly to *sayyid/sharīf*s or those that caused persons to act benevolently to *sayyid/sharīf*s after they occurred.[3] However, no reader of the stories recorded in the chapter will miss the fact that what Kammūna means by "incidents" are, in fact, instances of interaction between the visible and the invisible worlds, mostly via dreams.[4] To those "modern" minds who are no longer able to share the belief in the dream's role as a bridge between these two worlds (or the existence of the invisible world per se for that matter), the dream accounts that Kammūna presents read as miracle tales.

Let us read one of the "incidents" presented by Kammūna:

> ʿAbd Allāh b. al-Mubārak used to go on pilgrimage or participate in a religious expedition (*yaghzū*) in alternate years. He continued this practice for as long as fifty years. One year he departed for the pilgrimage and at one station found an ʿAlid lady cleaning a dead duck. So he approached her and said, "Why are you doing this?" She said, "O' ʿAbd Allāh, do not ask about something that does not concern you!" [Ibn al-Mubārak] said, "Her remark said something to my mind, so I insisted on asking the question. Then she said, 'O' ʿAbd Allāh, you have forced me to reveal my secret to you. I am an ʿAlid and I have four orphaned ʿAlid daughters. Their father has died recently. Today is the fourth day we have not eaten anything, so meat that has not been ritually slaughtered has become lawful to us. This is why I have picked up this duck. I will prepare it and carry

> it to my daughters so they can eat it.'" [Ibn al-Mubārak] said, "I said to myself, 'Woe to you Ibn al-Mubārak, what are you doing at this opportunity (*furṣa*),' and said to her, 'Open your *izār* [loincloth].' I poured gold coins to the side of her *izār* [that she had opened] while she bent her head without [even] turning [to me.]" [Ibn al-Mubārak] said, "I went to the place I was staying and God took away from my heart the desire for the pilgrimage that year. Then I prepared myself for my trip home and stayed there until people had performed the pilgrimage and came back. I went out to meet my neighbors and friends. Then, everybody to whom I said 'May God accept your pilgrimage and acknowledge your endeavors' began [to say, 'The same to you.] We were together at such and such a place.' I heard the same thing from so many people. I continued wondering [about that]. Then, I saw the Apostle of God – may God bless him and grant him salvation – in my dream. He said, 'O' ʿAbd Allāh, you helped my daughter who was in distress. So, I asked God – mighty and great – to create an angel in your shape so that he would perform pilgrimage for you every year until the Day of Resurrection and you might choose to go or not to go on pilgrimage as you like.'" This is the reward for one who gives up his pilgrimage and helps a distressed one of the daughters of the Apostle of God – may God bless him and grant him salvation – with his money for the pilgrimage.[5]

As is shown by the comment at the end, mere presentation of Ibn al-Mubārak's praiseworthy deed is clearly not the aim of this story. Rather, the story aims at edifying its readers as to how to behave toward *sayyid/sharīf*s by recounting the miraculous experience of Ibn al-Mubārak as a role model. In fact, most of the stories recounting "incidents" that Kammūna presents share this feature. It is this kind of edifying story comprising dream accounts that forms the focus of this study.[6] Kammūna is only one recent example of the many authors through the centuries who have recorded related stories. It is thus an enduring tradition of collecting and recording such stories that we are dealing with in this study. As far as I know, the present study represents the first serious attempt to study that tradition.[7]

This study has two goals. One is to clarify what the edifying stories are trying to convey; what special characteristics of *sayyid/sharīf*s do they emphasize and what deeds do they recommend or prohibit to believers? By answering these questions, this study aims to contribute to a better understanding of Muslim discourse concerning *sayyid/sharīf*s, which, as I have argued elsewhere, is prerequisite for a fuller understanding of their station in Muslim societies.[8]

The other aim is to identify the contours of a trans-sectarian tradition of recording these stories. In fact, many stories are presented in the works of both Sunnite and Shiʿite authors.[9] This stems from the fact that Shiʿite authors, including Kammūna, took the stories from their Sunnite counterparts. It is owing to this fact that the protagonist of the above story, recorded by Kammūna, is Ibn al-Mubārak (d. 181/797), who is not associated with Shiʿism in any particular way.[10] This trans-sectarian tradition offers an excellent example of how the boundary separating the two major sects becomes blurred when it comes to the question of the status of the *sayyid/sharīf*s. There indeed are differences in Sunnite and Shiʿite dogmas as to their status – and some of these differences are indeed reflected in the variations found in some of the stories discussed below. Nonetheless, the shared tradition of edifying stories strongly suggests that at the level these stories are concerned with, that is, at the level of the day-to-day practice of believers, there has been no significant difference between the behaviors that advocates of the special treatment of *sayyid/sharīf*s in either sect have promoted.

This study consists of three sections. In the first, we will take a closer look at the stories with dream accounts presented by Kammūna in order to clarify the basic traits they – and other related stories not recorded by Kammūna – share. Special attention will be paid to how the stories achieve their persuasive power. The second section will be devoted to the question of transmission. Here we will discuss not only the transmission within the two groups of authors – Shiʿite, then Sunnite – but also the connection between the two. We will then return to an analysis of the stories' contents in the third section. Actions recommended or denigrated, as well as sectarian divergences discernable in some stories will be presented.

The anatomy of the dream accounts

Whence do our edifying stories derive their persuasive power? The edifying stories with dream accounts, divergent as their particular plots are, share more or less the same structure when it comes to how they achieve persuasiveness. The stories presented by Kammūna will be used here as examples to elucidate that shared structure.

The first notable feature of the edifying stories with dream accounts is that they invariably feature the holy figures of the Prophet's family – the Prophet Muḥammad and ʿAlī b. Abī Ṭālib being the most common – in their dream accounts.[11] Dreams allow the holy figures to affect the course of events in the present time of the dream accounts, in spite of the long period of time separating them in reality. Amīr Dāwūd Bayk, in one story, meets ʿAlī in his dreams for two consecutive nights. It was Dāwūd's wrongdoing (that is, imprisonment of a Ḥusaynid and confiscation of his money), which prompted those apparitions. As the story goes, ordering restitution, ʿAlī hits Dāwūd with a stick in the second dream. With the marks of ʿAlī's beating on his body, Dāwūd releases the Ḥusaynid and begins to act respectfully toward him.[12] As seen here, incidents in the dreams involving holy figures can physically infiltrate the life of this world: Dāwūd Bayk's wounds demonstrate that what happened to him in the dreams was "real" indeed.

Other dreams take the dreamer away from the story's present and have him/her witness his/her fate on the Day of Resurrection.[13] A Muslim "king" (*malik*) in Balkh, in one story, finds in a dream that the Day of Resurrection has come. Arriving at the pool of Kawthar, he asks the Prophet to give him a drink from its water. But the Prophet, to the great dismay of the king, tells him to prove that he is really one of his followers. This is because earlier on that same day the king had refused to help a poor ʿAlid lady from Qum, with her daughters shivering in the cold weather, precisely by telling her to prove her ʿAlid descent.[14]

However, dreams in these stories are not merely convenient tools to bridge different time periods. Significant here is the fact that Islamicate dream cultures have treated dreams, albeit with due qualifications, as authentic conduits of communication from the invisible world, the realm of the truth.[15] It is obvious that the dreams in our edifying stories are presented as such. Moreover, the appearance of the Prophet – and of the Imams in the Shiʿite case – has been regarded as a strongest element to vouch for the truthfulness of the content of a particular dream, because it has been transmitted on the Prophet's authority that Satan cannot take his/their form(s). Such dreams in which Muḥammad (and/or the Imam[s]) appears have therefore been accorded authority comparable to that of hadiths.[16] Thus, a dream account in an edifying story validates the realistic nature of that story's contents while also serving as an integral building block of its plot.

Further, it is thanks to the use of dreams that the holy figures can be represented as responding to individual cases with specific and divergent contexts; for example, Ibn al-Mubārak's praiseworthy action or the Balkhi king's misbehavior. This flexibility would certainly be less feasible if the available tool of authentication was limited, for example, to the more or less solid corpus of hadiths. In addition, it is the intense sense of the immediate presence of the holy figures, also enabled by the dreams, that makes these stories especially emotive and, therefore, effective. The roles dream accounts play in our edifying stories, thus, cannot be overemphasized.

A further point to be noted in relation to the apparition of holy figures in dreams is that these figures are not represented as impartial demonstrators of universal norms but as affectionate forebears personally concerned with the fate of their family members. In the above-mentioned story involving the Balkhi king, Muḥammad instructs ʿAlī to give a drink to the person who kindly sheltered the ʿAlid lady after the king's rejection. What Muḥammad is reported as saying to ʿAlī is pertinent here:

> O' ʿAlī, you indeed owe him something. He sheltered your daughter so and so along with her daughters, protected them from the cold weather, dispelled their hunger, and she is still staying in his house. So, it is incumbent upon you to honor him.[17]

Thus, *sayyid/sharīf*s in these stories are the people who can count on the care and protection of the holy figures of matchless religious authority simply because they have the personal contact *par excellence*, namely, blood relationship.

It is not only the ongoing attention and protection by the holy figures manifested through dreams that the stories recount. Just as important is the fact that *sayyid/sharīf*s are also often represented as active participants in this process. The experience of an Egyptian blacksmith is an excellent case in point. This blacksmith was, so to speak, a fire-proof man who could handle burning iron with his bare hands. It was the right action he took with a female descendant of the Prophet that gave him this miraculous power. He had released a poor, beautiful woman – whose hungry children were waiting for her at home – when he saw her shivering and weeping out of fear of God after he had gotten her to agree to sell herself for money. Her entreaty, "If you let me go for God's sake, I will assure you that God will never torment you with His fire, either in this world or in the hereafter," was the reason for the miracle. After letting the woman go, the blacksmith met Fāṭima in a dream. Fāṭima revealed the woman's *sayyid/sharīf* identity and made a supplication from God so that what the woman had promised him would be realized.[18]

Thus, just as the holy figures of the Prophet's family are presented as capable of intervening in the affairs of the stories' present-day events through dreams, *sayyid/sharīf*s are depicted as being able to prompt such ancestral interventions.[19] It is this idea of the existence of a trans-temporal supernatural circuit between *sayyid/sharīf*s and their holy and affectionate forebears in all later times that underpins the edifying stories.

The shared tradition

As mentioned in the Introduction, many of the stories recorded by Kammūna originate from Sunnite works, the story of Ibn al-Mubārak and the poor ʿAlid lady being a case in point. Kammūna cites the story from Sibṭ b. al-Jawzī's (d. 654/1257; Sunnite) *Tadhkirat al-khawāṣṣ* and notes that the same story is recorded also in Muḥammad-Ashraf al-Ḥusaynī's (d. 1133/1720–1 or 1145/1732–3; Shiʿite) *Faḍāʾil al-sādāt*. Muḥammad-Ashraf cites (1) al-ʿAllāma al-Ḥillī's (d. 726/1325; Shiʿite) *Kashf al-yaqīn fī faḍāʾil Amīr al-Muʾminīn*, which again cites Sibṭ's *Tadhkira*, as well as (2) "*Ṣāḥib kitāb* Maqāmāt al-najāt" (i.e., Niʿmat Allāh al-Jazāʾirī [d. 1112/1700–1; Shiʿite]), who, Muḥammad-Ashraf writes, relied on Ibn Abī Jumhūr al-Aḥsāʾī's (d. 901/1495–6; Shiʿite) *ʿAwālī al-laʾālī al-ʿazīziyya fī al-aḥādīth al-dīniyya* where it is again al-Ḥillī's *Kashf* that is drawn upon. This way, all the transmission paths mentioned by Kammūna go back to Sibṭ's *Tadhkira*, whether directly or indirectly.[20] The reliance on an earlier Sunnite work in this way is, as mentioned above, a standard pattern among Shiʿite authors.

Shi῾ite story collections

Let us begin by clarifying the degree to which Shi῾ite authors depend on Sunnite sources. Table 1.1 shows the sectarian derivations of the related stories presented in four Shi῾ite sources from the seventeenth to the twentieth century. Stories presented in the chapter on the merit of supporting *sayyid/sharīf*s in al-Majlisī's (d. 1111/1700) *Biḥār al-anwār* and al-Nūrī al-Ṭabarsī's (d. 1330/1911–2) *Kalima ṭayyiba,* in the chapter on the "incidents" in *Faḍā'il al-ashrāf* (published in 1970), and throughout Muḥammad-Ashraf al-Ḥusaynī's (d. 1133/1720–1 or 1145/1732–3) *Faḍā'il al-sādāt* form the basis of the data presented. "Sectarian derivation" here is judged upon the affiliation of the first author to write down the story in question, that is, from whose work the authors of the four sources cited the story, whether directly or indirectly.

Table 1.1 Sectarian derivations of the edifying stories recorded in four Shi῾ite sources (seventeenth–twentieth centuries)[21]

Source	*Total number of stories*	*(I) Deriving from a Sunnite work*	*(II) Rework(s) of the story(-ies) in Sunnite works*	*(III) Deriving from a Shi῾ite work*
Chapter on "the Noble Progeny and the Merit of Supporting Them" in al-Majlisī, *Biḥār al-anwār*	5	4 (80%)	1 (20%)	–
Muḥammad-Ashraf al-Ḥusaynī, *Faḍā'il al-sādāt*	20	14 (70%)	2 (10%)	4 (20%)
Chapter on "the Merit of Supporting the Great Family of *Sayyids*" in al-Nūrī al-Ṭabarsī, *Kalima ṭayyiba*	16	12 (75%)	1 (6%)	3 (19%)
Chapter on "the Incidents Which Occurred to Those Who Supported the Family of the Apostle" in Kammūna al-Ḥusaynī, *Faḍā'il al-ashrāf*	13	8 (62%)	2 (15%)	3 (23%)

The table shows an unequivocal trend: in the three works excluding *Biḥār al-anwār*, whose value as a sample is lower on account of the limited number of stories, roughly 80 percent of the stories derive from a Sunnite work (Columns [I] and [II]).[22] Those who open these Shiʿite books to learn how to behave toward *sayyid/sharīf*s will actually read so many stories originating from Sunnite sources, sometimes even without noticing it.

It is certainly arguable that Shiʿite authors cited extensively from Sunnite sources intentionally. It may indeed be surmised that at least some of the Shiʿite authors were aware that they could make a point of the trans-sectarian nature of the positive attitude toward *sayyid/sharīf*s by citing stories from Sunnite sources. Al-ʿAllāma al-Ḥillī begins his transcription of related stories from *Tadhkirat al-khawāṣṣ* (see below) in the following manner, thereby emphasizing Sibṭ b. al-Jawzī's Ḥanbalite (*sic*) affiliation: "Ibn al-Jawzī [*sic*], who was affiliated to the Ḥanbalites, related in *Tadhkirat al-khawāṣṣ*: . . ."[23] This statement is reproduced in most of the later works that draw on *Kashf*. Moreover, there is even a case of the use of related stories by a Shiʿite author in a polemical context, that is, in order to criticize a Sunnite position by citing Sunnite sources. Fatḥ Allāh b. Muḥammad al-Jawād al-Iṣfahānī (d. 1339/1920–1), in his *al-Qawl al-ṣurāḥ fī al-Bukhārī wa-Ṣaḥīḥihi al-jāmiʿ*, cites two stories in such a context.[24]

This, however, does not explain why Shiʿite authors did not juxtapose more stories of Shiʿite provenance with Sunnite ones. An excellent case in point here is al-Nūrī al-Ṭabarsī's *Dār al-salām fī mā yataʿallaqu bi-ruʾyā wa-l-manām*, which also indicates the dominance of the stories of Sunnite origin.[25] For one thing, there appears to be no point in suppressing stories of Shiʿite origin in this book which focuses on dreams and dreaming in general. Furthermore, the erudite author of *Mustadrak al-wasāʾil* is one of the last persons who would be ignorant of related materials of Shiʿite provenance, supposing their existence.[26] The Shiʿite authors' heavy reliance on Sunnite sources appears indeed to indicate the scantiness of available materials in the works of their own sect.

Of course, this does not mean that the Shiʿites do not have their own stories at all. Table 1.1 also shows that three of the four sources include stories originating from a Shiʿite source, albeit in small numbers. The recording of one such story can even be traced back conservatively to the fourth/tenth century.[27] It is a typical dream-account story that recounts the remuneration given to a poor person who gave to "the family (*qarābāt*) of Muḥammad and ʿAlī" what food he had, sacrificing the needs of his own family.[28] But the repertoire of such Shiʿite stories obviously did not see any significant growth. Shiʿite authors rather looked to the stories available in Sunnite sources.

A trace of trans-sectarian transmission is discernible already in Muntajab al-Dīn b. Bābūyah's (d. after 585/1189) *al-Arbaʿūn ḥadīth*, the first written work across the two sects to record a particular story (that of Abū Jaʿfar the merchant, discussed below). Muntajab al-Dīn heard the story with one intermediary from Abū Saʿīd ʿAbd al-Wāḥid b. ʿAbd al-Karīm al-Qushayrī, the second son of the author of *al-Risāla al-Qushayriyya* who himself was called "*Nāṣir al-Sunna*" (the Protector of the Sunna).[29] Traces of the Sunnites are also perceptible in the first Shiʿite work to collect multiple stories, *al-Durr al-naẓīm fī manāqib al-aʾimma al-lahāhīm* by Yūsuf b. Ḥātim al-Shāmī (seventh/thirteenth century). Presented there are (1) a story related from Ibn Ḥanbal (d. 241/855) in which he recounts his own experience; (2) a variant of Ibn al-Mubārak's story; (3) a story presenting the experience of a certain Sharaf al-Dīn Hilāl b. ʿĪsā which is in fact a parallel (reworking?) of a story featuring the Sunnite poet Ibn ʿUnayn (d. 630/1233) and (4) a story transmitted by a Niẓām al-Dīn, the imam of the Prophet's mausoleum at Medina, recounting the experience of his father al-Qurṭubī (possibly the renowned exegete?).[30]

The use of Sunnite written works as the main source of related edifying stories began with al-ʿAllāma al-Ḥillī (d. 726/1325) in the *Kashf al-yaqīn* mentioned above. Al-Ḥillī transcribed four stories from Sibṭ b. al-Jawzī's *Tadhkirat al-khawāṣṣ*, a work on the lives and merits of ʿAlī and the eleven other Imams compiled about half a century before.[31] After al-Ḥillī, Shiʿite authors came mostly to copy the stories already written down in Sunnite works or to recycle them among themselves. Table 1.2 presents the Sunnite written sources used, directly or indirectly, in more than one of the four sources taken up in Table 1.1.[32] As we shall see, the three sources of higher importance, from which more than one story was taken, namely Nūr al-Dīn al-Samhūdī's (d. 911/1506) *Jawāhir al-ʿiqdayn fī faḍl al-sharafayn* and Bā Kathīr al-Makkī's (d. 1047/1637) *Wasīlat al-maʾāl fī ʿadd manāqib al-Āl*, in addition to *Tadhkirat al-khawāṣṣ*, belong to a Sunnite tradition of presenting related stories in the form of a collection.[33]

Why did the Shiʿites not develop their own repertoire but rather chose to rely on the Sunnites instead? As is well known, they have no shortage of miracle tales in general, especially those concerning the Imams. One possible explanation is that it was exactly the centrality of those Imams in the Shiʿite dogma that impeded the development of the kind of stories we are discussing. In comparison with the miracle tales of Imams that are of direct relevance to a core doctrine of Shiʿism, namely, the Imamate, the stories dealing with ordinary *sayyid/sharīf*s are only of marginal importance. That quite a few Shiʿite authors record related stories as evidence of ʿAlī b. Abī Ṭālib's posthumous miracles, appears to support this interpretation.[34]

Furthermore, we also have to keep in mind that after they began to transcribe stories from Sunnite works, the Shiʿite authors had a plentiful supply of those stories: what demand they had for related stories appears to have been met by the supply from the Sunnite side. We will see below that the Shiʿite authors needed to make only limited adjustments to make the stories taken from Sunnite sources fit their position and that those adjustments actually did not affect how they advised their readers to behave: the Sunnite provenance of the stories appears not to have troubled the Shiʿite authors in the slightest.

Table 1.2 Sunnite sources of the stories presented in the four Shiʿite sources (seventeenth–twentieth centuries)

	Biḥār al-anwār	*Faḍāʾil al-sādāt*	*Kalima ṭayyiba*	*Faḍāʾil al-ashrāf*	*Note*
Ibn al-Jawzī (d. 597/1200), *Kitāb al-mudhish*		1		1	
Ibn ʿUnayn (d. 630/1233), *Dīwān*		1	1	1	Ibn ʿUnayn himself is the protagonist of the story in question.
Sibṭ b. al-Jawzī (d. 654/1257), *Tadhkirat al-khawāṣṣ*	4	5	4	2	
"al-Maqrīzī" (d. 845/1442)			1	1	The story, including the reference to "al-Maqrīzī," is in fact taken from *Jawāhir*.
Nūr al-Dīn al-Samhūdī (d. 911/1506), *Jawāhir al-ʿiqdayn*		2	1	1	
Aḥmad b. al-Faḍl Bā Kathīr (d. 1047/1637), *Wasīlat al-maʾāl*		8	1		

Notes: (1) Many of the stories are shared by more than one source (e.g., *Faḍāʾil al-sādāt* and *Faḍāʾil al-ashrāf* cite one and the same story from *Kitāb al-mudhish*); (2) See below for the dubious nature of the references to *Kitāb al-mudhish*.

Sunnite story collections

What was the situation on the Sunnite side then? The most salient feature of the transmission of edifying stories with dream accounts among Sunnite authors is the early emergence and enduring development of a tradition of forming collections of related stories, mostly as a part of a work on the merits of the Prophet's family.

As far as I have been able to clarify, this Sunnite tradition can be traced back to *Tadhkirat al-khawāṣṣ*, with six stories recorded in its final pages.[35] Three of the stories were transmitted orally to, and written down for the first time by, Sibṭ b. al-Jawzī, while the other three had been recorded previously in books of diverse subjects. The oldest of the works mentioned would appear to be al-Masʿūdī's (d. 345/956) *Murūj al-dhahab*.[36]

The next author to present dream-related stories in the form of a collection was al-Maqrīzī (d. 845/1442). He gathered, on the basis of oral transmission, six stories in *Maʿrifat mā yajibu li-Āl al-Bayt al-nabawī*, most of which were set in Mamluk society and therefore none of his stories overlapped with those recorded by Sibṭ.[37] The *Maʿrifa* is thus the first book on the merits of the Prophet's family that includes a collection of related stories. The rest of the works that will be mentioned in this sub-section all deal fully or partially with this subject.

The stories collected by al-Maqrīzī in *Maʿrifa* are also found in the collection included in al-Sakhāwī's (d. 902/1497) *Istijlāb irtiqāʾ al-ghuraf*, along with five other stories gathered from disparate works.[38] Thus al-Maqrīzī became a familiar name often mentioned as a source in later story collections.[39] Subsequently, Ibn Ḥajar al-Haytamī (d. 973/1566), in *al-Ṣawāʿiq al-muḥriqa*, reproduced al-Sakhāwī's collection (minus one story) while adding five more of his own on the basis of oral transmission.[40]

It was Nūr al-Dīn al-Samhūdī (d. 911/1506), the well-known historian of Medina, who combined Sibṭ b. al-Jawzī's collection and the collection developed by (al-Maqrīzī and) al-Sakhāwī. By combining Sibṭ's and al-Sakhāwī's collections and adding stories gathered individually, he formed a collection (in two parts) of twenty-four stories in his *Jawāhir al-ʿiqdayn*.[41] Al-Samhūdī's collection was then used extensively by Bā ʿAlawī al-Tarīmī (d. 960/1553) in his *Ghurar al-bahāʾ al-ḍawī*, who added stories of Ḥaḍramī origin to form a twenty-five-story collection.[42] The collections found in Aḥmad b. Muḥammad al-Khafājī's (d. 1069/1659) *Tafsīr Āyat al-Mawadda* (comprising fifteen stories) and Sulaymān al-Qundūzī's (d. 1294/1877–8) *Yanābīʿ al-mawadda* (twenty-two stories) also owe most or all of their materials to al-Samhūdī's collection, respectively.[43] Another work that appears to have relied heavily on *Jawāhir al-ʿiqdayn* is *Wasīlat al-maʾāl fī ʿadd manāqib al-Āl* by Aḥmad b. al-Faḍl Bā Kathīr al-Makkī (d. 1047/1637).[44]

Finally, most of the stories found in the collections mentioned so far were gathered by Abū Bakr al-ʿAlawī al-Ḥaḍramī (d. 1341/1922) in his *Rashfat al-ṣādī*, which also presented eight new stories collected individually from elsewhere (the collection comprises forty-one stories in total).[45] Yūsuf al-Nabhānī (d. 1350/1932) also recorded ten stories in *al-Sharaf al-muʾabbad*, most of which again overlapped with the ones found in the mentioned collections.[46]

In this way, a distinct tradition of including a collection of related and overlapping stories can be discerned among the Sunnite authors of the works on the merits of the Prophet's family. The tradition can be traced back to *Tadhkirat al-khawāṣṣ* in the thirteenth century and a core set of stories was formed already at the end of the fifteenth century when *Jawāhir al-ʿiqdayn* was compiled. As Table 1.2 indicates, it was mainly upon the works belonging to this Sunnite tradition that Shiʿite authors depended. Actually, after al-Ḥillī's *Kashf al-yaqīn*, we have to wait until the latter half of the seventeenth century for the next Shiʿite works including new material, namely either al-Majlisī's *Biḥār al-anwār* or Ibn Shadqam's *Tuḥfat al-azhār*.[47] It is clear now that by the time these and later Shiʿite works were written, a rich variety of stories were readily available in earlier Sunnite story collections.

Table 1.3 Overlapping of the stories among the Sunnite story collections

	Tadhkira	*Maʿrifa*	*Istijlāb*	*Jawāhir*	*Ghurar*	*Ṣawāʿiq*	*Rashfa*	*Sharaf*
Tadhkira (6/0)	–	0	0	6	6	0	5	1
Maʿrifa (6/0)	0	–	6	5	5	6	6	6
Istijlāb (11/0)	0	6; A	–	9	9	10	11	7
Jawāhir (24/0)	6; A	5; A	9	–	20	8	22	7
Ghurar (25/2)	6; A	5; A	9	20; A	–	8	23	7
Ṣawāʿiq (15/1)	0	6; A	10; B	8	8	–	14	7
Rashfa (41/8)	5; A	6; A	11	22; B	23; B	14; B	–	8
Sharaf (10/1)	1	6; A	7	7	7	7; A	8	–

Legend: For example, *al-Ṣawāʿiq* contains 15 stories (1 [the figure after the slash mark] of them is unique to it), six of which also appear in *Maʿrifa*; "A" after semicolon indicates that the author of the work above is cited as a source, while "B" indicates that the title of the work above is (also) cited.

Notes: (1) The works that do not make any addition to a collection in a previous work are not included; (2) The work cited by an author may not be the one the author actually used. For example, it is certainly via *Jawāhir* that the stories recorded in *Tadhkira* are transcribed in *Ghurar*; (3) See n. 39 for the irregular status of *Maʿrifa* in this table.

Whence, then, did the stories in these Sunnite story collections come? It is unfortunately difficult to give a definitive answer to this question because in a considerable number of cases what we know about the provenance of a given story is limited to the names of obscure oral transmitters or, worse, the mere fact that there were such transmitters. Two observations, however, should be mentioned in this regard.

Firstly, with regard to the sectarian provenance of the stories, none of the identifiable sources, whether oral or written, appears to be distinctly Shiʿite.[48] Al-Masʿūdī's history, *Murūj al-dhahab*, is actually the only written source that may possibly be called Shiʿite, although the book obviously enjoyed trans-sectarian circulation.[49] As for the oral sources, it appears that the authors' informants mostly hailed from among the people surrounding them in the Sunnite environments of Ayyubid Syria, Mamluk Egypt, Mamluk and Ottoman Hijaz, or the Ḥaḍramawt. The sense is that, contrary to the case of the Shiʿite sources after al-ʿAllāma al-Ḥillī, it is unlikely that the bulk of the materials in the Sunnite collections are actually Shiʿite in origin.

Secondly, there are indications that suggest the affinity these stories had with preaching (*waʿẓ*). One such indication is the role ascribed to Ibn al-Jawzī in the transmission of some stories. Ibn al-Jawzī is said to have recorded two stories in the source books for preaching he authored, i.e., *al-Multaqaṭ* and *al-Mudhish* (both mentioned above). Yet, not only do the printed editions of the books not record the stories but their overall contents suggest that it was fairly unlikely that they ever included such stories. This ascription to the preacher *par excellence* of his time appears to reflect the affinity these stories had with preaching in the minds of later recorders.[50] The fact that it was Sibṭ b. al-Jawzī, again a reputed preacher of his time, that collected the related stories for the first time, can be adduced in addition.[51] Whatever the case, there is no doubt that our edifying stories are quite appropriate as materials for preaching both in terms of contents and tone, as exemplified by the inclusion of one of them in al-Ḥarīfīsh's collection of sermons *al-Rawḍ al-fāʾiq*.[52] Our edifying stories might have emerged as materials for oral preaching and retained that aspect even after they came to be put down in writing in the works on the merits of the Prophet's family.

Morals of the edifying stories

Let us return now to examine the content of the stories. Since we have already elucidated how the stories derive their persuasive power, the task that remains is to clarify what morals the stories are being used to instill in believers. What are the proper and improper behaviors toward *sayyid/sharīf*s presented in the stories?

Before we discuss this question, however, it must be noted that these stories are multifaceted. When these stories are collected in one place, they are naturally presented as instructing believers as to how they should behave toward *sayyid/sharīf*s. But that is not the only meaning these stories can carry.

The story Sibṭ b. al-Jawzī cites from *Murūj al-dhahab* serves as an example, for it is in the context of highlighting the praiseworthy character of the person who met Muḥammad in his dream that the story is presented in *Murūj*.[53] It was Sibṭ who attached a new significance to the story. Also relevant is the story featuring a flour merchant named Abū al-Ḥasan, who continued to hand out flour for free to *sayyid/sharīf*s and was later repaid by the Prophet. It terminates with Abū al-Ḥasan's posthumous statement in a dream seen by fellow believers that he attained an elevated status in the afterlife because of his patience.[54] When read alone, the story will appear to promote the idea that one must be patient to receive reward for good deeds in general rather than to advise the readers to hand out their possessions for free to *sayyid/sharīf*s.[55] It should also be repeated that quite a few Shiʿite works record the related stories as instances of ʿAlī's posthumous miracles. It is with these qualifications that we are now focusing on the advice as to how to behave toward *sayyid/sharīf*s.

Basic features

The proper action that is presented most often in the stories is to support the livelihood of *sayyid/sharīf*s, especially the poor among them. The simplest way to provide support to them is to give money or material goods. This is the form of support mentioned most frequently in the stories. One may give a pension to *sayyid/sharīf*s as did the renowned vizier of the ʿAbbasids, ʿAlī b. ʿĪsā (d. 334/946) in one story.[56] At the same time, it is advisable not to fail to make spontaneous gifts and extend help at any time, e.g., at the sight of needy *sayyid/sharīf*s, especially female ones. We have seen this in the stories of Ibn al-Mubārak and the Balkhi king. This advice also applies even when giving out one's possessions will mean a considerable sacrifice on the part of one's self and family. In the Shiʿite story mentioned above as originating (conservatively) from the fourth/tenth century, the protagonist, at the sight of a hungry couple from "the family of Muḥammad and ʿAlī," thinks that "they are more entitled [to the food I have] than my family," and gives them what he has at hand. The food was, however, what he bought with the single *dirham* he had come by so as to quell the hunger of his own family. Of course, he is rewarded handsomely by Muḥammad and ʿAlī for this act of self-sacrifice. He not only becomes "the richest person in Medina" but is also promised further remuneration in the afterlife.[57]

If one is a merchant, one should even hand over one's merchandise to *sayyid/sharīfs* by putting them on the account of the holy figures of the Prophet's family. Abū Jaʿfar the merchant (*tājir*) and the aforementioned flour merchant named Abū al-Ḥasan, both of Kufa, are the two main role models in this regard. In the case of Abū Jaʿfar, he receives a visit by Muḥammad, ʿAlī, Ḥasan and Ḥusayn after he has become impoverished because of his benevolence. He is then repaid by ʿAlī what he is owed. Muḥammad (or ʿAlī, as we find in another version of this story) asks Abū Jaʿfar to continue this generosity, promising that he will never be impoverished again.[58]

The explicit display of respect is also presented as an appropriate action when encountering *sayyid/sharīfs*. In a story first recorded by al-Maqrīzī, the *raʾīs* al-ʿUmarī accompanies the *muḥtasib* Jalāl Maḥmūd al-ʿAjamī to the house of the *muʾadhdhin* al-Sharīf ʿAbd al-Raḥmān al-Ṭabāṭabāʾī.[59] Al-ʿAjamī then begins to apologize to the *sharīf*, who is already touched by the visit of such a dignitary. Al-ʿAjamī confesses that when, at the court of Sultan Barqūq (r. 784–791/1382–1389 and 792–801/1390–1399), the *sharīf* took a seat higher than his, he asked himself how this man could dare to do so. Thereafter, he was reprimanded by the Prophet, who asked if he minded "my child" (*waladī*) taking an upper seat.[60]

Another principle that a good many stories make a point of is the inviolability of *sayyid/sharīfs*. Those who violate them, or even intend to do so, will certainly be punished. After a violent clash between the ʿAbbasids and the Ṭālibids in Kufa, the Caliph al-Qādir (r. 381–422/991–1031) orders the Buyid *amīr* Sharaf al-Dawla (d. 379/989) to head for Kufa and eradicate the Ṭālibids. While the Ṭālibids at Kufa are horrified by this news, an ʿAbbasid woman, in a dream, sees ʿAlī descend from the skies on horseback in order to slay those aiming to murder the Ṭālibids. Then the news of Sharaf al-Dawla's sudden death arrives.[61] Some other stories underline the inviolability of *sayyid/sharīfs* by recounting the release of a *sayyid/sharīf* from prison because of the apparition of holy figures in a dream.[62]

When it comes to improper behavior, the point that is repeatedly emphasized in many stories is that one should not pay attention to the deeds and morality of individual *sayyid/sharīfs*. The story recounting the experience of ʿAlī b. ʿĪsā, mentioned above in passing, is typical in this regard. In this story, ʿAlī b.

ʿĪsā makes it a rule to distribute money among the ʿAlids every year. One day, ʿAlī b. ʿĪsā finds one of his recipients drunken in the street, and refuses to give him his share any longer. Muḥammad chastises the vizier in a dream. The Prophet, after refusing to return the greeting of ʿAlī b. ʿIsā, cites the case of the drunken man, and asks if he was doing favors to the ʿAlids for their own sake or for Muḥammad's sake. The vizier is told that he should have ignored the ʿAlid's deeds and remained silent for the Prophet's sake. ʿAlī b. ʿĪsā summons the man and gives double what he used to give. The man asks why ʿAlī b. ʿĪsā changed his mind and, upon hearing the story, he does his penance.[63]

Finally, complaining about or even harboring discontent with misdeeds perpetrated by *sayyid/sharīf*s is strongly discouraged. Thus, believers should not complain about the *maks* (commercial tax not prescribed in Islamic law) levied by the *Sharīf*s of Mecca.[64] One story even implies, based on the example of the poet Ibn ʿUnayn (d. 630/1233), who was robbed by a band of robbers with *sayyid/sharīf* descent, that one should be grateful for the damages caused by misbehaving *sayyid/sharīf*s.[65]

Sectarian differences

When compared with these common basic features, the sectarian differences manifest in the stories are only marginal. This is understandable since a great many of the materials that Sunnite and Shiʿite authors record actually overlap, and Shiʿite authors tend merely to transcribe the stories originating from Sunnite works. However, there are two significant differences worth special attention.

The first concerns the reason why *sayyid/sharīf*s must be given special treatment. It is the different configurations of the holy figures discernible in some stories that reveal this. Besides Muḥammad, who of course appears the most often, other members of the *Ahl al-Kisāʾ* (i.e., Muḥammad, ʿAlī, Fāṭima, Ḥasan and Ḥusayn), especially ʿAlī, tend to figure more prominently in the stories recorded in Shiʿite works, and even other later Imams sometimes play a role. The above-mentioned story recounting the fate of the Balkhi king, which in fact is a Shiʿite rework of a story taken from a Sunnite work, is a case in point.[66] While the version found also in Sunnite works talks only about the apparition of Muḥammad in a dream, this version has "*Ahl al-Bayt*," comprising ʿAlī, Ḥasan, Ḥusayn and "their descendants" (i.e., the descendants of Muḥammad, Ḥasan and Ḥusayn; presumably denoting the rest of the Imams) accompany the Prophet and portrays ʿAlī as playing a significant role.

Another interesting example – though lacking a dream account – is a story that recounts the experience of Aḥmad b. Isḥāq al-Ashʿarī, the administrator of *waqf*s at Qum. This story is strikingly similar to the story featuring ʿAlī b. ʿĪsā discussed above, although the differences between the two are telling. While ʿAlī b. ʿĪsā gets reprimanded by Muḥammad, it is Ḥasan al-ʿAskarī who corrects al-Ashʿarī. Moreover, Ḥasan al-ʿAskarī explicitly tells al-Ashʿarī that he must act benevolently to *sayyid/sharīf*s regardless of their morality because of "their kinship with me" (*li-intisābihim ilaynā*).[67] This story thus rationalizes the special treatment due to *sayyid/sharīf*s not so much by characterizing them as the Prophet's family as by emphasizing their kinship with the Imam.

The other difference to be noted has to do with stories that exhibit evidence of more extensive rewriting by Shiʿite authors. The Sunnite repertoire actually includes two stories that present the Shiʿism of Medinan *sayyid/sharīf*s as a misdeed that must be overlooked. One should not be affected by their *bidʿa*s (illicit innovations) or by the fact that they curse Abū Bakr and ʿUmar, the stories admonish. Some Shiʿite authors obviously found these observations problematic and made modifications. The modification made to one of them reveals the ingenuity of the modifier. In the original version of the story, a Maghrebi pilgrim is reprimanded in a dream for not handing money to a Shiʿite *sayyid/sharīf*. Shiʿism is bad, but one must not begrudge benevolence because of that, this version preaches. As expected, the Shiʿite *sayyid/sharīf* does penance and stops cursing the first two caliphs at the end of the story. This ending is, however, markedly modified in the Shiʿite version. Instead of doing penance, the Shiʿite *sayyid/sharīf* is made to say, "If you had not come to me [to hand over the money], I would have doubted the authenticity of my descent and that my creed was really the same as theirs [i.e., the creed of Muḥammad and Fāṭima]." The modified version thus presents Shiʿism as an authentic tradition of the Prophet's family.[68]

Yet, it needs to be noted again that these differences are manifest only in a small proportion of the stories. They, at the same time, do not make any difference when it comes to the practical dimension of what to do with *sayyid/sharīf*s. Trans-sectarian commonality of respect for the *sayyid/sharīf*s stably remains the most conspicuous feature when the morals put forth by Sunnite and Shiʿite authors in the edifying stories are compared.

Conclusion

The above examination of edifying stories that incorporate dream accounts has yielded findings in two main areas: what those stories are preaching and how they have been transmitted and recorded.

The fundamental message conveyed by the stories is fairly simple: believers must respect and support *sayyid/sharīf*s unconditionally for the sake of the Prophet (and for the sake of the Imams in the Shiʿite context). These stories seek to justify the special treatment due to *sayyid/sharīf*s not by claiming their innate superiority in morality or religiosity. Rather, it is the right of the Prophet and other holy figures of the Prophet's family that *sayyid/sharīf*s be paid due respect.

It is in the concrete instruction as to what to do, something that the dream's manipulability allows them to offer, that the strength of these stories lies. The edifying stories do not shy away from telling believers to give *dirham*s and *dīnār*s, to give away their merchandise for free, or to overlook a drunken *sayyid/sharīf*. It is therefore quite understandable that many works on the merits of the Prophet's family came to incorporate these stories, often in their final sections. The edifying stories are expected to show the readers how they should put into practice the principles already discussed in the preceding sections in a rather scholastic mode, on the basis mainly of Qur'ānic verses and hadiths. The overlap these stories probably had with preaching has also been suggested.

The more important finding of this study, however, consists in the uncovering of the trans-sectarian tradition of transmission and recording of related stories. These materials were transmitted beyond the boundaries separating Sunnites and Shiʿites, and their logic and teachings were shared by the pro-*sayyid/sharīf* elements within both sects. Moreover, it was in fact the Sunnite side that took the lead and, as noted, many of the stories recorded in the Shiʿite works after al-ʿAllāma al-Ḥillī derive from earlier Sunnite works. If it is our habit to seek Shiʿite influences in Sunnite discourses in favor of the Prophet's family, this study has shown that the flow of influence can sometimes be the opposite.

Still, these are findings based solely on a particular type of material. It is hoped that further studies on related materials, especially literature on the merits of the Prophet's family deriving from different times, places and religious orientations will lead us to a better and more nuanced understanding of the trajectories of the discourses about *sayyid/sharīf*s. This appears all the more desirable when we remember that the overall argument of an author may differ significantly from that of another, even when the individual components they use to construct their arguments are identical.

Acknowledgment

I would like to thank Professors William A. Graham and Kamada Shigeru for their comments and help. My gratitude is also due to Professors Akahori Masayuki and Tonaga Yasushi who let me present an earlier version of this study on their panel at WOCMES-2. The research for this study was supported by Inamori Foundation.

Notes

1 *Faḍā'il al-ashrāf* (Najaf: Maṭbaʿat al-Ādāb, 1390/1970), 311–346. Kammūna published extensively on the history and genealogy of the Prophet's family. His publications include: *Mawārid al-ithāf fī nuqabā' al-ashrāf*, 2 vols (Najaf: Maṭbaʿat al-Ādāb, 1388/1968); *Mashāhid al-ʿitra al-ṭāhira wa-a'yān al-ṣaḥāba wa-l-tābiʿīn* (Najaf: Maṭbaʿat al-Ādāb, 1387/1968).

2 The phrase is taken from *Faḍā'il al-ashrāf*, 311.

3 "*Sayyid/sharīf*s" in this study denotes those people who are putatively related to the Prophet Muḥammad and thus are often called by such honorific titles as "*sayyid*" or "*sharīf*." Those people mostly claim affiliation with the ʿAlids (or, the Ḥasanids or the Ḥusaynids for that matter), but the concept allows the inclusion of other lines originating from different close relatives of the Prophet (demarcations do vary).

4 One story, presented in ibid., 316–317, may in fact recount a case of a waking vision. As only a negligible proportion of the stories discussed in this study seem

to include accounts of waking visions (distinguishing them from dreams is not possible in some cases) and both dreams and waking visions invariably function as the bridge between the visible and the invisible world, this study uses the word "dream" to cover both phenomena. For the ambiguity of the border between the two, see Elizabeth Sirriyeh, "Dreams of the Holy Dead: Traditional Islamic Oneirocriticism versus Salafi Scepticism," *Journal of Semitic Studies* 45/1 (2000): 116 [115–130].

5 Kammūna, *Faḍāʾil al-ashrāf*, 335–336. I have consulted Sibṭ b. al-Jawzī (d. 654/1257), *Tadhkirat al-khawāṣṣ*, prefaced by Muḥammad-Ṣādiq Baḥr al-ʿUlūm (Najaf: al-Maktaba wa-l-Maṭbaʿa al-Ḥaydariyya, 1964, repr., Tehran: Maktabat Nīnuwī al-Ḥadītha, n.d.), 367–368, where the same story is recorded, in order to fill lacunae in Kammūna's text.

6 Incorporation of (1) an account of communication with the invisible world through a dream and (2) edification as to how to behave toward *sayyid/sharīf*s in general are the two common features of the stories under examination in this study. Stories including only one of the two items are not considered unless otherwise noted.

7 The only instance of a reference to the kind of stories put under examination in this study is found in C. van Arendonk [W. A. Graham], "Sharīf," in H. A. R. Gibb et al. eds, *The Encyclopaedia of Islam*, new ed., 13 vols (Leiden: Brill, 1960–2009; hereafter *EI2*), IX:336 [329–337], where Graham mentions the existence of "a number of anecdotes" recorded by al-Maqrīzī and al-Nabhānī (for those accounts, see below).

8 See my article "Toward the Formation of Sayyido-Sharifology: Questioning Accepted Fact," *The Journal of Sophia Asian Studies* 22 (2004): 87–103. Available online at: http://ci.nii.ac.jp/naid/110004497103 (accessed 20 July 2011).

9 I will use "Shiʿism" to denote Twelver Shiʿism in this study. Whether the same stories are recorded in the texts of other branches of Shiʿism, especially the Zaydites, remains an open question for future studies.

10 For this scholar cum ascetic, see J. Robson, "Ibn al-Mubārak," in *EI2*, III:879.

11 The different configurations of groups of holy figures noticeable in the stories reflecting Sunnite and Shiʿite positions respectively will be discussed below. In any case, the holy figures appearing in most dream accounts consist of the *Ahl al-Kisāʾ* (Muḥammad, ʿAlī, Fāṭima, Ḥasan and Ḥusayn). I am not asserting that ordinary *sayyid/sharīf*s lack any element of holiness by allocating this appellation to the limited members of the Prophet's family.

12 Kammūna, *Faḍāʾil al-ashrāf*, 339.

13 A further type of dreams, insignificant in number, are those in which the protagonist's fate in the afterlife is revealed posthumously in a dream seen by a third party. See, e.g., the story featuring Abū al-Ḥasan the flour merchant, discussed below.

14 Ibid., 325–330. The ʿAlid lady, after being coldly rejected by the king, was kindly received by a Zoroastrian retainer of the king. When the king wakes up the next morning and, after a frantic search, finds the ʿAlid lady at that retainer's place, he finds that the retainer has converted to Islam. Thanks to his commendable deed and the supplication (*duʿāʾ*) the ʿAlid lady made to God to guide her host and his family to Islam, the Zoroastrian saw a similar dream, was allowed to drink water from the Kawthar by Muḥammad and ʿAlī, and then converted to Islam. For another story involving the conversion of a Zoroastrian, see Sibṭ b. al-Jawzī, *Tadhkira*, 371; Ḥusayn al-Nūrī al-Ṭabarsī (d. 1330/1911–2), *Dār al-salām fī mā yataʿallaqu bi-ruʾyā wa-l-manām*, 4 vols, 2nd ed. (Beirut: Dār al-Balāgha, 1412/2007 [*sic*]), I:291–292 (for the purpose of brevity, only some sample sources are cited for each story).

15 For a useful overview of the findings of the scholarship on Islamicate dream cultures, see Louise Marlow's "Introduction" to her edited book, *Dreaming across*

Boundaries: The Interpretation of Dreams in Islamic Lands (Boston: Ilex Foundation, 2008), 1–11 [1–21].

16 Leah Kinberg, "Literal Dreams and Prophetic *Ḥadīṯ*s in Classical Islam: A Comparison of Two Ways of Legitimation," *Der Islam* 70 (1993): 279–300 (though Kinberg's point is rather to emphasize the authority accorded to literal dreams in general); Khalid Sindawi, "The Image of ʿAlī b. Abī Ṭālib in the Dreams of Visitors to His Tomb," in Marlow ed., *Dreaming across Boundaries*, 185–186, 187–188 [179–201]; al-Nūrī, *Dār al-salām*, IV:281–293.

17 Kammūna, *Faḍāʾil al-ashrāf*, 328. The benefactor in question is the Zoroastrian retainer mentioned in n. 14 above.

18 Ibid., 333–335.

19 Although this particular story presents a complicated process involving the *sayyid/sharīf*'s promising and the holy figure's supplication, the most common means of *sayyid/sharīf*s' active approach to the invisible world is through their own supplications. See, e.g., n. 14 above. See also Sibṭ b. al-Jawzī, *Tadhkira*, 373; al-Nūrī, *Dār al-salām*, I:293–294.

20 *Tadhkira*, 370–371; *Faḍāʾil al-sādāt* (Qum: Sharikat al-Maʿārif wa-l-Āthār, 1380/1960–1), 361–363; *Kashf al-yaqīn*, ed. by Ḥusayn Dargāhī (Tehran: Vizārat-i Farhang va Irshād-i Islāmī, 1415/1995), 485–486; *ʿAwālī al-laʾālī*, ed. by Mujtabā al-ʿIrāqī, vol. 4 (Qum: Maṭbaʿat Sayyid al-Shuhadāʾ, 1405/1985), 140–142.

21 Sources: Muḥammad-Bāqir al-Majlisī, *Biḥar al-anwār al-jāmiʿ li-durar akhbār al-aʾimma al-aṭhār*, 110 vols, 3rd ed. (Beirut: Dār Iḥyāʾ al-Turāth al-ʿArabī, 1403/1983), XCIII:217–236 (*Bāb madḥ al-dhurriyya al-ṭayyiba wa-thawāb ṣilatihim*); Muḥammad-Ashraf, *Faḍāʾil al-sādāt*, 229, 239–242, 301–302, 337–338, 341–367, 393, 493–495; Ḥusayn b. Muḥammad-Taqī al-Nūrī al-Ṭabarsī, *Kitāb kalima ṭayyiba* (Tehran: Kitābfurūshī-yi Islāmiyya, n.d.), 423–452 (*Bab . . . dar fażl-i iʿānat-i silsila-yi jalīla-yi sādāt*); Kammūna, *Faḍāʾil al-ashrāf*, 311–346 (*al-Faṣl . . . waqāʾiʿ li-ashkhāṣ awṣalū Āl al-Rasūl*). All of the relevant chapters in *Biḥār*, *Kalima ṭayyiba* and *Faḍāʾil al-ashrāf* also include materials which are outside the scope of this study (e.g., hadiths or historical accounts). The same will be true, to different extents, with many of the "story collections" discussed below. *Faḍāʾil al-sādāt* and *Kalima ṭayyiba* are written in Persian (the former, however, presents the stories in both Arabic original and Persian translation). The rest of the primary sources discussed in this study are in Arabic, unless noted otherwise.

22 The four sources used in the table share the strong point that they are collections of related stories intentionally gathered in one place by respective authors in the view to promoting the special treatment of *sayyid/sharīf*s (most of the stories presented in *Faḍāʾil al-sādāt* are also concentrated at 337–338, 341–367). It can thus be expected that they somehow represent the knowledge of the authors, including such erudite scholars as al-Majlisī and al-Nūrī al-Ṭabarsī, with regards the stories useful for their purposes. But limiting the sources to these four items inevitably confines the source basis, too. Some additional data are presented here for the purpose of offsetting this weakness. (1) I identified eight related stories in Ḍāmin b. Shadqam (alive in 1090/1679–80), *Tuḥfat al-azhār wa-zulāl al-anhār fī nasab abnāʾ al-aʾimma al-aṭhār*, a genealogy of the Ḥasanids and the Ḥusaynids (ed. by Kāmil Salmān al-Jabūrī, 3 vols in 4 [Tehran: Mīrāṡ-i Maktūb, 1420/1999], II-1:174, 191–197, 208–211, 332). The breakdown of those stories in accordance with the columns in Table 1.1 is: (I) 5 (62.5 percent); (II) 1 (12.5 percent); (III) 2 (25 percent). (2) I also identified twenty-five stories in *Dār al-salām*, a work on dreams and dreaming compiled by al-Nūrī al-Ṭabarsī, the author of *Kalima ṭayyiba* used in the table (I:126–127, 148–149, 213–217, 225–226, 273–275, 278–279, 285, 291–294, 360–361, 379–381, 398–402, II:5–15). The breakdown is: (I) 16 (64 percent); (II) 2 (8 percent); (III) 7 (28 percent). (3) *Biḥār al-anwār* includes another

chapter where six related stories are presented (four of them overlap with those found in the chapter covered by the table), i.e., XLII:1–16 (*Bāb mā ẓahara fī al-manāmāt min karāmātihi* [i.e., *karāmāt ʿAlī*] . . .). I also identified two other related stories at XXIII:263–265 and XLIX:119. This brings up the total number of the stories presented in the work to nine. The breakdown of the nine stories is: (I) 5 (56 percent); (II) 1 (11 percent); 3 (33 percent). Obviously, none of these findings challenges the findings in Table 1.1. The other Shiʿite works from the period I consulted include only a few related stories.

23 Al-Ḥillī, *Kashf*, 485.

24 Ed. by Ḥusayn al-Harsāwī (Qum: Muʾassasat al-Imām al-Ṣādiq, 1422/2001–2), 49–53.

25 See n. 22 above.

26 Al-Nūrī al-Ṭabarsī cites three related stories in *Mustadrak*, too. *Mustadrak al-wasāʾil*, 18 vols, 3rd ed. (Beirut: Muʾassasat Āl al-Bayt li-Iḥyāʾ al-Turāth, 1411–1412/1991), XII:374–375, 381–382.

27 The story is found in the Qurʾān exegesis attributed to Ḥasan al-ʿAskarī (d. 260/874). Although the attribution of this book to the eleventh Imam is disputed, it is certain that this *tafsīr* was already being transmitted as early as the fourth/tenth century. See *al-Tafsīr al-mansūb ilā al-Imām Abī Muḥammad al-Ḥasan b. ʿAlī al-ʿAskarī* (Qum: Muʾassasat al-Imām al-Mahdī, 1409/1988), 714–736. The story is presented at ibid., 337–338.

28 It is also useful to mention the case of another story, first recorded in *Tārīkh-i Qum*, compiled in the fourth/tenth century. This story shares the fundamental traits of our edifying stories except that it lacks the dream account for an obvious reason: the holy figure in the story, Ḥasan al-ʿAskarī, was still alive when the story was set. Both stories will be discussed in the next section.

29 *Al-Arbaʿūn ḥadīth ʿan arbaʿīn shaykh min arbaʿīn ṣaḥābī fī faḍāʾil Amīr al-Muʾminīn ʿAlī b. Abī Ṭālib* (Qum: Madrasat al-Imām al-Mahdī, 1408/1987–8), 95–96. For ʿAbd al-Wāhid, see al-Ṣarīfīnī (d. 641/1243), *al-Muntakhab min al-Siyāq li-Taʾrīkh Naysābūr*, ed. by Muḥammad Aḥmad ʿAbd al-ʿAzīz (Beirut: Dār al-Kutub al-ʿIlmiyya, 1409/1989), 339–340; Abū al-Ḥasan al-Fārsī (d. 529/1134–5), *al-Mukhtaṣar min kitāb al-Siyāq li-Taʾrīkh Naysābūr*, ed. by Muḥammad-Kāẓim al-Maḥmūdī (Tehran: Mīrāṯ-i Maktūb, 1384 AHS/2005–6), 237–238.

30 Al-Shāmī, *al-Durr al-naẓīm* (Qum: Muʾassasat al-Nashr al-Islāmī, 1420/1999–2000), 801–805.

31 Al-Ḥillī, *Kashf*, 485–492.

32 Only the stories in Column (I) of Table 1.1 are considered.

33 References to Ibn al-Jawzī's *Kitāb al-mudhish* and Ibn ʿUnayn's *Dīwān* pertain to one single story recorded in multiple Shiʿite sources, respectively.

34 Some cases in point are: Muntajab al-Dīn b. Bābūyah, *al-Arbaʿūn ḥadīth*, 95–96; Shādhān b. Jibraʾīl al-Qumī (d. 660?/1261?), *Kitāb faḍāʾil Amīr al-Muʾminīn*, ed. by Muḥammad al-Mūsawī and ʿAbd Allāh al-Ṣāliḥī (Qum: Muʾassasat Walī al-ʿAṣr, 1422/2002), 247–248; al-Ḥillī, *Kashf*, 485–492 (in the chapter "*Faḍāʾiluhu* [i.e., *faḍāʾil ʿAlī*] *al-thābita lahu baʿda wafātihi*"; note, however, that it is Muḥammad, not ʿAlī, who appears in the dream accounts. The merits of ʿAlī and those of his descendants are apparently confounded); al-Majlisī, *Biḥār*, XLII:1–16 (*Bāb mā ẓahara fī al-manāmāt min karāmātihi* [i.e., *karāmāt ʿAlī*] . . .).

35 Sibṭ b. al-Jawzī, *Tadhkira*, 367–373.

36 The two remaining works are Abū al-Faraj b. al-Jawzī (d. 597/1200), *al-Multaqaṭ* and "*Kitāb al-Jawharī*" ("*Kitāb al-Jawharī ʿan Ibn Abī al-Dunyā*"). I could not find the story presented as originating from *al-Multaqaṭ* (with the intermediary of an oral transmitter) in "Multaqaṭ al-ḥikāyāt," in *Majmūʿat rasāʾil Ibn al-Jawzī fī al-khiṭab wa-l-mawāʿiẓ*, ed. by Hilāl Nājī and Walīd b. Aḥmad al-Ḥusayn Abū ʿAbd Allāh al-Zubayrī (London: Majallat al-Ḥikma, 1421/2000). Muwaffaq al-Dīn b.

Qudāma (d. 620/1223), however, cites the same story from *al-Multaqaṭ* in *Kitab al-tawwābīn*, ed. by Jūrj al-Maqdisī (Damascus: al-Maʿhad al-Faransī li-l-Dirāsāt al-ʿArabiyya, 1961), 286–287.

37 Al-Maqrīzī, *Maʿrifat mā yajibu li-Āl al-Bayt al-nabawī min al-ḥaqq ʿalā man ʿadāhum*, ed. by Muḥammad Aḥmad ʿĀshūr, 2nd ed. (n.p.: Dār al-Iʿtiṣām, 1393/1973), 80–86. The two stories not staged in the Mamluk society feature Timur (d. 807/1405).

38 *Istijlāb irtiqāʾ al-ghuraf bi-ḥubb aqribāʾ al-Rasūl wa-dhawī al-sharaf*, ed. by Khālid b. Aḥmad al-Ṣummī Bābṭīn, 2 pts (Beirut: Dār al-Bashāʾir al-Islāmiyya, 1421/2000), 679–693. Al-Sakhāwī draws on Taqī al-Dīn al-Fāsī (d. 832/1429), *al-ʿIqd al-thamīn* and Ibn Nūḥ (d. 708/1308–9), *al-Muntaqā min kitāb al-Waḥīd fī sulūk ahl al-tawḥīd*, in addition to oral transmission.

39 It is interesting to note, however, that al-Sakhāwī does not seem to have taken the six stories as a ready-made set from *Maʿrifa*: the wording of three stories he records corresponds far better with the version recorded in another work of al-Maqrīzī's than the version in *Maʿrifa*. See al-Sakhāwī, *Istijlāb*, 683–684 (corresponding with *Durar al-ʿuqūd al-farīda fī tarājim al-aʿyān al-mufīda*, ed. by Maḥmūd al-Jalīlī, 4 vols [Beirut: Dār al-Gharb al-Islāmī, 1423/2002], III:537; cf. *Maʿrifa*, 81–82), 687–688 (*al-Sulūk li-maʿrifat duwal al-mulūk*, ed. by Muḥammad ʿAbd al-Qādir ʿAṭā, 8 vols [Beirut: Dār al-Kutub al-ʿIlmiyya, 1417/1998], VII:199; cf. *Maʿrifa*, 82–83), 689–690 (*al-Sulūk*, VII:219–220; cf. *Maʿrifa*, 83–85). The wording of the story recorded in *Istijlāb*, 691–692 is also significantly different from the version recorded at *Maʿrifa*, 81. (But, note that the wording of the story in *Istijlāb*, 684–685 corresponds better with that of the version at *Maʿrifa*, 85–86 than those at *Durar*, II:252–253 and *al-Sulūk*, V:329–330.) Among the later Sunnite authors mentioned in this sub-section, only al-Nabhānī (d. 1350/1932), in *al-Sharaf al-muʾabbad li-Āl Muḥammad* ([Cairo]: Muṣṭafā al-Bābī al-Ḥalabī, 1381/1961–2), 195–199, consulted *Maʿrifa* and cited the stories directly from it. The others are based, directly or indirectly, on *Istijlāb*.

40 *Al-Ṣawāʿiq al-muḥriqa ʿalā ahl al-rafḍ wa-l-ḍalāl wa-l-zandaqa*, ed. by ʿAbd al-Raḥmān b. ʿAbd Allāh al-Turkī and Kāmil Muḥammad al-Kharrāṭ, 2 pts (Beirut: Muʾassasat al-Risāla, 1417/1997), 689–701. The section of which these pages form a part is actually an abridgment of *Istijlāb*. Al-Haytamī indicates his oral sources only in ambiguous ways, e.g., "one of the seekers of religious knowledge" (*baʿḍ ṭalabat al-ʿilm*).

41 *Jawāhir al-ʿiqdayn fī faḍl al-sharafayn*, ed. by Mūsā Bunāy al-ʿAlīlī, 2 vols in 3 ([Baghdad]: Wizārat al-Awqāf wa-l-Shuʾūn al-Dīniyya, 1405–1407/1984–1987), II:268–277, 285–309. The same author's *al-Jawhar al-shaffāf fī faḍāʾil al-ashrāf* presents the same story collection (MS Maktabat al-Ḥaram al-Makkī 2629, 100b–103b, 106b–118a; I thank Dr Yahya ibn Junaid, Prof. Bernard Haykel, Mr Nadav Samin and Dr Goto Emi for helping me gain access to this source). Al-Samhūdī took as many as six stories from Hibat Allāh b. ʿAbd al-Raḥīm al-Bārizī (d. 738/1337–8), *Tawthīq ʿurā al-īmān fī tafḍīl ḥabīb al-Raḥmān*, a work on the merits and miracles of the Prophet. I have been able to spot those stories in the Berlin manuscript of *Tawthīq* (in 2 pts: MSS. Orientalabteilung, Staatsbibliothek zu Berlin, Pruess. Kulturbesitz, Sprenger 127a and 127b; the relevant folios are 127b: 11a–11b, 13a–13b, 64a–64b, 68b–69b, 86b–87a), but no story collection as such. For further details on *Jawāhir*, a work advancing the merits of *ʿilm* and the prophetic descent, see my "The Prophet's Family as the Perennial Source of Saintly Scholars: Al-Samhudi on *ʿIlm* and *Nasab*," in Catherine Mayeur-Jaouen and Alexandre Papas eds, *Family Portrait with Saints: Hagiography, Sanctity and Family in the Muslim World* (Berlin: Klaus Schwarz Verlag and CNRS, forthcoming in 2012).

42 *Ghurar al-bahā' al-ḍawī wa-durar al-jamāl al-badī' al-bahī*, prefaced by ʿAbd al-Qādir al-Jīlānī b. Sālim (n.p.: ["*aḥfād al-muʾallif*"], 1427/2007), 728–752.
43 Al-Khafājī, *Tafsīr Āyat al-Mawadda*, ed. by Muḥammad-Bāqir al-Maḥmūdī (Qum: Majmaʿ Iḥyā' al-Thaqāfa al-Islāmiyya, 1412/1992), 191–201; al-Qundūzī, *Yanābīʿ al-mawadda li-Dhawī al-Qurbā*, ed. by ʿAlī Jamāl Ashraf al-Ḥusaynī, 4 vols ([Qum]: Dār al-Uswa, 1416/1995–6), III:175–193. *Yanābīʿ* also contains two other stories separately as far as I could spot (ibid., III:133–135, 174).
44 I have not been able to consult a manuscript of this work. That this work relies heavily on *Jawāhir* as far as the edifying stories are concerned can be understood from the lineup of the stories cited from this work in Shiʿite works as well as references to *Jawāhir* found in those stories. See al-Nūrī, *Dār al-salām*, II:6–14, esp. 7; al-Nūrī, *Kalima ṭayyiba*, 430–438, esp. 438.
45 *Rashfat al-ṣādī min baḥr faḍā'il banī al-Nabī al-hādī*, ed. by ʿAlī ʿĀshūr (Beirut: Dār al-Kutub al-ʿIlmiyya, 1418/1998), 247–287. Al-Ḥaḍramī cites an especially gripping story from Shuʿayb b. Saʿd al-Miṣrī al-Makkī al-Ḥarīfīsh (d. 810/1407–8), *al-Rawḍ al-fā'iq fī al-mawā'iẓ wa-l-rawā'iq* (ed. by ʿĀṣim Ibrāhīm al-Kayyālī [Beirut: Dār al-Kutub al-ʿIlmiyya, 1425/2004], 288).
46 *Al-Sharaf al-muʾabbad*, 193–203.
47 For *Tuḥfa*, see n. 22 above. Al-Ḥasan b. Muḥammad al-Daylamī's (eighth/fourteenth century) *Irshād al-qulūb* (2 pts [Qum: Manshūrāt al-Sharīf al-Raḍī, n.d.], 443–445) and Ibn Abī Jumhūr's *ʿAwālī* (140–147), the two works from the period in between that I noticed present related stories, only present two of the stories found in *Tadhkirat al-khawāṣṣ* and *Kashf al-yaqīn*.
48 See preceding notes for the (important) sources mentioned by the authors.
49 There appears to be a consensus as to al-Masʿūdī's Shiʿite inclinations, but opinions vary as to whether he adhered to any of the "formal" branches of Shiʿism. See Ahmad Shboul, *Al-Masʿudi and his World: A Muslim Humanist and his Interest in non-Muslims* (London: Ithaca Press, 1979), 38–41; Tarif Khalidi, *Islamic Historiography: The Histories of Masʿūdī* (Albany: SUNY Press, 1975), 127–128, 145; Rasūl Jaʿfariyān, *Manābiʿ-i tārīkh-i Islām* (Qum: Anṣāriyān, 1376 AHS/1997), 176. *Murūj* (al-Masʿūdī, *Murūj al-dhahab wa-maʿādin al-jawhar*, ed. by M. M. ʿAbd al-Ḥamīd, 4 vols, 4th ed. [Cairo: al-Maktaba al-Tijāriyya al-Kubrā, 1385/1965], III:356–357) is also cited by al-Samhūdī in *Jawāhir*, II:297–299, as the source of a story featuring Mūsā al-Kāẓim.
50 For Ibn al-Jawzī's stature as a preacher, see Angelika Hartmann, "La prédication islamique au Moyen Age: Ibn al-Ǧawzi et ses sermons (fin du 6e/12e siècle)," *Quaderni di studi arabi* 5–6 (1987–1988): 337–346.
51 For Sibṭ b. al-Jawzī as a preacher, see Daniella Talmon-Heller, *Islamic Piety in Medieval Syria: Mosques, Cemeteries and Sermons under the Zangids and Ayyūbids (1146–1260)* (Leiden and Boston: Brill, 2007), 128–139.
52 See n. 45 above.
53 Sibṭ b. al-Jawzī, *Tadhkira*, 373; al-Masʿūdī, *Murūj al-dhahab*, IV:95–96.
54 Al-Samhūdī, *Jawāhir*, II:305–306; al-Nūrī, *Dār al-salām*, II:10–11.
55 Also compare al-Ḥaḍramī, *Rashfa*, 276–277 and al-Ḥarīfīsh, *al-Rawḍ*, 288.
56 Al-Samhūdī, *Jawāhir*, II:306–308; al-Nūrī, *Dār al-salām*, II:11–12.
57 Al-Majlisī, *Biḥār*, XXIII:263–265; Muḥammad-Ashraf, *Faḍā'il al-sādāt*, 337–338. See also n. 27 above. For another story advancing the virtue of self-sacrifice in favor of *sayyid/sharīf*s, see al-Samhūdī, *Jawāhir*, II:302.
58 Al-Samhūdī, *Jawāhir*, II:285–286; Kammūna, *Faḍā'il*, 336–337.
59 All these are historical figures. See al-Sakhāwī, *Istijlāb*, 684, nn. 5–7.
60 Al-Maqrīzī, *Maʿrifa*, 85–86; al-Ḥaḍramī, *Rashfa*, 272. The act of yielding the upper seat also appears in a story (not comprising a dream account) found in al-Nabhānī, *al-Sharaf*, 203–204.

61 Quṭb al-Dīn al-Rāwandī (d. 573/1178), *al-Kharāʾij wa-l-jarāʾiḥ*, 3 vols (Qum: Muʾassasat al-Imām al-Mahdī, 1409/1989), I:220–221; Kammūna, *Faḍāʾil al-ashrāf*, 333. Note that in reality al-Qādir assumed the caliphate after Sharaf al-Dawla's death.

62 See, e.g., the story of Dāwūd Bayk discussed above and the story featuring the Mamluk sultan Muʾayyad Shaykh (r. 815–824/1412–1421) and the *amīr* of Medina ʿAjlān b. Nuʿayr (al-Maqrīzī, *Maʿrifa*, 82–83).

63 Al-Samhūdī, *Jawāhir*, II:306–308; al-Nūrī, *Dār al-salām*, II:11–12. Pigeon-keeping (*laʿb bi-l-ḥamām*) is also presented as a misdeed to be overlooked in one story (al-Samhūdī, *Jawāhir*, II:268–269; al-Nūrī, *Dār al-salām*, I:13–14). Relevant is al-Maqrīzī's comment (*al-Sulūk*, VII:199; also cited in al-Sakhāwī, *Istijlāb*, 688–689): "Be careful not to violate them, whatever [moral] state they are in, because a child is a child regardless of whether being righteous or immoral." See also al-Samhūdī's comment at *Jawāhir*, II:277–278. References to *sayyid/sharīf*s' Shiʿism as another such misdeed in stories of Sunnite provenance will be discussed below.

64 Al-Haytamī, *al-Ṣawāʾiq*, 700; al-Ḥaḍramī, *Rashfa*, 281. See also the story in al-Tarīmī, *Ghurar*, 752; al-Ḥaḍramī, *Rashfa*, 267 (though the tax levied is named *ʿushr*).

65 Al-Samhūdī, *Jawāhir*, II:274–277; Muḥammad-Ashraf, *Faḍāʾil al-sādāt*, 493–495.

66 The story appears for the first time in Ibn Abī Jumhūr, *ʿAwālī*, 142–147, where "*Minhāj al-yaqīn fī faḍāʾil Amīr al-Muʾminīn*" by al-ʿAllāma al-Ḥillī is cited as the source. Judging from the lineup of the two stories quoted by Ibn Abī Jumhūr from the work (the other runs pp. 140–142) as well as the fact that al-Ḥillī's work with a similar title, *Manāhij al-yaqīn fī uṣūl al-dīn* (ed. by Yaʿqūb al-Jaʿfarī al-Marāghī [[Qum]: Dār al-Uswa, 1415/1994–5]), does not contain those stories (the book's subject also does not fit), it is clear that this is a corruption of *Kashf al-yaqīn fī faḍāʾil Amīr al-Muʾminīn*. But, the story recorded in *Kashf al-yaqīn*, 486–489 is a parallel version quoted from Sibṭ b. al-Jawzī, *Tadhkira*, 370–371, featuring a Muslim *raʾīs al-balad* and a Zoroastrian *ḍāmin al-balad* at Samarqand. The difference is thus attributable to reworking. There is, at the same time, a likelihood that a recension of *Kashf al-yaqīn* carried the Balkhi king version, since al-Nūrī al-Ṭabarsī, after presenting the *raʾīs al-balad* version, states in *Kalima ṭayyiba*, 435, that the version found in *Kashf al-yaqīn* is significantly different. The rewrite in this case should be attributed to a copyist of *Kashf al-yaqīn*. To compare the two versions handily, see al-Majlisī, *Biḥār*, XCIII:225–231; al-Nūrī, *Dār al-salām*, II:6–7, 213–217.

67 The story derives from *Tārīkh-i Qum*, originally written in Arabic in the fourth/tenth century but extant in Persian translation only. Here, the phrase is taken from Muḥammad-Ashraf, *Faḍāʾil al-sādāt*, 383, where an (original?) Arabic version is presented. For the Persian version, see Ḥasan b. Muḥammad Qumī, *Tārīkh-i Qum*, ed. by Muḥammad-Riżā Anṣārī Qumī (Qum: Kitābkhāna-yi Marʿashī, 1385 AHS/2006), 556–564.

68 For the original version, see al-Samhūdī, *Jawāhir*, II:269–271. For the modified version, see Kammūna, *Faḍāʾil al-ashrāf*, 343–344. Muḥammad-Ashraf's *Faḍāʾil al-sādāt*, though being a Shiʿite work, presents the original version (393). For the original and modified versions of the other story featuring the Shiʿite *sayyid/sharīf*, see al-Samhūdī, *Jawāhir*, II:273–274; Kammūna, *Faḍāʾil al-ashrāf*, 341–342.

2 Qur'ānic commentary on the verse of *khums* (al-Anfāl VIII:41)

Roy Parviz Mottahedeh

A famous Qur'ānic verse grants an economic benefit in the form of the *khums* or one-fifth to *sayyid*s and *sharīf*s. This essay surveys the interpretation of this verse in Qur'ān commentaries, a task which, as far as I know, has not been done before. The verse in question, verse 41 of Sūra VIII, al-Anfāl, is very often called "the verse of *khums*."[1]

An English understanding of this verse is:

> Know that anything in the way of booty/benefit you have taken, one-fifth of it belongs to God and to His Messenger and to the relatives and the orphans and the poor and the wayfarer, if you have believed in God and what We have revealed to Our servant on the Day of Separation, the day in which the two gatherings will meet. And God is Mighty over all things.

The dimensions of interpretation

As with so many questions concerning entitlements to money and, perhaps, honor, the breadth of disagreement is astonishing. The problems in interpreting this verse are laid out elegantly and succinctly by al-Māwardī, a very celebrated Sunnī jurist of the Shāfi'ī school who died in 450/1058. There are, he says, three theories as to the relationship of the word *ghanīma*, which means "booty/benefit" to *fay'*, a word implied by the verb used in verse 7 of Sūra LIX, al-Ḥashr, which begins: "What God granted as *fay'* from the people of the towns belongs to God and His messenger and the relatives and the orphans and the poor and the wayfarers."

The first theory is that the *ghanīma* and *fay'* are the same thing, and that the verse in Sūrat al-Anfāl abrogated the verse in Sūrat al-Ḥashr.

The second theory is that *ghanīma* is booty taken by force, whereas property taken by treaty is *fay'*. This theory is supported by the early jurists Sufyān al-Thawrī (d. 161/778) and al-Shāfi'ī (d. 204/820).

The third theory is that *ghanīma* represents the movable property (*māl*) of the nonbelievers and *fay'* represents their landed property.

Furthermore, people disagree as to whether the verse specifies a share for God. Some believe the phrase "belongs to God" is a prologue to the five categories of people mentioned subsequently. This is the opinion of several early Sunnī jurists, including al-Shāfiʿī.

A second opinion, attributed to Abū ʿĀliya al-Riyāḥī, a Basran Qurʾān expert of the end of the first Islamic century, is that the portion belonging to God is a separate sixth category and should be given to the Kaʿba.

Yet another issue concerns the understanding of what happens to the Prophet's share after his death. One view gives it to the caliphs. A second view, which believes that the Prophet could have heirs, assigned his share to his kin group. A third view adds the Prophet's share to the four categories mentioned subsequently. A fourth view holds that it should be used for the common good of the Muslims. Al-Māwardī mentions that this is the view of al-Shāfiʿī, the founder of al-Māwardī's own legal school. Finally, some say the share should be used for weapons and horses.

There are three different understandings as to who the Prophet's "relatives" are. The first is that they are the Banū Hāshim, descendants of the Apostle's great-grandfather. The second makes them the Banū Hāshim and the Banū Muṭṭalib, descendants of Muḥammad's great grand uncle, Muṭṭalib. This is the view of al-Shāfiʿī and al-Ṭabarī (d. 310/923). A third opinion is that they are the entirety of the Quraysh, the tribe at Mecca to which the Prophet belonged.

Al-Māwardī offers four opinions about use of the relatives' share after the Prophet's death. Al-Shāfiʿī believes that it belongs to the relatives of Muḥammad forever. A second school holds that it belongs to the relatives of the ruling caliph. A third school believes that the Imam , the leader of the Muslim community, can use it as he wishes. A fourth view, followed by the Ḥanafīs, adds the relatives' share and the Prophet's share to the three categories mentioned subsequently, namely, the orphans, the poor and the wayfarer.[2]

Early Qurʾān commentaries

This rather legalistic presentation of al-Māwardī opens most of the questions that are considered in earlier and later commentaries. A very early Qurʾān commentary by Muqātil b. Sulaymān (d. 150/767) explains "relatives" as the "kin (*qirāba*) of the Prophet," without further discussion.[3] Two other early commentaries, one by Mujāhid (d. 104/722) and another ascribed to Zayd b. ʿAlī (d. 122/740) have nothing to say about the verse.

Al-Ṭabarī in his classic *tafsīr*, written a century and a half before al-Māwardī, adds many traditions to the opinions. In refuting the views that the share of the relatives can go to the ruler (*walī al-amr*), he recites a hadith which becomes a standard frequently cited by later commentators:

> I [Jubayr b. Muṭʿim] and ʿUthmān b. ʿAffān saw the Prophet giving the share of the relatives to the Banū Hāshim and the Banū Muṭṭalib after the victory at Khaybar and we said "O Messenger of God, these are our brothers, the Banū Hāshim. We do not deny their excellence because of

> the place God has given you amongst them. Do you think it right for the Banū Muṭṭalib [to get a share]? You give it to them and leave us out! We [as descendants of Nawfal and ʿAbd al-Shams, Hāshim's brothers] and they [the Banū Muṭṭalib, also descending from a brother of Hāshim's] are in the same position in regard to [genealogical closeness to] yourself!" [Muḥammad] said, "They [the Banū Muṭṭalib] did not separate themselves from us either in the Jāhiliyya or in Islam. The Banū Hāshim and Banū Muṭṭalib are one and the same."

Al-Ṭabarī says:

> The most correct view, in my opinion, is that the share of the relatives belongs to the relatives of Banū Hāshim and their allies (*ḥulafāʾ*), the Banū Muṭṭalib – because this hadith is sound and because the sworn allies (sing. *ḥalīf*) of a people belong to that people.

Al-Ṭabarī mentions a Prophetic hadith "Nobody inherits from us! What we leave behind will be *ṣadaqa*." He also mentions the contrary opinion, namely, the opinion of the Shīʿīs. Al-Ṭabarī tells us that Zayn al-ʿĀbidīn ʿAlī b. al-Ḥusayn (d. 94/712 or 95/713) was asked about the *khums* and ʿAlī said, "It belongs to us." And the questioner said to ʿAlī, "God speaks of orphans and poor and wayfarers." ʿAlī said "Our orphans and our poor." Al-Ṭabarī also reports that Ibn ʿAbbās wrote to Najda: "We are them [the relatives]; and our people have done this [act of deprivation] to us and have said, 'All the Quraysh are the relatives.'"

Al-Ṭabarī strongly supports Sunnī opinion that *ghanīma*, the booty/benefit referred to in the verse is battlefield booty and not, as Shīʿīs believed, immoveable property of non-Muslims or the income from it. He mentions several times the strong statist opinion which he ascribes to "a group of ʿIrāqīs" (meaning the proto-Ḥanafīs) who say that after Muḥammad's death the *khums* was divided only among the orphans, poor and wayfarers. A similar statist opinion states that the share of the relatives goes to the "guardian of the affairs of the Muslims" (*walī amr al-muslimīn*).

Al-Ṭabarī, who was the founder of his own law school, believed that the Prophet's share goes back into the divisible booty, which is then divided four ways, with one for the relatives. He did not think it permissible "for persons [explicitly] mentioned in the Book not to get their share," though of booty only.[4]

Hūd b. Muḥakkam al-Huwwārī, an ʿIbāḍī commentator approximately contemporaneous with al-Ṭabarī, has fewer disagreements with the Sunnī tradition than might have been anticipated. Like al-Ṭabarī, he says that Abū Bakr and ʿUmar transferred the share of the relatives to "the Path of God." We get a slight taste of Khārijite egalitarianism and piety when Hūd gives a hadith about a man asking the Apostle "Is any one person entitled to more booty (*ghanāʾim*) than another?" Muḥammad answered, "No, even the portion he takes personally is not something that he has a special right to."[5] To jump many centuries forward, the commentary of Muḥammad b. ʿĪsā Aṭṭafayyish, an ʿIbāḍī who died in 1332/1913, also does not differ much from the Sunnī accounts. It agrees with those Sunnīs, principally Shāfiʿīs, who feel that one-fifth of the *khums* should be given to relatives of the Prophet, whether they be rich or poor.[6]

A Shīʿī contemporary of al-Ṭabarī is Muḥammad b. Masʿūd al-ʿAyyāshī. His death date is unknown, but his works can be dated to the late third/ninth century. He lived at Samarqand and belonged to an Eastern school of Shīʿism, which preserves many traditions attributed to the Prophet and the Imams not to be found in the Iraqi and Qummī schools. Some of these traditions are not picked up by the central Twelver Shīʿī tradition until the enormous seventeenth-century collection called *Biḥār al-anwār*. Al-ʿAyyāshī quotes Muḥammad al-Bāqir, the Fifth Imam, as saying "We have a scriptural right to the *khums*. Even if some were to crush it, or claim it is not from God, or claim that they do not know about it, that would make no difference." He quotes the same Imam as explaining "[ʿAlī, the First Imam] said that God has forbidden the Family the *ṣadaqa* and revealed the *khums* for their benefit, an obligation owed to them, a mark of their nobility, and a matter lawful for them." Al-ʿAyyāshī also anticipates the later Twelver Shīʿī position in that he believes the Imam has a claim to the *khums* over everything classified as *fayʾ* (immoveable property) and *anfāl* (booty). He adds that the Family has a claim to everything in this world, but mentions a contrary hadith to the effect that *khums* is payable only on booty (*ghanāʾim*). He does not define the sources of wealth subject to *khums*.[7]

The Iraqi and Western Iranian Twelver Shīʿī tradition is represented by ʿAlī b. Ibrāhīm al-Qummī, who flourished around 300/900. Al-Qummī tells us that the *khums* is divided into six parts, a standard Twelver Shīʿī position thereafter. He explains that it is the Imam's duty to act as a father for the community, just as the Prophet did. As a consequence, the Imam acts as the Prophet's trustee or executor, and receives three parts of the six because of his position. Therefore he collects the monies to be redistributed among the categories assigned by the Qurʾān.[8]

If we turn to the later Shīʿī commentary by al-Ṭūsī, who was a contemporary of al-Māwardī and died in 460/1067, we find a more developed treatment of the Twelver Shīʿī tradition. Al-Ṭūsī's eminent position in the development of Twelver Shīʿī law is so great that he is called "*Shaykh al-Ṭāʾifa*" ("Leader of the Sect," i.e., Shīʿīs). Al-Ṭūsī says that immoveable property (*fayʾ*) is subject to *khums*, which the Imam is free to distribute as he pleases. He distinguished it from booty from battle, *ghanīma*, three-sixths of which (must) go to the Imam and the rest to the orphans and poor and wayfarers of the House of the Prophet. Again, he tells us that the Banū Hāshim are forbidden *ṣadaqa*, and that the *khums* replaces this benefit. He notes that some Twelver Shīʿīs disagree about this, but holds that they are wrong. He holds what will become the standard Twelver Shīʿī position hereafter, that the *khums* is an obligatory

20 percent tax on every legitimate source of profit, whether made through trade, treasure trove, mines, diving and the like.[9]

Al-Ṭabarānī (d. 360/971), of Syrian origin, and supposedly a pupil of al-Ṭabarī, wrote his "Great Commentary" (*al-Tafsīr al-kabīr*) about a half century after his teacher. He explicitly names the Ḥanafīs as believing that the Prophet's share died with him because the Prophets do not have heirs. This principle also rules out the relatives, which leaves three categories that deserve the *khums*. Al-Ṭabarānī quotes Shāfiʿī as saying that there are still five categories, the share of the Prophet going to the most urgent needs of the Muslims, and the other shares as specified, in the case of the relatives, both the rich and poor.[10]

A commentator of the Eastern Ḥanafī school, Abū al-Layth Naṣr b. Muḥammad al-Samarqandī, is a near contemporary of al-Ṭabarānī (d. between 373/983 and 393/1002–3). His work continued to have wide currency, as Joseph Schacht has said, "from Morocco to Indonesia." He follows the opinion of Abū Ḥanīfa (d. 150/767) and his school that the *khums* after the Prophet's death is to be divided in three portions, the relatives only benefitting if they can be classified as poor.[11]

An Eastern commentator of slightly later date is Aḥmad b. Muḥammad al-Thaʿlabī al-Nīsābūrī (d. 427/1035) whose enormous *al-Kashf wa-l-bayān* has only recently been published. Although many of his sources are similar to al-Ṭabarī, he quotes Ibn ʿAbbās as saying that the Prophet never took his share and that the *khums* in Muḥammad's time was divided among the remaining four categories.

Al-Thaʿlabī relates on the authority of al-Zuhrī (d. 124/742) the well-known account that Fāṭima and ʿAbbās went to Abū Bakr requesting their inheritance in Khaybar and Fadak. Abū Bakr told them that he had heard the Prophet say: "We stand in the company of Prophets and do not have heirs. What we have left as inheritance is *ṣadaqa*." Yet he quotes ʿAlī's contrary opinion: "Every person should be given his [proper] share of the *khums* which does not go to anyone else; and the Imam is in charge of the portion belonging to God and His Messenger." He even quotes the opinion – presumably Shīʿī – that all of the *khums* is for the relatives (*qirāba*) of the Prophet.[12] A student of al-Thaʿlabī, ʿAlī b. Aḥmad al-Wāḥidī al-Nīsābūrī (d. 468/1076), perhaps the most famous pre-modern expert on "occasions of revelation," follows his Shāfiʿī law school in giving a fifth of the fifth for relatives to Banū Hāshim and Banū Muṭṭalib.[13]

The outstanding philologist and commentator, al-Zamakhsharī, died 538/1144, is often said to be the last Sunnī Muʿtazilī. The extremely widely used commentary of al-Bayḍāwī (d. 685/1286) is essentially the commentary of al-Zamakhsharī with the Muʿtazilī and some rhetorical discussions removed. Al-Zamakhsharī repeats much of the material in al-Ṭabarī, including the three schools of thought on the distinction between *ghanīma* and *fay'* – either they are identical, that *fay'* implies real estate, or that *fay'* implies wealth taken under a treaty. He explicitly gives a hadith attested in much earlier sources that "It is not legal to give *ṣadaqa* to the people of the House, when God has allotted them one-fifth of the *khums*." Interestingly, he acknowledges that the Twelver Shīʿī position exists and records that "some say the whole of the *khums* belongs to the relatives of the Apostle of God." He even quotes the saying of Zayn al-ʿĀbidīn ʿAlī mentioned above, but he himself supports the view that "orphans and poor and wayfarers" applies to all Muslims.[14]

Another Eastern commentator is Abū al-Muẓaffar Manṣūr b. Muḥammad al-Samʿānī (d. 489/1096) of Marv. He puts forward the standard Shāfiʿī view that, of the booty, the share of Prophet is spent on the welfare of the Muslims, and the share of the relatives goes to them whether they are poor or wealthy. He mentions the opinion of the Ḥanafīs, that the relatives' share is added to the last three categories, and of Mālik, that the Imam has discretion over all shares and can or cannot distribute them, as the groups mentioned are permitted to have these shares but do not have them "by entitlement." There is no mention of the Ḥanbalī school, which was not strongly represented in Khurasān and Transoxiana at this time.[15]

A later scholar, Abū Muḥammad al-Ḥusayn b. Masʿūd al-Baghawī (d. 510/1117 or 516/1122), author of one of the most admired works on hadith, wrote an extensive commentary. Surprisingly, he believes that Mālik and al-Shāfiʿī agree that the share of the booty for the relatives still is an established right down to the present. Al-Baghawī adds:

> The Book [the Qurʾān] and the Sunna both indicate the permanence [of the right of the relatives to a share of the *khums*] and the caliphs succeeding the Prophet used to distribute it, and the poor were not given preference over the rich because the Prophet and the caliphs gave a share to ʿAbbās b. ʿAbd al-Muṭṭalib in spite of his abundant wealth.[16]

A near contemporary of al-Baghawī is the scholar al-Maybudī who flourished around 520/1126. His commentary is one of the largest pre-modern works in Persian. Al-Maybudī, somewhat surprisingly, says that *khums* comes out of both wealth acquired as booty and wealth in immoveable property acquired from non-Muslims through conquest or treaty, including the categories of *jizya* and *kharāj*. He describes the Prophet's share as going to the treasury for the welfare of the Muslims for such purposes as securing the frontier posts and the salaries of judges and muezzins.[17]

Commentaries of the middle period

The seventh century of the Hijra (thirteenth century CE) was a rich period for Islamic scholarship, and one of the great commentators of this period was the Spanish jurist al-Qurṭubī (d. 671/1272), who was of the Mālikī school. He begins with an interesting philological discussion: *ghanīma* is "that which a man or a group attains by an effort from the unbelievers." *Fayʾ* is all wealth or property that comes to Muslims without war, such as the canonical taxes of *kharāj* and *jizya*. Characteristically of the Mālikīs, he says "portions under the *khums* are at the discretion of the leader of the Muslims." He holds that the four first caliphs acted in this way.[18]

In the following century, one of the most important and respected commentaries is by the conservative scholar Ibn Kathīr, who died in 775/1373. As a specialist in the biography of the Prophet, he is particularly concerned with the occasion of revelation. He holds that the verse of *khums* was revealed after the battle of Badr, while the verse of *fay'* was revealed after the occupation of the quarter of Banū Naḍīr. But the verses do not really contradict one another. He quotes in several different forms letters from the Apostle of God to groups submitting to Islam. For example, there is a letter that reads "To Banū Zuhayr b. Qays: If you bear witness that there is no god but God, and establish the prayer, and pay the *zakāt*, and separate from the heathen and pay the *khums* of the *ghanā'im* and the *ṣafī* [i.e., the object or objects which the leader of the victorious army may select for himself], then you are protected by the safe-conduct of God and of the Apostle!" Ibn Kathīr judges this hadith to be sound. Interestingly, in the context of the early Mamluk state, he says the *walī al-amr*, the general legatee of the Prophet, has the right of disposal over the *khums*. He judges another hadith sound in which the Apostle of God said to the Banū Hāshim, "I wish you to be free from washing other people's hands, because you have a fifth of the fifth, which will make you rich, or at least self-sufficient."[19]

The major Twelver Shīʿī commentary of the sixth century was written by al-Ṭabarsī – or, more correctly, al-Ṭabrisī (d. 548/1154). He says that the tradition transmitted from the Imams agrees with al-Shāfiʿī that *ghanīma* is what is taken in battle and *fay'* is what is taken without fighting. This verse therefore does not abrogate similar verse in Sūrat al-Ḥashr [Qur'ān, LIX:7] that specifies *fay'* for the relatives (among other categories). Al-Ṭabarsī says that according to his school (Shīʿism), *khums* is to be divided into six categories, of which the first three, God's share, the share of the Prophet and the share of the relatives goes to the Imam who stands in the place of the Prophet. The last three categories, the orphans, the poor and the wayfarer, all refer to the Family of the Prophet, as God has forbidden them the *ṣadaqāt*. The Twelvers agree with Ibn ʿAbbās and Mujāhid that the Banū Hāshim alone are intended, to the exclusion of the Banū Muṭṭalib. The Twelvers also believe that the *khums* is to be paid on any profit made from transactions, profits of trade, treasure trove, mines, diving and the like. Al-Ṭabarsī quotes two opinions that agree with his own, namely that three of the six shares go to the Imam arising after the Prophet. Finally, he quotes Ibn ʿAbbās as saying: "The *khums* is licit for us and the mark of honor (*karāma*) is licit for us."[20]

In his commentary, the Ḥanbalī polymath Ibn al-Jawzī (d. 597/1201) says that one of the three opinions on the fifth not distributed to the fighting men is that the share of God and of the Prophet is added to that of the relatives. This opinion is transmitted by the Companion Ibn Abī Ṭalḥa from Ibn ʿAbbās. Ibn al-Jawzī then discusses opinions about the Prophet's share, and says that the founder of his school, Aḥmad b. Ḥanbal (d. 241/855), agreed with al-Shāfiʿī that the Prophet's share after his death went to the welfare of the Muslims. He also understands Aḥmad b. Ḥanbal to be supporting the view of al-Shāfiʿī that the relatives are the Banū Hāshim and the Banū Muṭṭalib, even if they are rich.[21]

The commentator al-Nasafī (d. 710/1310) is a typical member of the Central Asian Ḥanafī school from far off Soghdiana. He flatly states as most Ḥanafīs do that the shares of the Prophet and the relatives are canceled with the Prophet's death. Yet he adds that a share goes to the poor relatives, not the rich relatives of the Prophet. It is not clear whether he considers their entitlement to come from this verse or from the share of the poor, although as a Ḥanafī he probably means the latter.[22]

The Sufi commentators

A separate strand of interpretation is found among the Sufi commentators. Al-Qushayrī (d. 465/1072), one of the most important mystics of the Islamic tradition, in his commentary relates the verse to the greater *jihād* in which the *ghanīma* is the recapture of the self or soul from desire and Satan. Inwardly, the place of seeking one's desires becomes the place of seeking God's satisfaction. In this way the servant of God is freed from the slavery of owning any share.[23]

Sufi commentary by ʿAbd al-Razzāq al-Kāshānī (d. 736/1336), often attributed to the great Ibn al-ʿArabī (d. 638/1240), discusses the verse in the same spirit. The five portions mentioned in the verse are the elements in the "comprehensive unicity [of man]" (*al-tawḥīd al-jamʿī*); the heart belongs to the Prophet, the share of the relatives means "the secret" (*al-sirr*) (which is given to them); the orphans are the theoretical and practical rational faculties; the poor are the faculty of sense perception; and the wayfarer is the inner traveling self in exile, traveling far from its original place.[24]

The later commentators

The Ottoman commentator Abū al-Saʿūd, who died in 982/1574, served as *Shaykh al-Islām* under Süleyman the Magnificent. He was a Ḥanafī, like all holders of that office. He believed that the Imam has the right to do as he likes with prisoners as well as with land seized as plunder. This theory was important for Ottoman rule, because it sanctioned the *devşirme*, a levy of the Christian youths of the Balkans, to form the elite army corps called Janissaries. On the issue of the rights of the House of the Apostle, he quotes Zayd b. ʿAlī (d. 122/740), who is supposed to have said "We [ʿAlids] do not have the right to build forts or buy mounts from [the *khums*]." Doubtless the Ottomans, who saw themselves faced with the Safavid Twelver Shīʿī movement to their east, which championed the rights of the Family of the Prophet, wished to hear that defending their lands had priority over the claims of the Family.[25]

A Safavid commentator, al-Fayḍ al-Kāshānī, died 1091/1680, is one of the great intellects of the Shīʿī tradition. His commentary on this verse, however, is completely traditional and shows strong continuity with the commentary of al-Ṭūsī. He writes, "I say that *ghanīma* means the income from wealth (*māl*) of any sort whatever." He quotes not only al-Ṭūsī but also al-ʿAyyāshī, who by this time had been integrated into the mainstream Twelver Shīʿī tradition. He makes it clear that payment of the *khums* is necessary for the individual believer's salvation, writing "If you have believed in God, know that the *khums* is obligatory in order to draw near to Him, and be satisfied with the four-fifths [that remain for you]."[26]

Conclusion

It will be no surprise to any specialist in Qur'ān commentary that the commentators draw heavily on each other, particularly as the tradition develops. Nevertheless, some of the later commentators go back to collections of hadith as does Ibn Kathīr whose commentary stands as one of the most extensive *tafsīr*s *bi-l-ma'thūr* or "commentary explicated by tradition." In the commentaries less exhaustive of hadith, there continues to be a difference in the choice of hadith used as proof text. Only the longer commentaries are interested in preserving established points of *ikhtilāf*, "difference," such as whether the phrase "for God" implies a sixth portion – a view nearly universally rejected by the Sunnīs and nearly universally adopted by the Shīʿīs.

The adhesion of commentators to their respective Islamic law-school dominates the commentaries from the middle Islamic period almost to the present, but this adhesion is not absolute. The insistence of the Shāfiʿī al-Baghawī that the Mālikī position agrees with the Shāfiʿī position is both contradicted by some scholars (e.g., al-Qurṭubī, a Mālikī, and Ibn Kathīr, a Shāfiʿī). Among Ḥanafīs the most important modification of the original opinion of that school is offered by Abū al-Saʿūd who adds to the Imam's rights the land seized as plunder.

Among Twelver Shīʿīs there is general agreement although with some modifications. Al-ʿAyyāshī, except for affirming the Imam's right to *khums*, does not describe the sources of wealth to which it applies. Al-Qummī states the Twelver Shīʿī case more plainly: there are six parts to the *khums*, three of which go to the Imam. The Imam also collects the other three parts to give to those named in the Qur'ān. In the commentary written over a hundred years later by al-Ṭūsī, we are given a presentation of subsequent Twelver belief without, however, explaining to whom *khums* is paid in the absence of the Imam. The seventeenth-century commentary by al-Fayḍ al-Kāshānī is also silent on this point.[27]

The Sufi commentaries are remarkable for the largely individual ways in which they interpret the inner meaning of the verse. Not one of the three Sufi commentators draws on another.

Modern Shīʿī scholars point out that none of the schools restrict *khums* to the spoils of battle. All law schools recognize that buried treasure is *ghanīma*, and Ḥanafīs and Twelver Shīʿīs agree that mines are subject to *khums*.[28] But the Ḥanafīs regard wealth from mines not fully exploited as well as buried treasure to be plunder abandoned by pre-Muslim peoples.

An interesting discussion in many commentaries bears on the reasons that the Qur'ān gives the relatives a claim to the *khums*. No commentary known to me says that all the *sayyid*s or *sharīf*s have inherently better inherited characteristics (or, to use contemporary language, better genetic material). Clearly, for many authors, it is a mark of respect for the Prophet that his heirs should have special rights. Both Sunnī and Shīʿī commentaries say that it replaces the *ṣadaqa*, which is forbidden for the descendants of the Prophet. It is significant that only the *ṣadaqa* and not the *zakāt* is mentioned in these contexts and, because when the two terms are not used interchangeably, *ṣadaqa* means voluntary alms.

Al-ʿAyyāshī quotes Jaʿfar al-Ṣādiq, the sixth of the twelve Imams, as saying: "The *khums* for us is a duty (*farīḍa*), and the mark of honor/grace (*al-karāma*) bestowed on us is a licit matter."[29]

Al-Ṭabarsī, as mentioned above, repeats this sentiment, again referring to the mark of honor/grace that the payment of the *khums* embodies. As al-Maybudī observes above, this right of the relatives has nothing to do with the poverty or wealth of the recipients. Yet Ibn Kathīr quotes the Prophet as saying that he wished the Banū Hāshim "to be free of washing other people's hands," because the *khums* will make them rich or at least self-sufficient.

Is the *khums*, even that minor *khums* granted by Ḥanafīs out of treasure trove, meant to keep the relatives of the Prophet from poverty? Is it meant to honor the Prophet by honoring his kinsmen, regardless of their need? Is it a privilege to pay the kinsmen of the Prophet? Or, is it all or some or none of these? This question is in part addressed by the commentaries as well as other sources. It is a distinct question but related to the question of the sociological function of *sayyids*/*sharīfs*. These respected kinsmen of the Prophet wished to maintain their collective right to some sort of income and also to preserve their role as sanctified members of the societies in which they lived. A fuller answer to the questions as to why they "deserve" this distinction will provide insight into the presence of this privileged category in Muslim societies.

Notes

1 Some material from Qur'ānic commentaries is given in the excellent article "Khums" by A. Zysow and R. Gleave in H. A. R. Gibb et al. eds, *The Encyclopaedia of Islam*, new ed., 13 vols (Leiden: Brill, 1960–2009; hereafter *EI2*), XII:531–535.
2 ʿAlī b. Muḥammad al-Māwardī, *al-Nukat wa-l-ʿuyūn*, ed. by al-Sayyid b. ʿAbd al-Maqṣūd b. ʿAbd al-Raḥīm, 6 vols (Beirut: Dār al-Kutub al-ʿIlmiyya and Mu'assasat al-Kutub al-Thaqāfiyya, 1413/1992), II:318–321.
3 Muqātil b. Sulaymān, *Tafsīr Muqātil b. Sulaymān*, ed. by ʿAbd Allāh Maḥmūd Shiḥāta, 5 vols (Cairo: al-Hay'a al-Miṣriyya al-ʿĀmma li-l-Kitāb, 1399–1410/1979–1989), II:116.
4 Al-Ṭabarī, *Jāmiʿ al-bayān*, 30 vols, 3rd printing (Cairo: Muṣṭafā al-Bābī al-Ḥalabī, 1388/1968), X:1–9.

5 Hūd b. Muḥakkam al-Huwwārī, *Tafsīr Kitāb Allāh al-ʿazīz*, ed. by Bālḥājj b. Saʿīd Sharīfī, 4 vols (Beirut: Dār al-Gharb al-Islāmī, 1411/1990), II:90–94.
6 Muḥammad b. ʿIsā Aṭṭafayyish, *Tafsīr himyān al-zād ilā dār al-maʿād*. www.altafsir.com (accessed 25 June 2011).
7 Muḥammad b. Masʿūd al-ʿAyyāshī, *al-Tafsīr*, ed. by Qism al-Dirāsāt al-Islāmiyya, Mu'assasat al-Baʿtha, 3 vols (Qum: Mu'assasat al-Baʿtha, 1421/2000), II:199–203.
8 ʿAlī b. Ibrāhīm al-Qummī, *Tafsīr al-Qummī*, ed. by Ṭayyib al-Mūsawī al-Jazā'irī, 2 vols (Beirut: Dār al-Surūr, 1412/1991), I:204–205.
9 Muḥammad b. al-Ḥasan al-Ṭūsī, *al-Tibyān fī tafsīr al-Qur'ān*, ed. by Aḥmad Shawqī al-Amīn and Aḥmad Ḥabīb Quṣayr al-ʿĀmilī, 10 vols (Najaf: al-Maṭbaʿa al-ʿIlmiyya, 1377–1383/1957–1963), V:143–146.
10 Sulaymān b. Aḥmad al-Ṭabarānī, *al-Tafsīr al-kabīr*, ed. by Hishām b. ʿAbd al-Karīm al-Badrānī al-Mawṣilī, 6 vols (Irbid: Dār al-Kitāb al-Thaqāfī and Dār al-Mutanabbī, 1429/2008), III:260–261.
11 Abū al-Layth al-Samarqandī, *Tafsīr al-Samarqandī*, ed. by ʿAlī Muḥammad Muʿawwaḍ, ʿĀdil Aḥmad ʿAbd al-Mawjūd, Zakariyyā ʿAbd al-Majīd al-Nawutī, 3 vols (Beirut: Dār al-Kutub al-ʿIlmiyya, 1414/1993), II:18–19. See J. Schacht, "Abū'l-Layth al-Samarḳandī," in *EI2*, I:137.
12 Aḥmad b. Muḥammad al-Thaʿlabī, *Al-Kashf wa-l-bayān al-maʿrūf bi-Tafsīr al-Thaʿlabī*, ed. by Abū Muḥammad b. ʿĀshūr and Naẓīr al-Sāʿidī, 10 vols (Beirut: Dār Iḥyā' al-Turāth al-ʿArabī, 1423/2002), IV:357–361.
13 ʿAlī b. Aḥmad al-Wāḥidī, *al-Wasīṭ fī tafsīr al-Qur'ān al-majīd*, ed. by ʿĀdil Aḥmad ʿAbd al-Mawjūd et al., 4 vols (Beirut: Dār al-Kutub al-ʿIlmiyya, 1415/1994), II:460–463.
14 Al-Zamakhsharī, *al-Kashshāf ʿan ḥaqā'iq ghawāmiḍ al-tanzīl*, 4 vols (Beirut: Dār al-Kitāb al-ʿArabī, 1366/1947), II:221–223.
15 Abū al-Muẓaffar al-Samʿānī, *Tafsīr al-Qur'ān*, ed. by Abū Tamīm Yāsir b. Ibrāhīm and Abū Bilāl Ghanīm b. ʿAbbās b. Ghanīm, 6 vols (Riyadh: Dār al-Waṭan, 1418/1997), II:265–266.
16 Abū Muḥammad al-Ḥusayn b. Masʿūd al-Baghawī, *Tafsīr al-Baghawī*, ed. by Muḥammad ʿAbd Allāh al-Nimr, ʿUthmān Jumʿa Ḍumayriyya, Sulaymān Muslim al-Ḥarash, 8 vols (Riyadh: Dār al-Ṭibah, 1418/1997), III:357–359.
17 Al-Maybudī, *Kashf al-asrār wa-ʿuddat al-abrār*, 10 vols (Tehran: Dānishgāh-i Tihrān, 1331–1339 AHS/1952–3–1960–1), IV:49–64.
18 Al-Qurṭubī, *al-Jāmiʿ li-aḥkām al-Qur'ān*. www.altafsir.com (accessed 5 March 2011).
19 Ibn Kathīr, *Tafsīr Ibn Kathīr*, ed. by Ṣalāḥ ʿAbd al-Fattāḥ al-Khālidī, 6 pts (Amman: Dār al-Fārūq, 1429/2008), III:1483–1487.
20 Faḍl b. al-Ḥasan al-Ṭabrisī, *Majmaʿ al-bayān*, 10 vols in 5 (Qum: Maktabat al-Marʿashī, 1403/1983), II:543–545.
21 Abū al-Faraj ʿAbd al-Raḥmān b. ʿAlī ibn al-Jawzī, *Zād al-masīr fī ʿilm al-tafsīr*, ed. by ʿAbd al-Razzāq al-Mahdī, 4 vols (Beirut: Dār al-Kitāb al-ʿArabī, 1422/2001), II:211–212.
22 ʿAbd Allāh b. Aḥmad al-Nasafī, *Tafsīr al-Nasafī: Madārik al-tanzīl*, ed. by Marwān Muḥammad al-Shaʿʿār, 4 vols (Beirut: Dār al-Nafā'is, 1417/1996), II:41.
23 ʿAbd al-Karīm b. Hawāzin al-Qushayrī, *Laṭā'if al-ishārāt*, ed. by Ibrāhīm Basyūnī, 3 vols, 2nd ed. (Cairo: al-Hay'a al-Miṣriyya al-ʿĀmma li-l-Kitāb, 1401–1404/1981–1983), I:625.
24 Ibn al-ʿArabī (attr.), *Tafsir al-Qur'ān al-karīm*, ed. by Muṣṭafā Ghālib, 2 vols, 2nd ed. (Beirut: Dār al-Andalus, 1398/1978), I:477. Another important commentary in the Sufi tradition is by Ibn ʿAjība (d. 1224/1809).
25 Abū al-Saʿūd Muḥammad b. Muḥammad, *Tafsīr Abī al-Saʿūd*. www.altafsir.com (accessed 15 March 2011).

26 Al-Fayḍ al-Kāshānī, *Kitāb al-ṣāfī fī tafsīr al-Qur'ān*, ed. by Muḥsin al-Ḥusaynī al-Amīnī, 7 vols (Tehran: Dār al-Kutub al-Islāmiyya, 1419/1998–9), III:340–342.
27 For the discussion of *khums* among the Shīʿī jurists, see the learned appendix on the subject by Abdulaziz Sachedina, *The Just Ruler in Shīʿite Islam* (New York: Oxford University Press, 1988), esp. 239–243.
28 See, e.g., Sayyid Muḥammad Rizvī, *Khums: An Islamic Tax* (Qum: Ansariyan Publications, 1992).
29 Al-ʿAyyāshī, *Tafsīr*, II:202.

3 Debate on the status of *sayyid/sharīfs* in the modern era

The ʿAlawī–Irshādī dispute and Islamic reformists in the Middle East

Yamaguchi Motoki

Introduction

Elucidating the Muslim discourses that have surrounded the Prophet's family, in addition to clarifying the historical experiences of the family members, is a task that is essential to the furthering of our understanding of the roles and statuses of *sayyid/sharīf*s across different eras and locations.[1] A significant event for a study in this area is the large-scale debate on the status of *sayyid/sharīf*s that spread across the Islamic world in the early twentieth century. It originated from a polemic among the Arabs in Southeast Asia, the majority of who were immigrants from Ḥaḍramawt, a region in Southern Arabia, and their descendants.[2] In their homeland, the *sayyid/sharīf*s, named ʿAlawīs or Bā ʿAlawīs, had been entitled to a high social status owing to their noble pedigree. Within Southeast Asia's Arab community, however, a group influenced by Islamic reformism began to deny the privilege granted to the ʿAlawīs, or the *sayyid/sharīfs* in general, advocating equality among all Muslims. Their activities later crystallized into the establishment of an organization – the Arab Association for Reform and Guidance (Jamʿiyyat al-Iṣlāḥ wa-l-Irshād al-ʿArabiyya, henceforth, al-Irshād) – in Batavia in 1914. A great debate raged between the two parties, which also involved non-Ḥaḍramī Muslims and continued into the 1930s.

Studies to date have described this dispute as a competition over leadership in the Ḥaḍramī community of Southeast Asia.[3] As a result, since it has been recognized only within the local context, little attention has been paid to the dispute in terms of its value to the study of *sayyid/sharīf*s. The arguments over the special position of the Prophet's descendents have been regarded as superficial, and the roles of Muslims other than the Ḥaḍramī have almost been ignored.

Thus, this study proposes to examine the dispute in a larger context. It will pay special attention to interventions in the dispute by Muslims outside the Ḥaḍramī community in Southeast Asia or Ḥaḍramawt, and examine their arguments on the status of *sayyid/sharīf*s. In particular, it focuses on two prominent thinkers of Islamic reformism, who were influential in many parts of the Islamic world including Southeast Asia. The first is Muḥammad Rashīd

Riḍā (d. 1935), the chief editor of the Egyptian journal *al-Manār* who was himself a descendant of the Prophet.[4] The other is Shakīb Arslān (d. 1946), who was born into a distinguished Druze family in Lebanon. Both studied under Muḥammad ʿAbduh (d. 1905) and were closely associated with one another.[5] Initially, only Riḍā was involved in the dispute, but by the early 1930s, both thinkers were attempting to reconcile Southeast Asian Arabs.[6] In the course of such attempts, several issues relevant to the special position of *sayyid/sharīf*s were raised. I will examine the opinions of both Riḍā and Arslān on these issues to elucidate how the position of the Prophet's descendants was redefined in modern Muslim thought as well as the actual impact of this redefinition on the lives of *sayyid/sharīf*s in Southeast Asia.

This study is primarily based on contemporary Arabic periodicals. The dispute in question was for the most part conducted through these periodicals, which enabled it to have an expansive geographical range. These periodicals can be divided into two groups. The first consists of the Egyptian periodicals *al-Manār* (1898–1935) and *al-Fatḥ* (1926–48),[7] both of which had wide circulation in Southeast Asia. The second comprises periodicals published by Arabs in the Netherlands East Indies and Singapore in the 1930s, such as the pro-ʿAlawī *Ḥaḍramawt* (1923–33, Surabaya) and *al-ʿArab* (1931–35, Singapore) and the pro-Irshādī *al-Hudā* (1931–34, Singapore) and *al-Kuwayt wa-l-ʿIrāqī* (1931–32, Batavia/Buitenzorg).[8]

Outset of the dispute

The conflict within the Southeast Asian Arab community began with arguments over two practices that had been regarded as privileges of the descendants of Prophet Muḥammad, especially in Ḥaḍramawt. They were the marriage restriction on a *sharīfa* (an honorific title for female descendants of the Prophet in Ḥaḍramawt, i.e., an ʿAlawī woman) and the practice of "kissing hands" (*taqbīl* or *shamma*)[9] of the ʿAlawīs.

It has generally been accepted that the society in Ḥaḍramawt was divided on the basis of lineage.[10] The ʿAlawīs – the descendants of Muḥammad – were placed at the top of the social ladder. Owing to a custom that banned a person from marrying his daughter to a man of a lower stratum, a marriage between a *sharīfa* and a non-*sayyid/sharīf* was strictly prohibited there. Nevertheless, the early twentieth century witnessed some marriages that disregarded this restriction among the Arabs in Southeast Asia.

In 1905, a *sharīfa* in Singapore married an Indian Muslim who claimed to be a descendant of the Prophet. Yet, because the authenticity of his pedigree was questionable, the ʿAlawīs denounced the marriage. In response to the letter of a reader from Singapore, Riḍā published an opinion on the case in question in *al-Manār*, and stated that the marriage could be legal regardless of the pedigree of the groom, although he acknowledged the lack of information available to him. In contrast, Sayyid ʿUmar al-ʿAṭṭās, an ʿAlawī scholar in Sumatra, declared the marriage illegal in his *fatwā* (legal opinion), to which

Riḍā, in turn, published a rejoinder in *al-Manār*, further elaborating on the legality of the marriage.[11]

After a lapse of several years, the controversy over such marriages provoked a greater problem within the Arab community, which stirred up divisions. In 1911, an organization in Batavia, Jamᶜiyyat Khayr (the Association for Welfare),[12] most of whose members were Arabs of Ḥaḍramī descent, recruited three scholars from Mecca to be teachers at its schools. Among them, a Sudanese by the name of Aḥmad b. Muḥammad al-Sūrkatī (or Sūrkittī)[13] earned a reputation and consolidated his position because of his deep knowledge and skillful school management. Despite his prominence, during his visit to Solo in 1913, he stated that the marriage between a *sharīfa* and a non-*sayyid/sharīf* was legal. This led to angry reactions from the conservative ᶜAlawīs in the association. The dissension between al-Sūrkatī and the leading circle of the association, dominated by the ᶜAlawīs, became severe. As a result, al-Sūrkatī tendered his resignation and broke away from Jamᶜiyyat Khayr in September 1914.

The disagreement between ᶜAlawīs such as ᶜUmar al-ᶜAṭṭās and reformist scholars such as Riḍā and al-Sūrkatī highlighted the different interpretations of *kafāʾa* (suitability of the groom to the bride) in Islamic law. Al-ᶜAṭṭās maintained that it was necessary to fulfill the *kafā'a* of pedigree (*nasab*) in marriage.[14] In his view, because of their link to "the intrinsic nobility" (*sharaf dhātī*) of the Prophet, which can never be attained by anyone other than them, the *sayyid/sharīf*s were placed at the highest stratum on account of their pedigree. In addition, among Arabs, it is common to believe that marrying a woman to a man inferior to her would bring dishonor (*ᶜār*) to her as well as her agnates. On the basis of these arguments, al-ᶜAṭṭās concluded that, because a marriage between a *sharīfa* and a man of non-*sayyid/sharīf* pedigree was equivalent to harming the Prophet himself, it should never be permitted, even if the woman and her guardian(s) (*walī*) consented to it. ᶜUmar al-ᶜAṭṭās also insisted, on the basis of a hadith, that the descendants of Ḥasan and Ḥusayn, the Prophet's two grandchildren, were the masters of mankind. Accordingly, he compared a marriage between an ordinary Muslim man and a *sharīfa* to that between a slave and his mistress. Although his opinion sounds rather extreme, it should be noted that the observance of *kafāʾa* in pedigree was not specific to al-ᶜAṭṭās or Ḥaḍramī ᶜAlawīs. The interpretation of *kafāʾa* is indeed said to have been stricter in Ḥaḍramawt than other Muslim regions,[15] but it was also a widely accepted stipulation among those following classic Sunnī family law.[16] In addition, the descendants of the Prophet outside Ḥaḍramawt tended to intermarry among themselves.[17]

In contrast to his more conservative opponents, Riḍā asserted that all Muslims were basically equal in the Islamic jurisprudence and that it was not indispensable to consider *kafā'a* of pedigree in marriage.[18] According to him, the marriage of a daughter of *sayyid/sharīf*s to a man of non-*sayyid/sharīf* pedigree was legal even in regions where such a marriage would be considered dishonorable, provided that the woman and her guardian(s) agree to that marriage. He classified marriages as *muʿāmalāt* (interpersonal acts), which are based on *maṣlaḥa* (welfare), and held that the parties concerned in a marriage best understood their own *maṣlaḥa*. Al-Sūrkatī also emphasized the equality of all Muslims and maintained that, if some items such as pedigree were not equivalent between spouses, a woman was likely to give her consent only if she could discern the groom's merits and demerits. Accordingly, he continued that, as long as the groom was a Muslim, the condition of a legal marriage was the woman's consent if she had come of age and could deliberate (*rashīda*); on the other hand, if she was still a minor, the condition would be the approval of her guardian(s).[19]

The other practice that led to discord in the Arab community in Southeast Asia was the "kissing hands" of *sayyid/sharīf*s, a practice that had been generally followed in Ḥaḍramawt. This became a source of contention in the early twentieth century when ʿUmar b. Yūsuf Manqūsh, a non-ʿAlawī Ḥaḍramī businessman who served as the *kapitein* (head of a community appointed by the Dutch colonial government) in Batavia, refused to kiss the hands of ʿUmar al-ʿAṭṭās.[20] Manqūsh was a supporter of Jamʿiyyat Khayr and later became one of the founding members of al-Irshād.

This latter problem tended to assume less importance in the dispute over the position of the Prophet's descendents because some of the ʿAlawīs also considered the practice improper.[21] Nevertheless, we should not ignore the fact that non-Ḥaḍramī Muslims also engaged in the discussion regarding this matter. For instance, Ahmad Hassan (d. 1958), a leading figure in Persatuan Islam (Persis), a reformist organization in the Dutch East Indies, condemned the practice in *Utusan Melayu*, a Malay newspaper published in Singapore.[22]

Riḍā also expressed his opinion on this issue, again in reply to a question posed by a Singaporean reader of *al-Manār*.[23] He argued that if the *sayyid/sharīf*s allege that the practice is a legitimate right of the descendants of the Prophet established by Sunna and that those who renounced it offend Sunna, "they are adding to the law of Allah something which does not belong to it. This is one of the most grievous sins." Sunna of greeting, argued Riḍā, was to say "*salām*" and shake hands, not to "kiss hands." The practice of "kissing hands" would be permissible (*mubāḥ*) as long as it was not attributed to the religion and instead merely regarded as a custom (*ʿāda*), and kept from becoming the cause of any evil (*mafsada*). However, if the practice was treated as part of the religion, as it actually was by the *sayyid/sharīf*s in Ḥaḍramawt, it would become harmful and, for that reason, such treatment should be prohibited.

It was these issues that caused a split within the Arab community in Southeast Asia. It is noteworthy that, at the outset of the dispute, the opponents of the ʿAlawīs relied upon influential reformist scholars outside the Southeast Asian Ḥaḍramī community or Ḥaḍramawt, such as Riḍā and al-Surkatī, to rationalize their assertion. As Bujra points out, within the Ḥaḍramī society the ʿAlawīs had been the ultimate Islamic authority; hence, the Ḥaḍramīs who tried to object to them had to appeal to outside authorities who could be considered "higher" than the ʿAlawīs.[24]

After his secession from Jamʿiyyat Khayr, al-Sūrkatī opened a private school in Batavia in September 1914. He and his supporters formed a new organization, al-Irshād, in order to raise funds for the school. With support and assistance from anti-ʿAlawī Ḥaḍramīs, reform-minded indigenous Muslims, and even some ʿAlawīs sympathetic to the idea of al-Irshād, the organization grew rapidly, opening branches in other cities. In the meantime, although the ʿAlawīs continued the activities of the Jamʿiyyat Khayr, they established a new representative body – the ʿAlawī Union (al-Rābiṭa al-ʿAlawiyya) – in Batavia in 1927.[25]

Changes in the issues

Although the discord within the Arab community in Southeast Asia escalated and even resulted in some violent encounters in the late 1920s and early 1930s,[26] several attempts at reconciliation were also made during the same period. It was in this period that Arslān first intervened in the dispute. In 1931, at the request of Yūnus al-Baḥrī, one of the editors of *al-Kuwayt wa-l-ʿIrāqī*, Arslān published an open letter in which he offered advice to each of the two parties and suggested the formation of a committee for arbitration as a concrete step toward settling the dispute. It seems, however, there was little response to Arslān's appeal from the Arabs in Southeast Asia. This was probably because, at that time, the settlement talks mediated by an Egyptian organization called the Eastern Union (al-Rābiṭa al-Sharqiyya)[27] were in their final stage and attracting much attention.[28]

The Eastern Union embarked upon negotiations to accommodate the dispute among the Arabs in Southeast Asia in early 1930.[29] It appointed al-Sūrkatī, a central figure of al-Irshād, and Sayyid Ibrāhīm b. ʿUmar al-Saqqāf,[30] an influential ʿAlawī resident in Singapore, as negotiators (*wasīṭ*) in the capacity of representatives. After about eighteen months of secret correspondence, the two reached an agreement in October 1931. In November, they published the terms of settlement that had been signed by representatives of both sides.[31] The signatory of al-Irshād was its Secretary-General, ʿAbd Allāh b. ʿAqīl Bā Juray, while al-Sūrkatī was only a negotiator. As for the ʿAlawī Union, while al-Saqqāf concurrently held the position of representative,[32] his agreement to participate in the reconciliation had been approved by one of the leaders of the ʿAlawī Union, ʿAlawī b. Ṭāhir al-Ḥaddād.[33] Further, the two editors of *al-Kuwayt wa-l-ʿIrāqī*, Yūnus al-Baḥrī and ʿAbd al-ʿAzīz al-Rashīd, also participated in the negotiations and attended the signing. This appears to be the first time the terms of a settlement were published with signatures of representatives from both groups. However, the terms were met with dissatisfaction from a rather large number of people.

It must be pointed out here that the issues of dispute among Southeast Asia's Arabs had changed by the time of these negotiations. The two issues that had been most prominent at the outset of the conflict – the marriage restriction on *sharīfa*s and "kissing hands" of *sayyid/sharīf*s – were no longer the main topics of discussion. They were replaced by two new issues: the application of the title "*sayyid*" and the authenticity of the pedigree of the ʿAlawīs.[34]

The first of these new issues concerned the use of the title "*sayyid*" and whether it should be restricted to the descendants of the Prophet.[35] In May 1931, the congress of al-Irshād decided that, henceforth, the title would also be applied to people other than the descendants of the Prophet as a common honorific for men, just like "mister" in English or "*tuan*" in Malay.[36] This decision entailed a revision of nothing other than the constitution of al-Irshād. The constitution included the sentence, "no one from the *sayyid*s (*sāda*) is allowed to become a member of the executive," where the word "*sayyid*" was used to indicate a descendant of the Prophet. Therefore, the sentence was rewritten to convey that "no one from the Bā ʿAlawī family (*Āl Bā ʿAlawī*) is allowed to become a member of the executive or his deputy."[37] The decision resulted in the ʿAlawīs submitting petitions to both the Dutch and British colonial governments for legally restricting the use of this title to only the descendants of the Prophet. The Irshādīs, in turn, tried to dissuade the colonial authorities from intervening in this issue. In the end, the British government did not make any decision to restrict the title legally. In February 1933, the Dutch government also rejected the ʿAlawīs' petition and suggested that the last name (*nisba*) "*ʿAlawī*" should be used to distinguish between the ʿAlawīs and non-ʿAlawīs instead.[38]

The other issue was that the Irshādī discredited the authenticity of the ʿAlawīs' claim to have descended from the Prophet. The term "*ʿAlawī*" generally implies "a descendant of ʿAlī." Yet, because the *sayyid/sharīf*s in Ḥaḍramawt have an ancestor named ʿAlawī b. ʿUbayd Allāh, the term also indicates his descendants.[39] Both "*ʿAlawī*" and "*Bā ʿAlawī*" had been used synonymously to identify a *sayyid/sharīf* of Ḥaḍramwt origin. The Irshādīs, however, began to differentiate between the two words deliberately.[40] According to the Irshādīs, the people called "*ʿAlawī*" were certainly the descendants of the Prophet, but their opponents were not "*ʿAlawī*" but "*Bā ʿAlawī*," the descendants of ʿAlawī b. ʿUbayd Allāh who could not be identified as descendants of the Prophet.[41] In a word, the Irshādīs, in using the word "*Bā ʿAlawī*," implicitly claimed to be referring to someone who was not a descendant of the Prophet.[42] Consequently, the Irshādī side reacted negatively to the above-mentioned proposal by the Dutch colonial government to use the last name "*ʿAlawī*" instead of the title "*sayyid*." *Al-Hudā*, for instance, commented as follows:

> Here, this addition [of the last name "*ʿAlawī*"] has provoked a new controversy. And the point is summed up in its legitimacy. Are they [the Bā ʿAlawīs] entitled to use it [the last name "*ʿAlawī*"]? Without doubt, there remain obscurity and ambiguity of any kind which resist every effort to take them away. The Bā ʿAlawīs continue to strive in vain to confirm that their pedigree traces back to the ʿAlawī *sayyids*.[43]

The Irshādīs' attack on the authenticity of their pedigree brought forth harsh rebuttals from the ʿAlawīs. An article in *al-ʿArab* insisted that the difference between the two words was merely on the level of wording (*lafẓī*) and had nothing to do with "the essential nature" (*jawhar*). It defined the term "*ʿAlawī*" as "the true *nisba*" (*nisba ḥaqīqiyya*) and "*Bā ʿAlawī*" as "a colloquialism in Ḥaḍramawt" (*iṣṭilāḥ Ḥaḍramī*). It explained the following: "we are the ʿAlawīs according to the *Fuṣḥā* (classical standard Arabic) and are Bā ʿAlawī family according to the Ḥaḍramī dialect." In addition to this, the ʿAlawīs made a case for the authenticity of their pedigree as follows:

> Now, we ask them [the Irshādīs] whether they know that before the genealogy of the ʿAlawīs reached the perfection of accuracy, many scholars had traveled around several regions, corresponded, examined, and strove for accuracy. There was among them the great traveler, Sayyid ʿAlī b. Shaykh b. Shihāb, who reached Marrakesh in his journey. Do they know anything about him? Do they know any of his writings about this?[44]

It is assumed that the attack against the authenticity of the pedigree of the ʿAlawīs began around 1930, as did the new movement regarding the title "*sayyid.*" Because the attack is obviously not compatible with the questions concerning the privileges of *sayyid/sharīf*s, such as the marriage restriction on *sharīfa*, it is improbable that it would have started at the time when the older questions were under dispute.[45] More conceivably, at around the same time that they modified the constitution, the Irshādīs began to insist that their opponents were not descendants of the Prophet. In addition, it should also be noted that not all of the Irshādīs questioned the authenticity of the ʿAlawīs' descent. For example, al-Sūrkatī was not willing to take up this matter; he used the term "*ʿAlawī*" even when he was arguing fiercely with the ʿAlawīs.[46]

Let us now return to the terms of settlement, which were drawn up through the intermediation of the Eastern Union. The treatment of the two issues in the terms is so delicate and subtle that it could even escape the eyes of a careful reader during the first reading. However, in light of the situation of the dispute at that time, a close examination of the words used therein permits a relatively exact interpretation. First, the terms of settlement do not use the disputable title "*sayyid*" at all, even when they mention the ʿAlawīs. This can be understood as a favorable gesture toward the Irshādīs, in that the terms at least made no distinction between how the *sayyid/sharīf*s and non-*sayyid/sharīf*s should be addressed. Second, we can safely state that the terms of settlement implicitly accepted the authenticity of the ʿAlawīs' pedigree. The terms not only contained a passage that stated, "Do not defame the genealogies" (*ʿadam al-ṭaʿn fī al-ansāb*),[47] but also used the word "*ʿAlawī*" and not "*Bā ʿAlawī.*" This, however, does not imply that the ʿAlawīs obtained what they had sought. In fact, the ʿAlawī side had demanded insertion of the passage that recognized the authenticity of their pedigree more clearly: "Because the genealogies of the ʿAlawīs are authentic, do not defame them. Because the genealogies of the Irshādīs are also authentic, do not defame them." This passage was omitted in the end owing to the Irshādīs' objection.[48]

There is another point that should not be overlooked. The first term stipulates "the equality of all cultural, religious, and social rights" (*musāwāt fī jamīʿ al-ḥuqūq al-adabiyya wa-l-dīniyya wa-l-ijtimāʿiyya*) between the two parties. This term was obviously in line with the position of al-Irshād, which had campaigned for equality of all believers ever since its establishment and denied the notion of superiority based on lineage. However, what is most important here is the attitudinal change that occurred on the ʿAlawī side. The ʿAlawīs did not show any opposition to the inclusion of the term "equality" in the document.[49] This indicated that a large enough number of ʿAlawīs had renounced the notion of superiority on the basis of lineage that ʿUmar al-ʿAṭṭās had fervently defended at the outset of the dispute.

These terms of settlement disappointed quite a number of people from both parties, especially on the ʿAlawī side. While some urged their colleagues to accept the terms of settlement,[50] others – represented by the editor of *Ḥaḍramawt*, ʿAydarūs al-Mashhūr – protested against the head office of the ʿAlawī Union in Batavia.[51] Some of the Irshādīs also opposed the terms of settlement, citing the terms' recognition of the authenticity of the ʿAlawīs' descent. However, their leader, al-Sūrkatī, traveled around the branches of al-Irshād to persuade them to share his point of view, even saying that if they did not agree to the reconciliation, he would resign from his position in al-Irshād.[52]

In the end, these terms of settlement did not meet with wide enough approval among the ʿAlawīs. As a result, the ʿAlawī Union claimed that what al-Saqqāf signed was only a basic agreement, which meant that further discussion and final approval from the ʿAlawī side would be required,[53] and published its "explanation" of the terms of settlement in April 1932.[54] The "explanation" provided that the title "*sayyid*" was a privilege of the descendants of the Prophet, though, as mentioned previously, the terms of settlement had stipulated equality between the parties regarding all rights. This "explanation," however, differentiated between general rights (*ḥuqūq ʿāmma*) and special rights (*ḥuqūq khāṣṣa*). Although all believers were equal as far as the general rights were concerned, the right to bear the title "*sayyid*" belonged to the latter category, in which there was no room for equality. Because of this "explanation," the dispute between the two parties recurred and the agreement that had brought on the initial reconciliation broke down.[55]

Reconciliation attempts by two Islamic reformists

After the intermediation of the Eastern Union resulted in a total deadlock, other figures and organizations attempted to settle the dispute from the end of 1932 until the end of 1934. Among such attempts, the efforts of Riḍā and Shakīb Arslān, in particular, led to documented opinions on the two issues and records of the reactions these opinions received from the Arabs in Southeast Asia.[56] The two thinkers began their attempts to settle the controversy around the same time, prompted by Ibrāhīm al-Saqqāf. Al-Saqqāf departed from Singapore in May 1932 and called on Arslān in Geneva before visiting Riḍā in Egypt.[57]

Rashīd Riḍā

As previous studies have pointed out, Riḍā appears to have had a close relationship with al-Irshād. It is obvious that al-Irshād was strongly influenced by Riḍā's ideology. The name "al-Irshād" itself is said to have been derived from Riḍā's School for Propagation and Guidance (Madrasat al-Daʿwa wa-l-Irshād) in Egypt.[58] In addition, Riḍā supported the activities of al-Irshād in a more practical way. In the early 1920s, at the request of al-Irshād, Riḍā sent two teachers from Egypt to the Netherlands East Indies.[59] The close relationship between Riḍā and al-Irshād was also borne out of the latter's actions during the negotiations mediated by the Eastern Union. When the two parties discussed the assignment of arbitrator(s) in case they could not resolve the issues by themselves, the Irshādī side recommended none other than Riḍā, while the ʿAlawī side opposed the idea. As a result, no arbitrator was assigned.[60] Considering these facts and Riḍā's opinions on the status of the descendants of the Prophet, published at the outbreak of the dispute, we can suppose that Riḍā sided with the Irshādīs.

Therefore, it is somewhat surprising that it was not an Irshādī but an ʿAlawī, Ibrāhīm al-Saqqāf, who called on Riḍā to ask him to arbitrate the dispute. Upon his departure from Singapore, al-Saqqāf did not clearly state the purpose of his travel, and he later said that his visit to Egypt had not been originally scheduled. Involving Riḍā was probably al-Saqqāf's personal decision, because a consensus among the ʿAlawīs to ask Riḍā for arbitration would be unthinkable. In any case, around the end of 1932, Ibāhīm al-Saqqāf brought copies of the new terms of settlement to al-Irshād and the ʿAlawī Union, along with Riḍā's letter that called on the leaders of the two sides to make mutual adjustments.[61] The new terms were published in some periodicals in Southeast Asia and later in *al-Manār*.[62]

The contents of Riḍā's terms largely adhered to those previously published under the intermediation of the Eastern Union. Yet Riḍā made some amendments and additions. It is in the first term that he expressed his opinion on the two matters in hand. Similar to the previous version, it stipulates "the legal equality on detail" (*musāwāt sharʿiyya tafṣīliyya*). Then, however, it continues as follows:

> The ʿAlawīs' exclusive right (*ikhtiṣāṣ*) to the title "*sayyid*" is a part of the customary rights (*ḥuqūq ʿurfiyya*) just as that of all those whose genealogies to the two noble grandsons [i.e., Ḥasan and Ḥusayn] have been proven by independent acceptances by good many people (*tawātur*) or other things which make the genealogies proven in the Islamic law.

It should be noted that this new term permits the use of the title "*sayyid*" as a privilege of the ʿAlawīs, albeit as a customary right.[63] In addition, it is also clear from the next passage that the ʿAlawīs were recognized as the descendants of the Prophet. That is to say, Riḍā expressed opinions that supported the ʿAlawīs' stance on both issues.

Nevertheless, the point Riḍā emphasized was that the two parties had to cease their dispute and cooperate for the benefit of Islam and the Muslim Umma. This was made clear from the fact that Riḍā added a new term that stipulates the following:

> The two parties will help one another in order to serve Islam and its language [i.e., Arabic], and to resist its enemies who defame it, such as propagandists of heterodoxy (*ilḥād*), creeds (*adyān*), and sects (*niḥal*) which are contradictory to the consensus (*ijmāʿ*) of Muslims whose Islam the Sunnī people rely on. And they will not help one another in order to support any one of the enemies, according to His word "Help one another to piety and godfearing; do not help each other to sin and enmity" [Qurʾān, V:3].[64]

Furthermore, in the sixth term, Riḍā asserted that the "difference of opinions on the problems open to *ijtihād* (*masāʾil ijtihādiyya*) is natural for mankind and agreement on all of them is impossible." Therefore, he required that the two parties excuse each other and not regard problems as reasons for conflict unless they entailed a deviation from the four Sunnī *madhhab*s. The correct approach to those differences, according to Riḍā, was that "we help each other in what we agree on, and we forgive each other for what we disagree on." This tone was reiterated in his letter to the leaders of both sides and in his article published later in *al-Manār* along with the terms of settlement.

It seems that these terms put the Irshādīs in a difficult situation. Although Riḍā's judgments were hardly acceptable to the Irshādīs, they could not easily refuse them, partly because they had recommended Riḍā to be an arbitrator. They did not take a definite stance toward these terms immediately.[65] An article in *al-Hudā* avoided referring to Riḍā's judgment on the two issues and obliquely responded to the new plan for reconciliation negatively, claiming that the former reconciliation intermediated by the Eastern Union was still valid.[66] It explained that Riḍā had proposed the new plan for reconciliation because he thought the former one had been canceled. However, in reality, the ʿAlawīs had merely declined it unilaterally, as the article explained. It also criticized the inconsistent stance of the ʿAlawīs, pointing out that, while they were pretending to support Riḍā's proposal, some of them expressed opinions, either in the journal *Ḥaḍramawt* or other brochures its office distributed, that blamed him.

A few months after the terms were introduced, the Irshādī side ended up declining Riḍā's proposal more definitely. We can confirm this from an article in *al-Hudā*, which commented on a periodical in Jerusalem that had supported Riḍā's proposal and advised the two parties to follow it.[67] The article not only reiterated the validity of the former reconciliation but also declared that the judgments of Riḍā on both issues were unacceptable. The article also argued that the controversy between the two parties was "not as simple as many people think it to be, nor like a conflict between parties in Egypt." Although one could interpret the article as implicitly criticizing Riḍā's proposal because the name "Egypt" was mentioned, it still avoided hurling any direct accusations against him.[68]

Immediately after the announcement of Riḍā's proposal, the ʿAlawī side "did not hesitate to be glad, left the period of hatred and dispute, and willingly agreed to welcome the period of cooperation and harmony," declaring its acceptance of its terms.[69] An article in *al-ʿArab* of Singapore praised Riḍā and regarded his new terms of settlement "to be surely beneficial to both of the two parties." This article accused the Irshādīs of refusing many plans for reconciliation, including this one. With regard to the Irshādī's insistence on the validity of the former reconciliation, it said, "we do not want to return the discussion to the past."

After his proposal of the terms of settlement, Riḍā still continued his efforts to bring the Arab community in Southeast Asia to an agreement. Around March 1933, he held a session with some eminent Egyptian journalists and intellectuals, including ʿAbd al-Ḥamīd al-Khaṭīb (d. 1961) and Muḥammad al-Ghanīmī al-Taftāzānī (d. 1936), to talk about the problem. This resulted in the establishment of a committee to deal with the dispute among the Arabs in Southeast Asia.[70]

Shakīb Arslān

As mentioned above, when Ibrāhīm al-Saqqāf departed from Singapore in May 1932, he avoided making any definite statement about the purpose behind his trip. However, many of the Southeast Asian Arabs thought he intended to ask Arslān for arbitration,[71] because, when the ʿAlawī side had published its "explanation" of the terms of settlement in April 1932, al-Saqqāf had recommended Arslān as an arbitrator.[72] It seems reasonable to infer that one of the reasons for this recommendation was Arslān's letter, sent to the Arabs of Southeast Asia in 1931 at the request of Yūnus al-Baḥrī. In the letter, while he warned the ʿAlawīs not to regard non-*sayyid/sharīf*s as inferior to *sayyid/sharīf*s, he required the Irshādīs to recognize that the ʿAlawīs belonged to "the People of the House" (*Ahl al-Bayt*). That is to say, he had already stated his recognition of the authenticity of the ʿAlawī's pedigree. Perhaps the Irshādī side assumed a negative attitude toward this proposal for the same reason.[73]

In response to the request from al-Saqqāf, Arslān at first proposed in his letter, addressed to *Ḥaḍramawt* and dated 27 June 1932, that he would not reconcile the dispute directly but would entrust the arbitration to the General Islamic Congress (al-Mu'tamar al-Islāmī al-ʿĀmm) of Jerusalem.[74] "Because this congress has the greatest Islamic thinkers, and it is the only committee which can serve instead of the Islamic caliphate after its abolition by the Kemalists, and it is expected to remove the disease of Islam and treat its illness," Arslan opined that it was most qualified to settle the dispute among the Arabs in Southeast Asia. Thus, in December of the same year, the permanent bureau of the Congress put forth a plan of reconciliation in its letters sent to *al-Hudā* and *Ḥaḍramawt* as periodicals representative of each party.[75]

The plan suggested that both sides would immediately suspend hostilities, and each would present its explanation and opinion on the dispute to the permanent bureau, which would then render a decision after careful examination. Both groups, however, failed to achieve the unanimity needed to accept this plan, and the prospect of arbitration by the General Islamic Congress grew dim.[76] Thus, it was Arslān himself who came to arbitrate the dispute by releasing several articles in *al-Fatḥ*.

On the issue of the application of the title "*sayyid*," Arslān, contrary to Riḍā, said that the title should not be limited to the descendants of the Prophet.[77] For this, he offered the following reasons. First, even though the word "*sayyid*" was widely applied to the descendants of Ḥasan and Ḥusayn, as some authors such as Riḍā had acknowledged, "this application is," he argued, "only recognized as an idiomatic usage (*iṣṭilāḥ*) and not as the literal meaning (*maʿnā lughawī*)" of the term. He then defined the literal meaning of the word "*sayyid*" as "all those who have mastery (*siyāda*)." Of course, possession of mastery is not restricted to the kinfolk of the Prophet. Accordingly, his conclusion was that "it is reasonable to apply '*sayyid*' to all those who have mastery, whether they are from the House of the Prophet (*al-Bayt*) or not, even if they were to be non-Muslims." Arslān told the ʿAlawīs that "even if some person other than you is called '*sayyid*,' that will not diminish your mastery at all." Next, he referred to the situation of the descendants of the Prophet in other regions. According to him, even Christians bore the title "*sayyid*" in Syria; yet the descendants of the Prophet there were not irritated by that or inclined to protest against it. He also noted that those in Egypt and North Africa (*al-Maghrib*) did not prohibit others from using the title. Furthermore, Arslān explained that, from the historical point of view, it was not since early times that the term "*sayyid*" had been limited to the descendants of the Prophet.

As for the authenticity of the ʿAlawīs' pedigree, Arslān recognized it as he had done in his previous letter.[78] In his view, their pedigree had been proven by "the written records of the genealogy" (*sijillāt al-ansāb al-maktūba*) and by "being accepted independently by many people over the centuries" (*tawātur min qurūn ʿadīda*). Furthermore, Arslān even reprimanded the Irshādīs: "it is not only deplorable but makes people hostile toward the Irshādīs that some of them venture to deny the pedigree of the ʿAlawīs."

In addition, Arslān mentioned another issue: some pro-Irshādī periodicals had published articles that denied the legality of the marriage between ʿAlī and Fāṭima. Thus, Arslān sent a letter to al-Sūrkatī in November 1932, and reproached him for leaving the situation unaddressed, saying, "I do not acquit the ʿAlawīs of their fault, but your fault came to be graver."[79] This problem was then publicized by Arslān's article in *al-Fatḥ* in January 1933.[80] Responding to the article, in March 1933, the head office of al-Irshād wrote to *al-Fatḥ*, saying that neither the defamation of the "genealogy of any Muslims which has been proven" nor the aspersion cast on ʿAlī and Fāṭima was a matter relevant to the Irshādīs and that the editors of those periodicals did not have close ties with al-Irshād.[81] It also included al-Sūrkatī's statement denouncing the writer who had defamed ʿAlī.[82] In April 1933, Arslān indicated his acceptance of al-Irshād's explanation in *al-Fatḥ*, apologizing to al-Sūrkatī for his harsh reproach.[83]

Arslān's article prompted the ʿAlawī Union to release an article in *al-ʿArab*, arguing against Arslān's opinion on the problem of the application of the title "*sayyid*."[84] First, the article argued that the Southeast Asian Muslims had long considered the title exclusive to the ʿAlawīs, and only in recent years did "people with innovations and false sects" (*ahl al-bidaʿ wa-l-niḥal al-ḍālla*) begin to arrogate it, thus deceiving the public. Second, in Ḥaḍramawt, the ʿAlawīs, who traditionally lived among rivaling tribes without weapons, had received great reverence in society and their safety was guaranteed, which meant they could fulfill special roles, such as serving as guardians for caravans. There were also *waqf*s, whose profits were allotted to the ʿAlawīs. Because it was the title "*sayyid*" that distinguished the ʿAlawīs from others, the application of the title to those other than the ʿAlawīs would not only make the ʿAlawīs indistinguishable and seriously damage their status, but would also entail great confusion in society. In addition, the article stated that even though Arslān mentioned some cases in which those other than the Prophet's descendants bore the title in other regions or in previous eras, they were only exceptions. The vast majority of Muslims, and even Christians, had used the title only for the Prophet's descendants. The ʿAlawī Union agreed with Arslān in accepting that the literal meaning of the word "*sayyid*" was not the "*ʿAlawīs*," but they insisted that the title should be used to indicate "the People of the House." However, with the exception of this matter, the ʿAlawīs offered a positive assessment of Arslān's article as a whole, regarding it as favorable to their interests because it recognized the authenticity of their lineage and included a more severe rebuke of the Irshādī side.

On the other hand, the Irshādīs were also pleased with Arslān's opinion as far as the application of the title "*sayyid*" was concerned. They stated that "probably the opinion of the Amīr [Shakīb Arslān] will be the final decision. We turn the attention of the leaders of Bā ʿAlawī family to it," and "it [the title "*sayyid*"] is no longer a point in dispute and there is no need to resurrect it."[85] Regarding other issues, however, the Irshādīs argued against Arslān.[86] An article in *al-Hudā* repeated the formerly made assertion that the ʿAlawīs had unilaterally canceled the reconciliation intermediated by the Eastern Union and that the authenticity of the lineage of the ʿAlawīs had not been proven. In addition, an article in *al-Irshād*, a newly published organ of the association, claimed that one could deny kinship to the Prophet on the grounds of faults in deeds (*aʿmāl*) and morals (*akhlāq*), regardless of historical proof (*asānīd taʾrīkhiyya*). The article quoted the case of Canaan, who was banished by Allah from the family of Noah owing to his evil deeds. As for the defamation of the marriage between ʿAlī and Fāṭima, for which Arslān had criticized the Irshādīs sharply, the articles explained that, in fact, it was not an Irshādī but an ʿAlawī who had written about it and that *Ḥaḍramawt* had misattributed the opinions to the Irshādīs.[87]

Still, the Irshādīs avoided direct criticism of Arslān just as they had in their response to Riḍā. In their view, Arslān had severely reprimanded them because he was deceived by the false accounts of the ʿAlawī side. They complained that Arslān had not blamed the pro-ʿAlawī journals, even though they had also published some blameworthy articles. An article in *al-Hudā* appealed to Arslān: "all we want is only a just treatment (*inṣāf*), that is to say, we are listened to like others, and if others' charges are reduced, ours are also reduced." Yet the author of the article had great respect for Arslān saying, "because we look on him as our spiritual father, we accept his word even if it were colocynth (*ʿalqam*), for we believe that sincerity is his guiding principle and counsel concerning Islam is his intention and purpose." Nonetheless, the Irshādīs never accepted Arslān's arbitration.

Subsidence of the dispute

Neither the attempts at reconciliation by Riḍā nor those by Arslān could bring about a decisive solution to the dispute among the Arabs in Southeast Asia.[88] Yet it would be untrue to suppose that their attempts did not have any influence on the dispute's subsequent development. In fact, after the mid 1930s, the two issues between the Irshādīs and ʿAlawīs came to be less contested. In particular, the year 1934 marked a turning point in the dispute.

In that year, the ʿAlawīs abandoned further fighting over the problem of the title "*sayyid*." This decision was made at the ʿAlawī Sayyid Congress, held in Pekalongan in March 1934.[89] It is said that the organizers of the congress had intended to decide to send a further petition to the colonial authorities to legally restrict the use of the title, but the younger generation of ʿAlawīs were of the opinion that they should tackle more urgent problems instead of continuing a futile fight. As it happened, this younger generation took over the leadership of the congress in 1934, and the congress subsequently announced that it had "decided not to talk about the problem of the title '*sayyid*' nor to make a petition to the government as to the decision regarding it, for it is not the right time for it." Instead, its main resolutions included the establishment of a committee for improving the education of the ʿAlawīs' scions. It is highly likely that Arslān's judgment on the matter of the title "*sayyid*," which had been announced the previous year, had influenced their decision.

As for the Irshādī side, their denial of the plans for reconciliation proposed by Riḍā and Arslān resulted in al-Sūrkatī's announcement of his resignation from the activities of al-Irshād in 1934.[90] An article in *al-Hudā* explained that the direct cause of this resignation was "correspondence between the great professor [i.e., al-Sūrkatī] and many of the leaders of the Islamic world (*zuʿamāʾ al-ʿālam al-Islāmī*) who are concerned with the struggle occurring in these places of emigration (*hādhihi al-mahājir*)." In fact, it was Arslān who advised al-Sūrkatī to tender his withdrawal in order to take responsibility for the Irshādīs' refusal of the plans for reconciliation.[91]

This announcement was met with skepticism from some of the ʿAlawīs, and one of them, writing in *al-ʿArab*, warned that al-Sūrkatī's announcement was false, a trick to cheat the ʿAlawī side.[92] Still, it seems reasonable to assume that al-Sūrkatī sincerely intended to conciliate the ʿAlawī side. He sent his announcement to al-Saqqāf in Singapore, and then published it in the pro-ʿAlawī *al-ʿArab*. Even though *al-Hudā* had temporarily stopped publication at that time, al-Sūrkatī clearly showed his compassion for the ʿAlawī side by doing this. In addition, al-Sūrkatī hoped that *al-ʿArab* would not comment on his announcement. We may infer that he intended to prevent further hostility over his announcement.

The Irshādī side was apparently thrown into confusion by al-Sūrkatī's announcement. *Al-Hudā*, which by then had resumed publication, once again did not directly criticize Arslān but maintained that he had been deceived by false accounts derived from the ʿAlawīs.[93] It argued that the ʿAlawīs convinced him that "all the Irshādīs obey al-Sūrkatī. It is nothing other than his order that dissuades them from reconciliation." At the same time, representatives from al-Irshād branch offices held a meeting in Surabaya to discuss the matter. They resolved not to accept al-Sūrkatī's announcement and to summon a general meeting in Pekalongan for further talks.[94]

After this, although the feud continued among the Arabs in Southeast Asia, it gradually began to soften in the latter half of the 1930s. In 1936, al-Saqqāf began the publication of a new journal, *al-Salām* [Peace]. It has been argued that the increasing fraternity between the two groups induced its publication and influenced its naming.[95] By the end of the 1930s, periodicals regarded the dispute as a thing of the past. The former editor of *al-Hudā*, who had held contentious debates with the ʿAlawīs, asserted in his new periodical, *al-Akhbār*, that "newspapers and magazines are essentially irrelevant to factionalism and such problems that foment a controversy."[96] Furthermore, according to an ʿAlawī journal, *Ṣawt Ḥaḍramawt*, the spirit of reconciliation had spread in the Ḥaḍramī society of Southeast Asia to the extent that, for example, when al-Irshād opened its branch in Solo in 1940, ʿAlawī notables participated in the opening ceremony.[97]

Conclusion

Generally speaking, the arguments made by Riḍā and Arslān over the position of *sayyid/sharīf*s emphasized equality among all believers in Islam and negated the superiority of the descendants of the Prophet. It may seem that Riḍā and Arslān, in their attempts at reconciliation in the first half of the 1930s, supported the position of the ʿAlawīs rather than the Irshādīs, who insisted on full equality of all Muslims. However, we should note here that it was in the question of the authenticity of the *sayyid/sharīf* pedigree that both Riḍā and Arslān supported the ʿAlawīs' claim. Needless to say, the legitimacy of the privilege or the special position of *sayyid/sharīf*s was not at stake in this question.

As for the other issue, that is, the application of the title "*sayyid*," Riḍā and Arslān were divided. What has to be noted is that even Riḍā defended the title as being only a customary right of the descendants of the Prophet. He had used the same reasoning regarding the practice of "kissing hands" among *sayyid/sharīf*s, insisting that this should be allowed only if it is performed as a custom. Arslān also discussed the problem only in terms of custom, language, and history. In summary, Riḍā and Arslān fully agreed that privileges or superiority of *sayyid/sharīfs* could not be explained or accepted as part of the Islamic religion.[98]

It is obvious that the opinions of Riḍā and Arslān had a substantive influence on the dispute. The Irshādīs could not criticize Riḍā and Arslān directly even if the two thinkers expressed unfavorable judgments. It seems fair to suppose that the reason for this was that, at the outbreak of the dispute, the group opposing the ʿAlawīs, who later became Irshādīs, appealed to the non-Ḥaḍramī authorities of Islamic reformism, namely Riḍā and al-Sūrkatī. Their rejection of Ridā's and Arslān's arbitrations negatively affected their activities, as was made clear by al-Sūrkatī's resignation. As for the ʿAlawī side, it seems that Arslān's judgment was one of the reasons for their final acceptance of the unrestricted application of the title "*sayyid*." Furthermore, they did not dare to raise any objection to the cause of equality between all Muslims that Riḍā and Arslān championed in the first half of the 1930s. We must note that this represents a rather substantial change in their attitude: it was only about twenty-five years earlier that ʿUmar al-ʿAṭṭās insisted that Islam guaranteed the superiority of *sayyid/sharīf*s.

Thus, it was the egalitarianism advocated by Islamic reformists from outside the Ḥaḍramī community of Southeast Asia that governed this Umma-wide debate on the status of *sayyid/sharīf*s. Given this fundamental framework of the debate, it was only natural that the privileges of the Ḥaḍramī *sayyid/sharīfs* in Southeast Asia came to be denied or, at best, regarded as mere regional customs with no backing from Islam. The *sayyid/sharīf*s, who ended up abandoning their explicit insistence on the superiority of the descendants of the Prophet, were fighting with a serious handicap indeed.

Acknowledgment

I extend special thanks to Mr Geys Amar and Mr Arai Kazuhiro for providing the source materials.

Notes

1 Morimoto Kazuo, "Toward the Formation of Sayyido-Sharifology: Questioning Accepted Fact," *Journal of Sophia Asian Studies* 22 (2004): 96–97.

2 I use the term "Southeast Asia" to refer to the region that, in the present day, encompasses Indonesia, Malaysia, and Singapore; this is where most Arab immigrants and their descendants resided. It is estimated that, from the late nineteenth to the early twentieth century, over 90 percent of the Arabs in those

regions were from Ḥaḍramawt. See L. W. C. van den Berg, *Le Hadhramout et les colonies arabes dans l'archipel indien* (Batavia: Imprimerie du Gouvernement, 1886), 107–109; W. H. Lee Warner, "Notes on the Hadhramaut," *Geographical Journal* 77 (1931): 220.

3 Serjeant and Bujra portrayed the dispute as a conflict between the traditional ruling class and newly emerging opposing class. See R. B. Serjeant, *The Saiyids of Ḥaḍramawt* (London: Cambridge University Press, 1957); R. B. Serjeant, "Historians and Historiography of Ḥaḍramawt," *Bulletin of the School of Oriental and African Studies* 25 (1962): 238–261; Abdalla S. Bujra, "Political Conflict and Stratification in Ḥaḍramaut I," *Middle Eastern Studies* 3/4 (1967): 355–375. On the other hand, Mobini-Kesheh points out that both groups were oriented toward certain kinds of reform and defines the dispute as one between groups of reformers over the initiative and methods of reform. See Natalie Mobini-Kesheh, *The Hadrami Awakening: Community and Identity in the Netherlands East Indies, 1900–1942*, Studies on Southeast Asia 28 (Ithaca, New York: Cornell Southeast Asian Program Publications, 1999), chapter 5. Ho investigates the reasons behind why the dispute occurred in Javanese cities, and not in Ḥaḍramawt or other settlements, in relation to the proportion of local-born and immigrant populations as well as Dutch colonial policies. Engseng Ho, *The Graves of Tarim: Genealogy and Mobility across the Indian Ocean* (Berkeley: University of California Press, 2006), 173–187. Although they provide detailed descriptions that make full use of Arabic materials, Arabic works on the dispute are lacking in analysis. Yaʿqūb Yūsuf al-Ḥajjī, *al-Shaykh ʿAbd al-ʿAzīz al-Rashīd: Sīrat ḥayātihi* (Kuwait: Markaz al-Buḥūth wa-l-Dirāsāt al-Kuwaytiyya, 1993); ʿAbd Allāh Yaḥyā Zayn, *al-Nashāṭ al-thaqāfī wa-l-ṣuḥufī li-l-Yamaniyyīn fī al-mahjar: Indūnīsiyā-Mālīziyā-Singhapūra, 1900–1950* (Damascus: Dār al-Fikr, 2003).

4 Riḍā claimed that he was a descendant of Ḥusayn on his paternal side and of Ḥasan on his maternal side. See *al-Manār* 9/4 (May 1906): 300.

5 For the relationship between them, see, e.g., Raja Adal, "Constructing Transnational Islam: The East–West Network of Shakib Arslan," in Stéphane A. Dudoignon, Komatsu Hisao, and Kosugi Yasushi eds, *Intellectuals in the Modern Islamic World: Transmission, Transformation, Communication* (London and New York: Routledge, 2006), 176–210.

6 In this paper, I include non-Ḥaḍramī Arabs in Southeast Asia when I use the terms "Arabs" and "Arab community." The activities of non-Ḥaḍramī Arabs were remarkable even though they were very small in number. We should not neglect their presence, especially when discussing the ʿAlawī–Irshādī dispute.

7 *Al-Fatḥ* was founded and edited by Muḥibb al-Dīn al-Khaṭīb (d. 1969). Arslān published many articles in this journal.

8 For surveys of Arabic periodicals published in Southeast Asia in the early twentieth century, see William R. Roff, *Bibliography of Malay and Arabic Periodicals Published in the Straits Settlements and Peninsular Malay States 1876–1941* (London: Oxford University Press, 1972); Natalie Mobini-Kesheh, "The Arab Periodicals of the Netherlands East Indies, 1914–1942," *Bijdragen tot de Taal-, Land- en Volkenkunde* 152/2 (1996): 236–256; Zayn, *al-Nashāṭ*.

9 According to Ho, this practice, although usually referred to as "kissing hands" (*taqbīl*), is in fact a gesture of smelling (*shamma*). See Ho, *The Graves of Tarim*, 84–85. He explains that this act is performed in Ḥaḍramawt not only in interactions with descendants of the Prophet but also when meeting great scholars, pious persons, and family elders. Serjeant refers to the fact that this practice was common among the local religious class (*mashāʾikh*) before the arrival of the ʿAlawīs. See Serjeant, *The Saiyids*, 14.

10 The model that Bujra presented for the social strata of Ḥaḍramawt is well known, though recent studies have criticized or modified it. See Abdalla S. Bujra, *The*

Politics of Stratification: A Study of Political Change in a South Arabian Town (London: Oxford University Press, 1971).

11 For Riḍā's opinion on the problem, see *al-Manār* 8/6 (May 1905): 215–217; 8/15 (September 1905): 580–588; 8/24 (February 1906): 955–957. In 1904, a year before the incident occurred in Singapore, a similar marriage caused controversy in Egypt, and Riḍā also shared his opinion on this instance in *al-Manār*. Ṣafiyya, the daughter of Aḥmad al-Khāliq al-Sādāt, the Shaykh of the Wafā'iyya Sufi order with a *sayyid/sharīf* pedigree, married ʿAlī Yūsuf (d. 1913), the editor of an Egyptian daily called *al-Mu'ayyad* and who was not a *sayyid/sharīf*. Although her father should have been her legal guardian, she appointed another person as her guardian at the marriage. When her father demanded the cancelation (*faskh*) of the marriage, one of the reasons he offered was the lack of *kafā'a* (suitability of the groom to the bride) given the groom's pedigree. See *al-Manār* 7/10 (July 1904): 381–384.

12 Jamʿiyyat Khayr was founded around 1901, and was approved by the Dutch colonial government in July 1905. Its activities were prominent in the area of education, such as in its establishment of modern Islamic schools. For the early history of this association, see ʿAlī b. Aḥmad al-Saqqāf, *Lamaḥāt ta'rīkhiyya ʿan nash'at Jamʿiyyat Khayr* (n.p., 1953).

13 For information on Aḥmad al-Sūrkatī, see Bisri Affandi, *Syaikh Ahmad Syurkati (1874–1943): Pembaharu dan pemurni Islam di Indonesia* (Jakarta: Pustaka Al-Kautsar, 1999), 212; Ahmad Ibrahim Abushouk, "A Sudanese Scholar in the Diaspora: Life and Career of Aḥmad Muḥammad al-Surkittī in Indonesia (1911–1943)," *Studia Islamika* 8/1 (2001): 55–86.

14 For the opinions of ʿUmar al-ʿAṭṭās, see *al-Manār* 8/15:580–583.

15 Farhat J. Ziadeh, "Equality (*Kafā'ah*) in the Muslim Law of Marriage," *American Journal of Comparative Law* 6 (1957): 515–516.

16 Yanagihashi Hiroyuki, *Islamic Family Law: Marriage, Parentage and Kinship* (in Japanese) (Tokyo: Sōbunsha, 2001), 151–154.

17 Sometimes, the marriage of male descendants of the Prophet was also restricted to secure spouses for the daughters of *sayyid/sharīf*s. See Morimoto Kazuo, "Social Control of *Sayyid*s: The Formation of the Science of *Sayyid* Genealogies in the 10th and 11th Centuries" (in Japanese), *Shigaku Zasshi* 105 (1996): 588.

18 Riḍā still affirmed that there were exceptions to the equality, citing the prohibition on the sharing of *ṣadaqa* (alms) for *sayyid/sharīf*s.

19 Aḥmad b. Muḥammad al-Sūrkatī al-Anṣārī, *Ṣūrat al-jawāb* (Surabaya: al-Maṭbaʿa al-Islāmiyya, 1915). This was a rejoinder to an article in a Malay language periodical, *Soeloeh Hindia* 2 (28 October 1915).

20 *Al-Irshād* 1 (July 1933): 14–15.

21 Mobini-Kesheh, *The Hadrami Awakening*, 93.

22 See Deliar Noer, *The Modernist Muslim Movement in Indonesia 1900–1942* (Kuala Lumpur: Oxford University Press, 1973), 83–92; Howard M. Federspiel, *Islam and Ideology in the Emerging Indonesian State: Persatuan Islam (PERSIS), 1923 to 1957* (Leiden: Brill, 2001), 169. Persis was established in Bandung in 1923.

23 *Al-Manār* 9/4:304.

24 Bujra, "Political Conflict," 359–360, 370–371.

25 For basic information about the ʿAlawī Union, see Linda Boxberger, *On the Edge of Empire: Hadhramawt, Emigration, and the Indian Ocean, 1880s–1930* (New York: State University of New York Press, 2002), 56–58; Ulrike Freitag, *Indian Ocean Migrants and State Formation in Hadhramaut: Reforming the Homeland* (Leiden: Brill, 2003), 353–356.

26 See Ṣalāḥ [ʿAbd al-Qādir] al-Bakrī, *Ta'rīkh Ḥaḍramawt al-siyāsī*, 2 vols in 1 (Cairo: Dār al-Āfāq al-ʿArabiyya, 2001), II:335–336. A famous example is the fatal

skirmish that occurred in January 1933 in Bondowoso. For information on this event, see also Boxberger, *On the Edge of Empire*, 61; Freitag, *Indian Ocean*, 252.

27 The Eastern Union was established in 1922. In order to better understand this organization, see James Jankowski, "The Eastern Idea and the Eastern Union in Interwar Egypt," *The International Journal of African Historical Studies* 14/4 (1981): 643–666.

28 It is highly likely that Arslān's suggestion and advice affected the content of the terms of settlement published under the intermediation of the Eastern Union. The fifth term required the establishment of a committee to bring the reconciliation into effect. For the terms of settlement, see n. 31 below.

29 According to al-Bakrī, two members of the organization, Riḍā and Muḥammad al-Aḥmadī al-Ẓawāhirī (the Shaykh al-Azhar), engaged in the intermediation process. See al-Bakrī, *Ta'rīkh Ḥaḍramawt*, II:338. Al-Bakrī also explains the background to the intermediation in Ṣalāḥ ʿAbd al-Qādir al-Bakrī, *Ta'rīkh al-Irshād fī Indūnīsiyā* (Jakarta: Jamʿiyyat al-Irshād al-Islāmiyya, 1992), 149–150. In 1927, the Eastern Union had already sent its letter to the Muslims in the Netherlands East Indies and advised them to cease struggles and unite. See *Mir'āt Muḥammadiyya* 8 (12 May 1927): 175–177. Nonetheless, it appears that the struggle the letter mentioned was not defined as occurring among the Arabs, but within Muslim society in general.

30 Ibrāhīm b. ʿUmar al-Saqqāf is a Mecca-born Ḥaḍramī (d. ca. 1972). Some details on his career are given in *al-Nahḍa al-Ḥaḍramiyya* 5 (May 1933): 10–11; 6–7 (June–July 1933): 27, 52; Syed Mohsen Alsagoff, *The Alsagoff Family in Malaysia: A.H. 1240 (A.D. 1824) to A.H. 1382 (A.D. 1962)* (Singapore: Author, 1963), 29–31; ʿAbd al-Raḥmān b. Muḥammd b. Ḥusayn al-Mashhūr, *Shams al-ẓahīra fī nasab Ahl al-Bayt min Banī ʿAlawī*, ed. and commentated by Muḥammad Ḍiyā' Shihāb (Jidda: ʿĀlam al-Maʿrifa, 1984), 242–243; Syed Muhd Khairudin Aljunied, "Hadhramis within Malay Activism: The Role of al-Saqqāf(s) in Post-War Singapore (1945–1965)," in Ahmad Ibrahim Abushouk and Hassan Ahmed Ibrahim eds, *The Hadhrami Diaspora in Southeast Asia* (Leiden and Boston: Brill, 2009), 231–237.

31 The announcement of the agreement was published in *al-ʿArab* 3 (15 October 1931): 6; *Ḥaḍramawt* 305 (16 October 1931): 2, and the terms of settlement were published in *al-ʿArab* 6 (5 November 1931): 4; 8 (19 November 1931): 3; *al-Mishkāt* 17 (16 November 1931): 1, 3; and *al-Kuwayt wa-l-ʿIrāqī* 5 (January 1932): 248–249.

32 *Al-Kuwayt wa-l-ʿIrāqī* 5:249. Muḥammad b. ʿUbayd ʿAbūd is also cited as a representative of al-Irshād in *al-Hudā* 28 (1 December 1931): 12.

33 *Al-ʿArab* 3:4.

34 This can be gathered from the discussion between al-Sūrkatī and al-Saqqāf. See *al-ʿArab* 28 (15 April 1932): 1–4, 6; 38 (24 June 1932): 1–3, 7; *Ḥaḍramawt* 325 (18 April 1932): 1–2; 327 (5 May 1932): 1–2; 333 (23 June 1932): 1–2; 334 (30 June 1932): 1–2; *al-Kuwayt wa-l-ʿIrāqī* 9 (May 1932): 456–479; *al-Hudā* 51 (16 May 1932): 3–5, 11. Al-Bakrī also discusses this point. See al-Bakrī, *Ta'rīkh al-Irshād*, 150.

35 Many studies have referred to this problem. See, for example, Mobini-Kesheh, *The Hadrami Awakening*, 103–107; Boxberger, *On the Edge of Empire*, 58; Freitag, *Indian Ocean*, 255–258.

36 The resolution of this congress was published in several periodicals, including *al-Jaum* 1/12 (20 May 1931): 6; *al-Hoeda* 12 (1 June 1931): 439–441. However, in 1928, the annual congress held by the Surabaya branch had already made the same decision. In fact, some Irshādīs used the title before the resolution of 1931. See, for example, *al-Hoeda* 12:435.

37 Mobini-Kesheh, *The Hadrami Awakening*, 104. Before the modification, the constitution of al-Irshād was published as a brochure. Jamʿiyyat al-Iṣlāḥ wa-l-Irshād al-ʿArabiyya bi-Batāfiyā, *Qānūn Jamʿiyyat al-Iṣlāḥ wa-l-Irshād al-ʿArabiyya: Al-asāsī wa-l-dākhilī* (Surabaya: al-Maṭbaʿa al-Islāmiyya, 1919). The modified version is quoted in al-Bakrī, *Taʾrīkh Ḥaḍramawt*, II:257–261.

38 Mobini-Kesheh, *The Hadrami Awakening*, 106–107; Boxberger, *On the Edge of Empire*, 58.

39 ʿAlawī b. ʿUbayd Allāh was the grandson of Aḥmad b. ʿĪsā al-Muhājir, the first *sayyid/sharīf* who arrived in Ḥaḍramawt from al-Baṣra. See Ho, *The Graves of Tarim*, 37–38.

40 In this study, I use only the word "*ʿAlawī*" to avoid confusion.

41 For this argument made by the Irshādīs, see Aḥmad Ibrāhīm Abū Shawk ed., *Ta'rīkh ḥarakat al-Iṣlāḥ wa-l-Irshād wa-Shaykh al-Irshādiyyīn al-ʿAllāma al-Shaykh Aḥmad Muḥammad al-Sūrkittī fī Indūnīsiyya* (Kuala Lumpur: Research Centre, International Islamic University Malaysia, 2000), 1.

42 It seems that the Irshādīs only raised doubts and did not deny the authenticity of the ʿAlawīs' pedigree completely. This is perhaps because to deny the Prophetic pedigree would have required them to provide conclusive evidence. See C. von Arendonk [W. A. Graham], "S͟harīf," in H. A. R. Gibb et al. eds, *The Encyclopaedia of Islam*, new ed., 13 vols (Leiden: Brill, 1960–2009), IX:329–337; Morimoto Kazuo, "A Study on Technical Terms and Signs of the Science of *Sayyid* Genealogies: Their Significations and Significance" (in Japanese), *Rekishigaku Kenkyū* [Journal of Historical Studies] 743 (2000): 10.

43 *Al-Hudā* 89 (13 February 1933): 1.

44 *Al-ʿArab* 43 (29 July 1932): 2. For information on Sayyid ʿAlī b. Shaykh b. Shihāb (d. 1788–9), see al-Mashhūr, *Shams al-ẓahīra*, 146–148.

45 The authenticity of the genealogy of the ʿAlawīs has also been questioned in the past. See al-Bakrī, *Taʾrīkh Ḥaḍramawt*, I:78; Serjeant, *The Saiyids*, 10–11.

46 See, for example, *al-Kuwayt wa-l-ʿIrāqī* 9:461–469; *al-Hudā* 51:3–5.

47 The term "*ṭaʿn*" casts strong doubts on genealogy. See Morimoto "A Study on Technical Terms," 10.

48 *Al-ʿArab* 38 (24 June 1932): 2. Tentative drafts of the terms of settlement proposed by both sides before the agreement were published in *al-Kuwayt wa-l-ʿIrāqī* 4 (December 1931): 204–206.

49 The tentative draft of the terms of settlement proposed by the ʿAlawī side also stipulated "the equality of all cultural and social rights" (*musāwāt fī jamīʿ al-ḥuqūq al-adabiyya wa-l-ijtimāʿiyya*). See *al-Kuwayt wa-l-ʿIrāqī* 4:204.

50 See, for example, *al-ʿArab* 14 (31 December 1931): 1.

51 *Al-Hudā* 29 (7 December 1931): 7. The names of the Surabaya, Bangil, and Pekalongan branches are mentioned.

52 *Al-Hudā* 88 (6 February 1933): 7; 103 (29 May 1933): 1.

53 *Al-ʿArab* 19 (5 February 1932): 4; 20 (19 February 1932): 7.

54 Al-Saqqāf released two articles at the same time as the "explanation" of the terms of settlement: *al-ʿArab* 28:1–4, 6; *Haḍramawt* 325:1, 3.

55 It is likely that one of the main reasons for the rift in the negotiations was that the Eastern Union had ceased its activities by mid 1931. See Jankowski, "The Eastern Idea," 663.

56 In the early 1930s, other non-Ḥaḍramī Muslims also intervened in the dispute; among these were Zaydi Imam of Yemen, Yaḥyā b. Muḥammad Ḥamīd al-Dīn (d. 1948); the Shaykh al-Azhar, al-Ẓawāhirī; ʿAbd al-ʿAzīz b. Saʿūd (d. 1953); and the Indonesian traditionalist Muslim association, Nahdlatul Ulama. For their opinions on the dispute, see n. 88.

57 His travel to Europe was described in *Ḥaḍramawt* 362 (27 October 1932): 2–3; 363 (31 October 1932): 2.

58 G. E. Pijper, *Beberapa studi tentang agama Islam di Indonesia 1900–1950*, trans. by Tudjimah and Yessy Augustin (Jakarta: Universitas Indonesia Press, 1984), 114; Affandi, *Syaikh Ahmad Syurkati*, 212; Freitag, *Indian Ocean*, 251. Riḍā's school was established to train Islamic intellectuals and leaders but was closed because of the outbreak of World War I.

59 Al-Ḥajjī, *al-Shaykh ʿAbd al-ʿAzīz*, 259–260; al-Bakrī, *Taʾrīkh al-Irshād*, 182; Affandi, *Syaikh Ahmad Syurkati*, 21; Mobini-Kesheh, *The Hadrami Awakening*, 58. The two teachers soon returned for health reasons without making any progress.

60 In addition to Riḍā, the Irshādī side recommended two other candidates: a representative of the Eastern Union and the Shaykh al-Azhar (*mashyakha*), while the ʿAlawī side recommended only the Shaykh al-Azhar. *Al-ʿArab* 6:4; *al-Mishkāt* 17:1; *al-Kuwayt wa-l-ʿIrāqī* 4:204–206. Al-Sūrkatī alluded to the ʿAlawīs' opposition to Riḍā's appointment as an arbitrator in his writing. See *al-Hudā* 50 (May 9, 1932): 4.

61 Al-Saqqāf indirectly delivered the copy to al-Irshād through al-Sūrkatī. See *al-ʿArab* 66 (12 January 1933): 5.

62 In *al-ʿArab* and *Ḥaḍramawt*, the terms of settlement that Riḍā proposed were published with his letter to the leaders of both parties. In *al-Manār*, his other article was published along with the terms, but, in *al-Hudā*, only the terms were announced. *Al-ʿArab* 65 (29 December 1932): 1, 4, 8; *al-Hudā* 85 (9 January 1933): 10, 11; *Ḥaḍramawt* 384 (12 January 1933): 1; *al-Manār* 33/1 (March 1933): 73–78.

63 Still, the wording remains rather ambiguous. One might interpret it as meaning that the two groups have the equally customary right to hold the title "*sayyid*." However, the Arabs in Southeast Asia interpreted Riḍā as permitting the title's use exclusively to the descendants of the Prophet. See, for example, *al-Hudā* 86 (1 January 1933): 2; *al-ʿArab* 68 (27 January 1933): 1, 8.

64 The English translation of the Qurʾān used here is from Arthur J. Arberry, *The Koran Interpreted* (London: George Allen & Unwin, 1980).

65 An article in *al-ʿArab* pointed out that the Irshādī side did not take a definite position on Riḍā's terms of settlement. See *al-ʿArab* 68:1.

66 *Al-Hudā* 92 (6 March 1933): 1–3.

67 The name of the periodical is *al-ʿArab*. Its article is quoted in *al-Hudā* 104 (6 June 1933): 4, and in a pro-ʿAlawī journal in Singapore, *al-Nahḍa al-Ḥaḍramiyya* 5:29.

68 When this article was published, Arslān's comments on the dispute had already been issued. Therefore, it is likely that he was included in the "many people" mentioned here, too.

69 *Al-ʿArab* 68:1. The acceptance of the ʿAlawī Union was published in *al-ʿArab* 66:5.

70 This is based on an article in an Egyptian daily, *al-Balāgh* (24 March 1933): 5. It is quoted in *al-Nahḍa al-Ḥaḍramiyya* 5:29. ʿAbd al-Ḥamīd al-Khaṭīb was the son of Aḥmad al-Khaṭīb of Minangkabau (d. 1916), a prominent scholar of Sumatran origin. Muḥammad al-Ghanīmī al-Taftāzānī was one of the founders of the Eastern Union.

71 See, for example, *al-Hudā* 52 (23 May 1932): 1–6.

72 *Al-ʿArab* 28:2–3; *Ḥaḍramawt* 325: 1.

73 *Ḥaḍramawt* 330 (28 May 1932): 2. The article mentioned that the Irshādīs refused Arslān as an arbitrator because he had negatively commented on the Sudanese and their practice of Islam in one of his works, but Arslān denied this and asked *Ḥaḍramawt* to make a correction. See also *Ḥaḍramawt* 342 (18 August 1932): 1.

74 *Ḥaḍramawt* 342:1–2. For the General Islamic Congress of Jerusalem, see Martin Kramer, *Islam Assembled: The Advent of the Muslim Congresses* (New York: Columbia University Press, 1986), chapter 11.

75 *Ḥaḍramawt* 373 (5 December 1932): 1; *al-Hudā* 82 (28 December 1932): 1, 3.

76 The editor of *al-Hudā*, ʿAbd al-Wāḥid al-Jīlānī, responded to the plan affirmatively, whereas another Irshādī was against it, arguing that the former reconciliation should not be ignored. See *al-Hudā* 82:3; 88:7. As for the ʿAlawī side, a comment in *Ḥaḍramawt* expressed a negative attitude toward it, but an article in *al-ʿArab* seems to express its acceptance. See *Ḥaḍramawt* 373:1; *al-ʿArab* 67 (19 January 1933): 1.
77 *Al-Fatḥ* 329 (27 January 1933): 2; 342 (27 April 1933): 2–3.
78 *Al-Fatḥ* 342:3, 14.
79 The letter from Arslān to al-Sūrkatī is quoted in full in *al-Fatḥ* 342:14.
80 *Al-Fatḥ* 329:2.
81 The letter from the head office of al-Irshād was published in *al-Fatḥ* 336 (16 March 1933): 10–11.
82 Al-Sūrkatī's statement was originally published in *al-Miṣbāḥ* 7 (July 1929): 9.
83 *Al-Fatḥ* 342:14–15.
84 The comment from the ʿAlawī Union was published in *al-ʿArab* 79 and its abstract was published in *al-Fatḥ*. See al-Ḥajjī, *al-Shaykh ʿAbd al-ʿAzīz*, 414.
85 *Al-Irshād* 1:18, 20–25. Arslān's opinion on this issue is quoted in *al-Hudā* 101 (15 May 1933): 10; *al-Irshād* 1:20–25.
86 *Al-Hudā* 101:3; 103:3; 104:1, 3, 10; *al-Irshād* 1:6–13.
87 According to pro-Irshādī journals, this problem arose from *Ḥaḍramawt*'s misrepresentation of a quotation in the Malay newspaper *Pembela Islam*, published by Ahmad Hassan of Persis in Bandung, in which some Irshādīs had written articles. The quotation was allegedly taken from a book by an ʿAlawī, Abū Bakr b. Shihāb, *Rashfat al-ṣādī*. See, *al-Hudā* 103:3; *al-Irshād* 1:8–9. Most likely, the part that the pro-Irshādī journals pointed out is Abū Bakr Shihāb al-Dīn al-ʿAlawī al-Ḥaḍramī, *Rashfat al-ṣādī min baḥr faḍāʾil banī al-Nabī al-hādī*, ed. by ʿAlī ʿĀshūr (Beirut: Dār al-Kutub al-ʿIlmiyya, 1418/1998), 83–85.
88 For the opinions of parties from outside the Ḥaḍramī community intervening in discussions on the two issues, consider the following: (1) In about 1932, the Imam Yaḥyā offered to support the ʿAlawīs' position on both the problems. See Freya Stark, *The Southern Gates of Arabia* (London: Century Publishing, 1936), 247; Serjeant, *The Saiyids*, 11; Boxberger, *On the Edge*, 23. (2) In 1933, the Shaykh al-Azhar, al-Ẓawāhirī also recognized the title "*sayyid*" as a privilege of the descendants of the Prophet, although he did not address the problem of authenticating the ʿAlawīs' pedigree. See *al-Nahḍa al-Ḥaḍramiyya* 3–4 (March–April 1933): 22, 25; Fakhr al-Dīn al-Aḥmadī al-Ẓawāhirī, *al-Siyāsa wa-l-Azhar: Min mudhakkirāt Shaykh al-Islām al-Ẓawāhirī* (Cairo: Maṭbaʿat al-Iʿtimād, 1945), 320. (3) In the same year, Ibn Saʿūd intervened in the dispute through the mediation of Ibrāhīm al-Saqqāf. However, he only appealed to the two groups for reconciliation and did not reveal his opinion on the problems. See *al-Irshād* 1:45–49; *al-Hudā* 108 (14 October 1933): 3; al-Bakrī, *Taʾrīkh Ḥaḍramawt*, II:339–342. (4) In 1932–33, Nahdlatul Ulama repeatedly announced its support for the ʿAlawīs regarding the problem of the application of the title "*sayyid*." See *al-ʿArab* 63 (15 December 1932): 5; *al-Nahḍa al-Ḥaḍramiyya* 6–7:32, 51.
89 For the proceedings of this congress, see *Pandji Poestaka* 12/23 (20 March 1934): 389–340; 12/26–27 (30 March 1934): 437–438; Mobini-Kesheh, *The Hadrami Awakening*, 107.
90 Al-Sūrkatī announced his resignation in *al-ʿArab* 112. For this, see al-Ḥajjī, *al-Shaykh ʿAbd al-ʿAzīz*, 548–549.
91 *Al-Hudā* 128 (20 April 1934): 1.
92 *Al-ʿArab* 114 (5 April 1934): 1, 4.
93 *Al-Hudā* 128:1. *Al-Hudā* also reported that trouble and infighting occurred within some branches of al-Irshād, such as Batavia, Surabaya, and Pekalongan, but I cannot say for certain whether this had to do with the unfavorable judgments of

Riḍā and Arslān. Al-Ḥajjī is of the opinion that the trouble stemmed from the disagreement between al-Sūrkatī and ʿAbd al-ʿAzīz al-Rashīd. See al-Ḥajjī, *al-Shaykh ʿAbd al-ʿAzīz*, 546–548.

94 *Al-Hudā* 130 (4 May 1934): 4.

95 Zayn, *al-Nashāṭ*, 244–246.

96 *Al-Akhbār* 1 (13 September 1939): 1. We can find accounts in other periodicals of that time that consider the dispute to have ended. See, for example, *al-Dhikrā* 2 (20 September 1938): 1.

97 *Ṣawt Ḥaḍramawt* 14 (20 January 1941): 2.

98 Yet, as previously mentioned, the *ṣadaqa* and *zakāt* regulations are exceptions.

Part II

Sayyids and *sharīfs* in the Middle East

4 Genealogy, marriage, and the drawing of boundaries among the ʿAlids (eighth–twelfth centuries)

Teresa Bernheimer

Introduction

It is difficult to imagine Islamic history without the descendants of the Prophet Muḥammad. From the famous early rebels to the founders or eponyms of the major Islamic sects, to numerous rulers such as the Idrīsids in ninth-century Morocco, the Fāṭimids in tenth-century Egypt, the current-day king of Jordan, the Ayatollah Khomeini or the Aga Khan: descendants of the Prophet have played a major role throughout the history of the Islamic world. Despite considerable variation in the circumstances of the members of the ʿAlid family, an increasing sense of self-definition and self-identity of the family as a distinct social group is clearly discernible from the ninth century onwards. Indeed, *sayyid*s and *sharīf*s developed into what has been termed a "blood aristocracy without peer" in Islam.[1]

As Morimoto Kazuo points out in his article on the state of the field, the study of the kinsfolk of the Prophet Muḥammad in different Muslim societies is still a relatively unexplored area of research.[2] Because of the perceived importance of the family of the Prophet by all schools and sects, as well as the ʿAlids' own efforts to preserve and improve the position of the family, a diverse social group can be examined over a wide geographical and temporal spread. Indeed, this is perhaps the one family for whom we have some sort of information throughout Islamic history, from many parts of the Islamic world. Clearly, this is a large project, and the collaboration of scholars working on the role and position of people claiming an affiliation with the household of the Prophet Muḥammad, in different Muslim societies, is much desired. I would like to reiterate my thanks to the organizers of the Tokyo conference for providing such a pleasant and productive forum to discuss questions regarding the role and position of *sayyid*/*sharīf*s in Muslim societies.

Despite their importance in the history of Muslim societies, the prominence of the descendents of the Prophet was by no means a foregone conclusion. Though it may be argued that a special treatment for the descendants of the Prophet can be observed from the earliest period of Islam, I would like to suggest that crucial developments in the status and position of ʿAlids took place between the eighth and the twelfth centuries. In this period, we can trace the development of "ʿAlidism," characterized by a non-sectarian reverence and support for the family, as distinct from "Shīʿism," the political and religious claims of some of its members or others on their behalf.[3] Many of the aspects we now associate with *sayyid*s and *sharīf*s in Muslim societies, such as their geographical mobility and ubiquity, or indeed their exemption from some of the rules of ordinary society, are part of this development. The formation and spread of the *niqāba* or headship of the ʿAlid (or Ṭālibid) family, for instance, is an excellent example of the social changes that took place in this period, and a clear indication that the kinsfolk of the Prophet had come to be perceived as deserving – and sometimes demanded – special treatment on account of their genealogy. The origins of the *niqāba* are still little understood, but Morimoto has clearly shown that within a hundred years of their first appearance in the late ninth century, *nuqabāʾ* were found all over the Islamic world.[4] The extent of a *naqīb*'s power, his autonomy from the authorities, as well as his duties toward the ʿAlids varied from place to place and over time; significantly, however, this office gave the family a certain self-determination over its affairs, not least to administer some of its privileges. This is unparalleled in a society that places great emphasis on the equality of all believers – no other social group could claim such exceptions and exemptions. The ʿAlids were emerging as "the First Family of Islam."

In what follows, I discuss the marriage patterns of the kinsfolk of the Prophet as an important example of this development. As indicated above, members of the family themselves contributed to the efforts to preserve and improve their position – networks were established and boundaries drawn. Nowhere can we see this more clearly than in marriage relations: between the eighth and the twelfth centuries, the social circles were increasingly narrowed, as well as shifted. ʿAlid daughters especially were no longer given away to other families, Arab or non-Arab, but married off only to other ʿAlids, or sometimes other Ṭālibids. Increasingly, only a *sayyid* or *sharīf* was considered a suitable choice for a *sayyida* or *sharīfa*. Of course there must have been exceptions, but the sources do not record them. The men also married increasingly within the family; if they married out, they began to take wives from other elite families, often non-Arabs. As marriage is understood to be an expression of at least some measure of shared identity and hierarchic rank, these changes in marriage patterns reflect changes in the notions of the status of the family within the social hierarchy of medieval Islamic society more generally. Interestingly, an examination of the legal sources shows that the narrowing of possible marriage relations must be primarily considered social praxis: it is not reflected in the theory of the law. In fact, the early Imāmī works even explicitly sanctioned the marriage of ʿAlid women to non-ʿAlid men, a good example of a disengagement of ʿAlids and Shīʿites. Before discussing some of the theoretical and empirical findings in more detail, however, I would like to give a brief note on terminology, as well as on this study's sources and their limitations.

Terminology and sources

I repeatedly use the term "the ʿAlids" – so who precisely are "the ʿAlids," and should a study of the marriage patterns of the kinsfolk of the Prophet not more properly examine "the Ṭālibids," or even "the Hāshimites"? Strictly speaking, the only *descendants* of the Prophet Muḥammad are of course the offspring of his daughter Fāṭima and his cousin ʿAlī – descendants of their two sons Ḥasan and Ḥusayn, commonly called ʿAlids. ʿAlī, however, had other sons (Muḥammad b. al-Ḥanafiyya, ʿUmar, and ʿAbbās), also called ʿAlids, whose offspring sometimes became prominent *sayyid*s and *sharīf*s, despite having only an agnatic relation to the Prophet. There are other important agnates among the Ṭālibids – descendants of ʿAlī's father Abū Ṭālib through ʿAlī as well as his other sons Jaʿfar and ʿAqīl – and even other Hāshimites (the clan that included Ṭālibids and ʿAbbāsids). The terms and definitions of who belonged to the family of the Prophet were fluid and flexible. The sources themselves rarely agree, and frequently substitute one term for the other. Of course, there were also many attempts to define precisely which kinship groups could call themselves *sayyid*s and *sharīf*s, and were thus entitled to share in the varying privileges of the Prophet's family: the Egyptian scholar al-Suyūṭī (d. 911/1505) for instance, defines the *ahl al-bayt* widely as the descendants of Hāshim and al-Muṭṭalib, and discusses in some detail the status of the Zaynabīs, descendants of Zaynab, a daughter of Fāṭima and ʿAlī. He concludes that even the Zaynabīs are indeed *sharīf*s, as members of the wider family of the Prophet, and should be allowed to share in some of their endowments.[5]

Thus, the possible definitions were by no means rigid, but often dependent on the particular context. I have nonetheless chosen to stick to the term "ʿAlid," and also focus my analysis on the ʿAlid family, for two main reasons: first, to emphasize the contrast to the other important Hāshimite family, the ʿAbbāsids, against whom the ʿAlids (and other Ṭālibids) began to define themselves after the ʿAbbāsid Revolution of 750.[6] Second, the term "the ʿAlids" seeks to make clear that at the center of the emergence of an Islamic aristocracy were indeed the descendants of ʿAlī, first and foremost his offspring from the marriage with Fāṭima, the Ḥasanids and Ḥusaynids. ʿAlī's descendants through other sons, as well as other Ṭālibids certainly played a significant role at times; Roy Mottahedeh, for instance, has drawn attention to some important Jaʿfarids in Buyid Qazwīn.[7] But these Jaʿfarids, and other Ṭālibids, though also addressed as *sayyid*s and *sharīf*s, were not the ones driving the emergence of the family as an Islamic aristocracy, nor were they at the center of the non-sectarian veneration for the kinsfolk of the Prophet.

To add to the confusion about terminologies, our primary sources for the marriage patterns of the kinsfolk of the Prophet are the so-called "Ṭālibid genealogies," a group of works dating from the ninth to the fifteenth centuries that were first examined in detail by Morimoto Kazuo.[8] The Ṭālibid genealogies record the kinship relations of the Ṭālibid branch of the Banū Hāshim; they focus on the ʿAlid lineages, but other Ṭālibids are also discussed.[9]

It is thought that they are based on local registers, which in turn were the result of information gathered and tested by genealogists and their helpers. Apart from the well-known *ʿUmdat al-ṭālib* by Ibn ʿInaba (d. 828/1424–5), many of these works have only recently become available in printed form.[10] Although their focus and aim is rather different, the Ṭālibid genealogies continue and build on the earlier works of Arab genealogy, such as the *Jamharat al-nasab* by Hishām b. al-Kalbī (d. 204/819), or the *Kitāb nasab Quraysh* by Muṣʿab b. ʿAbdallāh al-Zubayrī (d. 236/851).[11] For the later generations, namely from the eighth century onwards, the Ṭālibid works offer a variety of genealogical and historical material rarely found elsewhere. Thus, these sources allow us to trace particular lineages over the centuries, especially in the Eastern Islamic lands. The material, however, also limits a study on marriage patterns in a number of ways. The first important limitation concerns the information on women.

As is customary for Arab genealogy (and lots of other kinds of genealogy, for that matter), the records follow the male line of the family. Women appear if they are listed as wives, and sometimes as daughters of a given ʿAlid; but in almost all of the cases, such information is not followed any further. The twelfth-century genealogist Fakhr al-Dīn al-Rāzī (d. 606/1209), for instance, lists all the twenty-seven daughters of Jaʿfar al-Kadhdhāb (a brother of Ḥasan al-ʿAskarī), but none of them re-appear elsewhere in the text. Either the daughters were all not married, or, more likely, their lineages did not make it into the genealogical works.[12] To give some sense of the disproportional nature of the material, the index in al-Rāzī's published *al-Shajara al-mubāraka fī ansāb al-Ṭālibiyya* may be helpful: the section on the women runs to five pages, whereas the men occupy 136 pages.

Moreover, not only are women only mentioned as mothers and wives, if at all, even this information is more plentiful for the earlier generations than the later ones. For the earlier period, often corresponding to the generations covered by the early genealogical works on the Arabs or Quraysh, the names of the wives or mothers of ʿAlids are generally given. Sometimes there is even information on the marriages of prominent women: some of the earlier works have short sections on "multi-marrying women."[13] For the later generations covered in the Ṭālibid genealogies, there is much less information on mothers, whether or not they were ʿAlids themselves. The explanation for this drop in information on women may simply be a pragmatic decision: there were increasing numbers of people to cover, so the authors were no longer able to include everyone. They began to focus on the surviving male lineages. Indeed, rather than giving a complete account of all the offspring of the kinsfolk of the Prophet, what mattered ever more was to record the lineages that survived, so no one could falsely claim to be a member of the Prophet's family.[14]

However, there is also another reason, which brings us to the second limitation for a study on marriage patterns: the information, also for the male lineages, is not comprehensive. While the earlier genealogical works seem to record all possible descent lines, including many women, this is no longer the case in the Ṭālbid genealogies. A full description of the lineages is usually given up to generation VII or VIII after ʿAli, which again corresponds largely to the material found in the earlier general works; but after that the Ṭālibid genealogies focus on particular branches, and no longer provide a complete account.[15]

So far one can only speculate as to the reasons for this change in genealogical record keeping. An important consequence for a study on marriage patterns is that the genealogical "data set" is much less complete than one would wish. Not only is information on women limited, generally attached to male lineages, and increasingly rare, even the records for men are patchy. A study of the marriage patterns of the kinsfolk of the Prophet is therefore necessarily impressionistic – it relies on cumulative records and a few external references. Nevertheless, given that these findings are largely based on Ṭālibid genealogies, often written by (and perhaps mainly for) the Ṭālibids themselves, they at the very least provide a picture that the family itself sought to preserve and convey.

Theoretical discussions

In theory, a Muslim adult male can freely chose his wife. Nonetheless, the law books give a series of rules and regulations regarding marriage (*nikāḥ* or *zawāj*), and the section of the *Kitāb al-nikāḥ* usually opens with a discussion on marriages that are prohibited. Prohibitions include relationships of affinity or consanguinity, as a man is generally not allowed to marry his female ascendants or descendants, his sisters, female descendants of his siblings, or his aunts and great-aunts; much of this is understood to be based on the Qurʾān, sūra IV.[16] There are further restrictions regarding relationships of fosterage and religion: a woman is always prohibited from marrying an infidel, whereas a man is in principle allowed. According to Joseph Schacht, however, the permission for men to marry even women of the *ahl al-kitāb* is, "at least by the Shāfiʿīs, so restricted by conditions as to be prohibited in practice."[17] Number is another factor: a free man can take up to four wives at the same time, a woman of course only one husband. The *Kitāb al-nikāḥ* goes on to discuss a variety of other topics such as the role of a woman's guardian (*walī*), the amount of the dower (*mahr*) and when and how it must be paid, prescriptions on sexual intercourse and so on. The most important section for the present purposes is the discussion on *kafāʾa*, equality or suitability in marriage, and its emphasis on descent (*nasab*).

Kafāʾa *and descent*

According to the *Lisān al-ʿArab*, *kafāʾa* in marriage means that the husband is to be equal to the woman in terms of honor (*ḥasab*), religion (*dīn*), descent (*nasab*) and family (*bayt*), and other such things (*wa-ghayr dhālika*).[18] *Kafāʾa* is thus directed at the woman's marriage relation: it intends to regulate her choice of husband, as a woman may not marry beneath herself.

The legal schools differ over the categories and regulations of *kafāʾa*, as well as its importance over all. In very general terms, it might be said that marriage regulations were elaborated in most detail by some Ḥanafī scholars, and are of least importance to the Mālikīs.[19] As Amalia Zomeño has shown, however, while the Mālikīs generally exclude *nasab* in theoretical legal discussions, there is some evidence that it did matter in practice.[20] Other schools are more explicit also in theory: in his discussion of the differing opinions on *kafāʾa* of Abū Ḥanīfa and al-Shāfiʿī, al-Ṭūsī (d. 460/1067) ascribes to Abū Ḥanīfa the statement that "all of Quraysh are equal (*akfāʾ*); the Arabs are not equal to Quraysh."[21] He further says that there is a disagreement between Ḥanafīs and Shāfiʿīs, as the latter add that "non-Arabs (*ʿajam*) are not suitable for the Arabs, the Arabs are not equal to Quraysh, and Quraysh is not equal to the Banū Hāshim."[22] This notion is repeated by the Shāfiʿī jurist al-Māwardī (d. 450/1058), who refers to a disagreement between the "school of the Baṣrans" and the "school of the Baghdādīs": the former say that all of Quraysh are equal in marriage, whereas the latter insist that the Banū Hāshim are preferred (*ashraf* or *afḍal*) on account of their closer relation with the Prophet.[23]

Beyond these broad discussions, however, the Sunnī schools are noticeably quiet on the question of Hāshimite marriages in general, and ʿAlid marriages in particular.

The Shīʿite view

Given the importance of the descendants of the Prophet in Shīʿite doctrine, it may be surprising that the Shīʿites similarly do not single out the ʿAlids as requiring special *kafāʾa* on account of their genealogy. Indeed, early Imāmī works not only fail to restrict ʿAlid marriages; contrary to what one might expect, some works even explicitly state that marriages by non-ʿAlid men to ʿAlid women are allowed. Thus, according to the great Imāmī authority of the Buyid period, the Sharīf al-Murtaḍā (d. 436/1044), marriage to an ʿAlid woman – called explicitly *imraʾa ʿAlawiyya Hāshimiyya* – may be seen as reprehensible in terms of governance and custom (*siyāsa wa-ʿāda*); but "it is not forbidden as far as the religion is concerned (*lam yakun maḥẓūran fī al-dīn*)."[24] Al-Murtaḍā's friend and student al-Ṭūsī (d. 460/1067) similarly states in the *Nihāya*:

> The Believers are of equal worth to one another in terms of marriage, just as they are equal in terms of lives, even if they differ in terms of lineage (*nasab*) and honor (*sharaf*). If a believer asks another for the hand of his daughter, has the means to support her, is satisfactory in religion and faith (*dīnuhu wa-īmānuhu*), and has not committed any crime, he [the father] is sinning against God and going against the Sunna of the Prophet if he does not marry him to her, even if he [the suitor] is of low origin (*ḥaqīr fī nasabihi*).[25]

The early Imāmī scholars thus do not support regulations of *kafāʾa* in the same way as some of the Sunnī schools; descent and honor are not important factors, and only faith and the ability to provide maintenance (*nafaqa*) must be considered.[26] This is also the view in the *Kāfī* of al-Kulīnī (d. 329/941): Jaʿfar al-Ṣādiq is reported to have said that the two criteria for suitability in marriage are virtue and means (*al-kufūʾān yakun ʿafīfan wa ʿindahu yasār*).[27] Ibn Bābūya (d. 381/991) – half a century later – says that if a man is good enough in religion, morality and faith (*dīnuhu wa-khulquhu wa-īmānuhu*), he should be accepted for marriage; he cites a Qurʾānic verse to say that means also matter little.[28] He says nothing about descent in either the *Hidāya* or the *Muqniʿ*, but elaborates a bit on the question in his *Iʿtiqādāt al-Imāmiyya*. There he argues that devotion to the descendants of the Prophet is obligatory, because it is the recompense for the Prophetic message; to substantiate his point he cites Qurʾān, XLII:23, "*Qul lā asʾalukum ʿalayhi ajran illā al-mawadda fī al-qurbā*" (Say: I ask of you no reward for it except the love of kin). There is nothing more explicit on marriages. Regarding *nasab*, he cites Jaʿfar al-Ṣādiq as having said that his devotion (*walāya*) to the Prophet was more dear to him than his descent from him.[29]

In short then, the Imāmīs do not consider Prophetic lineage to be an important criterion for suitability in marriage. Again, this is surprising: one would have expected it of the Imāmīs. Importantly, however, this clearly shows that the disengagement of ʿAlidism and Shīʿism goes both ways: not only could one be a supporter of the ʿAlids without being a Shīʿite, one could also be a Shīʿite without proposing any special treatment for the ʿAlids.

Marriage patterns and social praxis

While there is little in both Shīʿite and Sunnī law to explicitly restrict ʿAlid marriages, social convention made it increasingly impossible for an ʿAlid woman to marry outside her family – as al-Murtaḍā had said, it was seen as reprehensible in terms of governance and custom. This is clear from the evidence of the genealogical and historical sources, to which we will now turn. Social praxis clearly demanded that the ʿAlids – and especially ʿAlid women – married someone of acceptable status, a requirement generally met by marriage within the family: throughout the period studied, the ʿAlids married to a large extent endogamously, that is, within the family.[30] Ḥasanids married other Ḥasanids, and Ḥusaynids married other Ḥusaynids, or Ḥasanids and Ḥusaynids married each other or other Ṭālibids. Most common are first or second cousin marriages, a pattern found among many societies throughout history.[31]

There have been a number of studies on the phenomenon of cousin marriage, and various explanations can be offered, such as the coherence of the clan, the preservation of property, protection of the honor of the women, or simply geographical proximity. Emrys Peters in his 1940s study of the Bedouins of Cyrenaica still found that "the preferred spouse for a man is a father's brother's daughter."[32] For the women, who are the main concern, to marry a cousin was also desirable because she would not join a group of strangers, but rather remain among her extended kinship group, where a loss of status is less likely.[33]

However, even though the greatest number of marriages took place among the ʿAlids, they also married outside the family. Not only were there great numbers of relations with an *umm walad*[34]; marriages were contracted also with other, non-ʿAlid or non-Ṭālibid, families. Because these marriages outside the family are perhaps more illustrative of changes in the status of the ʿAlids and the hierarchy of Islamic society more generally, I will focus here on such exogamous marriages.

My research shows that in general terms, exogamous marriages in the early period (seventh and eighth centuries) were contracted with other families from Quraysh, and sometimes, though rarely, other Arab tribes. Both men and women intermarried with these families, that is, both ʿAlid men and women took partners from other families. However, if we take the examples of marriages with the Banū Makhzūm and the Banū ʿAbbās, we find that the ʿAlids married "out" in a position of relative weakness, and they married "in" in a position of relative strength. Thus, they accepted Makhzūmī brides, but did not themselves marry their daughters to the Banū Makhzūm; this may emphasize at the same time a shared identity, but perceived superior status on the part of the ʿAlids. On the other hand, they married their daughters off to the ʿAbbāsids, but took no ʿAbbāsid brides; this may reflect their relative weakness toward the ʿAbbāsids, particularly around the time of the ʿAbbāsid Revolution. Let us examine these points in some more detail.

Marriages with the Banū Makhzūm

The Banū Makhzūm were an important clan of Quraysh. Some of its members are said to have been among the Prophet's adversaries in Mecca, but differences between the families were soon overcome, it seems. From the earliest Islamic period there were ʿAlid–Makhzūmī relations, and Makhzūmīs intermarried particularly with the Ḥasanid branch of the Prophet's family.[35] These relations intensified in the late Umayyad and early ʿAbbāsid periods, with ʿAlids taking Makhzūmī brides. In generations V and VI after ʿAlī, there are at least six Ḥasanid–Makhzūmī marriages recorded – among them between ʿAbdallāh b. al-Ḥasan b. al-Ḥasan b. ʿAlī and ʿĀtika bt. ʿAbd al-Malik al-Makhzūmiyya. One of their sons was Idrīs b. ʿAbdallāh, the founder of the Idrīsid dynasty in North Africa. ʿAbdallāh's brother Ibrāhīm also took a Makhzūmī wife, and in the two generations that followed there are at least four more marriages between Ḥasanids and Makhzūmīs.[36] But there are no longer any examples, as far as I have seen, of an ʿAlid woman being married off to a Makhzūmī.

The reasons for such strong marriage connections with the Makhzūmīs cannot easily be discerned from the sources. During the Umayyad period the Banū Makhzūm were mostly supporters of the "fiercely anti-ʿAlid family of al-Zubayr," with whom the ʿAlids incidentally had marriage relations throughout this period. After the ʿAbbāsid Revolution, there are some Makhzūmīs among the supporters of Muḥammad al-Nafs al-Zakiyya, an older son of the above-mentioned ʿAbdallāh b. al-Ḥasan, who led an important anti-ʿAbbāsid uprising in the Ḥijāz.[37] The Makhzūmī women came from a number of different families, though mainly from the al-Mughīra branch, which Martin Hinds identified as the most important one in the early Islamic period.[38] Geographical proximity in the Ḥijāz, common economic interests, or political alliances may well have played a role. There is probably more to be discovered by further study. The readings thus far suggest that this change in marriage patterns, whereby the ʿAlids no longer gave their daughters to the Makhzūmīs in marriage after a certain point in the mid-eighth century, reflects a shift in the social hierarchy, or in the relative status of the two families – particularly as there clearly had been such intermarriages in earlier times. As the Makhzūmīs became less prominent in the ʿAbbāsid period, the ʿAlids no longer married their daughters to them. There was still a shared identity in that both families belonged to Quraysh, but they were no longer equals. Boundaries were beginning to be drawn around the kinsfolk of the Prophet.

Marriages with the Banū ʿAbbās

In contrast to ʿAlid marriages with the Banū Makhzūm, most ʿAlid–ʿAbbāsid marriages took place between Ḥusaynids and ʿAbbāsids.[39] There are some examples of intermarriages (that is, both ʿAlids and ʿAbbāsids taking in marriage the others' wives) in the early Islamic period.[40] When marriage relations increased in the late Umayyad and early ʿAbbāsid periods, however, it was ʿAlid women who were married off to the ʿAbbāsids. There are very few instances in which ʿAbbāsid women were offered as brides to an ʿAlid – one famous example is that of the caliph al-Maʾmūn: he gave two of his daughters in marriage to the Ḥusaynids, to ʿAlī al-Riḍā (d. 203/818), the later eighth Imam of the Imāmī Shīʿites, and his son Muḥammad. In view of the absence of any such marriages in the preceding generations, the gesture is significant: not only had the caliph named ʿAlī al-Riḍā as his successor, he also forged ties of kinship to underline the connection.[41]

The list of Ḥusaynid–ʿAbbāsid marriages is long. It includes two daughters of Jaʿfar al-Ṣādiq, who were both married, one after the other, to Muḥammad b. Ibrāhīm b. Muḥammad b. ʿAlī b. ʿAbdallāh b. al-ʿAbbās, the son of the first ʿAbbāsid caliph al-Ṣaffāḥ.[42] Muḥammad b. Ibrāhīm also had other Ḥusaynid wives, such as Fāṭima bt. al-Ḥusayn b. Zayd b. ʿAlī b. al-Ḥusayn. After he died Fāṭima married a son of al-Manṣūr, but he divorced her (*fāraqahā*).[43] The caliph Hārūn al-Rashīd (d. 193/809) also married a Ḥusaynid, if only very briefly: he divorced Zaynab bt. ʿAbdallāh b. al-Ḥusayn b. ʿAlī b. al-Ḥusayn b. ʿAlī after just one night, which gave her the name "*Zaynab laylatin*" among the people of Medina.[44]

There are more examples; clearly the ʿAlids married their daughters to the ʿAbbāsids, particularly around the time of the ʿAbbāsid Revolution. It is striking that there are noticeably more Ḥusaynid–ʿAbbāsid relations than Ḥasanid–ʿAbbāsid ones; this may indeed confirm that the former two clans were on better terms than the Ḥasanids and ʿAbbāsids.[45] To what extent the ʿAlids were coerced to marry their daughters is not known. According to Abū Naṣr al-Bukhārī's (d. mid tenth century) version of the one-night marriage between the caliph Hārūn and Zaynab bt. ʿAbdallāh, Zaynab did not want to be married to the ʿAbbāsid. There was already some suspicion that she might be trouble: in the night of the marriage (*laylat al-dukhūl*) a slave came to Zaynab, intending to bind her with a rope so she might "not be unapproachable" for Hārūn; but when the slave came near her she kicked him so hard that he broke two ribs. Hārūn let her go without having consummated the marriage, but still sent her four thousand *dīnār*s each year for her maintenance.[46] We should probably read this as a conciliatory gesture; but other marriages, such as the one between Zaynab bt. Muḥammad al-Nafs al-Zakiyya (the rebel against al-Manṣūr) and Muḥammad b. ʿAbdallāh (the son of al-Ṣaffaḥ), who had even taken an active part in the defeat of his father-in-law's revolt, were more likely, I would argue, another way to display ʿAbbāsid victory over the ʿAlids.

Marriages in the ninth century and after

As ʿAlid–ʿAbbāsid relations continued to deteriorate and status relations began to shift during the eighth century, the intermarriages between the two families decreased sharply. This was the case also for ʿAlid marriage relations with all other non-Ṭālibid families. Indeed, from the early ninth century onwards, the ʿAlids married increasingly within their own family. Endogamy came to be the desired form of marriage, prescribed for ʿAlid women, and recommended for ʿAlid men. In his discussion of the duties of the *naqīb al-ashrāf*, al-Māwardī (d. 450/1058) in the *Aḥkām al-sulṭāniyya* says that the *naqīb* must

> prevent their single women whether divorced or widowed, from marrying any but those of compatible birth owing to their superiority to other women, in order to protect their purity of descent and maintain inviolability against the indignity of being given away by someone other than a legal guardian or married to unsuitable men.[47]

According to the genealogist of the Saljuq period Ibn Funduq al-Bayhaqī (d. 565/1169–70), the *naqīb* should furthermore "prohibit the men from marrying common women (*al-ʿāmiyyāt*), so that no daughters of the Prophet remain unmarried."[48] It appears that in practice these prescriptions were generally followed. Indeed, the absence of legal limitations, as discussed above, may explain why the responsibilities of the *naqīb* had to include so emphatically the guardianship of ʿAlid marriages.

Thus the majority of ʿAlid marriages came to be contracted within the family. Nevertheless, there are some examples in the ninth to eleventh centuries of marriages between ʿAlid men and the daughters of local rulers, or other local notables. Some ʿAlid families came to be so highly regarded that it was evidently a mark of distinction and honor for these elite families to marry their daughters to the ʿAlids. I would thus finally like to introduce an ʿAlid family from the Eastern Islamic lands in the ninth and tenth centuries, a prominent Ḥasanid family from Nishapur, called the Āl Buṭḥānī, to illustrate these later changes in ʿAlid marriage patterns.

The Buṭḥānī family has been examined in some detail by Richard Bulliet in his *Patricians of Nishapur*.[49] They were descendants of al-Ḥasan b. Zayd b. al-Ḥasan b. ʿAlī, one of the few ʿAlids who continued to support the ʿAbbāsids after their rise to the caliphate. Al-Ḥasan was governor of Medina for the caliph al-Manṣūr, and "the first to wear black from among the ʿAlids"; he allegedly died in 168/784 at the age of 80.[50] His grandson Muḥammad b. al-Qāsim b. al-Ḥasan was the eponymous al-Buṭḥānī.[51] By the end of the ninth century, Buṭḥānī Ḥasanids had spread to many parts of the Muslim world: there still were distinguished members of the family in Medina, but also in Egypt (one Buṭḥānī was a genealogist in the *maḥḍar* incident of the Fāṭimids, where an official document was drawn up to disclaim their ʿAlid descent), in Ṭabaristān (there are two well-known supporters of the *dāʿī* al-Ḥasan b. Zayd, authors of important Zaydī works), as well as in various cities in the East. In Nishapur they rose to particular prominence, taking over the *niqāba* from a rival Ḥusaynid family, the Āl Zubāra, in 395/1004. They then held the office for at least 120 years. Most surprisingly, perhaps, the Buṭḥānīs may have been Sunnī. They made marriage alliances with elite families of the scholarly community, taking wives from both the rivalling Ḥanafī and Shāfiʿī factions: in generation IX, Abū Muḥammad Ḥamza married al-Ḥurra bt. al-Imām al-Muwaffaq Hibat Allāh b. al-Qāḍī ʿUmar b. Muḥammad, chief of the Shāfiʿīs (*muqaddam aṣḥāb al-Shāfiʿī*). Incidentally, the Shāfiʿīs in particular supported the transfer of the *niqāba* to this family. As Ibn Funduq says, "the followers of the Imam Muṭṭalibī Shāfiʿī, may God be pleased with him, considered it advisable to help the sons of the Sayyid Abū ʿAbdallāh [the Buṭḥānis], and the *niqāba* passed from this line to the other one . . ."[52] But the Buṭḥānīs' eggs were not all kept in one basket: a generation later, Abū al-Ḥasan ʿAlī is described as the son-in-law (*khatan*) of the prominent Ḥanafī shaykh al-Ṣandalī.[53]

Moreover, in addition to local support and strategic marriage alliances with both Nishapuri *madhhab*s, the Buṭḥānīs also took pains to cultivate their relations with the dynastic rulers, Ghaznavids and Saljuqs. One member of the family, Abū al-Qāsim Zayd, took part in the Somnath raids with Maḥmūd b. Sebuktekīn in 416/1025, and one source says that "for that reason he was then given the *niqāba* of Nishapur in the 420s."[54] In fact, this was a most significant appointment, as it was this very same ʿAlid who took a leading role in the first surrender of the city to the Saljuqs in 428/1036.[55] But he kept his loyalty to the Ghaznavids, so that when the Saljuqs established permanent control of the city in 431/1039 after a brief Ghaznavid re-conquest, the *niqāba* went to another branch of the family, to a nephew called Abū ʿAlī Muḥammad. The latter was entrusted with the *niqāba* (*fuwwiḍat ilayhi al-niqāba fī ʿahd* . . .) by the Saljuq Malikshāh (r. 465–485/1073–1092) and even appointed as the *naqīb al-nuqabāʾ al-Hāshimiyya*.[56] Both Ghaznavids and Saljuqs thus integrated this family into their own structures while recognizing their power at a local level.

Over all, the Buṭḥānīs conform to the marriage pattern described above: most of the recorded marriages were contracted within the family, with other ʿAlids or Ṭālibids. But there were some notable exogamous marriages as well. In the earlier generations, there is a marriage with a woman from the Banū Thaqīf, another Arab tribe; and in the eighth century there is a marriage between an ʿAbbāsid and a granddaughter of al-Ḥasan b. Zayd, the *amīr* in Medina (she is a daughter of al-Ḥasan's son ʿAbd al-Raḥmān al-Shajarī, the brother of Muḥammad al-Buṭḥānī).[57] In the later generations there is information almost exclusively for ʿAlid men who married within the family, or took wives from the local notables or other prominent families, not necessarily Arabs. Indeed, as the ʿAlids left the Ḥijāz and settled in cities all over the Islamic world, their political, scholarly and social affiliations reflected the changing makeup of the Islamic empire. Between the eighth and the twelfth centuries, social hierarchies changed considerably in Muslim societies all over the Islamic world, and included an increasing number of non-Arabs. The new elites were Persians and Turks, or, in the case of North Africa, sometimes Berbers; and like the old elites in the earlier centuries, they gave their daughters in marriage to *sayyid*s and *sharīf*s, so that their offspring would be part of the kinsfolk of the Prophet.

Conclusion

While the kinsfolk of the Prophet was held in high esteem by the Muslim community from an early period, the ʿAlids emerged in the centuries after the ʿAbbāsid Revolution as the undisputed aristocracy of Islam. They left the Ḥijāz and settled in cities all over the Islamic world, became part of the local elites, and began to delineate ever more clearly what it meant to be part of the kinsfolk of the Prophet. Especially in the Islamic East, genealogies were written to record the important branches of the family, and to clarify and verify who belonged to this family, and could thus claim a share in the social, religious, or indeed economic privileges.

The narrowing of ʿAlid marriage choices between the eighth and the twelfth centuries clearly reflects the heightened consciousness about the presumed special status of the family of the Prophet, and reveals an interest on part of the family to further it. As has been discussed above, there is little in the sources, including the Shīʿite literature, to explicitly restrict ʿAlid marriages to the family. Some of the Shīʿite sources, such as the eleventh century Imāmī authority al-Murtaḍā, even point out that the marriage of a *sayyida* to an ordinary Muslim was not forbidden on religious grounds. Nonetheless, as al-Murtaḍā already suggests, social convention came to make it virtually impossible for an ʿAlid woman to marry outside her family.

Indeed, an exogamous marriage of a *sayyida* could evoke serious conflict even in more recent times. One example is the famous case of the Ḥaḍramī community in the Middle East and South East Asia in the early twentieth century.[58] Beginning in 1905, a number of marriages between *sayyid* women and non-*sayyid* men were publicly denounced, because of their unsuitability. In his journal *al-Manār* in Egypt, the Islamic reformer Rashīd Riḍā publicly sanctioned the marriage of a Ḥaḍramī *sayyida* to a non-*sayyid* Indian Muslim, after a question on its permissibility had been posed to him by a reader in Singapore. He argued – in line with the early medieval sources surveyed above – that there was nothing in Islamic law to prohibit such a marriage. Riḍā's response, however, was strongly contradicted by the leading Ḥaḍramī scholar of the time, Sayyid ʿUmar al-ʿAṭṭās. Al-ʿAṭṭās declared that a marriage between a *sayyida* and a non-*sayyid* was unlawful, because descent was to be the basic criterion for *kafāʾa*.[59] The discussion had far-reaching consequences, and sparked a power struggle in the overseas Ḥaḍramī communities that had long adhered to a rigid system of social stratification based on descent. People began to openly question the century-long domination of the *sayyid*s, their status and system of social control, setting in motion events that arguably led to the Yemeni revolution and the abolition of the Zaydī Imamate in 1962.[60] To what extent the marriage relations of *sayyid*s and *sharīf*s, in Ḥaḍramī communities or elsewhere in Muslim societies, were lastingly changed as a result of this episode remains to be investigated. What is clear, however, is that marriage had become a means to emphasize the boundaries, as well as a way to question, the special status of the kinsfolk of the Prophet.

Notes

1 Richard Bulliet, *The Patricians of Nishapur* (Cambridge, MA: Harvard University Press, 1972), 234.

2 Morimoto Kazuo, "Toward the Formation of Sayyido-Sharifology: Questioning Accepted Fact," *Journal of Sophia Asian Studies* 22 (2004): 87–103.

3 As Shīʿites and ʿAlids are frequently conflated in the secondary literature, this important distinction cannot be overemphasized. Not only were there Sunnī as well as Shīʿite supporters of the kinsfolk of the Prophet, there were also Sunnīs and Shīʿites among the ʿAlids. As will be clear also from some of the examples below, not all ʿAlids were Shīʿites, as is often assumed.

4 Morimoto Kazuo, "A Preliminary Study on the Diffusion of the *Niqāba al-Ṭālibīyīn*: Towards an Understanding of the Early Dispersal of *Sayyids*," in Kuroki Hidemitsu ed., *The Influence of Human Mobility in Muslim Societies* (London: Kegan Paul, 2003), 3–42; Teresa Bernheimer, *The ʿAlids: The First Family of Islam, 750–1200* (Edinburgh: Edinburgh University Press, forthcoming).

5 Al-Suyūṭī, "al-ʿAjāja al-zarnabiyya fī al-sulāla al-Zaynabiyya," in al-Suyūṭī, *al-Ḥāwī*, 2 vols (Cairo: Idārat al-Ṭibāʿa al-Munīriyya, 1352/1933), II:31–34. This text was expertly discussed by Nebil Hussen during the 2010 Princeton workshop on Sayyids/Sharīfs*: The Kinsfolk of the Prophet in Muslim Societies*. The workshop was lead by Morimoto Kazuo, and I am grateful to him for bringing this text to my attention.

6 For an elaboration of this point, see Teresa Bernheimer, "Shared Sanctity: Early Tombs and Shrines of the ʿAlid Family in the Eastern Islamic Lands," in Ruba Kana'an and Zulfikar Hirji eds, *Places of Worship and Devotion in Muslim Societies* (Oxford: Berghahn Press, forthcoming), 6.

7 Roy Mottahedeh, "Administration in Būyid Qazwīn," in D. S. Richards ed., *Islamic Civilisation 950–1150* (Oxford: Oxford University Press, 1983), 33–45.

8 Kazuo Morimoto, "The Formation and Development of the Science of Talibid Genealogies in the 10th and 11th Century Middle East," *Oriente Moderno* n.s. 18 (1999): 541–570.

9 Very occasionally there is a short section on the ʿAbbāsids; see for instance Ibn Funduq al-Bayhaqī (d. 565/1169–70), *Lubāb al-ansāb*, 2 pts (Qum: Maktabat al-Marʿashī, 1410/1989), 716, on the ʿAbbāsids of Nishapur. Generally, however, the point is to exclude them.

10 Some of the most important ones used in this study are: Shaykh al-Sharaf al-ʿUbaydalī (d. 435/1043), *Tahdhīb al-ansāb* (Qum: Maktabat al-Marʿashī, 1413/1992); Abū al-Ḥasan al-ʿUmarī (d. 450/1058), *al-Majdī fī ansāb al-Ṭālibiyyīn* (Qum: Maktabat al-Marʿashī, 1409/1988); Ibn Funduq, *Lubāb al-ansāb*; Fakhr al-Dīn al-Rāzī (d. 606/1209), *al-Shajara al-mubāraka fī ansāb al-Ṭālibiyya* (Qum: Maktabat al-Marʿashī, 1409/1988); al-Marwazī al-Azwarqānī (d. after 614/1217), *al-Fakhrī fī ansāb al-Ṭālibiyyīn* (Qum: Maktabat al-Marʿashī, 1409/1988); Ibn ʿInaba (d. 828/1424–5), *ʿUmdat al-ṭālib al-ṣughrā fī nasab āl Abī Ṭālib* (Qum: Maktabat al-Marʿashī, 1425/2009).

11 Hishām b. al-Kalbī, *Ǧamharat an-nasab: das genealogische Werk des Hišām ibn Muḥammad al-Kalbī*, ed. by Werner Caskel, 2 vols (Leiden: Brill, 1966), and *Jamharat al-nasab*, ed. by Maḥmūd Firdaws al-ʿAzm, 3 vols (Damascus: Dār al-Yaqẓa al-ʿArabiyya, 1982–1986); Muṣʿab b. ʿAbdallāh al-Zubayrī, *Kitāb nasab Quraysh*, ed. by Evariste Lévi-Provençal (Cairo: Dār al-Maʿārif li-l-Ṭibāʿa, 1953). For an excellent discussion of some of the aims of Arab genealogy, see Asad Ahmed, "Prosopography and the Reconstruction of Ḥijāzī History for the Early Islamic Period: The Case of the ʿAwfī Family," in Katharine Keats-Rohan ed., *Prosopography: Approaches and Applications* (Oxford: Prosopographica et Genealogica, 2007), 418.

12 Al-Rāzī, *al-Shajara*, 93.

13 Al-Madāʾinī, *Kitāb al-murdifāt*, in ʿAbd al-Salām Muḥammad Hārūn ed., *Nawādir al-makhṭūṭāt*, 2 vols in 8 (Beirut: Dār al-Jīl, 1991), I:57–80; and Ibn Ḥabīb, *Kitāb al-muḥabbar*, ed. by Ilse Lichtenstädter (Hyderabad: Maṭbaʿat Jamʿiyyat Dāʾirat al-Maʿārif al-ʿUthmāniyya, 1361/1942), 435–455. Al-Madāʾinī is said to have had a number of books on women and marriages; see Ibn al-Nadīm, *Fihrist*, trans. by Bayard Dodge, 2 vols (New York: Columbia University Press, 1970), I:220–221.

14 Books on those ʿAlids and Ṭālibids who left no male offspring, called the *dārijūn*, seem to have existed as well; see Ibn Funduq, *Lubāb*, 721.

15 As Morimoto ("Diffusion", 12) rightly says, "the generation up to which such full descriptions are made is by no means uniform within a single work, or among different works." I have followed Morimoto in using Latin numerals to refer to the generation numbers, generation I being the first generation after ʿAlī (i.e., Ḥasan or Ḥusayn); see Morimoto, "Diffusion", 14, n. 33.

16 The relevant verses are Qurʾān, IV:20–25.

17 Joseph Schacht, "Nikāḥ," in H. A. R. Gibb et al. eds, *The Encyclopaedia of Islam*, new ed., 13 vols (Leiden: Brill, 1960–2009; hereafter *EI2*), VIII:26–29.

18 Ibn Manẓūr, *Lisān al-ʿArab*, 20 vols in 10 (Cairo: Būlāq, 1300–1307/1882–3–1889–90), I:134.

19 Yvon Linant de Bellefonds, *Traité de droit musulman comparé*, 3 vols (Paris and La Haye: Mouton et Cie, 1965–1973), II:171. Mālik is reported to have explicitly

authorized the marriage of non-Arab men to Arab women, and to have said that a previously married woman should be able to choose her husband regardless of his *sharaf* or *ḥasab*; see Saḥnūn (d. 240/854), *al-Mudawwana al-kubrā*, 16 vols in 4 (Cairo: Maṭbaʿat al-Saʿāda, 1323/1905), IV:13.

20 There is some indication that *nasab* was discussed even in the Mālikī *furūʿ* works. Zomeño cites the opinion of Khalīl (d. 776/1374) from his *Mukhtaṣar* that "a man without noble origin (*ghayr sharīf*) is not suitable for a noble woman (*sharīfa*)"; see Amalia Zomeño, "*Kafāʾa* in the Mālikī School: A *Fatwā* from Fifteenth-Century Fez," in Robert Gleave and Eugenia Kermeli eds, *Islamic Law: Theory and Practice* (London: I. B. Tauris, 1997), 91–95.

21 Al-Ṭūsī, *Kitāb al-khilāf*, 6 vols (Qum: Muʾassasat al-Nashr al-Islāmī, 1407–1417/1987–1996), IV:272.

22 For a discussion of the different criteria of *kafāʾa* of Ḥanafīs and Shāfiʿīs, see al-Ṭūsī, *Kitāb al-khilāf*, IV:271–273; also al-Ṭūsī, *al-Mabsūṭ fī fiqh al-Imāmiyya*, 8 vols in 7 (Tehran: Maktabat al-Murtaḍawiyya, 1387–1391/1967–1972), II:178.

23 He adds that the same hierarchy is reflected in the *dīwān* of ʿUmar: the Banū Hāshim and the Banū al-Muṭṭalib were equal (*akfāʾ*), as the Prophet put them together regarding their tax portion (*sahm dhawī al-qurbā*); see al-Māwardī, *al-Ḥāwī al-kabīr* (Beirut: Dār al-Fikr, 1414/1994), 102–103.

24 Al-Sharīf al-Murtaḍā, *Rasāʾil al-Sharīf al-Murtaḍā*, ed. by Mahdī al-Rajāʾī, vol. 1 (Qum: Dār al-Qurʾān al-Karīm, 1405/1984–5), 300.

25 Al-Ṭūsī, "*Bāb al-kafāʾa fī al-nikāḥ wa-ikhtiyār al-azwāj*," in al-Ṭūsī, *al-Nihāya fī mujarrad al-fiqh wa-l-fatāwā*, ed. by Muḥammad-Taqī Dānish-pazhūh, 2 pts (Tehran: Dānishgāh-i Tihrān, 1343 AHS/1964–5), 470; also al-Ṭūsī, *Kitāb al-khilāf*, IV:272.

26 Al-Ṭūsī, *Kitāb al-khilāf*, IV:272; see also Farhat Ziadeh, "Equality (*Kafāʾah*) in the Muslim Law of Marriage," *The American Journal of Comparative Law* 6/4 (1957): 507.

27 Al-Kulīnī (d. 329/941), *Uṣūl min al-Kāfī*, ed. by A. A. Ghaffārī, 8 vols (Tehran: Dār al-Kutub al-Islāmiyya, 1375–1381/1955–1961), V:347.

28 Ibn Bābūya, *al-Muqniʿ wa-l-hidāya*, ed. by Muḥammad Ibn Mahdī al-Wāʿiẓ (Tehran: Muʾassasat al-Maṭbūʿāt al-Dīniyya, 1377/1957), 101; he cites Qurʾān, XXIV:32, "If they are poor, God will make them rich through his mercy."

29 Ibn Bābūya, *al-Iʿtiqadāt fī dīn al-Imāmiyya* (Qum: Ghulām Riḍā al-Māzandarānī, 1412/1991–2), 86; many thanks to Morimoto Kazuo for sending me copies of this text. See Asaf A. A. Fyzee, *A Shiʿite Creed* (London and New York: Milford, Oxford University Press, 1942), 114–115; repr. (Tehran: World Organisation for Islamic Services, 1982), 100.

30 To what extent this differs from other important families in early Islam has not been investigated, though it is possible that the situation would have been similar. If that were the case, this would not change the argument presented here, but simply suggest that the ʿAlids in the early period behaved like many other Arab families.

31 Burton Pasternak, *Introduction to Kinship and Social Organisation* (Englewood Cliffs: Prentice-Hall, 1976), 68.

32 See Emrys Peters, *The Bedouin of Cyrenaica* (Cambridge: Cambridge University Press, 1990), 192, also 129 and 239.

33 In a recent study on the Arab tribes in the eighth and ninth centuries, Eva Orthmann points out that the bond with the *ʿamm* and *ibn ʿamm* is described in the sources as particularly close and important. Parallel cousin marriages, or "*bint ʿamm*" marriages, are thus very desirable. She also warns that the positive emphasis on this relationship should be treated with some caution, as the ʿAbbāsids emphasized their right to the caliphate through al-ʿAbbās, the *ʿamm* of the Prophet; see Eva Ortmann, *Stamm und Macht: Die arabischen Stämme im 2. und 3. Jahrhundert der Hiğra* (Wiesbaden: Reichert, 2002), 226.

34 There were great numbers of *ummahāt al-awlād* among the mothers of the ʿAlids (famous examples include the mothers of ʿAlī Zayn al-ʿĀbidīn, and Muḥammad al-Bāqir). The importance of female descent is invoked in the letters between al-Manṣūr and Muḥammad al-Nafs al-Zakiyya; see al-Ṭabarī (d. 310/923), *Taʾrīkh al-rusul wa-l-mulūk*, ed. by Michael J. de Goeje et al., 3 series in 15 (Leiden: Brill, 1879–1901), series III:532; Tilman Nagel, "Ein früher Bericht über den Aufstand von Muḥammad b. ʿAbdallāh im Jahre 145 H.," *Der Islam* 46 (1970): 251; also Renato Traini, "La corrispondenza tra al-Manṣūr e Muḥammad an-Nafs al-Zakiyya," *Annali dell Istituto Universitario Orientale di Napoli* n.s. 14 (1964): 1–26.

35 See al-Ṭabarī, *Taʾrīkh*, III:2465; Ibn Ḥabīb, *Kitāb al-munammaq* (Hyderabad: Maṭbaʿat Majlis Dāʾirat al-Maʿārif al-ʿUthmāniyya, 1384/1964), 457, 519 and 528; and Ibn Ḥabīb, *Kitāb al-muḥabbar*, 437–438.

36 Ibrāhīm's wife was Rabīḥa bt. Muḥammad b. ʿAbdallāh b. Abī Umayya b. Mughīra. For further examples, see Abū Naṣr al-Bukhārī, *Sirr al-silsila al-ʿAlawiyya*, ed. by Muḥammad Ṣādiq Baḥr al-ʿUlūm (Najaf: al-Maṭbaʿa al-Ḥaydariyya, 1383/1963), 18, 23 and 25. Relations with the Ḥasanids were certainly closer, but there are also some examples of Ḥusaynid–Makhzūmī marriages, particularly in generation IV; some references are al-Bukhārī, *Sirr al-silsila*, 35, and al-Zubayrī, *Nasab Quraysh*, 65, and 246; and 71 and 333 for earlier relations.

37 For the "fiercely anti-ʿAlid family of al-Zubayr," see Wilferd Madelung, "Yaḥyā b. ʿAbdallāh," in *EI2*, XI:242–243. Muḥammad al-Nafs al-Zakiyya, for example, had a Zubayrid wife, Fākhita bt. Fulaykh b. Muḥammad b. Mundhir b. al-Zubayr, whose father was perhaps a supporter of his rebellion; see al-Bukhārī, *Sirr al-silsila*, 8.

38 Martin Hinds, "Ma<u>kh</u>zūm," in *EI2*, VI:137–140: "there are in addition indications that in the early ʿAbbāsid period Ma<u>kh</u>zūmī links with the ʿAlids, notably the Ḥasanids, became closer."

39 Among the Ḥasanid women who were married to ʿAbbāsids, there is the famous example of Zaynab bt. Muḥammad al-Nafs al-Zakiyya. See for example al-Zubayrī, *Nasab Quraysh*, 54; Ibn Ḥabīb, *Kitāb al-muḥabbar*, 438.

40 Al-Zubayrī, *Nasab Quraysh*, 26, 28, 32; al-Bukhārī, *Sirr al-silsila*, 29.

41 For an excellent recent discussion of ʿAlī al-Riḍā see Tamima Bayhom-Daou, "ʿAlī al-Riḍā," in G. Krämer et al. eds, *The Encyclopaedia of Islam*, 3rd ed. (Leiden and Boston: Brill, 2007–), 2009–3, 69–74.

42 Al-Zubayrī, *Nasab Quraysh*, 63–65. Muḥammad b. Ibrāhīm also married Fāṭima bt. al-Ḥusayn b. Zayd b. ʿAlī b. al-Ḥusayn, and Khadīja bt. Isḥāq b. ʿAbdallāh b. ʿAlī b. al-Ḥusayn b. ʿAlī, after she separated from her first husband; al-Zubayrī, *Nasab Quraysh*, 65 and 67.

43 Ibid., 65–66.

44 Ibid., 73. Before Hārūn there had been another ʿAlid woman married to an ʿAbbāsid caliph, namely the daughter of Abū ʿAbdallāh al-Ḥusayn b. Zayd b. ʿAlī b. al-Ḥusayn b. ʿAlī, who was married to the caliph al-Mahdī (d. 169/785); see al-Bukhārī, *Sirr al-silsila*, 62.

45 This has been suggested mainly to explain the revolt of Muḥammad al-Nafs al-Zakiyya; see, for example, Marshall Hodgson, "How Did the Early Shīʿa Become Sectarian?" *Journal of the American Oriental Society* 75 (1955): 10; Amikam Elad, "The Siege of al-Wāsiṭ (132/749): Some Aspects of ʿAbbāsid and ʿAlīd Relations at the Beginning of ʿAbbāsid Rule," in Moshe Sharon ed., *Studies in Islamic History and Civilisation in Honour of Professor Ayalon* (Jerusalem: Magnes Press, 1986), 59–90. For a contrary view, see Nagel, "Ein früher Bericht," 262; similarly "The Rebellion of Muḥammad b. ʿAbd Allāh b. al-Ḥasan (Known as al-Nafs al-Zakīya) in 145/762," in James E. Montgomery ed., *ʿAbbasid Studies: Occasional Papers*

of the School of ʿAbbasid Studies, Cambridge, 6–10 July 2002 (Leuven: Peeters en Dept. Oosterse Studies, 2004), 179–189.

46 Al-Bukhārī, *Sirr al-silsila*, 61.

47 Al-Māwardī (d. 450/1058), *Kitāb al-aḥkām al-sulṭāniyya*, ed. by Max Enger (Bonn: Adolphum Marcum, 1853), 81; trans. by Wafaa H. Wahba, *The Ordinances of Government* (Reading: Garnet Publishing, 1996), 107.

48 Ibn Funduq, *Lubāb*, 722. See Kazuo Morimoto, "Putting the *Lubāb al-ansāb* in Context: *Sayyid*s and *Naqīb*s in Late Saljuq Khurasan," *Studia Iranica* 36 (2007): 163–183.

49 Bulliet, *Patricians*, 234–245.

50 Al-Bukhārī, *Sirr al-silsila*, 21.

51 There is some discussion over the correct form of his *laqab*; see for instance al-ʿUmarī, *al-Majdī*, 203–205.

52 Ibn Funduq al-Bayhaqī, *Tārīkh-i Bayhaq*, ed. by Aḥmad Bahmanyār (Tehran: Bungāh-i Dānish, 1317 AHS/1938), 55, trans. in Clifford E. Bosworth, *The Ghaznavids: Their Empire in Afghanistan and Eastern Iran, 994–1040* (Edinburgh: Edinburgh University Press, 1963), 197. The episode is also mentioned in Ibn Funduq, *Lubāb*, 608–609. For a fuller discussion see Teresa Bernheimer, "The Rise of *Sayyid*s and *Sādāt*: The Case of the Āl Zubāra in 9th–11th Century Nishapur," *Studia Islamica* 100–101 (2005): 58.

53 Ibn Funduq, *Lubāb*, 604.

54 Ibid.

55 Bosworth, *Ghaznavids*, 252–257 for the report on the surrender to the Ghaznavid court.

56 Ibn Funduq, *Lubāb*, 607. It is somewhat unclear to what extent this title signified greater responsibilities to those of an ordinary *naqīb*. My current impression is that the *naqīb al-nuqabāʾ al-Hāshimiyya* in this particular case was probably both a ceremonial exaggeration as well as some sort of higher office that may have included the supervision of other *nuqabāʾ* in Khurasan.

57 Al-ʿUmarī, *al-Majdī*, 215.

58 An excellent study of the diaspora community of Ḥaḍramī *sayyid*s and non-*sayyid*s is Engseng Ho, *Graves of Tarim: Genealogy and Mobility across the Indian Ocean* (Berkeley: University of California Press, 2006).

59 A translation of his response is given in Ho, *Graves of Tarim*, 174–176. Al-ʿAṭṭās identifies four levels of suitability in marriage (always for women, i.e., a man can marry someone from a lower rank, but a woman cannot): Arabs must not marry non-Arabs, Qurashīs must not marry non-Qurashīs, Hāshimites must not marry non-Hāshimites, and descendants of Ḥasan and Ḥusayn must not marry anyone other than other Ḥasanids or Ḥusaynids. The last level is worth emphasizing, as none of the early scholars make this distinction. See also Abdalla S. Bujra, "Political Conflict and Stratification in Ḥaḍramaut – I," *Middle Eastern Studies* 3 (1967): 355–375; for al-ʿAṭṭās, see for instance Ulrike Freitag, "Gelehrtenbeziehungen im Spannungsfeld von Tradition und Moderne: Der hadhramische ʿĀlim Aḥmad b. Ḥasan al-ʿAṭṭās (1841–1915)," in Rainer Brunner et al. eds, *Islamstudien ohne Ende: Festschrift für Werner Ende zum 65. Geburtstag* (Würzburg: Ergon, 2002), 87–96.

60 [Editor's note] See Yamaguchi's contribution to this volume.

5 A historical atlas on the ʿAlids

A proposal and a few samples

Biancamaria Scarcia Amoretti

Introduction

A few years ago I was asked by some Iranian friends to prepare the project of a history of the Shīʿa, similar in structure to *The Cambridge History of Iran*. At that time, as I envisioned a section dedicated to the *Ahl al-Bayt*, I began to entertain the idea of a historical Atlas on the ʿAlids as a necessary supplement. Mostly due to health problems, I was not able to undertake the full scope of work that such a history would require. I lost a good opportunity and its momentum, but I did not give up on the idea of an Atlas, particularly one whose perspective would not be limited to the Shīʿite ʿAlids. Today I am even more convinced of the utility of such an Atlas as an independent tool, given, on the one hand, the contemporary political context (one need only call to mind the role of the ʿAlid families in contemporary ʿIrāq), and, on the other hand, the actual implications of information technology. I feel that these proceedings offer the appropriate opportunity to present my project, or, more precisely, the "idea of my project."

The reason I am presenting this study here is twofold. On the one hand, I took into serious consideration the request by Morimoto Kazuo to lay out "the strategy for future studies" within "the comparative approach adopted by the colloquium" held in Rome in 1998, which was just an initial endeavor to make this specific "case study" – the study on *sayyid*s and *sharīf*s – visible.[1] Morimoto is absolutely right when he points out the "potential significance" of a coherent integration of the many implications of the ʿAlid phenomenon into the different branches of Islamic studies. The implementation of his suggestions will require research tools that are both easily available to scholars and suitable for addressing a broad range of questions. I believe that a historical Atlas on the *Ahl al-Bayt* could be one of these tools. On the other hand, there is the need for international cooperation, on both the scholarly and the financial levels. In both cases "publicity" is necessary. Scholarly interest and involvement are a precondition to launching a fundraising campaign. Arousing such interest is the main purpose of my paper. It consists of two parts. First, on the basis of the material provided by a few sources selected from within my area of expertise, I will present some examples of the kind of information that such an Atlas can supply. I will also exhibit a few samples of maps that "translate," so to speak, this information into map form. In the second part, in the form of "Notes on the Maps," I will try to explain the rationale and the criteria that I used in planning them and list the ʿAlid characters who, in my sources, are connected in different ways with the locations that appear in the maps.

The main sources

My choice of the sources is also twofold. I worked on a few chapters of two genealogical texts: the *Sirr al-silsila al-ʿAlawiyya* (middle of the tenth century) by a pro-Shīʿite author, Abū Naṣr al-Bukhārī, and *al-Majdī fī ansāb al-Ṭālibiyyīn* (first half of the eleventh century) by an affirmed Shīʿite, Najm al-Dīn Abū al-Ḥasan al-ʿUmarī.[2] These books are quite familiar to me, especially as regards the Ḥusaynī branch of the Family, and, more importantly, they – as is generally the case with the prosopographic literature – are considered to belong to a specialized genre that is not necessarily included among the primary historical sources, at least as far as Shīʿite history is concerned.

It seems to me that the historical significance of the ʿAlid diaspora throughout *Dār al-Islām* has been anything but fully and fairly investigated.[3] And, in my understanding, it is the genealogical books that provide the initial building blocks upon which such an investigation would be built: where the ʿAlids' presence is attested, who they are (at least the branch or branches of the Family at stake, if not always individual members), a rough count of the number of generations of different branches and a temporal outline of their presence. It becomes more and more clear that the historiography has underestimated the political and social roles of the Family.[4] The ʿAlids do indeed hold a peculiar rank. And in order to understand that rank, we must stop dwelling on their (religious?) privileges in general terms and instead examine their activities in their local socio-political contexts.

I also took one historical source into consideration. I deliberately chose *Tārīkh Qum* by al-Ḥasan b. Muḥammad b. al-Ḥasan al-Qumī (end of the tenth century), preserved in the late Persian translation (1403–4) of al-Ḥasan b. ʿAlī b. al-Ḥasan al-Qumī with the same title, *Tārīkh-i Qum*,[5] because this text offers a specific advantage. It is not a genealogical work, but two main chapters – dedicated to the Talibids and to the Ashʿarī clan – record genealogical information, as regional historical texts usually do. Indeed, such texts are intended to offer a reasonably precise portrayal of their given location, and hence we may glean some hints of the reasons for ʿAlid settlement there and of the possible impact of their presence in peripheral contexts.

A few years ago I began to study the ʿAlid presence in Qum from the ninth to the thirteenth centuries with the intention that it could serve as a case study for enquiry into the role of ʿAlids in a Shīʿite town located in a broader Sunnī environment. Qum was not an important town in a political or economic sense, but it was meaningful from a Shīʿite point of view, being the center of the devotional cult to the shrine of Fāṭima bt. Mūsā.[6] As I had expected, in one sense this investigation helped to identify some of the factors that may have informed the ʿAlids' choice of location in their diaspora, and in another sense it showed that, eventually, their political importance needs to be carefully evaluated.

I do not believe that the texts that I have drawn upon here will enable me to address the broader goals that I outlined above for this study in a satisfactory manner – the rudimentary examples presented here can be only indicative of the relevance of the Atlas which I am proposing. In fact, my purpose may be ambitious, but not overly sophisticated if we presume that a convincing geographical representation of a phenomenon is an illuminating way of highlighting the relationship between a specific territorial context and its socio-political order.[7] Let us come to the point.

Ḥasanīs in al-Bukhārī's text

I chose to begin with the descendants of al-Ḥasan b. ʿAlī b. Abī Ṭālib in al-Bukhārī's text,[8] and collected the names of the places mentioned in relation to them. Four typologies of information transferable on maps came out: places where a major historical event, such as a rebellion or a battle, occurred (Map 5.1a), places where Ḥasanīs were subjected to persecutions (Map 5.1b), places where their presence was attested or where their burial grounds are found (Map 5.1c) and places where they had progeny, however doubtful at times (Map 5.1d).[9]

Clearly of interest to the Ḥasanī branch, at least according to al-Bukhārī, are the Eastern regions of the caliphate. But Madīna and Makka are still important locations for the Family, more than either Baghdād or Baṣra. Concerning the historical events and persecutions, the text with which to evaluate our information is the famous *Maqātil al-Ṭālibiyyīn* by Abū al-Faraj al-Iṣfahānī (written in 923), which is not mentioned among the sources of al-Bukhārī by the editor of *Sirr al-silsila*.[10] My preliminary examination showed that the *Maqātil* seems to confirm al-Bukhārī's reliability.

Our text suggests that the cliché that portrays the *Ahl al-Bayt* as victims *par excellence* is historically accurate and that emphasizing this point is necessary, at least when speaking of the early generations of the ʿAlids. The author often simply states that a given individual was taken to or died in "the prison of al-Manṣūr" or "of Hārūn." Map 5.1b is particularly – not to say exclusively – relevant to the period of the first two centuries of the *hijra*. We have a certain number of cases where the author stresses the responsibility of local authorities, governors and the like, for the persecutions, but the reasons for this are not obvious. One plausible interpretation is that he did so due to the importance of the region or town where the event occurred. Iran seems particularly relevant to the author. In this perspective, Map 5.1c can be considered as a kind of addenda to Map 5.1b.

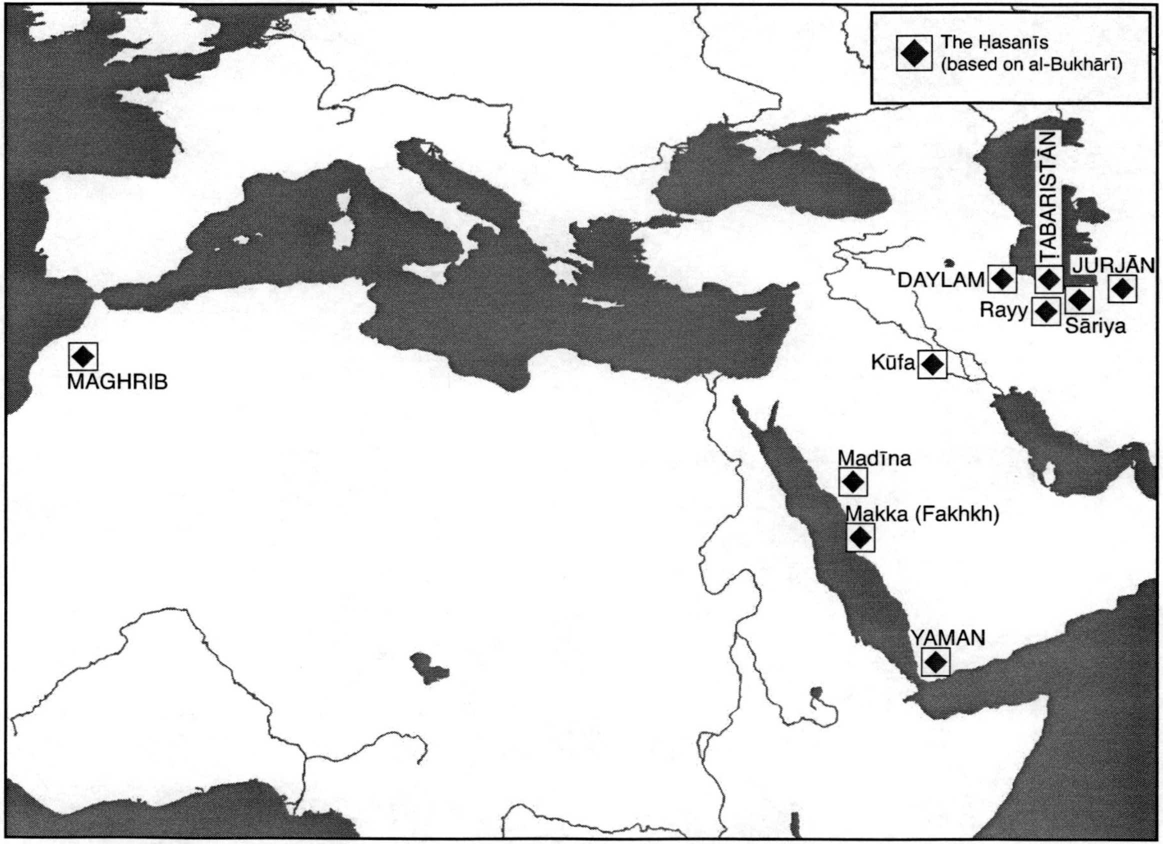

Map 5.1a Historical events involving the Ḥasanīs (based on al-Bukhārī, *Sirr al-silsila*, tenth century).

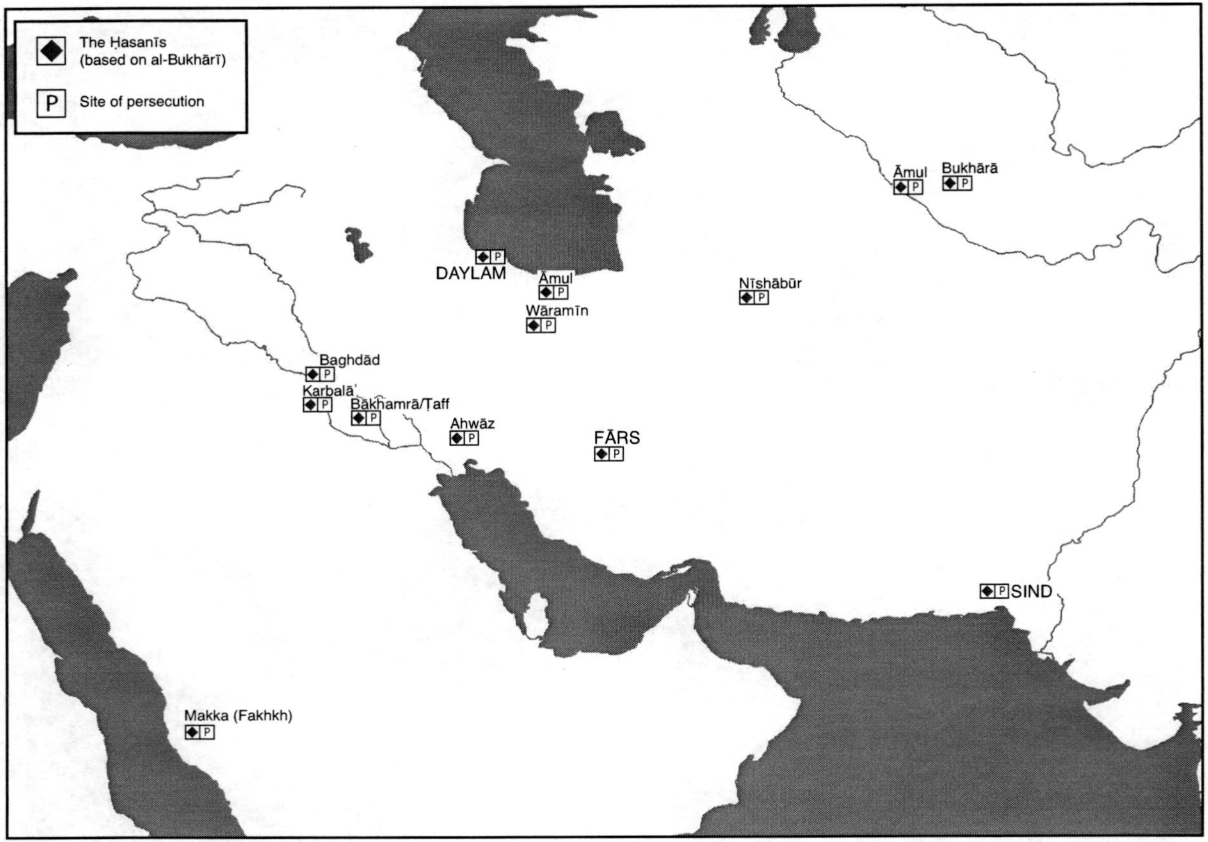
The Ḥasanīs
(based on al-Bukhārī)
Site of persecution
DAYLAM
Āmul
Wāramīn
Nīshābūr
Āmul
Bukhārā
Baghdād
Karbalā'
Bākhamrā/Ṭaff
Ahwāz
FĀRS
SIND
Makka (Fakhkh)

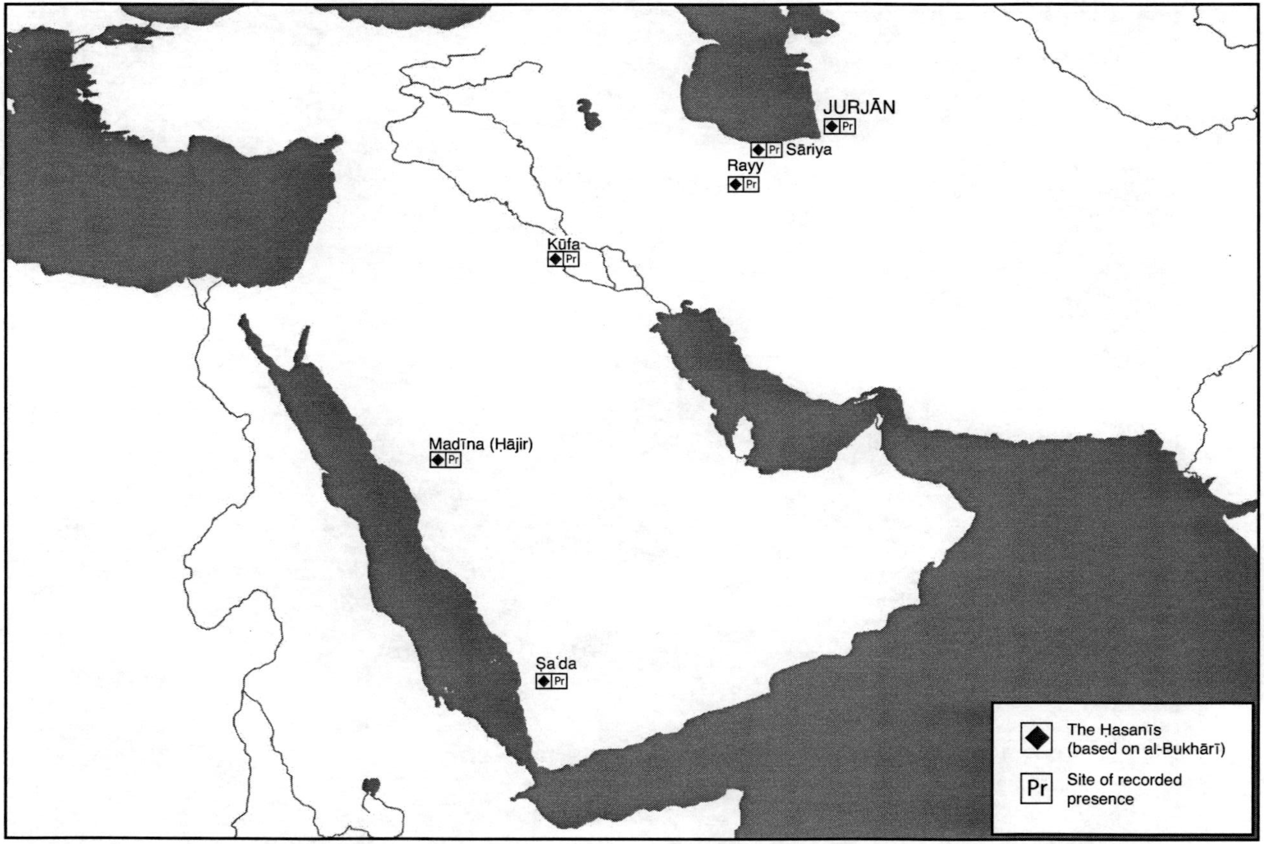

Map 5.1c Presence of Ḥasanī individuals (based on al-Bukhārī, *Sirr al-silsila*, tenth century).

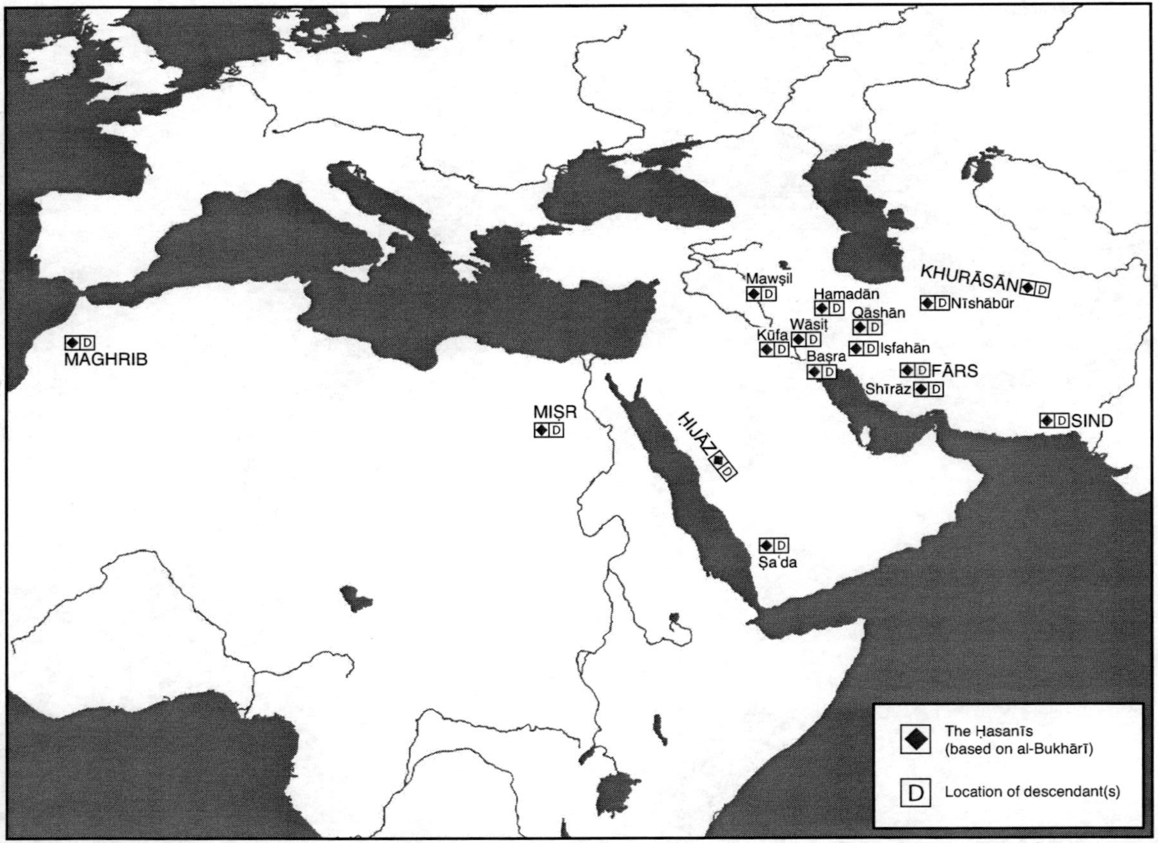

MAGHRIB
MIṢR
ḤIJĀZ
Mawṣil
Kūfa
Wāsiṭ
Baṣra
Hamadān
Qāshān
Iṣfahān
FĀRS
Shīrāz
KHURĀSĀN
Nīshābūr
SIND
Ṣaʿda
The Ḥasanīs
(based on al-Bukhārī)
Location of descendant(s)

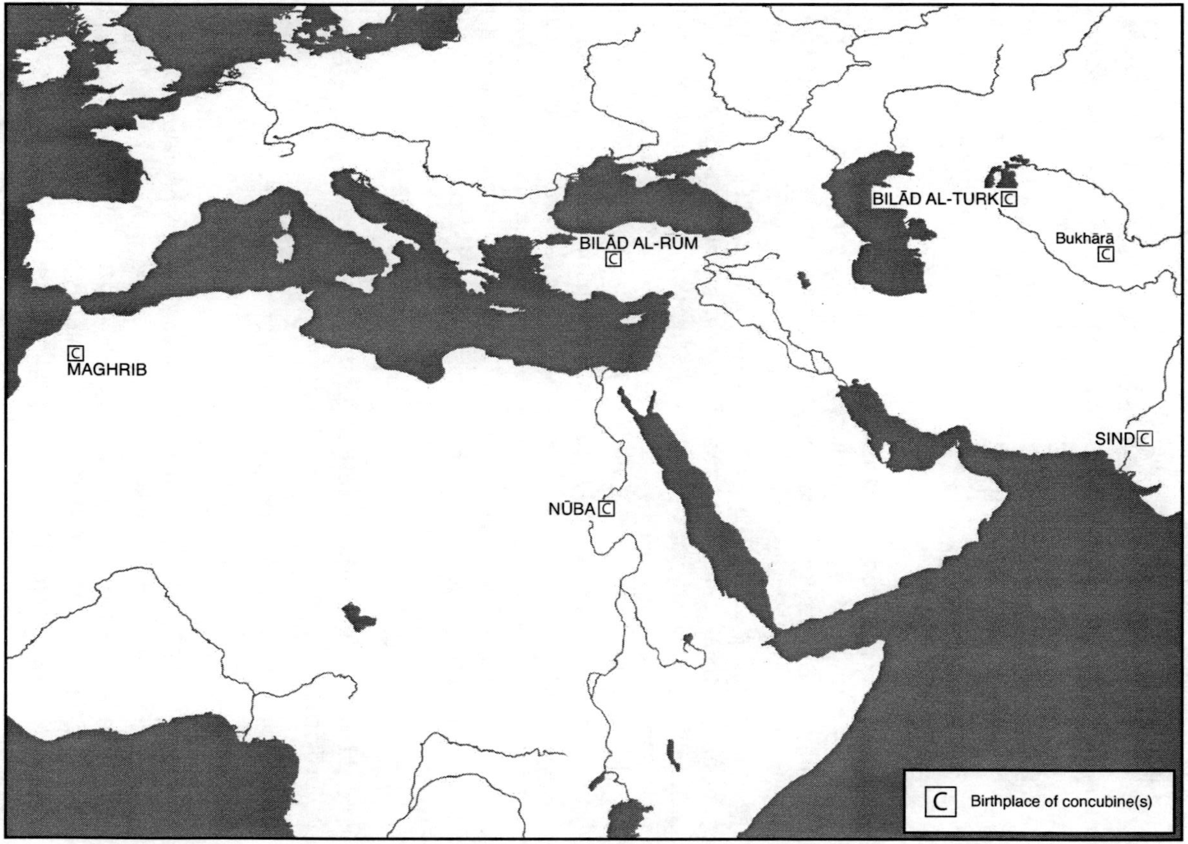

Map 5.2 Possible birthplaces of Ḥasanīs' concubines (based on al-Bukhārī, *Sirr al-silsila*, tenth century).

A question could be raised here. Our maps only tell us the information that our author (tenth century) intends to acknowledge. In this sense, he only rarely specifies the year of an event, although we are able at least to determine a date *ante quem* for them. In the Atlas that I am proposing, data missing in these maps will obviously be made available through search engines that will enable the simultaneous consultation of other maps. The same applies to Map 5.1d. Information on the Ḥasanī diaspora gleaned from al-Bukhārī, when combined with information from other genealogical or historical works, may enable us to sketch a plausible trend in the peregrinations of the ʿAlids. One of the most likely results of such an endeavor is that it may bring to light any correlation between this trend and the political destiny of the Zaydī dynasties in Ṭabaristān and the Caspian regions.

One of the most striking aspects of al-Bukhārī's work is that it pays particular attention to women, especially in the first generations of the ʿAlids. The author often mentions their pedigree, indicating whether they belong to the Family or to a great tribal clan. But determining the layout of the network of ʿAlid alliances both inside and outside of the Family will be possible only when we have at our disposal sufficient background information on the women in question and their families.[11] Moreover, the number of ʿAlid sons of concubines is sufficiently high to suggest the hypothesis that there may have been socio-political advantages (such as the avoidance of internal family conflicts) in being the son of an *umm walad* among the élites (caliphs and Imams included) during the early centuries of ʿAbbasid rule. The "gracious" name – such as Ghazāla, Zayn al-ʿĀbidīn's mother, or Khayzurān, Muḥammad al-Taqī's mother – assigned to the *umm walad* is often mentioned. In a few cases, they are identified by a *nisba*. Insofar as we may assume that the *nisba* designates their birthplace, this information may even aid in mapping out the slave trade of the era and "first pick markets" (Map 5.2).

Ismāʿīl b. Jaʿfar al-Ṣādiq's descendants in al-Bukhārī's and al-ʿUmarī's texts

Since the ʿAlid diaspora is a central concern of mine, I decided to check what kind of information our genealogical sources, the *Sirr al-silsila* and *al-Majdī*, offer on the diaspora of the descendants of Ismāʿīl b. Jaʿfar al-Ṣādiq (Maps 5.3a and 5.3b).[12] Although both texts are contemporary to the Fatimid *daʿwa*, they are more relevant to an understanding of the spread of other branches of Ismāʿīl b. Jaʿfar al-Ṣādiq's descendants than they are to the more controversial question of the genealogy (*nasab*) of the Fatimid dynasty.

The *Sirr al-silsila* does not pay great attention to Ismāʿīl's descendants. The author simply remarks that "people disagreed about the genealogy of the descendants of Ismāʿīl" (*ikhtalafa al-nās fī nasab awlād Ismāʿīl*), while pointing out that these disagreements do not concern what he presents in his work. It is impossible not to notice the absence of Ifrīqiyā and other places connected to the presence of the Imam and his missionaries.

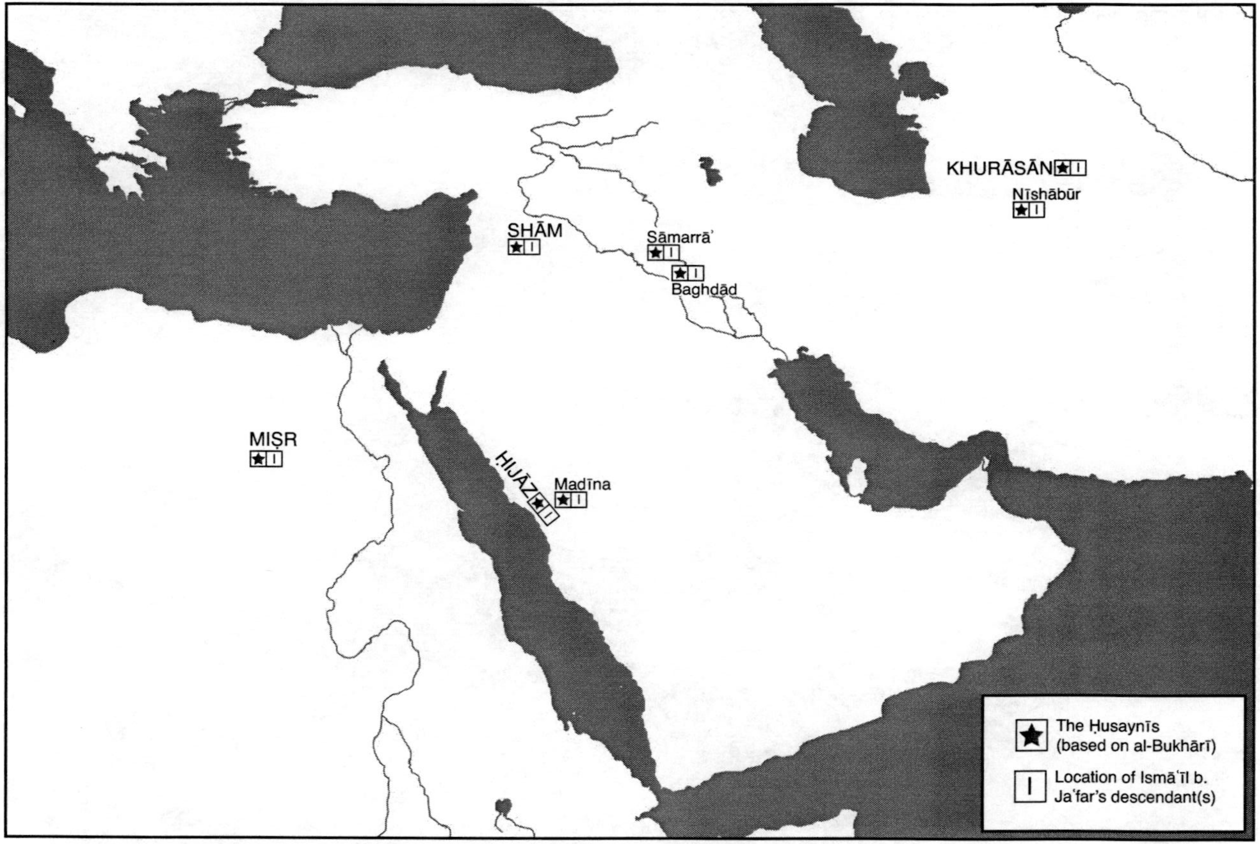

Map 5.3a Locations of Ismāʿīl b. Jaʿfar's descendants (based on al-Bukhārī, *Sirr al-silsila*, tenth century).

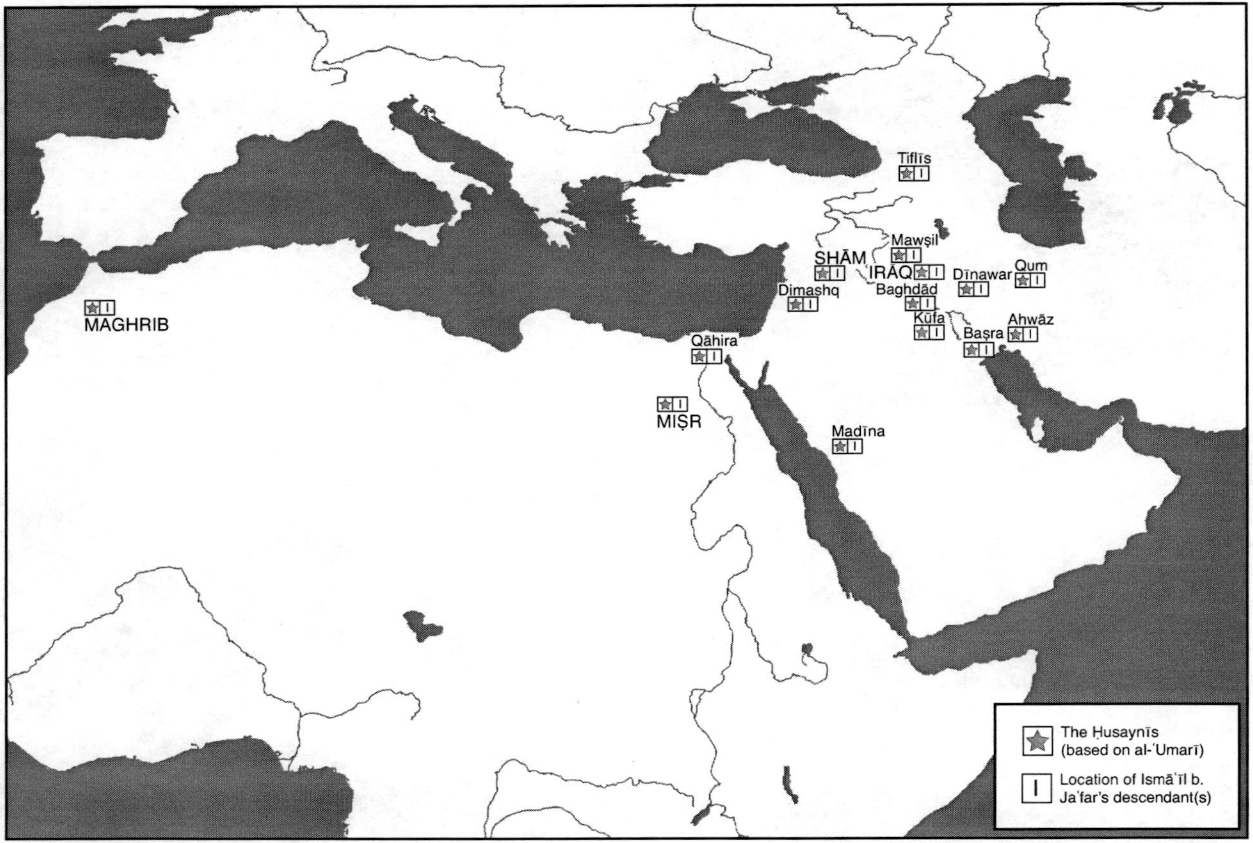
Tiflīs
Mawṣil
SHĀM
ʿIRĀQ
Dīnawar
Qum
Dimashq
Baghdād
Kūfa
Ahwāz
Baṣra
MAGHRIB
Qāhira
MIṢR
Madīna
The Ḥusaynīs
(based on al-ʿUmarī)
Location of Ismāʿīl b.
Jaʿfar's descendant(s)

Al-ʿUmarī's work presents a marked contrast in this regard. To begin with, he actually visited Cairo (*al-Qāhira*) during the Fatimid reign.[13] More importantly, his references are very accurate and since he specifies the sources of his information we can more readily assess its credibility. This means that a satisfactory map of this text would also include such information. I will not deal here with the question of the origins of the information that our sources present. Morimoto Kazuo has addressed this question for similar texts and we all know that he is interested in the "science" of Talibid genealogies. In particular, in the paper he presented in Rome, he pointed out the significance of the travels and journeys undertaken by the genealogists to gather information. Morimoto notes that a certain Abū al-Ghanāʾim al-Dimashqī, who was a contemporary of al-ʿUmarī and served as one of the sources for the early thirteenth century genealogist and author of *al-Fakhrī fī ansāb al-Ṭālibiyyīn*, Ismāʿīl b. al-Ḥusayn al-Marwazī al-Azwarqānī, traveled to Khurāsān, Fārs, ʿIrāq, Shām, Miṣr and the Maghrib.[14] These destinations align well with the locations of Ismāʿīl's descendants according to *al-Majdī*, as they are displayed in Map 5.3b, although al-ʿUmarī mentions a greater level of detail. Aside from places such as Egypt and Syria, where the Fatimids' presence is a matter of fact, the Eastern regions maintain their importance for the ʿAlids. The lack of any further specification in al-ʿUmarī's reference to the Maghrib leaves open the possibility that he may be referring to Ifrīqiyā, the birthplace of the Fatimid *daʿwa*.

Let us pursue the spread of Ismāʿīl's descendants further, since it is very significant for our purposes. As I mentioned, al-ʿUmarī offers a relatively detailed analysis of their diaspora, although he seems, at least to me, cautious when dealing with the Fatimids' *nasab* and their presence outside of Egypt. In my opinion he was coping with a problem that had already become contentious at his time, which was the question of the/an "official version" of the genealogy of the Fatimids. This would explain why, in his account of Ismāʿīl's Fatimid descendants, he seems to underline his neutrality when he records the different "versions" supplied by his authorities. On the other hand, as far as other Ismāʿīlī branches are concerned, al-ʿUmarī does not seem to proceed much differently from al-Bukhārī with regard to his criteria of selecting noteworthy people for attention and mentioning those places where their presence was attested. Evaluating my suggestion regarding al-ʿUmarī's treatment of Fatimid descent, which is clearly related to the problem of the relationship between Imāmī and Ismāʿīlī Shīʿites in the eleventh century, is one of the issues that I hope the Atlas that I am proposing may eventually shed light on.

To return to more general questions, we may assume (see the notes to Maps 5.3a, 5.3b, 5.4c, 5.5c) that the men who left progeny in more than one place are worthy of particular consideration even if they did not play any significant public role. Again, only a systematic enquiry can eventually substantiate this. In any case, it is clear that for al-ʿUmarī, Egypt and Damascus are the most relevant places for the descendants of Ismāʿīl and it is specifically in relation to these places that he mentions their position as *naqīb* or *qāḍī*. In other words, the impact of being related to the Fatimid family cannot be taken for granted. It is possible that such a relation could offer some kind of social or economic advantages, for example in Damascus or in Egypt, but we do not get any explicit information regarding the importance of Imāʿīlī affiliation of these figures from either of our sources.

ʿAlids' movements in *Tārīkh-i Qum*

Finally, I want to make some remarks based on *Tārīkh-i Qum*.[15] Here, my main concern is the peregrinations of the ʿAlids to and from Qum. Maps 5.4a and 5.5a depict a few examples of the locations from which the Ḥasanīs and the Ḥusaynīs migrated to Qum respectively, as Maps 5.4b and 5.5b depict some of the locations to which they migrated from Qum.

The question here is whether Qum was considered a "center" for Shīʿism in Iran[16] or if it was simply a location of convenience for ʿAlids – a question that has, in my view, not yet been answered clearly. In order to address this question, determining the nature of the distinction between Ḥasanī and Ḥusaynī clans will be necessary, especially if, as is indeed the case, some of the places where, apparently, most frequently Ḥasanīs and Ḥusaynīs had descendants are also listed and can thus be compared (see Map 5.4c and Map 5.5c).

The scant amount of information on the Ḥasanī branch indicates that it was not a central concern of the author of *Tārīkh-i Qum*. The sons of a certain number of Ḥasanīs are mentioned, but information concerning their descendants is scarce. Ṭabaristān is depicted as the privileged destination for the Ḥasanīs, at least before the persecution of the ʿAlids by the Zaydī *dāʿī* al-Ḥasan b. Zayd, while Qum appears to have been regarded more as a place of refuge than a minor point of transit.[17] However, this tendency cannot be regarded as something specific to the Ḥasanīs. Ṭabaristān and, second, Khurāsān seem to have been appealing to the Ḥusaynīs as well, who chose Qum as a destination when economic advantages may have been available, as in the case of Isḥāq b. Ibrāhīm b. Mūsā b. Jaʿfar al-Ṣādiq.[18]

The author's attitude changes when he deals with the Ḥusaynīs. Obviously, he wants to stress the Imāmī Shīʿite character of the town. In fact, he lists his figures according to their relation with one of the Imams, with the exception of the first Ḥusaynī who settled in Qum, Abū al-Jinn al-Ḥusayn b. Ḥusayn b. Jaʿfar b. Muḥammad b. Ismāʿīl b. Jaʿfar al-Ṣādiq. Our maps show quite well, I think, that the Ḥusaynīs circulated mostly in a limited area around the axis of Rayy–Qum. Ābah appears to have been somehow annexed to Qum, although our *Tārīkh* lists a certain number of Mūsā al-Kāẓim's descendants who settled there without passing through Qum.[19] The author highlights Qum's centrality by emphasizing the fact that a great number of prominent persons were buried in the famous Qum cemetery of Bābilān (not in our maps). The dates of important events, such as the death of a number of figures, are provided, especially if they were contemporary to the author.

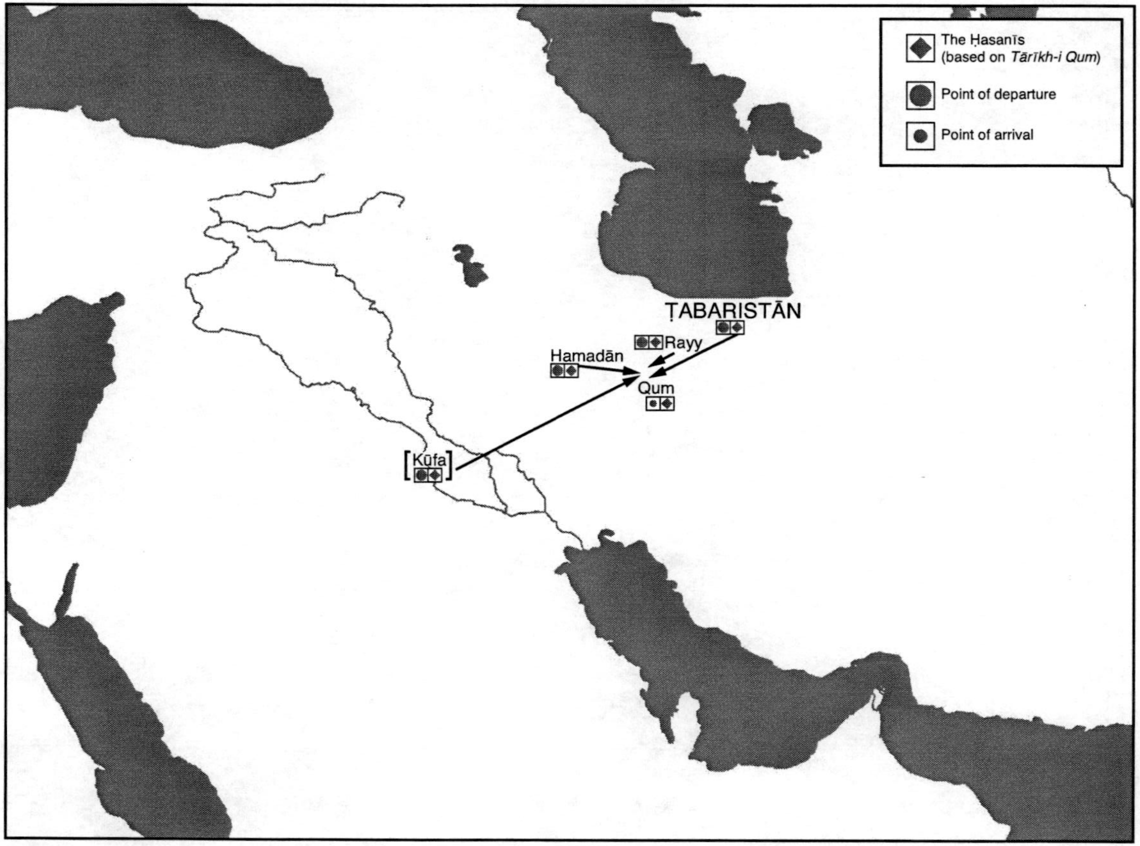

Map 5.4a Ḥasanīs' migrations to Qum (based on Qumī, *Tārīkh-i Qum*, tenth century).

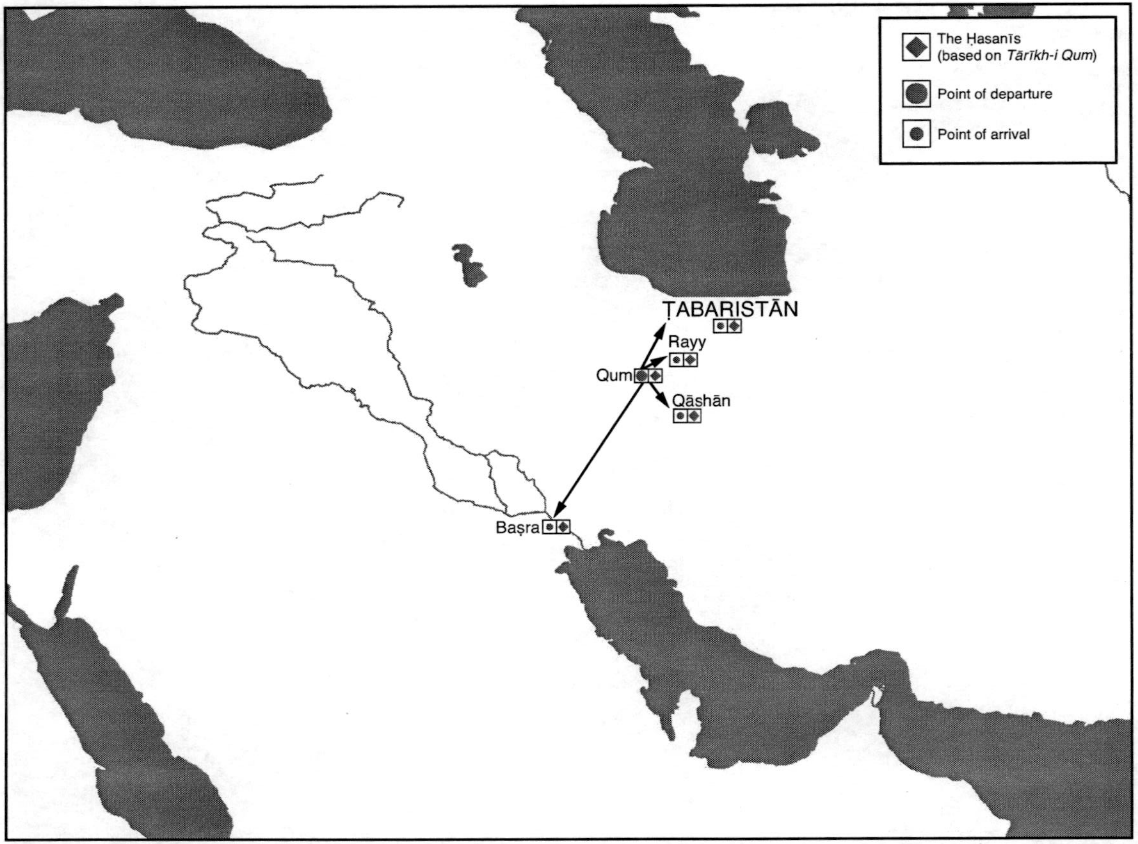
The Ḥasanīs
(based on *Tārīkh-i Qum*)
Point of departure
Point of arrival
ṬABARISTĀN
Rayy
Qum
Qāshān
Baṣra

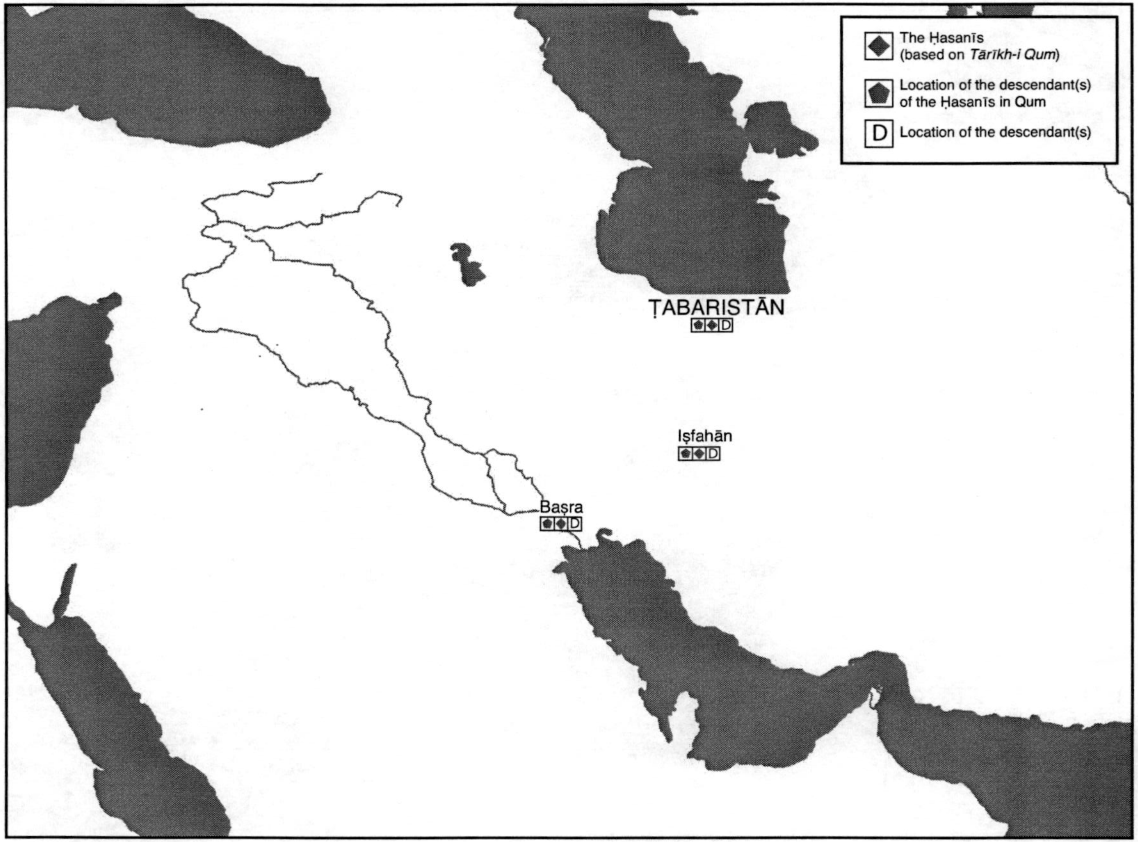

Map 5.4c Locations of the descendants of the Ḥasanīs in Qum (based on Qumī, *Tārīkh-i Qum*, tenth century).

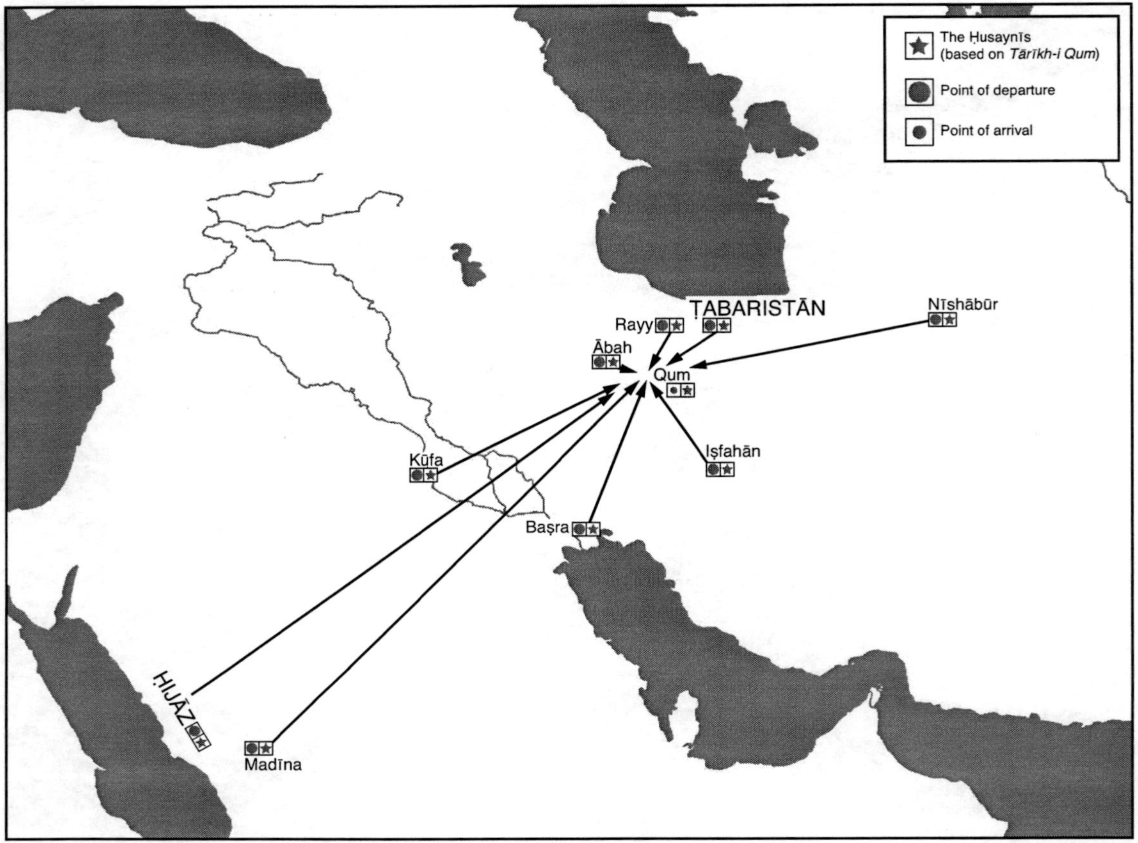
The Ḥusaynīs
(based on *Tārīkh-i Qum*)
Point of departure
Point of arrival
ṬABARISTĀN
Nīshābūr
Rayy
Ābah
Qum
Iṣfahān
Kūfa
Baṣra
ḤIJĀZ
Madīna

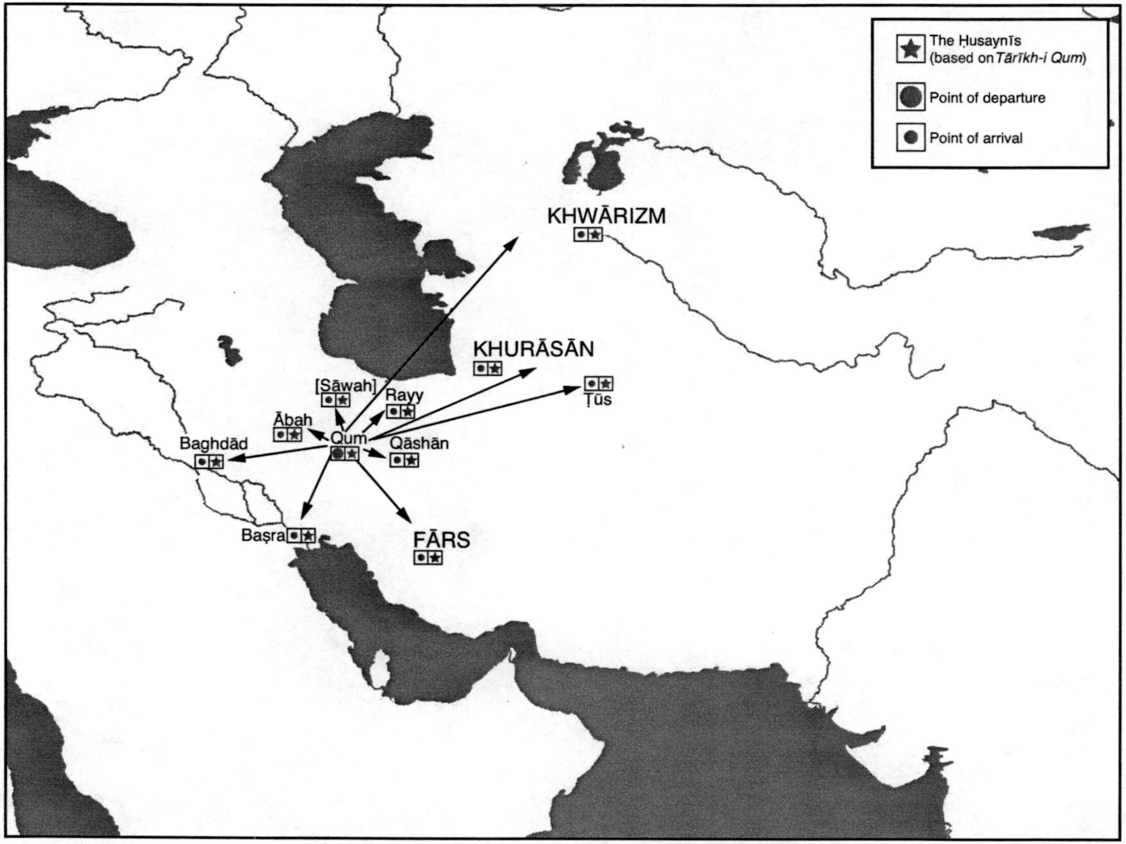

Map 5.5b Ḥusaynīs' migrations from Qum (based on Qumī, *Tārīkh-i Qum*, tenth century).

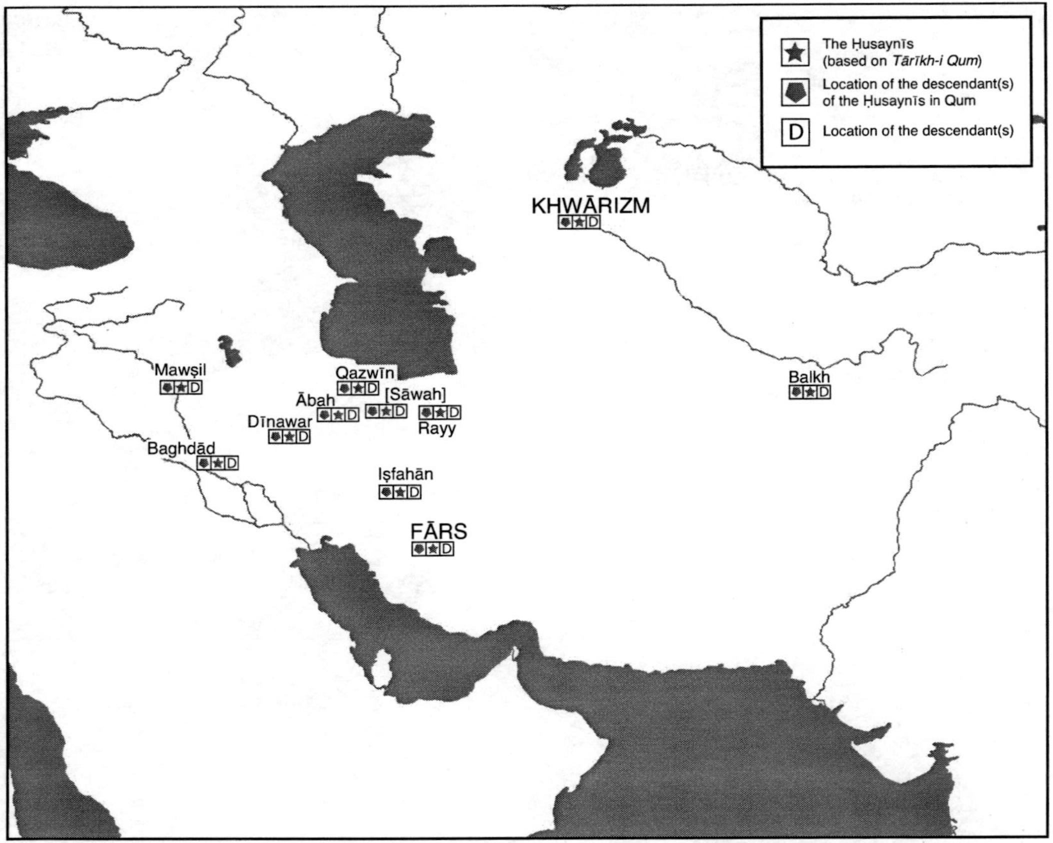
The Ḥusaynīs
(based on *Tārīkh-i Qum*)
Location of the descendant(s)
of the Ḥusaynīs in Qum
D
Location of the descendant(s)
KHWĀRIZM
D
Balkh
D
Mawṣil
D
Qazwīn
D
Ābah
D
[Sāwah]
D
Rayy
D
Dīnawar
D
Baghdād
D
Iṣfahān
D
FĀRS
D

The author of *Tārīkh-i Qum* pays a great deal of attention to ʿAlid women, in particular to the sisters of prominent figures, such as holders and administrators of family estates. Both Baghdād and Kūfa were central in *Tārīkh-i Qum*, in the sense that the Ḥusaynīs, men and women, who chose Qum as a place of residence often came from Kūfa, but when they were able, they also often migrated to Baghdād. The specific concern of our source for the Ḥusaynīs also extends to the locations of their progeny. Looking at the *Tārīkh* from this point of view, the author's purpose seems to be less to emphasize Qum's centrality than to demonstrate that, in Iran, Ḥusaynīs' presence, and through them, that of the Imāmī Shīʿites can be testified in all major towns, extending from Fārs to Khwārizm.

Conclusion

It is obvious that I cannot suggest any conclusions. I can only emphasize the fact that even our "rudimentary maps" provide much pertinent information regarding a number of long-standing subjects of historical enquiry. In my perspective, these subjects, listed in order of importance, are as follows: 1) The ʿAlid diaspora appears as a meaningful phenomenon for the Eastern lands of the caliphate while the Maghrib seems to have been an almost accidental destination. 2) The ʿAlid presence, in our sources, is not regularly traced with precision: the authors often mention only the region to which the ʿAlids emigrated. Why is this the case? If such a choice is proved to be frequent in other genealogical and historical works, then does the relationship between center/centers and periphery/peripheries in the medieval Islamic world have to be reconsidered? If so, taking into account the fact that the ʿAlids, wherever they settled, maintained strong family ties throughout *Dār al-Islām*, can we say that they gave a touch of cosmopolitanism to the places where they settled down, even if only temporarily? 3) While we normally stress their sectarian identity – Zaydī, Imāmī, Ismāʿīlī – our sources speak in terms of Family. Consequently, inter-ʿAlid marriages (and the role of the women) are an issue of primary interest if we want to understand the multifaceted implications of their family ties.

Notes on the maps

Methodology and criteria

The first question that guided my approach was the following: what is necessary to implement my idea of *A Historical Atlas on the ʿAlids*? The obvious answer was that I must present some examples of what I have in mind to begin with. A cartographer specialized in historical maps with sound IT skills was necessary. I met Dr Sandra Leonardi and together we undertook the following:

1) We prepared a few samples, which were not complicated in terms of their cartography. This was a deliberate choice. We thought that the priority in presenting our maps was to do so in such a way that scholars could see the possibility of (a) obtaining a range of specific historical information from them (such information might eventually be different from the sort we had in mind) and (b) proposing other similar maps in accordance with their own interests. Thus, each map presented here as a sample contains information that is meaningful in general terms to historians, although it was yielded by application of these methods to my own field of research.

2) We chose a system that could be developed further. At the beginning, I had Y. Bregel's *An Historical Atlas of Central Asia*[20] in mind as a model, and we started off in a "traditional" way, on the model of the *Tübingen Atlas* (where every map is almost independent in its usage of symbols, as is well known) with the aim of gathering drafts to "translate" into IT language. However, in the end, I was persuaded by Sandra Leonardi to think of a system which could fit into the GIS (Geographical Information System) because of the quantity and quality of information that can be gathered and assembled. As an example, all the maps dedicated to a book or to a topic can be visualized as an individual map, one overlapping the other.

In addition, in our view, it was even more important that the DBMS (Data Base Management System) – an aspect of GIS – can collect, catalogue and manage any kind of information. It seems to us that the main advantage is the fact that the DBMS, theoretically, has no limit to the amount of information that it can store and the progam can engage in sophisticated analyses of such information. This is not the case with a "traditional" historical Atlas. In Bregel's *Atlas*, for example, every map is accompanied by a page recording historical events, but references, indices etc., are all assembled in one place. Each map presented in this study is accompanied, under the name of all the registered places, by the name and genealogy of every related person as mentioned in the source, the generation he belongs to (counting the generation of the sons of ʿAlī b. Abī Ṭālib as generation I [i.e., I g.]),[21] biographical elements of the figure in question, as well as dates (given in CE) and, in some cases, information that the author regards as "doubtful" or "unreliable." Of course, all of these items need to be formalized in order to be integrated into the database. In the end, the "real" Atlas will be electronic, allowing the user to manipulate maps and data as he or she pleases.

3) Finally, we chose to propose a very simple *legenda* (see below). In fact, only a future/would-be "scientific committee" would be able to make appropriate proposals in this regard on the basis of a thorough list of desiderata provided by the different collaborators. This is why we decided to use very few symbols in each map, thinking that the simpler they are, the better they would illustrate the workings of "our idea."

Table 5.1 The symbols and shadings used in the maps

Symbols	
◆	The Ḥasanīs
★	The Ḥusaynīs
●	Point of departure
•	Point of arrival
⬟	Location of the descendant(s) of the Ḥasanīs in Qum
⬟	Location of the descendant(s) of the Ḥusaynīs in Qum
C	Birthplace of concubine(s)
D	Location of descendant(s)
I	Location of Ismāʿīl b. Jaʿfar's descendant(s)
P	Site of persecution
Pr	Site of recorded presence
Shadings to indicate the sources	
■	Al-Bukhārī, *Sirr al-silsila.*
■	Al-ʿUmarī, *al-Majdī.*
■	Qumī, *Tārīkh-i Qum.*

Data accompanying individual maps

Map 5.1a: Historical events involving the Ḥasanīs

Daylam: the place where al-Ḥasan b. Zayd b. Muḥammad b. Ismāʿīl b. al-Ḥasan b. Zayd (VII g.) took shelter (873) when he was obliged to leave Ṭabaristān, fleeing from Yaʿqūb b. Layth (al-Bukhārī, *Sirr*, 27); the uprising led by a son of Aḥmad b. Yaḥyā b. al-Ḥusayn b. al-Qāsim b. Ibrāhīm (IX g.) (ibid., 18).

Fakhkh (near Makka): al-Ḥasan b. Ismāʿīl b. Ibrāhīm al-Ghamr b. al-Ḥasan b. al-Ḥasan b. ʿAlī b. Abī Ṭālib (V g.) took part in the battle of Fakhkh (786) (ibid., 16).

Jurjān: ruled by the Zaydī Imam Muḥammad b. Zayd (VII g.) for some years during the last half of the ninth century (ibid., 27).

Kūfa: Muḥammad, brother of Ismāʿīl b. Ibrāhīm b. al-Ḥasan b. al-Ḥasan b. ʿAlī b. Abī Ṭālib (IV g.), as well as Abū Muḥammad ʿAbdallāh b. al-Ḥasan b. Zayd b. al-Ḥasan b. ʿAlī (IV g.) participated in Abū al-Sarāyā's insurrection (815) (ibid., 25); ʿUbaydallāh b. ʿAbdallāh b. al-Ḥasan b. Jaʿfar b. al-Ḥasan b. al-Ḥasan (VI g.) was *amīr* of the city under al-Maʾmūn (ibid., 19).

Madīna: the uprising (762) of Muḥammad al-Nafs al-Zakiyya b. ʿAbdallāh (IV g.) is mentioned (ibid., 7); Muḥammad b. Sulaymān b. Dāʾūd b. al-Ḥasan b. al-Ḥasan (V g.) revolted at the time of Abū al-Sarāyā (ibid., 18); al-Ḥasan b. Zayd b. al-Ḥasan b. ʿAlī b. Abī Ṭālib (III g.) was *amīr* of Madīna before al-Manṣūr (ibid., 21).

Maghrib: Idrīs b. Idrīs b. ʿAbdallāh (V g.) succeeded his father as head of the Idrīsid dynasty there (ibid., 13).

Makka: one of the cadet brothers of al-Nafs al-Zakiyya, Mūsā al-Jawn (IV g.) met the caliph al-Mahdī (ibid., 9); a descendant of Mūsā al-Jawn, Ismāʿīl b. Yūsuf b. Muḥammad al-Ukhayḍar b. Yūsuf b. Ibrāhīm (IX g.), was *amīr* of Makka, as well as his son al-Rafīq Ibrāhīm (X g.), and then his nephews Yūsuf b. Muḥammad b. Yūsuf and Aḥmad b. al-Ḥasan b. Yūsuf (X g.) (ibid., 10); for seven years the *khuṭba* was pronounced in the name of the Zaydī Imam Yaḥyā b. al-Ḥusayn b. al-Qāsim b. Ibrāhīm al-Hādī (VIII g.) (ibid., 18).

Rayy: al-Ḥusayn b. al-Qāsim b. ʿAlī b. Ismāʿīl b. al-Ḥasan b. Zayd b. al-Ḥasan (VII g.) was *naqīb* there (ibid., 28).

Sāriya: the *wilāya* of the town was in the hands of a Ḥusaynī, al-Ḥasan b. Muḥammad b. Jaʿfar al-ʿAqīqī (VI g.), who was the maternal cousin of Muḥammad b. Zayd (ibid., 27); see also Map 5.1c.

Ṭabaristān: al-Ḥasan b. Zayd, known as *al-dāʿī al-kabīr*, and his brother Muḥammad b. Zayd (VII g.) ruled the region in succession for much of the latter half of the ninth century and the beginning of the tenth (ibid., 26–27).

Yaman: Zaydī dynasty founded in Ṣaʿda by the above-mentioned Imam Yaḥyā al-Hādī, who was succeeded by his son al-Nāṣir li-Dīn Allāh Aḥmad b. Yaḥyā b. al-Ḥusayn b. al-Qāsim b. Ibrāhīm (IX g.). The sons of the latter continued to reign as *umarāʾ* and kings for 130 years (ibid., 17–18).

Map 5.1b: Persecutions of the Ḥasanīs

Ahwāz: the above-mentioned Abū Muḥammad ʿAbdallāh b. al-Ḥasan b. Zayd b. al-Ḥasan b. ʿAlī (IV g.) fled here from Kūfa after the revolt of Abū al-Sarāyā and was captured and executed by Dāʾūd b. ʿĪsā (al-Bukhārī, *Sirr*, 25).

Āmul (in Khurāsān): Muḥammad b. Jaʿfar b. Hārūn b. Isḥāq b. al-Ḥasan b. Zayd b. al-Ḥasan b. ʿAlī (VII g.) was killed here by Rāfiʿ b. al-Layth (ibid., 26).

Āmul (in Ṭabaristān): al-Ḥasan b. al-Qāsim b. al-Ḥasan b. ʿAlī b. ʿAbd al-Raḥmān b. al-Qāsim b. al-Ḥasan b. Zayd b. al-Ḥasan (IX g.) was killed here in 929 (ibid., 23).

Baghdād: Abū Muḥammad Yaḥyā b. ʿAbdallāh b. al-Ḥasan b. al-Ḥasan b. ʿAlī b. Abī Ṭālib, known as *ṣāḥib al-Daylam* (IV g.), died here in al-Rashīd's prison (ibid., 10–11); al-Ḥasan b. al-Ḥasan b. al-Ḥasan b. ʿAlī (III g.) and his two sons ʿAbdallāh and ʿAlī al-ʿĀbid (IV g.) were imprisoned here by al-Manṣūr (ibid., 14); ʿAlī b. al-Nafs al-Zakiyya (V g.) was taken to Egypt, then put in jail in Baghdād where he died (ibid., 8).

Bākhamrā (between Kūfa and Wāsiṭ): Ibrāhīm b.ʿAbdallāh (IV g.) was killed here by prince ʿĪsā b. Mūsā at the order of the ʿAbbasids, in 762–3 (ibid., 8).

Bukhārā: Zayd b. Muḥammad b. Zayd (VIII g.) was brought here as a prisoner (ibid., 27).

Daylam: al-Bukhārī records that al-Ḥasan b. Zayd killed a number of *ʿulamāʾ*, *ashrāf* and *sādāt ʿAlawiyya* (ibid., 26), in particular some members of the Ḥusaynī branch such as al-Ḥusayn b. Aḥmad b. Muḥammad b. Ismāʿīl al-Kawkabī (a descendant of Zayn al-ʿĀbidīn) and ʿUbaydallāh b. ʿAlī b. al-Ḥasan (a descendant of al-Ḥusayn al-Aṣghar b. Zayn al-ʿĀbidīn) whom he had appointed as governors but later defeated at Abhar, Zanjān and Qazwīn (ibid., 26–27).

Fakhkh (786): al-Ḥusayn b. ʿAlī b. al-Ḥasan b. al-Ḥasan b. al-Ḥasan b. ʿAlī (V g.) revolted against the ʿAbbasids here and was killed (ibid., 14), along with many other ʿAlids, including al-Ḥasan, a son of al-Nafs al-Zakiyya (V g.) (ibid., 8) and Sulaymān b. ʿAbdallāh b. al-Ḥasan b. al-Ḥasan b. ʿAlī (IV g.) (ibid., 12).

Fārs: ʿAbdallāh b. Jaʿfar b. Ibrāhīm b. Jaʿfar b. al-Ḥasan (VI g.) was killed here by the Khārijites (ibid., 20).

Karbalāʾ (680): al-Ḥasan b. al-Ḥasan b. ʿAlī (II g.) (ibid., 5) was wounded with his uncle al-Ḥusayn; ʿAbbās b. ʿAlī b. Abī Ṭālib was killed here with al-Ḥusayn (ibid., 29).

Nīshābūr: al-Ḥusayn b. Ibrāhīm b. ʿAlī b. ʿAbd al-Raḥmān b. al-Qāsim (VIII g.) died in the prison of al-Ṭāhir and was buried in Balājird in 873–4 (ibid., 22–23).

Sind: ʿAbdallāh al-Ashtar b. al-Nafs al-Zakiyya (V g.) was killed here. A captured slave-girl of his gave birth to a son after his death (ibid., 8).

Ṭaff (near Kūfa): Nafīsa bt. Zayd b. al-Ḥasan b. ʿAlī (III g.) was killed here, following al-Ḥusayn (ibid., 29).
Wāramīn: ʿAlī b. ʿAbd al-Raḥmān b. al-Qāsim b. al-Ḥasan b. Zayd (VI g.) was killed and buried here during the caliphate of al-Mahdī (ibid., 22).

Map 5.1c: Presence of Ḥasanī individuals

Jurjān: Muḥammad b. Zayd (VII g.) was killed and buried here (al-Bukhārī, *Sirr*, 27), although his head was taken to Marw (ibid., 27).
Ḥājir (between Makka and Madīna): Zayd b. al-Ḥasan b. ʿAlī (II g.) died here (ibid., 20).
Kūfa: Muḥammad b. Ibrāhīm b. al-Ḥasan b. al-Ḥasan b. ʿAlī (IV g.) died and was buried here in 815 (ibid., 16).
Madīna: Mūsā al-Jawn, the brother of al-Nafs al-Zakiyya (IV g.) (ibid., 10), Dāʾūd b. al-Ḥasan b. al-Ḥasan (III g.) (ibid., 18), and Jaʿfar b. al-Ḥasan b. al-Ḥasan b. ʿAlī b. Abī Ṭālib (III g.) (ibid., 19) all died here.
Rayy: Abū al-Qāsim ʿAbd al-ʿAẓīm b. ʿAbdallāh b. ʿAlī b. al-Ḥasan b. Zayd (VI g.) was buried in the Masjid al-Shajara of the town (ibid., 24).
Ṣaʿda: the Imam Yaḥyā b. al-Ḥusayn b. al-Qāsim b. Ibrāhīm (VIII g.) died there (ibid., 17).

Map 5.1d: Locations of Ḥasanīs' descendants

Baṣra: descendants of Muḥammad b. Ṭāhir b. Zayd (VI g.) (al-Bukhārī, *Sirr*, 23).
Fārs: descendants of Muḥammad b. Aḥmad b. Abī Sulaymān Muḥammad b. ʿUbaydallāh b. ʿAbdallāh (IX g.) (ibid., 20).
Hamadān: descendants of al-Ḥasan b. al-Ḥasan b. al-Qāsim b. Muḥammad b. al-Qāsim b. al-Ḥasan b. Zayd b. al-Ḥasan b. ʿAlī (IX g.) (ibid., 23).
Ḥijāz: putative descendants of Idrīs b. Idrīs b. Muḥammad b. Yaḥyā (who the author states are "not accepted" by the scholars) (VII g.) (ibid., 12); descendants of Muḥammad b. Sulaymān b. ʿAbdallāh (although they are unknown [*lā yuʿrafūn*]) (V g.) (ibid., 12); of Muḥammad b. Ṭāhir b. Zayd (VI g.) (ibid., 23); of Muḥammad b. Zayd b. ʿAbdallāh b. al-Ḥasan b. Zayd b. al-Ḥasan b. ʿAlī (VI g.) (ibid., 25); of Aḥmad b. ʿAbdallāh b. ʿAlī b. al-Ḥasan b. Zayd (VI g.) (ibid., 24).
Khurāsān: descendants of Abū al-Ḥasan ibn al-Ṣūfī, uncle of Abū ʿAbdallāh al-Ḥusayn b. ʿAlī b. al-Ḥasan b. al-Ḥasan b. al-Qāsim b. Muḥammad b. al-Qāsim b. al-Ḥasan b. Zayd b. al-Ḥasan b. ʿAlī (X g.) (ibid., 23); of ʿAbdallāh b. Muḥammad b. Ibrāhīm b. Ibrāhīm b. al-Ḥasan (VII g.) (ibid., 25).
Iṣfahān: Muḥammad b. Aḥmad b. Muḥammad b. Aḥmad b. Ibrāhīm Ṭabāṭabā b. Ismāʿīl b. Ibrāhīm al-Ghamr b. al-Ḥasan b. al-Ḥasan (IX g.) (ibid., 17).
Kūfa: putative descendants of Zayd b. Muḥammad b. Ismāʿīl b. al-Ḥasan b. Zayd (VI g.) (ibid., 27); descendants of Abū Jaʿfar [Muḥammad] al-Adraʿ b. ʿUbaydallāh b. ʿAbdallāh b. al-Ḥasan b. Jaʿfar (VII g.) (ibid., 19–20); of ʿUbaydallāh al-Adraʿ, who may (or may not) be ʿUbaydallāh b. ʿAbdallāh b. al-Ḥasan b. Jaʿfar b. al-Ḥasan b. al-Ḥasan (IX g.?) (ibid., 19–20).
Maghrib: descendants of Idrīs b. ʿAbdallāh al-Aṣghar b. al-Ḥasan b. al-Ḥasan b. ʿAlī (IV g.) (more precisely, at Fās and Ṭanja; ibid., 12); of al-Ḥasan b. Isḥaq b. al-Ḥasan (V g.) (ibid., 26).
Mawṣil: false claimants to descent from Ṭāhir b. al-Nafs al-Zakiyya (V g.) (ibid., 8).
Miṣr: putative descendants of Idrīs b. Idrīs b. Muḥammad b. Yaḥyā (who the author states are "not accepted" by the scholars) (VII g.) (ibid., 12).
Nīshābūr: descendants of ʿUbaydallāh b. ʿAbdallāh b. al-Ḥasan b. Jaʿfar (VI g.) (ibid., 20).

Qāshān: descendants of ʿUbaydallāh b. ʿAbdallāh b. al-Ḥasan b. Jaʿfar (*ut supra*) (ibid., 20).
Ṣaʿda: descendants of the Imam Yaḥyā b. al-Ḥusayn b. al-Qāsim b. Ibrāhīm (VIII g.) were *umarāʾ* and kings of Yaman (ibid., 18).
Shīrāz: false claimants to descent from ʿAbdallāh b. Jaʿfar b. Ibrāhīm b. Jaʿfar b. al-Ḥasan (VI g.) (ibid., 20).
Sind: ʿAbdallāh al-Ashtar b. al-Nafs al-Zakiyya (V g.) was killed in Sind where he probably left descendants (ibid., 8).
Wāsiṭ: alleged descendants of Zayd b. Muḥammad b. Ismāʿīl b. al-Ḥasan b. Zayd quoted above (VI g.) (ibid., 27).

Map 5.2: Possible birthplaces of Ḥasanīs' concubines

Bilād al-Rūm: Ḥabība Rūmiyya is the mother of two sons, Dāʾūd and Jaʿfar, from al-Ḥasan b. al-Ḥasan b. ʿAlī (III g.) (al-Bukhārī, *Sirr*, 7), both of whom had descendants; ʿAnān, the mother of Ibrāhīm b. Jaʿfar b. al-Ḥasan b. al-Ḥasan b. ʿAlī (IV g.) (ibid., 19).
Bilād al-Turk: Bārnūl (?), a Turkiyya, is the mother of Muḥammad b. Zayd b. Muḥammad b. Zayd b. Muḥammad b. Ismāʿīl (IX g.) (ibid., 27).
Bukhārā: Bukhāriyya is the mother of the one-eyed (*aʿwar*) Abū al-Ḥasan Isḥāq b. al-Ḥasan b. Zayd b. al-Ḥasan al-Kawkabī (IV g.) (ibid., 22).
Maghrib: Umm Khālid Barbariyya is the mother of the above-mentioned Abū Sulaymān Dāʾūd b. al-Ḥasan b. al-Ḥasan b. ʿAlī (III g.) (ibid., 18).
Nūba: Nūbiyya is the mother of Abū Ṭāhir Zayd b. al-Ḥasan b. Zayd b. al-Ḥasan (IV g.) (ibid., 22).
Sind: a *jāriya bi-l-Sind* (slave-girl in Sind) gave birth to Muḥammad b. ʿAbdallāh b. Muḥammad b. ʿAbdallāh b. al-Ḥasan b. al-Ḥasan (VI g.) (ibid., 8).

Map 5.3a: Locations of Ismāʿīl b. Jaʿfar's descendants (based on al-Bukhārī, Sirr al-silsila, *tenth century)*

Baghdād/ʿIrāq: Muḥammad b. Ismāʿīl b. Jaʿfar (VI g.) died there (al-Bukhārī, *Sirr*, 36); Jaʿfar b. Muḥammad b. Ismāʿīl b. Jaʿfar (VII g.) was born here and thus received the *nisba* al-Salāmī (ibid., 35).
Ḥijāz: Muḥammad b. Ismāʿīl b. Jaʿfar met al-Rashīd here with his uncle Mūsā al-Kāẓim (ibid., 35).
Khurāsān: more precisely in Farshiyān, in a village called Nirw, descendants of ʿAlī b. Muḥammad b. ʿAlī b. Ismāʿīl b. Jaʿfar (VIII g.) (ibid., 36).
Madīna: Ismāʿīl b. Jaʿfar (V g.) died in al-ʿUrayḍ, a village near Madīna and was buried in al-Baqīʿ (ibid., 34).
Miṣr (al-Qāhira?): the *umarāʾ* of Egypt are descendants of ʿAlī b. Muḥammad b. Jaʿfar b. Muḥammad b. Ismāʿīl (IX g.) (ibid., 36).
Nīshābūr: Aḥmad b. Ismāʿīl b. Muḥammad b. Ismāʿīl b. Jaʿfar died here (VIII g.) (ibid., 36).
Sāmarrāʾ: descendants of ʿAlī b. Muḥammad b. ʿAlī b. Ismāʿīl b. Jaʿfar (VIII g.) (ibid., 36).
Shām: putative descendants of Ismāʿīl b. Muḥammad b. Ismāʿīl (VII g.) (ibid., 36).

Map 5.3b: Locations of Ismāʿīl b. Jaʿfar's descendants (based on al-ʿUmarī, al-Majdī, *eleventh century)*

Ahwāz: Abū al-Ḥasan ʿAlī al-Shāʿir (XIII g.), a descendant of Ismāʿīl al-Thālith b. Aḥmad Ibn al-ʿUmariyya[22] (IX g.) and his descendants (al-ʿUmarī, *al-Majdī*, 103);

descendants of al-Ḥasan b. al-Ḥusayn b. ʿAlī b. Muḥammad b. ʿAlī b. Ismāʿīl b. Jaʿfar al-Ṣādiq (X g.) (ibid., 104); of Ḥamza b. al-Muḥsin b. ʿAlī al-Dīnawarī b. al-Ḥasan b. al-Ḥusayn b. ʿAlī Abī al-Jinn b. Muḥammad b. ʿAlī b. Ismāʿīl b. Jaʿfar al-Ṣādiq (XIII g.) (ibid., 104).

Baghdād: Muḥammad b. Ismāʿīl b. Jaʿfar was buried here (ibid., 99–100); descendants of Abū al-Ḥasan ʿAlī al-Shāʿir (XIII g.?), who is a descendant of Ismāʿīl al-Thālith b. Aḥmad Ibn al-ʿUmariyya (ibid., 103); of al-Ḥasan b. al-Ḥusayn b. ʿAlī b. Muḥammad b. ʿAlī b. Ismāʿīl b. Jaʿfar al-Ṣādiq (X g.) (ibid., 104).

Baṣra: descendants of above-mentioned Abū al-Ḥasan ʿAlī al-Shāʿir (see Ahwāz and Baghdād) (ibid., 103).

Dimashq: Banū al-Mantūf, descendants of al-Ḥusayn al-Mantūf b. Aḥmad Ibn al-ʿUmariyya (among them is the *naqīb*, son of *naqīb*, known as Ibn Maʿtūq, Abū al-Ḥasan Mūsā b. Ismāʿīl al-Dimashqī who died in 958–9) (XI g.) (ibid., 102); descendants of al-Ḥasan b. al-ʿAbbās b. al-Ḥasan b. ʿAlī Abī al-Jinn b. Muḥammad b. ʿAlī b. Ismāʿīl b. Jaʿfar al-Ṣādiq were *qāḍīs* and *naqībs* (ibid., 105); descendants of al-ʿAbbās b. al-Ḥasan b. al-ʿAbbās b. al-Ḥasan b. al-Ḥusayn b. ʿAlī b. Muḥammad b. ʿAlī b. Ismāʿīl b. Jaʿfar (XIII g.) (ibid., 105).

Dīnawar: descendants of Abū Muḥammad al-Ḥasan b. al-Ḥusayn al-Maqtūl b. ʿAlī b. Muḥammad b. ʿAlī b. Ismāʿīl b. Jaʿfar al-Ṣādiq (X g.) (ibid., 104).

ʿIrāq: descendants of Abū al-Ḥasan Muḥammad b. al-Ḥusayn b. al-Ḥasan Ṣubaywakha (?) b. Muḥammad b. Muḥammad b. Ismāʿīl al-Thānī b. Muḥammad b. Ismāʿīl al-Awwal b. Jaʿfar (XII g.) (ibid., 101–102).

Kūfa: Abū Ṭālib ʿAqīl, a descendant of al-Ḥasan b. al-Ḥusayn Asbīdjāma b. Aḥmad Ibn al-ʿUmariyya (XI g.) was buried here (ibid., 102); descendants of ʿAlī b. Ismāʿīl b. Jaʿfar al-Ṣādiq (VI g.) (ibid., 103).

Madīna: Ismāʿīl b. Jaʿfar (V g.) died in al-ʿUrayḍ (755–6) and was buried here (ibid., 99–100).

Maghrib: ʿAbdallāh b. Muḥammad, a descendant of Muḥammad b. Ismāʿīl, went to the Maghrib where he died and had descendants among whom was al-Naṣr b. al-Ḥusayn b. ʿAlī b. Muḥammad b. Jaʿfar b. Muḥammad b. Ismāʿīl b. al-Ṣādiq (XI g.) (ibid., 100); three sons, Abū al-Shalghalgh Aḥmad, Jaʿfar and Ismāʿīl, of Muḥammad b. Jaʿfar b. Muḥammad b. Ismāʿīl b. Jaʿfar al-Ṣādiq (IX g.?), whose descent from him was uncertain (ibid., 101).

Mawṣil: [Aḥmad b.?] al-Ḥusayn al-Maqtūl b. ʿAlī b. Muḥammad b. ʿAlī b. Ismāʿīl b. Jaʿfar al-Ṣādiq was *naqīb* of the town (IX or X g.) (ibid., 104).

Miṣr (al-Qāhira?): among the descendants of Muḥammad b. Muḥammad b. Ismāʿīl b. Jaʿfar (VII g.) are the *aʾimma bi-Miṣr* (ibid., 100); in 971–2, ʿAlī b. Muḥammad b. Jaʿfar b. Muḥammad b. Ismāʿīl (IX g.) moved to Egypt with his sons Jaʿfar and al-Ḥusayn. Al-Ḥusayn was with his son Naṣr al-Ṣaghīr (XI g.) (ibid., 100); the sons of al-Baghīḍ (among them was Mūsā b. Jaʿfar b. Muḥammad who died in 958–9) (ibid., 101); descendants of al-Muḥassin b. ʿAlī b. Ismāʿīl al-Aḥwal b. Aḥmad b. ʿĀqilīna b. Ismāʿīl al-Thālith b. Aḥmad Ibn al-ʿUmariyya b. Ismāʿīl al-Thānī b. Muḥammad b. Ismāʿīl al-Awwal b. al-Ṣādiq (XIV g.) (ibid., 102); Abū Jaʿfar Muḥammad b. al-Ḥusayn al-Maqtūl b. ʿAlī b. Muḥammad b. ʿAlī b. Ismāʿīl b. Jaʿfar al-Ṣādiq (X g.) died here (ibid., 104); descendants of al-Ḥasan b. al-Ḥusayn b. ʿAlī b. Muḥammad b. ʿAlī b. Ismāʿīl b. Jaʿfar al-Ṣādiq (ibid., 104); al-Ḥasan b. al-ʿAbbās b. al-Ḥasan b. ʿAlī b. Muḥammad b. ʿAlī b. Ismāʿīl b. Jaʿfar al-Ṣādiq (XI g.), as well as other members of the clan, were *naqībs* here (ibid., 105).

Qum: descendants of al-Ḥasan b. al-Ḥusayn al-Maqtūl b. ʿAlī b. Muḥammad b. ʿAlī b. Ismāʿīl b. Jaʿfar al-Ṣādiq (X g.) (ibid., 104).

Shām: descendants of al-Ḥasan b. al-Ḥusayn b. ʿAlī b. Muḥammad b. ʿAlī b. Ismāʿīl b. Jaʿfar al-Ṣādiq (X g.) (ibid., 104).

Tiflīs: al-Ḥusayn b. ʿAlī b. Muḥammad b. ʿAlī b. Ismāʿīl b. Jaʿfar al-Ṣādiq (IX g.) was killed here by the Saffarids (ibid., 104).

Map 5.4a: Ḥasanīs' migrations to Qum

Hamadān: descendants of al-Ḥasan b. al-Ḥasan b. ʿAlī (II g.), also settled in the village of Rāwand (Qāshān); among them: ʿUbaydallāh b. al-Ḥasan b. ʿAlī b. Muḥammad b. al-Ḥasan b. Jaʿfar b. al-Ḥasan b. al-Ḥasan (VIII g.) (Qumī, *Tārīkh-i Qum*, 545).

Rayy: Abū al-Qāsim Aḥmad al-Rāzī b. ʿĪsā (X g.) (ibid., 551); al-Ḥusayn b. Muḥammad al-Shishdīw b. al-Ḥusayn b. ʿĪsā b. Muḥammad al-Buṭḥānī b. al-Qāsim b. al-Ḥasan b. Zayd b. al-Ḥasan (IX g.) (ibid., 554, *nasab* in n. 3).

Ṭabaristān: Aḥmad b. Muḥammad b. Jaʿfar b. ʿAbd al-Raḥmān b. al-Qāsim b. al-Ḥasan b. Zayd b. al-Ḥasan b. ʿAlī (VIII g.) moved to Qum (ibid., 546–547); also Ṭāhir b. Abī al-Qāsim Aḥmad b. Muḥammad b. Jaʿfar b. ʿAbd al-Raḥmān al-Shajarī b. al-Qāsim b. al-Ḥasan b. Zayd b. al-Ḥasan (IX g.) (ibid., 550).

Map 5.4b: Ḥasanīs' migrations from Qum

Baṣra: Abū Muḥammad al-Ḥasan b. Abī Hāshim Muḥammad b. ʿAlī b. Ubaydallāh b. ʿAbdallāh b. al-Ḥasan [b. Jaʿfar] b. al-Ḥasan [b. al-Ḥasan] b. ʿAlī b. Abī Ṭālib (IX g.) (Qumī, *Tārīkh-i Qum*, 543–544), one of the sons of the first Ḥasanī settled in Qum, who moved here, probably from Kūfa, during the reign of Muʿizz al-Dawla (915–966; r. in ʿIrāq 945–966) and became *naqīb-i sādāt.*

Qāshān: Abū al-ʿAbbās Aḥmad b. Ṭāhir b. Abī al-Qāsim Muḥammad (descendant of ʿAbd al-Raḥmān al-Shajarī b. al-Qāsim b. al-Ḥasan b. Zayd b. al-Ḥasan) (X g.) (ibid., 550), but one of his children, Abū al-Qāsim ʿAlī (XI g.) came back to Qum (ibid., 550).

Rayy: Abū al-Qāsim ʿAlī al-Rāzī b. Ṭāhir b. Abī al-Qāsim Aḥmad al-Rāzī (X g.) went here, then moved to Nīshābūr (ibid., 551).

Ṭabaristān: Abū al-Qāsim Aḥmad al-Rāzī b. Muḥammad (VIII g.) returned here and remained until his death (ibid., 549); two of his children, Jaʿfar and Ḥamza, also moved here (IX g.) (ibid., 552).

Map 5.4c: Locations of the descendants of the Ḥasanīs in Qum

Baṣra: descendants of Abū Muḥammad al-Ḥasan b. Abī Hāshim Muḥammad b. ʿAlī (descendant of al-Ḥasan b. al-Ḥasan b. ʿAlī) (IX g.) (Qumī, *Tārīkh-i Qum*, 543–544).

Iṣfahān: descendants of Abū Hāshim Muḥammad (probably the father of the first Ḥasanī who settled in Qum) (VIII g.) (ibid., 544, but see also 541ff.).

Ṭabaristān: descendants of ʿAbbās b. Aḥmad [Abī al-Qāsim b. Muḥammad b. Jaʿfar b. ʿAbd al-Raḥmān al-Shajarī] (IX g.) (ibid., 551; *nasab* in n. 1); of Jaʿfar and Ḥamza b. Abī al-Qāsim Aḥmad b. Muḥammad (IX g.) (ibid., 552).

Map 5.5a: Ḥusaynīs' migrations to Qum

Ābah: Muḥammad b. ʿAlī b. ʿAlī b. al-Ḥasan al-Afṭas b. ʿAlī b. ʿAlī (VII g.) (Qumī, *Tārīkh-i Qum*, 637).

Baṣra: ʿAbdallāh b. al-ʿAbbās b. ʿAbdallāh b. al-Ḥasan al-Afṭas (VII g.) (ibid., 631–632; *nasab* in 631, n.1).

Ḥijāz: Abū al-Faḍl al-Ḥusayn b. al-Ḥasan b. al-Ḥasan b. ʿAlī b. ʿAlī Zayn al-ʿĀbidīn (VI g.) (with a group of "*mardum-i Daylam*") (ibid., 628).

Iṣfahān (?): al-Ḥasan b. ʿAlī b. ʿUmar b. al-Ḥasan b. ʿAlī b. ʿAlī Zayn al-ʿĀbidīn (VII g.) (ibid., 636).

Kūfa: the first descendant of ʿAlī al-Riḍā who moved to Qum was Abū Jaʿfar Muḥammad b. Mūsā b. Muḥammad b. ʿAlī al-Riḍā in 869–70 (IX g.) (ibid., 575–577), followed by three of his sisters, Zaynab, Umm Muḥammad (d. 954–5) (ibid., 590) and Maymūna (ibid., 581), and their aunt Burayha (ibid., 581); Abū ʿAlī Muḥammad b. Aḥmad b. Mūsā b. Muḥammad b. ʿAlī al-Riḍā (X g.) (d. 927–8) also moved here with two of his daughters, Fāṭima (d. 954–5) (ibid., 590) and Umm Salama (ibid., 585); one of Abū ʿAlī Muḥammad's sisters, Umm Ḥabīb, moved to Qum after his death to stay with his sons (ibid., 589).

Madīna: Fāṭima bt. Mūsā, sister of ʿAlī al-Riḍā in 816–7 (ibid., 565) and generally speaking the descendants of Muḥammad b. ʿAlī al-Riḍā (ibid., 600); al-Ḥusayn b. ʿĪsā b. Muḥammad b. ʿAlī b. Jaʿfar al-Ṣādiq (VIII g.) and his son ʿAlī (IX g.) (ibid., 611).

Nīshābūr: Abū ʿAlī Aḥmad b. ʿAlī b. Muḥammad b. ʿAlī b. ʿUmar b. ʿAlī b. al-Ḥusayn b. ʿAlī (VII g.) (ibid., 646–647).

Rayy: ʿAlī b. al-Ḥusayn b. ʿĪsā b. Muḥammad [b. ʿAlī] b. Jaʿfar al-Ṣādiq (IX g.) (ibid., 613); Ḥamza b. ʿAbdallāh b. al-Ḥusayn [al-Kawkabī] b. Aḥmad b. Muḥammad b. Ismāʿīl b. Muḥammad b. ʿAbdallāh [al-Bāhir] b. ʿAlī b. al-Ḥusayn b. ʿAlī (X g.) (ibid., 625, see also n. 8).

Ṭabaristān: Ḥamza b. Aḥmad b. Muḥammad b. Ismāʿīl b. Muḥammad b. ʿAbdallāh al-Bāhir b. ʿAlī b. al-Ḥusayn b. ʿAlī (VIII g.) (ibid., 619; see n. 6, where the genealogy of his brother Abū Jaʿfar Muḥammad is given).

Map 5.5b: Ḥusaynīs' migrations from Qum

Ābah: Abū ʿAlī Aḥmad b. Abī ʿAbdallāh Isḥāq b. Ibrāhīm b. Mūsā b. Ibrāhīm b. Mūsā b. Jaʿfar al-Ṣādiq (X g.), although he returned to Qum (Qumī, *Tārīkh-i Qum*, 602); Muḥammad al-Jawrānī b. al-Ḥusayn b. ʿAlī b. Muḥammad b. Jaʿfar al-Ṣādiq (VIII g.) who moved here and died in Rayy (ibid., 606); the sons of Muḥammad b. ʿAlī b. ʿAlī b. al-Ḥasan al-Afṭas b. ʿAlī b. ʿAlī, Ibrāhīm and ʿAlī, who had descendants here (VIII g.) (ibid., 638).

Baghdād: Muḥammad al-ʿAzīzī b. ʿAbdallāh b. al-Ḥusayn b. ʿAlī b. Muḥammad b. Jaʿfar al-Ṣādiq (IX g.), who died at Nahrawān (ibid., 606); three sons of ʿAlī b. al-Ḥusayn b. ʿĪsā b. Muḥammad b. ʿAlī b. Jaʿfar al-Ṣādiq (IX g.), Muḥammad, Ḥamza and Aḥmad (X g.) (ibid., 612); Abū ʿAlī al-Shaʿrānī b. Abī ʿAbdallāh al-Ḥusayn b. Aḥmad b. ʿAlī b. Jaʿfar al-Ṣādiq (VIII g.) (ibid., 613); Abū al-Ḥusayn Muḥammad al-Kawkabī b. ʿAlī b. Muḥammad b. ʿAbdallāh al-Bāhir b. ʿAlī b. al-Ḥusayn b. ʿAlī b. Abī Ṭālib, appointed by Muʿizz al-Dawla as *naqīb-i ʿAlaviyya* here (VI g.) (ibid., 617–618; see n. 8); Abū ʿAbdallāh al-Ḥusayn b. Muḥammad b. ʿAlī b. ʿUmar [al-Ashraf] b. al-Ḥasan al-Afṭas b. ʿAlī b. ʿAlī Zayn al-ʿĀbidīn (VIII g.) (d. 984–5) (ibid., 635); Abū Jaʿfar Muḥammad b. al-Ḥasan b. Aḥmad [al-Shajarī] b. ʿAlī b. Muḥammad b. ʿUmar b. ʿAlī b. ʿUmar al-Ashraf (X g.) (ibid., 649; *nasab* in n. 3); Abū al-Qāsim ʿAlī b. Aḥmad al-Shajarī b. ʿAlī b. Muḥammad b. ʿUmar b. ʿAlī (VII g.) (ibid., 649ff.).

Baṣra: Abū al-Ḥusayn Muḥammad al-Kawkabī b. ʿAlī b. Muḥammad b. ʿAbdallāh al-Bāhir b. ʿAlī b. al-Ḥusayn b. ʿAlī b. Abī Ṭālib was appointed by Muʿizz al-Dawla as *wālī* here (VI g.) (ibid., 618).

Fārs: above-mentioned sons of ʿAlī b. al-Ḥusayn b. ʿĪsā b. Muḥammad b. ʿAlī b. Jaʿfar al-Ṣādiq, Muḥammad, Ḥamza and Aḥmad (X g.) (ibid., 612).

Khurāsān: a nephew (XII g.) of Umm Salama bt. Abī ʿAlī Muḥammad b. Aḥmad (XI g.) (ibid., 592–593); Abū al-Qāsim [ʿAlī] b. Abī ʿAbdallāh Aḥmad b. Abī ʿAlī Muḥammad b. Aḥmad b. Mūsā b. Muḥammad b. ʿAlī al-Riḍā (XII g.) (ibid., 593).

Khwārizm: al-Ḥasan b. al-Ḥasan b. ʿAlī b. ʿUmar b. al-Ḥasan b. ʿAlī b. ʿAlī (VIII g.) (ibid., 636–637).

Qāshān: Abū Jaʿfar Muḥammad b. Mūsā b. Muḥammad b. ʿAlī al-Riḍā (IX g.) (ibid., 577ff.), although he returned to Qum (ibid., 577–578).

Rayy: Muḥammad, Mūsā, ʿAlī and al-Ḥasan (XII g.), the four sons of Abū ʿAbdallāh Aḥmad b. Abī ʿAlī Muḥammad b. Aḥmad b. Mūsā b. Muḥammad b. ʿAlī al-Riḍā, moved here to seek the protection of Rukn al-Dawla [al-Daylamī] and later returned to Qum (ibid., 592); ʿAbdallāh b. Ḥamza b. ʿAbdallāh b. al-Ḥusayn al-Kawkabī b. Aḥmad b. Muḥammad b. Ismāʿīl b. Muḥammad b. ʿAbdallāh [al-Bāhir] b. ʿAlī b. al-Ḥusayn b. ʿAlī (XI g.) (ibid., 626); Abū al-Faḍl al-Ḥusayn b. al-Ḥasan b. al-Ḥasan b. ʿAlī b. ʿAlī Zayn al-ʿĀbidīn (VI g.), who returned to Qum (ibid., 630); Abū ʿAbdallāh al-Abyaḍ b. al-Ḥusayn b. ʿAbdallāh b. al-ʿAbbās b. ʿAbdallāh al-Ḥasan b. al-Ḥasan al-Afṭas (IX g.) (ibid., 633).

Ṭūs: Abū al-Qāsim [ʿAlī] b. Abī ʿAbdallāh Aḥmad b. Abī ʿAlī Muḥammad b. Aḥmad b. Mūsā b. Muḥammad b. ʿAlī al-Riḍā (see also Khurāsān) (XII g.) (ibid., 593).

Map 5.5c: Locations of the descendants of the Ḥusaynīs in Qum

Ābah: descendants of ʿAlī b. al-Ḥusayn [Barṭala] b. ʿAlī b. ʿUmar b. al-Ḥasan b. ʿAlī b. ʿAlī Zayn al-ʿĀbidīn (VIII g.) (Qumī, *Tārīkh-i Qum*, 636, 640); Ibrāhīm and ʿAlī, both sons of Muḥammad al-Khazarī b. ʿAlī b. ʿAlī b. al-Ḥasan al-Afṭas b. ʿAlī b. ʿAlī (VIII g.) (ibid., 638, 643); the descendants of Abū al-Faḍl al-Ḥusayn b. ʿAlī b. al-Ḥusayn b. ʿĪsā b. Muḥammad b. ʿAlī b. Jaʿfar al-Ṣādiq (X g.) held the *niqābat al-sādāt* (ibid., 612).

Baghdād: descendants of ʿAlī Ṭāwūs b. Muḥammad b. al-Ḥasan b. al-Muḥsin b. al-Ḥusayn b. ʿAlī b. Muḥammad b. Jaʿfar al-Ṣādiq (XI g.) (ibid., 608); Muḥammad, Ḥamza and Aḥmad (X g.), sons of ʿAlī b. al-Ḥusayn b. ʿĪsā b. Muḥammad b. ʿAlī b. Jaʿfar al-Ṣādiq (ibid., 612); Abū ʿAlī al-Shaʿrānī b. Abī ʿAbdallāh al-Ḥusayn b. Aḥmad b. ʿAlī b. Jaʿfar al-Ṣādiq (VIII g.) (ibid., 613); Abū Muḥammad al-Ḥasan, a descendant of Muḥammad b. ʿAbdallāh al-Bāhir b. ʿAlī b. al-Ḥusayn b. ʿAlī (*nasab* with many omissions, ibid., 623).

Balkh: descendants of ʿAlī b. al-Ḥusayn [Barṭala] b. ʿAlī b. ʿUmar b. al-Ḥasan b. ʿAlī b. ʿAlī Zayn al-ʿĀbidīn (VIII g.) (ibid., 636).

Dīnawar: descendants of Abū al-Ḥasan ʿAlī b. al-Ḥasan b. al-Ḥasan b. ʿAlī b. ʿAlī Zayn al-ʿĀbidīn (VI g.) (ibid., 627–628).

Fārs (but also Baghdād): descendants of three brothers Muḥammad, Ḥamza and Aḥmad, who were all sons of ʿAlī b. al-Ḥusayn b. ʿĪsā b. Muḥammad b. ʿAlī b. Jaʿfar al-Ṣādiq (X g.) (ibid., 612).

Khwārizm: the presence of *sādāt* descending from Qumīs, also in Ābah and Qāshān (ibid., 596).

Iṣfahān: descendants of al-Ḥasan b. ʿAlī b. ʿUmar b. al-Ḥasan b. ʿAlī b. ʿAlī (VII g.) (ibid., 636).

Mawṣil: descendants of ʿAlī Ṭāwūs b. Muḥammad b. al-Ḥasan b. al-Muḥsin b. al-Ḥusayn b. ʿAlī b. Muḥammad b. Jaʿfar al-Ṣādiq (XI g.) (ibid., 608).

Qazwīn: descendants of Muḥammad b. al-Ḥusayn b. ʿAlī b. Muḥammad b. Jaʿfar al-Ṣādiq (VIII g.) (ibid., 606); a group of ʿAlids under the guide of Aḥmad b. ʿĪsā (ibid. 641) or, according to some sources, of al-Ḥusayn al-Kawkabī b. Aḥmad b. Ismāʿīl b. Muḥammad b. Ismāʿīl b. Muḥammad b. ʿAlī b. al-Ḥusayn (VIII g.) (ibid., 641; see n. 1) who is said to have been their *amīr*.

Rayy: descendants of ʿAbdallāh b. Ḥamza b. ʿAbdallāh b. al-Ḥusayn al-Kawkabī, a descendant of ʿAbdallāh b. ʿAlī Zayn al-ʿĀbidīn (XI g.) (ibid., 626); Abū ʿAbdallāh al-Abyaḍ b. al-Ḥusayn b. ʿAbdallāh b. al-ʿAbbās b. ʿAbdallāh b. al-Ḥasan al-Afṭas (IX g.) (ibid., 633).

Notes

1 Morimoto Kazuo, "Toward the Formation of Sayyido-Sharifology: Questioning Accepted Fact," *The Journal of Sophia Asian Studies* 22 (2004): 87–103.

2 Abū Naṣr al-Bukhārī, *Sirr al-silsila al-ʿAlawiyya*, ed. by Muḥammad-Ṣādiq Baḥr al-ʿUlūm (Najaf: al-Maktaba al-Ḥaydariyya, 1383/1963); Abū al-Ḥasan al-ʿUmarī, *al-Majdī fī ansāb al-Ṭālibiyyīn*, ed. by Aḥmad al-Mahdawī al-Dāmghānī (Qum: Maktabat al-Marʿashī, 1409/1988).

3 See for example, B. Scarcia Amoretti, "The Migration of the Ahl al-Bayt to Bukhara in Genealogical Books: Preliminary Remarks," in C. Silvi Antonini and D. K. Mirzaakhmedov eds, *Ancient and Mediaeval Culture of the Bukhara Oasis* (Samarkand: The Institute of Archaeology of the Academy of Sciences of the Republic of Uzbekistan and Rome: Rome University "La Sapienza," Department of Oriental Studies, 2006), 74–85.

4 Such a lacuna does not concern only the *Ahl al-Bayt*, although we have some examples of new awareness: see M. Davie, *Atlas historique des orthodoxes de Beyrouth et du Mont Liban 1800–1940* (Beirut: Publications de l'Université de Balamand, 1999).

5 Ḥasan b. Muḥammad Qumī, *Tārīkh-i Qum*, trans. by Ḥasan b. ʿAlī b. Qumī, ed. by Muḥammad-Rižā Anṣārī Qumī (Qum: Kitābkhāna-yi Marʿashī, 1385 AHS/ 2006). The text – as we know – presents many gaps; this new edition is in a sense too accurate and often integrates and rectifies the text using later sources, so that it is hard to restore in a reliable way the genealogical tree proposed by the author.

6 See B. Scarcia Amoretti, "Definire il 'centro': Qualche osservazione sul possibile ruolo dell'*Ahl al-Bayt*," in G. Contu ed., *Centre and Periphery within the Borders of Islam: Proceedings of the 23rd Congress of L'Union Européenne des Arabisants et Islamisants (UEAI), (28/9–1/10 2006)*, Orientalia Lovaniensia Analecta, 207 (Leuven: Peeters, 2011), 69–92.

7 To clarify what I mean, see D. Harvey, *Spaces of Global Capitalism: Towards a Theory of Uneven Geographical Development* (London and New York, NY: Verso, 2006).

8 Al-Bukhārī, *Sirr*, 4–29.

9 Detailed explanations as to how these maps were developed and what rich data they actually may contain in their digital format are to be found in "Notes on the Maps" below.

10 Al-Bukhārī, *Sirr*, 10–11.

11 See B. Scarcia Amoretti, "Women's Names in Early Islamic Pro-Shiʿite Texts on the Genealogy of the Talibiyyin," in M. Marín ed., "Arab-Islamic Medieval Culture," special issue, *Medieval Prosopography: History and Collective Biography* 23 (2002): 141–165; idem, "Genealogical Prestige and Mariage Policy of the *Ahl al-Bayt* (1): Status quaestionis," in S. Bowen Savant and E. de Felipe Rodriguez, eds, *Genealogy and Knowledge in Muslim Societies: Understanding the Past* (Edinburgh: Edinburgh University Press, forthcoming).

12 Al-Bukhārī, *Sirr*, 34–36; al-ʿUmarī, *al-Majdī*, 99–106.

13 Al-ʿUmarī, *al-Majdī*, 100.

14 Kazuo Morimoto, "The Formation and Development of the Science of Talibid Genealogies in the 10th and 11th Century Middle East," in B. Scarcia Amoretti and L. Bottini eds, "The Role of the *Sâdât/Ašrâf* in Muslim History and Civilization: Proceedings of the International Colloquium (Rome 2–4/3/1998)," special issue, *Oriente Moderno* n.s. 18 (1999): 550.

15 For Ḥasanīs, see Qumī, *Tārīkh-i Qum*, 541–555; for Ḥusaynīs, see ibid., 556–652.

16 See B. Scarcia Amoretti, "L'imamismo in Iran nell'epoca selgiuchide: a proposito del problema della 'comunità'," in G. Scarcia ed., "La Bisaccia dello Sheikh:

Omaggio ad Alessandro Bausani islamista nel sessantesimo compleanno," special issue, *Quaderni del Seminario di Iranistica, Uralo-Altaistica e Caucasologia dell'Università degli Studi di Venezia* 19 (1981): 127–139.

17 See, e.g., Qumī, *Tārīkh-i Qum*, 547–549.

18 Ibid., 601.

19 Ibid., 603.

20 Y. Bregel, *An Historical Atlas of Central Asia*, Handbuch der Orientalistik, VIII: Central Asia, 9 (Leiden: Brill, 2003). Cf. the review of E. de la Vaissière, in *Journal asiatique* 291/1–2 (2003): 295–300.

21 [Editor's note] The author's original starting point of generation count (I g.) was the generation of ʿAlī b. Abī Ṭālib. I thank the author for kindly accepting this system.

22 Ibn al-ʿUmariyya indicates that he was the son of Fāṭima bt. ʿAlī al-Ṭabīb b. ʿAbdallāh b. Muḥammad b. ʿUmar al-Aṭraf b. ʿAlī b. Abī Ṭālib.

6 The reflection of Islamic tradition on Ottoman social structure

The *sayyid*s and *sharīf*s[1]

Rüya Kılıç

Introduction

The descendants of the Prophet, known as the *sayyid*s or *sharīf*s, have always enjoyed high esteem within Islamic societies. The continuation of the old Arab tribal titles and nobility together with the struggle revolving around the institution of the caliphate played a role in their appearance as a social group after the creation of the Islamic religion. The "descendants of the Prophet" (*evlād-ı Resūl*) were considered to have been oppressed during this struggle. This accelerated the feelings of loyalty to the Prophet and the *sayyid*s and *sharīf*s became more popular. Furthermore, the presence of the *sayyid*s or *sharīf*s in the history of Islam can be said to be a reflection of the stratification of society due to various political and social circumstances. There have been detailed studies concerning how the special position within society of this "aristocracy of sacred descent" was accepted as legitimate by Islamic tradition.[2]

The Turkish people's encounters with the *sayyid*s and *sharīf*s date back to the tenth and eleventh centuries when they converted to Islam in the Transoxiana basin, Khwarezm and Khorasan. The Turks, who were enthusiastic about their new religion, embraced these people with great respect and love, considering them to be the living mementos of the Prophet Muḥammad. The *sayyid*s and *sharīf*s, who had dispersed over a vast area extending throughout the Islamic world from Spain to Central Asia, existed in Anatolia in great numbers even before Ottoman times. Once the Ottoman state was established, the *sayyid*s and *sharīf*s were granted social and economic privileges and this attracted many more of their number who migrated from other Islamic countries. Thus, the *sayyid*s and *sharīf*s became one of the main social elements that bound the Ottoman state to the Islamic tradition.

The objective of this study is to examine, within the Ottoman context, who the *sayyid*s and *sharīf*s were and why they were of such great importance for all Islamic societies. However, there are two dangers in this research; one is falling completely under the influence of the information contained in historical documents and the other is becoming enthralled with the appeal of sociological theories and thus adapting documents to these theories, especially when discussing the issue of social status. So it is important to emphasize that the topic will be examined from a socio-historical perspective, within a conceptual and theoretical framework applied to the large number of materials that were uncovered in the research for this study. Especially relevant are the registers of the *naqīb al-ashrāf*, which allow the identification of the *sayyid*s and *sharīf*s.

Institutionalization

In order to oversee the rapidly increasing numbers of *sayyid*s and *sharīf*s, the Ottoman state drew upon the experience of the Islamic states that had preceded it and established the position of *naqīb al-ashrāf*. The first person appointed to oversee the *sayyid*s and *sharīf*s, at the time of Sultan Yıldırım Bayezid (r. 1389–1402), was Sayyid Nattāʿī, who had come from Baghdad to Bursa with the famous Ottoman saint Emir Sultan Buhari (d. 1429?). ʿĀşık Çelebi (d. 1572), who is known for his work *Meşāʿir üş-Şuʿarā*,[3] was a member of Sayyid Nattāʿī's family and provides important information on the history of the position of *naqīb al-ashrāf* in the Ottoman period.[4] According to ʿĀşık Çelebi, Sayyid Nattāʿī was appointed the "*nāzır* of the *sādāt*" after he came to Anatolia and he was succeeded by his son, Sayyid Zeynelabidin. However, after the son's death, the position was left vacant for several years.[5] According to sources, as some people did not behave in a way befitting the concept of the *sayyid*s and *sharīf*s in the time of Sultan Bayezid (r. 1481–1512), Sayyid Mahmud (d. 1536–7) was appointed to oversee the *sayyid*s and *sharīf*s. Sayyid Mahmud was the first to use the title of *naqīb al-ashrāf* as in the Arab countries, instead of the Ottoman title the *nāzır* of the *sādāt*.[6]

The next *naqīb al-ashrāf* to be appointed after Sayyid Mahmud was Muhterem Efendi and it is to him that the oldest existing *naqīb al-ashrāf* registers belong. Unfortunately, these registers do not constitute a complete collection of records. Nevertheless, important data can be obtained from them as to who was accepted as a *sayyid* or a *sharīf*, the terminology used and in particular, the sensitivity within administrative circles concerning the distinction between the *sayyid/sharīf*s and the *mutasayyid*s (false claimants to membership of the family of the Prophet).

The registers can be classified as those containing copies of the credentials (sing. *hüccet*) regarding the *sayyid/sharīf* status conferred by the *naqīb al-ashrāf*, their summaries (sing. *icmal*), inspection (*teftiş*) registers and the registers concerning the appointment of the deputies (sing. *kāimmakām*) of the *naqīb*s. The summaries contain an alphabetical list of the people who received credentials from the *naqīb al-ashrāf*. These summary registers were drawn on the basis of existing credentials, with the aim of facilitating the confirmation of whether certain people were registered or not during investigations of people who claimed to be *sayyid*s or *sharīf*s. As can be inferred from the name, the inspection registers were compiled to record the examination of the *sayyid*s and *sharīf*s in the various regions and concomitant identification and removal of *mutasayyid*s from the registers. More recent registers contained various records regarding *sayyid*s and *sharīf*s, notably those concerning the appointment of the deputies of the *naqīb al-ashrāf*.

The first register is dated 17 Şevval 942/9 April 1536,[7] and in a simple format records the names of the *sayyid*s and *sharīf*s, those of their fathers, where they were from and the names of the *şuhūd* (witnesses).[8] Subsequent registers adhere to a similar format, although they contain more detail. For example, they trace the lineage beyond the father to the grandfather and even to the great-grandfather, and mention whether a family member possessed documents confirming their *sayyid/sharīf* status issued by a previous *naqīb al-ashrāf*.[9] There are exceptions in the first register; for example, sometimes there is no information as to where a *sayyid* or a *sharīf* had come from and sometimes there is only one witness named.[10] The second *naqīb al-ashrāf* register contains the names of the *sayyid*s and *sharīf*s provided in the first register, but lists them alphabetically. These first two registers are important since they contain interesting examples concerning the use of the title "al-ʿAbbasi" in the Ottoman state. It is significant that in the few records where "al-ʿAbbasi" is recorded there is no reference to the title of "*sayyid*" or "*sharīf*," such as in "Süleyman b. Behşayiş al-ʿAbbasi."[11]

Following this short introduction to the history and records of the institution of *naqīb al-ashrāf* in the Ottoman state, it is useful to consider the social base of the *naqīb*s and the conditions that played an important role in their appointment. Establishing the role of the *naqīb*s within society and their relationship with other groups would no doubt be of great interest, but this information is generally lacking in the available sources. The interpretations that follow are based on the list of twenty-five *naqīb*s dating from the time of Sayyid Mahmud Efendi at the end of the fifteenth century to the end of the seventeenth century (Table 6.1). Biographical works provide an outline of these people's professional lives, but do not offer much data regarding their social relations. Thus, these twenty-five records do not permit a general assessment of the social base of all the *naqīb*s. However, they do contribute to the formation of an opinion on the subject. As there is more data regarding later *naqībs*, the period researched was extended to the end of the seventeenth century. Of the thirteen *naqīb*s beginning with the initial *nāzır* of the *sādāt* to Sayyid Mehmed Efendi in the first half of the seventeenth century, two resigned of their own accord but all the others carried out their duty till the end of their lives. Beginning in 1634, dismissals became more frequent, although there were still *naqīb*s who remained in office for long periods of time. In the seventeenth century the political, social and economic changes within the Ottoman Empire began to affect the institution of *naqīb al-ashrāf* and the general tendency for official appointments to change hands more often seems to have affected the institution of *naqīb al-ashrāf*, too.

Table 6.1 contains further interesting information. For example, three of the first *naqīb*s came from outside of the Ottoman Empire. Muhterem Efendi was from Tashkent and Mirzā Mahdūm was from Tabriz. Bağdadīzade Hasan Efendi's father, Kıvameddin Yusuf, came from Shiraz and because of the Safavid menace migrated to the Ottoman Empire after having been employed as the *qadi* of Baghdad. However, subsequent *naqībs* were generally raised in

Table 6.1 The list of *naqīb*s in the Ottoman Empire

Name (Date of Death)	*Hometown*	*Father's Occupation*	*Previous Occupation(s)*	*Appointment and Termination of Office*	*Sources (Other than Devhatu'n-Nukabā)*
Sayyid Mahmūd Efendi (1534–5 or 1536–7)	Bursa	*Mudarris*	–	1534–5 or 1536–7 Death*1	Kınalızade Hasan Çelebi, I:185–186; Mecdī, 342.
Muhterem Efendi (1572)	Tashkent	–	–	1572 Death	Atāī, 175–176.
Bağdadīzāde Sayyid Hasan Efendi (1578)	Shiraz (father's)	*Qadi*	*Mudarris*, *Müfti*	1576 Resignation	Atāī, 247–248; Mecdī, 326–327.
Sayyid Mehmed Efendi (Malūlzāde Efendi) (1585)	–	*Kazasker*	*Mudarris*, *Qadi*, *Kazasker*	1585 Death	Müstakimzade, 29–30; Atāī, 281–282; Mecdī, 484–485.
Mirza Mahdūm Efendi (1587)	Tabriz	–	*Qadi*	1587 Death	Atāī, 297–299.
Yahya Efendi (Keçi/ Kiçi Mirza-zāde) (1599)	Bursa	–	*Mudarris*	1599 Death	Atāī, 431–432; Kınalızade Hasan Çelebi, II:944–946.
Abdülkādir Efendi (1604)	Kayseri	–	*Qadi*	1604 Death	Atāī, 497.
Sayyid Mehmed Naqīb (Yavuz Çelebi) (1605)	–	–	*Mudarris*, *Qadi*	1605 Death	Atāī, 498–499.
Emir Ali Efendi (1616)	Bursa	–	*Mudarris*, *Qadi*	1616 Death	Atāī, 582.
Kasım Gubārī Efendi (1625)	Amid	–	*Mudarris*	1625 Death	Atāī, 693.
Sayyid Mehmed Efendi (1631)	–	*Qadi*	*Mudarris*, *Qadi*, *Kazasker*	1629–30 Resignation	Atāī, 742–743; Kınalızade Hasan Çelebi, I:515–517.
Sayyid Mehmed (Allāme Şeyhi Efendi) (1635)	Eğridir	–	*Mudarris*, *Qadi*	1634 Dismissal	Şeyhī, I:18–20.
Sayyid Mehmed Esʿad Emir Efendi (Ankaravī Emir Efendi) (1647)	Ankara	–	*Qadi*	1647 Death	Şeyhī, I:135.
Seyrekzāde Yūnus Efendi (1652)	–	*Mudarris*, *Qadi*	*Mudarris*, *Qadi*	1647–8 Dismissal	Şeyhī, I:201–202; Atāī, 432–433.
Sayyid Mehmed b.	Ankara	*Qadi*, *Naqīb*	*Qadi*	1648 Dismissal	Şeyhī, I:347–348.

Abdurrahman b. Ahmed b. Emrullah (1674)		*Qadi*	*Mudarris*, *Qadi*	1648 Taking Office 1656 Dismissal	Şeyhī, I:413–414.
Sheikh Mehmed b. Mehmed Kudsī (1674)	–	*Kazasker*	*Mudarris*, *Qadi*, *Kazasker*	1657 Taking Office 1674 Death	Şeyhī, I:409–411; Atāī, 642–643.
Sayyid Mehmed Said ibn Mehmed Esʿad Efendi (1687)		*Mudarris*, *Qadi*, *Kazasker*	*Mudarris*, *Qadi*, *Kazasker*	1674 Taking Office 1680 Dismissal 1686 Taking Office 1687 Death	Şeyhī, I:241–242, 541–543.
Sayyid Cafer Efendi (1697)		*Qadi*	*Mudarris*	1680 Taking Office 1686 Dismissal	Şeyhī, II:135–136.
Sayyid Feyzullah Efendi (1703)	Erzurum	*Müfti*	Teacher of *şehzade*	1687 Taking Office 1688 Dismissal	Müstakimzade, 74–76; Şeyhī, II:247–249.
Sayyid Abdurrahman Efendi (Nefes-zāde) (1696)	Ankara	*İmam*, *Hatip*	*Mudarris*	1688 Taking Office 1690 Dismissal	Şeyhī, II:125–126.
Paşmakçı-zāde Sayyid Ali Efendi (1712)		*Qadi*	*Mudarris*, *Qadi*	1690 Taking Office 1694–5 Dismissal	Şeyhī, II:336–340, I: 500–501; Müstakimzade, 79–80.
Sayyid Mehmed Efendi (1696)		*Mudarris*, *Qadi*	*Mudarris*, *Qadi*, *Kazasker*	1694–5 Taking Office 1695 Dismissal	Şeyhī, I:121–122, II:128–130.
Sayyid Osman Efendi (1700)	–	*Kazasker*	*Qadi*, *Kazasker*	1695 Taking Office 1699 Dismissal	Şeyhī, I:25–26, II:173–174.
Sayyid Fethullah Efendi (1703)		*Naqīb al-ashrāf*, *Sheikh al-Islam*	*Kazasker*	1699 Taking Office 1703 Death	Şeyhī, II:249–250.

This table is based on the data from Ahmed Rıfʿat Efendi, *Devhatu'n-Nukabā* (Istanbul: Karahisari Esat Efendi'nin Litografya Destgahı, 1283/1866-7). References to other biographical works, i.e., (Nevʾīzade) Atāī, *Hadaik'l-Hakaik fī Tekmileti'ş-Şakaik*, ed. by A. Özcan as *Şakaik-ı Nuʿmaniye ve Zeyilleri*, vol. 2 (Istanbul: Çağrı, 1989); Kınalızade Hasan Çelebi, *Tezkiretü'ş-Şuarā*, ed. by İ. Kutluk, 2 vols (Ankara: Türk Tarih Kurumu, 1989); Mecdī Mehmed Efendi, *Hadaiku'ş-Şakaik*, ed. by A. Özcan as *Şakaik-ı Nuʿmaniye ve Zeyilleri*, vol. 1 (Istanbul: Çağrı, 1989); Müstakimzade (Süleyman Saadeddin), *Devhatü'l-Meşāyih* (Istanbul: Çağrı, 1978); Şeyhī, *Vekayiü'l-Fudalā I*, ed. by A. Özcan as *Şakaik-ı Nuʿmaniye ve Zeyilleri*, vol. 3 (Istanbul: Çağrı, 1989) are given only by the authors' names to save space.

*1 Sources give different dates for his death: Mecdī (*Hadaiku'ş-Şakaik*, 342) and Ahmed Rıfżat (*Devhatu'n-Nukabā*, 10) give 943/1536–7; Atāī, (*Hadaiku'l-Hakaik*, 175, 176) mentions 941/1534–5).

Ottoman lands, although the emphasis on Istanbul, which is recognizable in the later centuries, was not seen until the eighteenth century. Another interesting point is that the families of *naqīb*s were generally members of the ʿulama. Of twenty-five *naqīb*s, all but nine whose social status cannot be established, belonged to this class. Although it was not a clear-cut process, the *naqīb al-ashrāf* appears to have generally been selected from the ʿulama, such as *mudarris* (teacher), *qadi* (Muslim judge), *şehzāde hocası* (teacher of prince) and *kazasker* (chief military judge). Apart from the first three *naqīb*s, the position constituted only part of the title holder's professional life. Before becoming *naqīb* and after his duty was over, these people were *qadi*s or *kazasker*s. Indeed, some were even able to conduct both duties simultaneously.[12]

When considered as a whole, it is clear that being a *sayyid* or a *sharīf* was a prerequisite for being appointed as a *naqīb*; however, this prerequisite was not sufficient for obtaining this prestigious position. Another equally important requisite was that these people and their families were members of the ʿulama. Although it cannot be absolutely stated that certain families were particularly favored when it came to appointments, the blood kinship between (1) *naqīb al-ashrāf* Sayyid Mehmed Efendi and Allāme Şeyhī Efendi, (2) between Ankaravī Sayyid Mehmed Efendi and Sayyid Mehmed Efendi, (3) between Seyrekzade Yūnus Efendi and Abdurrahman b. Ahmed and (4) between Sayyid Feyzullah Efendi and Fethullah Efendi, for example, does seem to support the idea that blood kinship played a role in the selection.[13]

Concerning the duties of the *naqīb al-ashrāf*, the traditions of other Islamic states were basically maintained. So, they can be summarized as dealing with the affairs of the *sayyid*s and *sharīf*s. However, upon a closer examination, the most important duty of the *naqīb al-ashrāf* seems to have been distinguishing the true *sayyid*s and *sharīf*s from the *mutasayyid*s. Together with the general social changes that started taking place in the Ottoman Empire in the seventeenth century, there was a rapid increase in the number of *mutasayyid*s, which resulted in various difficulties for the administration, particularly in terms of tax income and maintaining social order.[14] The records found in *Kanūnnāme-i Sultānī li ʿAziz Efendi* reveal there were complaints that in return for some *akçe*s (silver coins) some *reʿāyā* had obtained documents, which they used to become part of the group of *sayyid*s and *sharīf*s and to gain exemption from taxes, and that this conduct was spreading like an epidemic throughout the Ottoman Empire.[15]

The institution of the *naqīb al-ashrāf* oversaw the *sayyid*s and *sharīf*s not only from an economic perspective but also to preserve social harmony. On the one hand they were appointed by the state and hence were representing the state. On the other hand they were acting on behalf of their own group. In dealing with the affairs of *sayyid*s and *sharīf*s, the *naqīb*s would act in collaboration with their deputies (sing. *kāimmakām*), who represented the *naqīb*s in the provinces, sub-provinces and districts. As there had to be a specific number of *sayyid*s and *sharīf*s in a particular area for a deputy to be appointed, at times one deputy was appointed to oversee two or more areas.[16] Suitable candidates for the position of the deputy of the *naqīb* were selected from the families of *sayyid*s and *sharīfs* that were respected and considered to be influential by the population.[17]

A deputy of the *naqīb* was appointed by a *naqīb al-ashrāf* letter and then this was most probably recorded in the *Sharīʿa* court records (*şerʿiye sicili*) of the relevant district, in order that the appointment could be considered official. These registers contain a great number of appointment letters, in which the duties of a deputy are described.[18] According to these letters, the main duties of the deputies consisted of verifying those who were *sayyid*s or *sharīfs* in their areas from the *mutasayyid*s, dealing with the affairs of the *sayyid*s and *sharīf*s and, in particular, not allowing local officials to intervene when the *sayyid*s or *sharīf*s needed to be penalized.[19] The latter duty was most probably aimed at preventing damage to the *sayyid/sharīf* status within society. This seems to have arisen also from the concern that there might be a negative public reaction to needless intervention with those who according to Islamic tradition were deemed to be the most sacred lineage. Moreover, it was emphasized that only the *naqīb al-ashrāf* of Istanbul was authorized to give the final approval of the status of *sayyid/sharīf*.[20]

Terminology[21]

The essential criterion for the right to the title of "*sayyid*" or "*sharīf*" was membership of Muḥammad's family, namely, the *Ahl al-Bayt*.[22] This term is used in a broad sense in the Islamic world to refer to the members of the Prophet's family, and in a narrow sense to refer to the descendants of Ḥasan and Ḥusayn.[23] Undoubtedly, the members of the *Ahl al-Bayt* regarded as the most noble by birth are the descendants of Ḥasan and Ḥusayn. The records in the contemporary sources used in this research confirm this general understanding. For example, the title of *sayyid* is used not only for the descendants of Ḥasan and Ḥusayn but also, though not so commonly, for those of Muḥammad b. al-Ḥanafiyya, who was directly connected to the Prophet only via his father, ʿAlī.[24] Moreover, as mentioned above, the term "al-ʿAbbasi" appears in Muhterem Efendi's (d. 1572) registers.[25] This gives rise to the idea that the ʿAbbasids enjoyed a special status according to the Sunni interpretation of the Ottoman state. However, such a distinction is not encountered in later registers, either because it was not necessary to indicate it, or because what was already a small group had been absorbed into the larger group.

Although it is generally accepted that the term "*sharīf*" is used for the descendants of Ḥasan, and "*sayyid*" for the descendants of Ḥusayn,[26] this distinction is not always very clear. For the Ottomans, the status of the father is sufficient for the son to claim to be a *sayyid* or a *sharīf* even if the child's mother is a slave. The *Sharīʿa* court records and the *naqīb al-ashrāf* registers also show that the maternal line could also be accepted as proof of the *sayyid/sharīf* status. A good example of the status of *sayyid/sharīf* through the female line is to be found in the Harput *Sharīa* court register for 1632. According to that record, Mehmed Efendi, appointed by the *naqīb al-ashrāf* to inspect the *sayyid*s and *sharīf*s, questioned whether a certain person called Mustafa Çelebi, who wore a green turban, was really a *sayyid* or a *sharīf*, and if he indeed was, whether this was on his father's or his mother's side. Mustafa Çelebi stated that it was on his mother's side. After witnesses corroborated the evidence of the lineage he provided, Mustafa Çelebi's claim was accepted.[27]

The acceptance of women's lineage is of great importance. In the Ottoman state, as in other patriarchal societies, when a woman married she acquired her husband's social status, but a man would not acquire his wife's status. One of the exceptions to this rule was, however, *sayyida*s and *sharīfa*s (female *sayyid*s and *sharīf*s), because in this case, the woman, after being married, retained her status on the basis of her nobility of blood and her child would thus enjoy the social status attained through the mother. Furthermore, it is interesting to note that in various examples from the Ottoman state, mothers and even grandmothers are mentioned in the lineage for the status of *sayyid/sharīf*, while fathers or husbands are not. Although it was preferred that *sayyida*s or *sharīfa*s married men of corresponding nobility, the existence of the husbands of *sayyida*s or *sharīfa*s who were not included in the documents because they were not *sayyid*s or *sharīf*s can be seen as evidence of the fact that this rule was not always complied with. Below is an example of the lineage of the Sharīfs Hasan, Emrullah and Ali:[28]

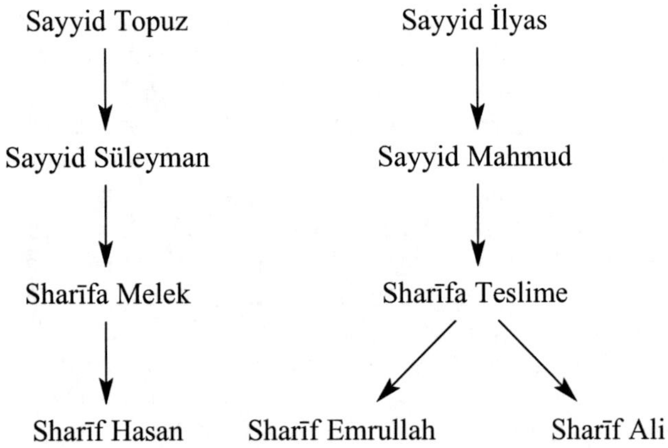

In some entries in the *Sharīa* court registers and in the *naqīb al-ashrāf* registers, the fathers and brothers are called "*sayyid*," while daughters and sisters are called "*sharīfa*."[29] Indeed, sometimes within the same family, mothers are called "*sayyida*," while daughters and granddaughters are called "*sharīfa*."[30] There are many documents concerning the use of the title "*sharīf*" for the children of "*sharīfa*s," but records also indicate that the title "*sayyid*"

was used in such cases.[31] For example, the daughter of Sayyid Mahmud Efendi is Sharīfa Teslime and her son is Sayyid Ismail.[32] It does not seem possible to establish a criterion to explain this variety in the female line. Nevertheless, a tendency can be seen toward the use of the titles of "*sharīf*" and "*sharīfa*." This makes it imperative to reconsider, in the case of the Ottoman state, the supposition that "*sharīf*" and "*sharīfa*" were formerly used for descendants of Ḥasan, because it is simply impossible that in the same family the father should be a *sayyid* in the sense of a Ḥusaynī and the daughter a *sharīf* in the sense of a Ḥasanī.

In fact, according to a record in a *naqīb al-ashrāf* register, a *sharīf* whose father's or grandfather's mother was a *sayyida* or *sharīfa* was considered to be different in his status from a *sayyid* descended from a male lineage.[33] The *naqīb al-ashrāf* register no. 2 contains a section with the heading "This reports the names of the children of *sharīfa*s" (*sharīfazādelerin esāmilerin beyān eder*). This section presents entries related to the children of "*sharīfa*s" and is clearly distinguished from the other sections dealing with "*sayyid*s" from their father's side.[34] Another register records an answer to the question, "Do those with a mother descended from the Prophet have the right to wear the green turban?" This answer is of great importance. It allows those whose mothers are "*sharīfa*s" to display a token (*ʿalāmet*) to distinguish themselves from other people, but states that the right to wear the green turban is a privilege conferred only on those whose father is a "*sayyid*."[35] This suggests that while in the Ottoman state, the female line was accepted in claims to the *sayyid/sharīf* status, the terms "*sharīf*" and "*sharīfa*" were sometimes used to distinguish those in the female line from those in the much nobler male line. Moreover, the distinction between "*sharīfazāde*s" (descendants of *sharīfa*s) and "*sayyid*s" was made visible via a restrictive decree regarding the wearing of a green turban.

Restrictions and privileges

In the Ottoman state, anyone who felt they had a right to the title of *sayyid* or *sharīf*, and thus, to benefit from related material and spiritual privileges, needed first to obtain the approval of the state. Theoretically, the only way to do this was before the *naqīb al-ashrāf* who would look for two conditions: the confirmation of the status by witnesses and credentials issued by previous *naqīb al-ashrāf*s for members of the same family. The first of these two conditions was the absolute prerequisite and in some cases, statements by witnesses were considered sufficient.[36] For example, Sharīf Mehmed b. Sharīf Kara Yusuf was recognized as having descended from Sheikh Sayyid Ibrahim et-Tennurī simply through declarations made by witnesses; his name was recorded in the register and he was permitted to wear a green turban.[37] After the first registration by an individual, other family members within the next one or two generations who claimed to be *sayyid*s or *sharīf*s would then present the credentials as proof of their descent. It was quite common for the credentials of close relatives such as fathers, grandfathers, uncles, brothers, cousins, or even cousins or uncles of fathers to be used in the verification of such claims.[38]

Some *sayyid*s and *sharīf*s had economic difficulties[39] and they were able to take advantage of their status to gain financial support. One such person was Sayyid Ahmed, who, in 1579, requested an income from the Sultan Süleyman Foundation (*vakf*) in Damascus.[40] There is also a register referring to the year 1670 that contains the amounts from the revenue of the Murad Pasha Foundation in Damascus to be distributed to needy people and *sayyid*s and *sharīf*s in Medina. Ten *sayyid*s and *sharīf*s were given a total of 280 *akçe* and the descendents of Sayyid Husayn er-Rifāi were given 400 *akçe*.[41] Apart from this kind of financial contribution, the most important privilege enjoyed by *sayyid*s and *sharīf*s was tax exemption. A document dated 1640 and addressing the provincial governor (*sancakbeyi*) and *qadi* of Antep lists the taxes from which *sayyid*s and *sharīf*s were exempt as follows: *avārız* (tax, originally collected irregularly to finance war), *tekālif-i örfiyye* (customary taxes), *sürsat* (irregular wartime tax of supplies for the army), *bennāk*, *mücerred*, *duhān*, *tekālif-i şakka* and *resm-i çift* (a form of tax assessed both in terms of land and per household).[42]

The fact that *sayyid*s and *sharīf*s benefited from their privileges to the full or even wished to increase them greatly annoyed the administration since it reduced their tax income. It is quite clear from the court registers that the conflict between the two parties sometimes resulted in matters being taken to court. For example, in 1590, the *sayyid*s and *sharīf*s of Antep were troubled because of the pressure brought on them regarding *avārız*, *nüzul* (irregular wartime tax of grain for the army) and *tekālif-i örfiyye*.[43] Two records dated 1595, within the same court register of Antep, show quite clearly the pressure brought on the *sayyid*s and *sharīf*s by local governors, regarding *avārız* and *rüsūm-ı raiyyet* (the taxation of the subjects).[44] In 1634, men from the *beylerbeyi* (the highest rank in the provincial government of the Ottoman Empire) and the *sancakbeyi* in Harput forced two *sayyid/sharīf*s, Mustafa and Husayn, to pay *tekālif-i şakka*. However, the fact that the *sayyid/sharīf*s conveyed their complaints to the central government and asked for help shows that they were aware of their rights and were not ready to forfeit them.[45] In 1690, the *sayyid*s and *sharīf*s of Konya expressed their discomfort because of the requests made by the *beylerbeyi*, *sancakbeyi*, *subaşı* (a provincial officer responsible for law and order) and their men.[46]

The examples cited above, taken from different periods and regions, demonstrate the importance of the issue for both sides. Although local governors tended not to recognize the privilege of *sayyid*s and *sharīf*s concerning taxes, the central government continued to protect them. It was the *reʿāyā* (tax-paying subjects) that bore the increased burden brought about by the tax exemption granted to *sayyid*s and *sharīf*s. There are examples of *reʿāyā* who petitioned the courts especially concerning *avārız* and objected to the people who wanted to benefit from tax exemption although they were not actually *sayyid*s or *sharīf*s.[47]

The question of status

In the Ottoman state, society was divided into two classes; the first was the *ʿaskerī*, who, by imperial decree, were granted religious or administrative authority by the sultan and the second were the *reʿāyā*, consisting of Muslims and non-Muslims who paid taxes but did not participate in the administration.[48] The *ʿaskerī* did not pay taxes and had imperial decrees. The *sayyid*s and *sharīf*s also had tax immunities, which is why in the *Kanunnāme-i Cedid* (the second half of the sixteenth century), the *sayyid*s and *sharīf*s were described as *ʿaskerī*.[49] Theoretically, in the Ottoman state, the concept of class was related to the status of individuals in terms of their specific administrative, economic, religious or political functions in the state. However, the *sayyid*s and *sharīf*s did not constitute a homogeneous group, and individuals could fulfill any number of different functions. They could be merchants, farmers, story-tellers, poets, *sheikh al-Islam*s, *mudarris*es, *qadi*s, sheikhs or viziers.[50] *Sayyid*s and *sharīf*s could even be vinegar-makers, candle-makers or peddlers and, therefore, belong to the lower social classes.[51]

*Sayyid*s and *sharīf*s cannot be easily placed into the religious class or the ʿulama. Not all *sayyid*s and *sharīf*s belonged to the religious class, though there was the wish that this be so. In spite of the importance attached to *sayyid*s and *sharīf*s in Sufi circles, people could not become sheikhs simply because they were related to the Prophet. First, they had to acquire the education and culture that was characteristic of a sheikh, just as it was the case with those aspiring to be the ʿulama.

In the Ottoman state people could change their status by serving the religion or the state, that is to say, via education or a military career.[52] One more item can be added, that is, being a *sayyid* or a *sharīf*. In fact, this method was easier since there was no obligation to render services in return for the financial, political and social power obtained and there was no danger of these privileges being rescinded. Once the claim to be a *sayyid* or a *sharīf* was validated, the privileges could be maintained for many generations. This was especially useful at times of social and economic problems in the empire. A common complaint in the political works (*siyasetname*s) of the second half of the sixteenth century was the fusion of the *reʿāyā* with the *ʿaskerī*. In the political discussion about problems of the Ottoman Empire such as *Āsāfnāme*, *Hırzü 'l-Mülūk* and *Kanūnnāme-i Sultānī li ʿAzīz Efendi*, one of the major issues was the deep discomfort arising from the fact that many *reʿāyā* had changed their social status by becoming *sayyid*s and *sharīf*s.[53]

The way in which the *sayyid*s and *sharīf*s were regarded by the remainder of the population was complex, since *sayyid*s and *sharīf*s from the ʿulama or Sufi class or those who came from highly educated families and the *sayyid*s and *sharīf*s who were peddlers of a low social status were not regarded in the same way and accorded the same respect. On the other hand, the fact that the closer people were to the lower classes in the population, the higher was their ambition to be a *sayyid* or a *sharīf*, cannot be explained simply via economic reasons. Indeed, it is not surprising that the number of people making such claims should be higher within these circles. *Sayyid*s and *sharīf*s belonging to the higher levels in society, such as *sheikh al-Islam*s, *kazasker*s or famous sheikhs, could expect to command high regard not only because of their descent but also because of their positions. However, for the *sayyid*s and *sharīf*s belonging to the lower socio-economic levels in society, being recognized as a *sayyid* or a *sharīf* and thus being considered as nobility was often the only possible way to change their position within society. The desire to acquire prestige within the society may at times have been stronger than that of obtaining financial benefits. *Sayyid*s and *sharīf*s would boast of their noble descent whenever the occasion arose. It is quite clear that they were quite successful at doing so. Indeed, this was probably the real reason for the power they enjoyed within society.

It is also interesting to consider how the *sayyid*s and *sharīf*s saw themselves in the context of a wider society. The awareness of being a *sayyid* or a *sharīf* is acquired from childhood on, from one's family and from society. Their lineages went back to *Ahl al-Bayt*; thus, they belonged to *ırk-ı tahir* (pure and noble descent) and identified themselves as such, often publicly. For example, ʿĀşık Çelebi indicated that his stammer and lisp was a feature of the lineage of Imam Ḥasan and boasted that it was a proof of his status as a *sayyid/sharīf*. According to ʿĀşık Çelebi, this feature, conferred by God to his predecessors, appears in almost all generations; if not in one, definitely in the successive one.[54] While talking about a poet with the pseudonym of Emīrī, ʿĀşık Çelebi states that although he was a Hāshimī he had inherited great eloquence and rhetoric.[55] In fact, many poets of *sayyid/sharīf* descent used pseudonyms such as Emīr, Emīrī, Hüseynī, Şerif, Şerifī, or Hāşimī, which indicated their status.[56]

Conclusion

The aim of this study in social history was to examine the *sayyid*s and *sharīf*s within the Ottoman society from as many perspectives as possible. Although the position of the *sayyid*s and *sharīf*s within society did not arise as a consequence of a religious rule firmly inscribed in the Qur'ān or Sunna, it was elaborately built around the concept of *Ahl al-Bayt* in the Islamic tradition. Throughout the history of Islam the *sayyid*s and *sharīf*s occupied a strong position in society. Many dynasties made use of the *sayyid/sharīf* status for political benefits, to obtain the support of the population and to have their legitimacy approved. On the other hand, in the Ottoman state, although the *sayyid*s and *sharīf*s maintained their prestigious position within society and were accorded various social and economic privileges, they were not permitted to exploit their status in the political arena.

Since the *sayyid*s and *sharīf*s maintained their existence within a variety of professional groups, they did not have a homogeneous structure with specific characteristics. Thus, it is not possible to call them a social stratum. They constituted a group that was so exclusive and different that it could not blend in with the hierarchical *ʿaskerī–reʿāyā* division of the society under Ottoman rule. The *sayyid*s and *sharīf*s, who were always conscious of their nobility of blood, sought material and spiritual support from the state and the society. This attitude, of course, existed more strongly among those people of lower social status and income level. However, when it came to the use of privileges, this group clashed from time to time with the government, especially local government, and also with the population. Upon the realization that descending from the family of the Prophet brought about various privileges, the *sayyid/sharīf* status became greatly desired by a large number of people who were not happy with their position within society.

Notes

1 This study includes some parts from the author's book, *Osmanlıda Seyyidler ve Şerifler* (Istanbul: Kitap, 2005).
2 The effect of different political and social circumstances in the appearance within the history of Islam of the *sayyid*s and the *sharīf*s has been analyzed in detail in the author's book, *Osmanlıda Seyyidler ve Şerifler*.
3 This important work has been published by G. M. Meredith-Owens, together with a preface on the author. ʿĀşık Çelebi, *Meşāʾir üş-Şuʿarā or Tezkere of ʿĀşık Çelebi* (London: Luzac, 1971).
4 For general information on *sayyid*s and *sharīf*s as well as their *naqīb*s in the Ottoman state, see İ. H. Uzunçarşılı, *Osmanlı Devleti'nin İlmiye Teşkilatı* (Ankara: Türk Tarih Kurumu, 1988), 161–172.
5 ʿĀşık Çelebi, *Meşāʾir üş-Şuʿarā*, 182a–182b, 49b–50a; Nevʿīzade Atāī, *Hadaik'l-Hakaik fī Tekmileti'ş-Şakaik*, ed. by Abdülkadir Özcan as *Şakaik-ı Nuʿmaniye ve Zeyilleri*, vol. 2 (Istanbul: Çağrı, 1989), 161, 176.
6 ʿĀşık Çelebi, *Meşāʾir üş-Şuʿarā*, 49b–50a; Atāī, *Hadaik'l-Hakaik*, 176.
7 Istanbul Müftülüğü, Şerʿiye Sicilleri Arşivi, Naqīb al-ashrāf registers (NED), no. 1:3a.
8 A typical entry, taken from NED, no. 1:3b, reads as follows:

> Seyyid Mehmed b. Seyyid İshak el-Niğdevī
> Şuhūd————
> Mevlana Halil b. Seyyid Mustafa b. Seyyid Şuayb
> and Mehmed b. Baba Şemseddin.

9 There are thirty-eight registers in the Archive of Istanbul Müftülüğü. Credentials: 17; summaries: 6; credentials and summaries: 3; inspection: 6; registers about the appointment of the deputies and so on: 6.
10 For both examples, see NED, no. 1:3b.
11 NED, no. 1:5b. For other records, see NED, no. 1:6a, 7a, 7b. Since I have never seen other instances where this title is used in a similar way, it is not possible to compare and contrast these records with other documents and verify whether "al-ʿAbbasi" is used in place of the titles "*sayyid*" or "*sharīf*" or whether it has other implications.
12 For examples of the duties conducted alongside the position of *naqīb al-ashrāf*, see Ahmed Rıfʿat Efendi, *Devhatu'n-Nukabā* (Istanbul: Karahisari Esat Efendi'nin Litografya Destgahı, 1283/1866–7), 15.
13 (1) Ahmet Rıfʿat Efendi, *Devhatu'n-Nukabā*, 19–20; (2) ibid., 21, 22–23; (3) ibid., 22, 23; (4) ibid., 28, 30–31.

14 For the crises of the seventeenth century, see S. Faroqhi, "Politics and Socio-economic Change in the Ottoman Empire of the Later Sixteenth Century," in M. Kunt and C. Woodhead eds, *Süleyman the Magnificent and His Age* (London and New York: Longman, 1995), 91–113; C. H. Fleischer, *Bureaucrat and Intellectual in the Ottoman Empire, The Historian Mustafa Ali* (Princeton, N.J.: Princeton University Press, 1986); W. J. Griswold, *The Great Anatolian Rebellion, 1000–1020/1591–1611* (Berlin: Klaus Schwarz Verlag, 1983); M. A. Cook, *Population Pressure in Rural Anatolia 1450–1600* (London: Oxford University Press, 1972).

15 *Kanūn-nāme-i Sultānī li ʿAziz Efendi*, ed. and trans. by R. Murphy (Cambridge, MA: Harvard University Press, 1985), 38.

16 Başbakanlık Osmanlı Arşivi (BOA) (Prime Ministerial Ottoman Archives), İbnü'l-Emin, Ensāb, no. 658; Karaman Şerʿiye Sicili (ŞS), no. 278:71.

17 For examples of the selection of the deputy of the *naqīb al-ashrāf*, see. H. A. R. Gibb and H. Bowen, *Islamic Society and The West*, 2 pts (London and New York: Oxford University Press, 1965), I:100–102.

18 Harput ŞS, no. 331:169; Karaman ŞS, no. 278:71; Konya ŞS, no. 20:5; no. 25:8; no. 30:3; Antep ŞS, no. 16:3; no. 171:6.

19 Karaman ŞS, no. 278:71; Harput ŞS, no. 384:185; Kayseri ŞS, no. 106:199; no. 31:324.

20 R. Kılıç, "Sayyids and Sharīfs in the Ottoman State: On the Borders of the True and False," *The Muslim World* 96 (2006): 30–31.

21 The question of terminology was discussed in my previous article ("Sayyids and Sharīfs in the Ottoman State"). Here the issue is revisited using new materials that generate new ideas.

22 C. van Arendonk, "Sharīf," in M. Th. Houtsma et al. eds, *Brill's First Encyclopaedia of Islam 1913*–1936, 9 vols (Leiden: Brill, 1987), VII:324–329; C. van Arendonk [W. A. Graham], "Sharīf," in H. A. R. Gibb et al. eds, *The Encyclopaedia of Islam*, new ed., 13 vols (Leiden: Brill, 1960–2009; hereafter *EI2*), IX:329–337 .

23 The definition of *Ahl al-Bayt* is an important issue among Islamic scholars. The Shiʿite view is that the term covers the five members of the *Ahl al-ʿAbā*, namely the daughter of the Prophet, his son-in-law and his two grandsons (Fāṭima, ʿAlī, Ḥasan and Ḥusayn). According to Sunni scholars, it is possible to divide the *Ahl al-Bayt* into two groups. One group would be confined to the wives of the Prophet, while the other would include, besides the wives of the Prophet, the Prophet's grandsons, uncles and their descendants or even all their relatives, namely the Banū Hāshim. See A. Özel, "Âl," in *Türkiye Diyanet Vakfı İslâm Ansiklopedisi (TDVİA)*, vol. 2 (Istanbul: DİVANTAŞ. Diyanet Vakfı Neşriyat Pazarlama ve Ticaret, 1989), 306; S. Uludağ, "Âl-ı Abâ," in *TDVİA*, vol. 2:307; M. Öz, "Ehl-i Beyt," in *TDVİA*, vol. 10 (1994): 499.

24 The name most familiar is that of Ahmed Yesevī, known by the title *Sayyid al-Sādāti'l-Alevī*, whose *sayyid/sharīf* status is based on his connection with Muḥammad b. al-Ḥanafiyya. See Hazinī, *Cevāhiru'l-Ebrar*, MS İstanbul Üniversitesi, Türkçe Yazmalar 3893, 33b, 25a–25b.

25 The first of these registers, NED, no. 1 contains credentials and the second, NED, no. 2 is a summary register. See NED, no. 1:5b, 6a, 7a, 7b; no. 2:16a; no. 4:73a.

26 İ. H. Uzunçarşılı, *Mekke-i Mükerreme Emirleri* (Ankara: Türk Tarih Kurumu, 1972), 6.

27 Harput ŞS, no. 384:185.

28 NED, no. 1:5b; no. 2:26a.

29 Konya ŞS, no. 35:63; Kayseri ŞS, no. 97:1; no. 106:116; Antep ŞS, no. 34:60.

30 For examples, see NED, no. 14:4a; no. 27:17a.

31 NED, no. 1:3b, 4a, 5b, 10b; no. 4:5b, 19b; no. 8:2a; no. 9:3b; no. 10:4b, 6a; no. 12:3a, 6b, 7b; no. 17:4b; no. 20:31b, 33a; no. 23:8b, 9a; no. 26:21b; no. 27:6a, 7a, 7b, 16b, 17a; no. 29:5a; no. 31:5b, 6b; no. 32:2b, 12a, 15a, 17a, 24a.
32 NED, no. 29:4b.
33 NED, no. 5:45b.
34 NED, no. 2:12a–15b, 26a.
35 NED no. 3:1b. Regarding the wearing of the color green, see no. 5:41b, 45b.
36 NED, no. 3:5a, 6a; no. 5:5a, 6a, 27a; no. 8:20b, no. 9:9b; no. 20:28b, 31a, 32a; no. 23:8b; no. 26:21b, 23b.
37 NED, no. 8:26a.
38 NED, no. 5:22a, 26b; no. 8:23b–24a, 28b; no. 9:9a, 15b, 16a, 20a; no. 14:4b, 5a; no. 26:22b; Harput ŞS, no. 386:422.
39 For examples, see BOA Mühimme Defterleri (MD) (Registers of outgoing decrees of Imperial Diwan), no. 1:195; no. 14:25; BOA İbnü'l-Emin, Ensāb, no. 166:22, 318.
40 MD, no. 37:98.
41 BOA Maliyeden Müdevver (MM), no. 1704:1, 2, 4, 6, 8, 9, 10, 14, 16.
42 Antep ŞS, no. 20:241–242. Many of these are the taxes imposed in accordance with the *çift-hane* system. Under this system, the state organized rural society and economy by appropriating grain-producing land and distributing it under the *tapu* system to peasant families (*hane*s). In theory each family in possession of a pair of oxen was given a farm (*çiftlik*) sufficient to sustain the family and meet its tax obligations. This was the basic fiscal unit that the state endeavored to maintain. Families with less than half a *çift* or *çiftlik*, or unmarried peasants, were separately categorized as *bennāk* or *mücerred* and subjected to lower rates of *çift*-tax (H. İnalcık and D. Quataert eds, *An Economic and Social History of the Otoman Empire 1300–1914* [Cambridge: Cambridge University Press, 1994], 996). In addition, those *sipahi*s who came to spend the winter in their *timar*s would collect a *resm* (fee, tax) of six *akçe* known as *duhān* or *tütün resmi* as the fee for "lighting their fireplaces" (M. Kütükoğlu, "The Structure of the Ottoman Economy," in *History of the Ottoman State, Society and Civilization*, 2 vols (Istanbul: IRCICA, 2001), I:580–581).
43 Antep ŞS, no. 8:51.
44 Antep ŞS, no. 42:184.
45 Harput ŞS, no. 386:302.
46 Konya ŞS, no. 35:257.
47 Harput ŞS, no. 331:88–89.
48 H. İnalcık, "Osmanlı Toplum Yapısının Evrimi," *Türkiye Günlüğü* 1990 Yaz:11, 31.
49 "Kanun-nāme-i Cedid," in S. Pulaha and Y. Yücel eds, *I. Selim Kānūnnāmesi (1512–1520) ve XVI. Yüzyılın İkinci Yarısının Kimi Kanunları* (Ankara: Türk Tarih Kurumu, 1988), 43, 45.
50 Bursalı İsmail Beliğ, *Güldeste-i Riyāz-ı İrfān* (Bursa: Hüdavendigar Matbaası, 1302/1884–5), 528, 531; Sehī, *Āsār-ı Eslāfdan Tezkire-i Sehī* (Istanbul: Matbaa-i Amedi, 1325/1907–8), 20, 42, 85, 88; ʿĀşık Çelebi, *Meşāʿir üş-Şuʿarā*, 49b–50b, 182a–183a, 253b; Kınalızade Hasan Çelebi, *Tezkiretü'ş-Şuarā*, ed. by İbrahim Kutluk, 2 vols (Ankara: Türk Tarih Kurumu, 1989), I:186, 515–516, 529, II:589, 748–749, 1057; Müstakimzade Süleyman Saadeddin, *Devhatü'l-Meşāyih* (Istanbul: Çağrı, 1978), 29–30, 74–76, 79–80; Mecdī Mehmed Efendi, *Hadaiku'ş-Şakaik*, ed. by Abdülkadir Özcan as *Şakaik-ı Nuʿmaniye ve Zeyilleri*, vol. 1 (Istanbul: Çağrı, 1989), 342; Atāī, *Hadaik'l-Hakaik*, 126, 161–164, 247, 313, 498–499, 562, 582, 742–743.
51 M. Baudier, *Histoire générale de la religion des Turcs* (Paris: C. Cramoisy, 1625), 206–207; Chalcondyle, *Histoire générale des Turcs*, trans. by B. de Vigenaire, 2 vols (Paris: Augustin Courbé, 1662), II:27.

52 B. Yediyıldız, "Osmanlı Toplumu," in E. İhsanoğlu ed., *Osmanlı Devlet ve Medeniyeti*, vol. 1 (Istanbul: IRCICA, 1994), 486–487.
53 Lütfü Paşa, "Āsāfnāme," in A. Akgündüz ed., *Osmanlı Kanunnāmeleri ve Hukukī Tahlilleri*, vol. 4 (Istanbul: Fey Vakfı Yayınları, 1992), 275; Anonym., "Hırzü'l-Mülûk," in Y. Yücel ed., *Osmanlı Devlet Teşkilātına Dair Kaynaklar* (Ankara: Türk Tarih Kurumu, 1988), 63a; *Kanūn-nāme-i Sultānī li ʿAzīz Efendi*, 38.
54 ʿĀşık Çelebi, *Meşāʿir üş-Şuʿarā*, 182b–183a.
55 Ibid., 50b.
56 Ibid., 49b–50b; Kınalızade Hasan Çelebi, *Tezkiretü'ş-Şuarā*, I:185–186, 515–516; II:1057.

7 The *ashrāf* and the *naqīb al-ashrāf* in Ottoman Egypt and Syria

A comparative analysis

Michael Winter

Introduction

As is well known, the term *sharaf* (lit., honor, nobility) means the descent from the Prophet Muḥammad through the children of his daughter Fāṭima with ʿAlī ibn Abī Ṭālib, the fourth caliph. The descendents of Ḥasan are called *ashrāf*, and those of Ḥusayn are the *sāda*. According to the usage in Ottoman Egypt and Syria, the distinction was usually blurred, although not unknown. Some *waqf* documents from Damascus in the early sixteenth century describe as beneficiaries *ashrāf* who are *Ḥusayniyyūn* (never *Ḥasaniyyūn*). Unfortunately, the sample is too small to draw wider conclusions, but this is noteworthy. A man of such descent was known as a *sharīf*, but he was called personally a *sayyid*: *Sayyid Fulān ibn Sayyid Fulān* (for example, in the biographies and the chronicles). In the tax registers of early Ottoman Damascus that I have studied, where people's names are not mentioned, it is written that a certain man in a certain street or city neighborhood is a *sharīf*. The fact is registered, because as a *sharīf* he enjoyed certain tax exemptions and was entitled to some allowances.[1]

With the Ottoman conquest, Egypt and Syria, which had been united under the Mamluks, became distinct provinces of the Ottoman Empire, whose center was outside these Arabic-speaking countries. Egypt, the largest Ottoman province, was treated by Istanbul differently than the Syrian provinces, owing to its size, economic importance, and its role as the cultural center of the Arabic-speaking lands. The *timar* "feudal" regime, the Ottoman version of the classical *iqṭāʿ*, was applied in Syria, as in most Ottoman provinces, but not in Egypt, for economic and fiscal reasons. In another sphere, the Ottomans granted the Egyptian ʿulama almost a full independence, much more than in Syria.

Bilād-i Shām (the modern Greater Syria) under the Ottomans was a geographic term, not an administrative one. Unlike Egypt, it consisted of separate *vilayet*s (provinces) that were different in character, despite their common Arab character, which they also shared with Egypt. Therefore, Damascus and Aleppo, the principal provincial capitals, and also the smaller provincial towns of Syria, had their own characteristics. This had an impact on the nature of the *ashrāf* community in each town, and the politics of their leadership, represented by the *nuqabā᾽ al-ashrāf*, the chief executive officers. While the *naqīb al-ashrāf* in Cairo was the chief of all *ashrāf* in Egypt to whom all the *nuqabā᾽* of the small towns were subordinate, each of the major Syrian cities and of the smaller towns had a separate independent *naqīb*. All *nuqabā᾽ al-ashrāf*, both in Egypt and Syria, were officially under the control of the *naqīb* of the Empire. It is unclear how effective that control was.

Ottoman Egypt[2]

The origins of the ashrāf *of Egypt*

Many *ashrāf* families settled in Egypt after emigrating from other countries. The historical sources record traditions that these people who claimed *sharīfi* descent came from Arabia, North Africa, or Iraq. In Egypt, whole villages whose inhabitants claimed the title were settled in many parts of the land. Often the founder was believed to have been a mythological *sharīf*. The inhabitants of several villages in Upper Egypt claimed descent from Jaʿfar al-Ṣādiq; they were *ashrāf*, and known collectively as Jaʿāfira.[3]

As is well known, the historical sources about the Mamluk period are arguably the richest in the pre-modern Middle East. Yet the information about our subject is scanty. The *ashrāf* get much more attention during the Ottoman centuries, for reasons that will be discussed below.

Al-Malik al-Ashraf Shaʿbān, a Mamluk Sultan, decreed in the year 773/1371–2 that all the *ashrāf* affix a green badge to their turbans.[4] The custom of wearing a green turban was adopted only toward the end of the sixteenth century.[5] *Ashrāf* who were rich or learned could choose to wear a white turban.

The status of the ashrāf *in Ottoman Egypt before the nineteenth century*

As was the case in other Muslim countries, *ashrāf* in Ottoman Egypt and Syria were respected, and enjoyed social and economic privileges. They were considered in theory as a distinct social class and different from the commoners, *ʿawāmm*.[6] Although many *ashrāf* were poor and uneducated, great numbers of them were ʿulama and Sufis.

For Ottoman Egypt, there are descriptions of *ashrāf* parading in religious and public occasions, sometimes with the *naqīb al-ashrāf* leading them. In a few cases, they marched at the orders of the pasha along other military contingents to suppress a rebellious Mamluk bey. Yet it is obvious that the *ashrāf*'s role was ceremonial and symbolic, not truly military.

On the other hand, *ashrāf* in Ottoman Egypt were willing and capable of organizing and acting in order to protect their honor and interests. There are quite a few reports about violent clashes between *ashrāf* and groups or individuals who harmed them. They fought it out with Bedouins who took their livestock, or insulted them, or quarreled with them. Wounded or killed victims fell on both sides, with resolutions of peace settlements and blood revenge. Typical cases of brawls in Cairo happened as a result of a quarrel on the price of a watermelon between a *sharīf* who had a stand in the marketplace and a soldier, a Mamluk, a member of the Janissaries or other Ottoman regiment. Such an argument could lead to the murder of the unarmed *sharīf*.[7]

The following incident illustrates the tensions between the *ashrāf* of Cairo and the soldiers. In 1124/1712, a *sharīf* named Sayyid Wafā quarreled with a Mamluk who killed him and then escaped. The *ashrāf* put Sayyid Wafā in a coffin and went up to the divan (the council that convened under the pasha to discuss the important matters of state), and proved the murder. They closed down the city's bazaars, stoning the shop owners who did not close quickly enough, and beat anyone whom they met, even emirs. This went on for two days. The *ashrāf* of Cairo summoned *ashrāf* from the neighboring villages and marched toward the Husayni Mosque. Carrying the "Prophet's banner," they headed to the house of Qayṭās Bey, the Treasurer, and fought against his Mamluks. This became too serious, and the emirs decided to send a group of *ashrāf* leaders into exile. Several ʿulama and Sufi shaykhs interceded, and they were pardoned. After the incident, the *ashrāf* considered it prudent to wear white turbans instead of the green ones.[8]

In 1089/1678, the qadi of Jerusalem named ʿAbdullāh Efendi was ordered to go to Egypt to inspect the *ashrāf*, namely, to investigate the allowances that were paid to them. They protested vehemently, claiming that such inspection was unprecedented. They sent a delegation to al-Azhar and obtained a *fatwā* from the chief ʿulama that it was illegal to take their money. The *ashrāf* then went to the divan to protest. Since their demands were not met immediately, they again forced the closing down of the shops and marched toward al-Azhar. They took the Prophet's flag and hoisted it on the minaret of al-Azhar. Finally, the governor (pasha) canceled the inspection, and the qadi escaped.[9]

The Egyptian ashrāf *in the nineteenth century*

The best source about the *ashrāf* (and other aspects of popular religion) in nineteenth century Egypt is the comprehensive topographical encyclopedia of the country by ʿAlī Bāshā Mubārak, the famous administrator and educator.[10] He describes the *ashrāf* as true elite who stayed away from blameworthy customs of the common people. Many of them were ʿulama and Sufi shaykhs. Many *ashrāf* families were prosperous; their income came from *iltizām* tax farms. After Muḥammad ʿAlī abolished the *iltizām* system, many ʿulama and *ashrāf* lost their main income. Mubārak observes that even after losing their wealth, the *ashrāf* were still considered as social elite and lived comfortably, since many of them were appointed to high positions in the service of the state.[11]

In the twentieth century, the *ashrāf*'s economic conditions declined further, but in many places their social status was still respected. This is true mainly in the villages, much less in Cairo.

Naqīb al-ashrāf

The office of *naqīb al-ashrāf* under the Mamluks was not very important, and information about the subject is not abundant. With the Ottoman occupation of 923/1517, Ibn Iyās, the chronicler of the first five years of Ottoman rule in Cairo, reports that the Ottomans appointed a *naqīb* for Cairo, according to their custom.[12] It is noteworthy that Ibn Iyās refers to this appointment as a matter-of-fact, without comment, although his work is full of harsh criticism of the Ottoman regime and its innovations. This suggests that the event did not seem important or harmful. The detailed historical coverage stops at Ibn Iyās's death for almost one century, yet from the information that is available for the rest of the sixteenth century from other literary and archival sources, it seems that the *nuqabāʾ al-ashrāf* had little impact on Egyptian social and religious affairs. Nevertheless, they were considered as respectable religious functionaries, and were present in the meetings of the divan. They controlled with the assistance of their deputies the lists of the *ashrāf* for the authenticity of their claim of descent, and performed the usual functions under the authority of the chief *naqīb al-ashrāf* of the Ottoman Empire in Istanbul.

In theory, the appointment of each *naqīb al-ashrāf* was for one year and could be extended, as was the practice regarding the governor of the province himself, or the chief qadi (*qāḍī al-ʿaskar, kazasker*). In fact, however, the *niqābat al-ashrāf* in Egypt was the monopoly of an Ottoman Anatolian family for almost a century. In the second half of the seventeenth century, Evliyā Çelebi, the famous Ottoman traveler, describes one of the *nuqabāʾ* as a rich and generous man, who controlled numerous *waqf*s and had tax farms, some of which consisted of whole villages. According to Evliyā Çelebi, Burhāneddīn Efendi's origin was the town of Eğri in the Sanjak of Hamid. He died in 1040/1630–1. He was succeeded by his son Mehmed, a graduate from the Süleymaniye in Istanbul.[13] When Ḥasan Efendi, another Ottoman *naqīb*, died in 1121/1709, Aḥmad Shalabī, the chronicler, notes that with him their dynasty came to an end (*bi-mawtihi inqaraḍat dawlatuhum*). A Sufi shaykh was appointed until Istanbul sent another *naqīb*. The new appointee was welcomed by the *ashrāf*, but he was murdered during the next night. Other *naqīb*s were sent from Istanbul, but again, they left little impact.[14]

The change in the position of the *niqāba* took place during the eighteenth century, when the office was transferred to local Egyptian notables. These were the Bakrīs and the Wafāʾīs, two aristocratic Sufi family orders with a history of several centuries in Egypt. The Bakrīs claimed descent from Abū Bakr al-Ṣiddīq, the first caliph, and from Ḥasan ibn ʿAlī. They were rich, educated, and maintained close ties with the Ottoman rulers. They were in charge of the organization of *mawlid al-nabī*, the festival in honor of Prophet Muḥammad.

The house of al-Sādāt al-Wafāʾiyya claimed descent from the Idrīsī royal dynasty of the Maghreb, and like the Bakrīs, they were *ashrāf* of the house of ʿAlī. The Wafāʾīs were a branch of the Shādhiliyya *ṭarīqa*, and came to Egypt from Tunis and Sfaks in the early eighth/fourteenth century. They were famous for their wealth, poets, and gatherings, where Sufis played musical instruments in spite of the displeasure of the orthodox. The head of the Sādāt al-Wafā'iyya acted as a counterbalance to Shaykh al-Bakrī, although the latter enjoyed a higher social and religious status. The Wafā'iyya were responsible for the Ḥusayni *mawlid*. There was rivalry between the two great Sufi houses for the office of *naqīb al-ashrāf.*

It is remarkable that in the second half of the eighteenth century, the *niqābat al-ashrāf* passed to illustrious local Egyptian families; the office had never been connected with Sufism before. Only then, the *niqāba* became influential in Egypt's religious life. That was another expression of the emergence of a conscious Egyptian Islam, as distinct from the Turkish-Ottoman version.[15]

ʿUmar Makram as naqīb al-ashrāf

When *naqīb al-ashrāf* Muḥammad al-Bakrī died heirless in 1208/1793–4 the two Mamluk emirs who were the de facto rulers of Egypt appointed ʿUmar Makram, a native of Asyūṭ in Middle Egypt as the new *naqīb*. They owed him a political debt for having negotiated with the Cairo authorities their return and ultimately their seizure of power. ʿUmar Makram was an unusual candidate for the post, being an outsider without contacts in Cairo. He was neither an *ʿālim* nor a Sufi.

ʿUmar Makram proved himself an independent and courageous man, however. He opposed injustice and oppression regardless of their source. During the French occupation of Egypt, he refused to cooperate with the French, and went into exile to Palestine. The French appointed Khalīl al-Bakrī, who unlike ʿUmar Makram and *Shaykh al-Sādāt* (a shortened title of *Shaykh Sādāt al-Wafā'iyya*), agreed to cooperate with them.

Students of the history of modern Egypt are familiar with the heroic leadership of ʿUmar Makram as the leader of an anti-French rebellion, his crucial contribution to the appointment of Muḥammad ʿAlī as the *vali* (governor) of Egypt, and his leadership in opposing the British in the invasion of 1807. During the political vacuum between the evacuation of the French army and the consolidation of Muḥammad ʿAlī's rule, ʿUmar Makram was a popular and courageous leader. His control of Cairo was complete. Yet without his title as *naqīb al-ashrāf* he could not have attained his power.

When ʿUmar Makram discovered that Muḥammad ʿAlī was a tyrant, he turned against the Pasha. Failing to bribe the *naqīb*, Muḥammad ʿAlī made the chief ʿulama send a petition to Istanbul accusing him of deleting from the lists names of genuine *ashrāf* and entering names of converted Jews and Copts. He was also falsely accused in the petition of inciting against the Ottomans. ʿUmar Makram was dismissed and exiled.

Nuqabā' al-ashrāf*'s lack of leadership*

In the previous section, the demonstrations and riots of the *ashrāf* have been discussed, especially before the nineteenth century. It is important to point out that never were the *nuqabāʾ al-ashrāf* involved in them in any way. This observation applies to the first two centuries of Ottoman rule in Egypt, when the *naqīb* was an Ottoman official, and also to that part of the eighteenth century when *niqābat al-ashrāf* was in the hands of the Bakrīs or the Sādāt al-Wafāʾiyya.

The explanation is simple: The *nuqabāʾ al-ashrāf* were a part of the ruling class and of the religious-bureaucratic establishment. They benefited from their position which was very lucrative. Therefore, they were reluctant to be associated with any violent actions that threatened the public order. They were close to the rulers and were loyal Ottoman subjects. As we have seen, the short incumbency of ʿUmar Makram was different. Yet he did not act for the sake of the *ashrāf*, or any other special interest group, but for the people of Cairo generally. It is noteworthy that there is no evidence that he owed his influence to the *ashrāf*.

Naqīb al-ashrāf *in the modern period*

Under Muḥammad ʿAlī, the post of *naqīb al-ashrāf* became the monopoly of the Bakrīs until the end of the monarchy in Egypt. Shaykh al-Bakrī now held the three positions of the head of the Bakrī order, the head of all the Sufi *ṭarīqa*s in Egypt – a position created by Muḥammad ʿAlī as a part of his centralizing politics – and the *naqīb al-ashrāf*. The *niqāba* became quite meaningless, and the headship of the Sufi *ṭarīqa*s turned to be the important position. This also reflects the decline of the power and influence of the *ashrāf*, a process that was noted by observers as the nineteenth century was coming to an end.

Not surprisingly, there were no demonstrations or other expressions of defiance of *ashrāf* in Egypt in the nineteenth and twentieth centuries. Both the country and the *ashrāf* were totally transformed.

Ottoman Damascus

The information about the *ashrāf* in Ottoman Syria is not as full as one would wish. Nevertheless, Ottoman Syria – particularly Damascus, and to a lesser extent Aleppo – has a rich historical literature. The biographical dictionaries and chronicles for Damascus during the sixteenth century and possibly for the seventeenth century are fuller and more detailed than those in Cairo at the same period. The eighteenth century too is described by important contemporary sources. Since Egypt and Syria were both Sunni and provinces of the same empire, the similarities in both lands concerning our topic are obvious. Yet, there were also significant differences.

Two dynasties of nuqabāʾ al-ashrāf *in Damascus?*

The detailed chronicles and biographical dictionaries of Damascus provide much information about the *nuqabāʾ al-ashrāf*. Although there were more than twenty *ashrāf* clans in the city, apart from a few that came from North Africa, two families virtually dominated all the appointments of *nuqabāʾ al-ashrāf* – Banū Ḥazma and Banū ʿAjlān. The two families' careers extended from the late Mamluk period until the eighteenth century. The ʿAjlān clan emigrated from Egypt, and settled in the large *zāwiya* of the Rifāʿiyya Sufi *ṭarīqa* in the Maydān al-Ḥaṣā quarter.[16] They were associated with that Sufi order. The Ḥamzas' origins are more obscure, but representatives of this family also already held central religious positions in the Mamluk Sultanate.

The ʿAjlānis are praised by the great seventeenth-century historian al-Muḥibbī for their undisputed lineage of *sharaf*, their scholarship, leadership, and the continuity of their service as *nuqabāʾ* in the same family.[17] Almost identical words were written of the Banū Ḥamza.[18] There is no evidence of serious struggles for the *niqāba* between the two clans (of the kind that existed between the Bakrīs and Wafāʾīs in Egypt), nor can we see that any one of the two families controlled the *niqāba* for a long time, excluding the other. All this leads to the assumption that the ʿAjlānis and the Ḥamzas were merging into one clan.[19]

The strongest evidence in support of this assumption that the Ḥamzas and the ʿAjlānis were, or became, one clan is in an obituary by al-Murādī, the author of *Silk al-durar*, the centennial biographical dictionary of twelfth-century Damascus, of ʿAlī b. Ismāʿīl b. Ḥamza al-Ḥusaynī (d. 1183/1769–70). Al-Murādī writes:

> He was the most successful *naqīb al-ashrāf*. He held the office for long periods. No other ʿAjlānī has achieved so much. He was wealthy and powerful, with land, property, *madrasa*s, and a high Ottoman scholarly rank (*rutbat mūṣile-i Süliymāniye*). He was a developer and an expert in agriculture. Like his ancestors, he was known as al-ʿAjlānī al-Dimashqī. In sum, the Banū ʿAjlān have been a clan (*ṭāʾifa*) of *sharaf* and *siyāda* in old times and new.[20]

Awqāf *for* ashrāf

As can be learned from the chronicles and the archival documents, significant numbers of *ashrāf* also lived in villages in the province of Damascus. Many of them had *waqf* and *milk* entitlements.

Waqf documents in the Ottoman archives list *waqf*s founded for the benefit of the Mālikīs in Damascus, under the heading *waqf al-sādāt al-Mālikiyya*. As is well known, Sufis were often called *sāda* as a token of respect, whether or not they were real *ashrāf*. Nearly all the Mālikīs in Damascus were Maghrebis, North Africans. The *waqf*s that are listed were rich, and consisted of a variety of revenue-yielding properties. The significance of these *waqf*s lies in the fact that they were the only ones that are thus singled out. *Waqf*s for Sufis or for *ashrāf* were common. The beneficiaries are not called Maghrebis or Sufis, but identified as Mālikīs. Possibly the founders believed that this was a better way to legalize the rights of the present and future beneficiaries. Clearly, the founders wanted to support the Maghrebis, who were foreigners in Syria.[21]

Social and economic conditions

Many men called *Sayyid* were wealthy. The seventeenth-century chronicler Ibn Kannān tells that some of his friends, who were *ashrāf* with "*Sayyid*" as a part of their names, had spacious houses with nice gardens. They invited him and other friends to spend a pleasant and cultured time with talks, poetry reading, and refreshments and seasonal fruits from their gardens.[22] Many *ashrāf* and *nuqabāʾ al-ashrāf* were ʿulama and served as *madrasa* professors and deputy judges (*nāʾib qāḍī*); the chief qadiship in all the Ottoman towns was invariably reserved for a Turkish-speaking Ḥanafī jurist graduate of the top *medreses* of the Ottoman Empire. Typically, the *naqīb al-ashrāf* of Damascus was a *sharīf* who was a respectable *ʿālim*. Some had a reputation as educated men who wrote poetry. Many of those who were appointed as *naqīb al-ashrāf* were employed at some point in the local court system. In the year 1025/1616, when a delegation went to plead with a pasha in Aleppo to reduce the levy for a military campaign that was imposed on the people of Damascus, it included several distinguished ʿulama and Sufis, among them Muḥammad b. ʿAjlān, the *naqīb al-ashrāf*.[23] Despite the high status of *nuqabāʾ*, they did not attain the same social and political position as the Bakrīs and the Wafāʾīs in Cairo.

The *naqīb al-ashrāf* also had ceremonial functions. A deposed *sharīf* from Mecca was welcomed by the governor of Damascus. He was honored by a procession of the local *ashrāf* led by their *naqīb*.[24] The occasions for ceremonies in which the Damascene *ashrāf* participated were much fewer than the case in Egypt. Evliyā Çelebi provides many examples.[25]

The *naqīb al-ashrāf* was one of the outstanding notables, although he was considerably less powerful than the chief qadi. Usually, the *nuqabāʾ* were respected, but examples of maltreatment by military commanders also occurred. In Damascus, rough behavior of a *defterdār* (an officer responsible for the finances of a province) toward a *naqīb* is reported. A former *naqīb al-ashrāf* in early Ottoman Damascus was arrested in the Citadel for financial reasons.[26]

Shaykh mashāʾikh al-ḥiraf wa-l-ṣanāʾiʿ

Several *nuqabāʾ al-ashrāf* or members of their family held the title *shaykh mashāʾikh al-ḥiraf wa-l-ṣanāʾiʿ*, "the head of the trades and crafts." The chroniclers explain that the functions of the incumbent were controlling the guilds (*ḥiraf*) in the city, and administering the initiation ceremonies (*ʿaqd* oath, and *shadd*, fastening the girdle around the body of the artisan when he becomes a master in the guild).[27] The chronicler explains that, in the past, the office was called *sulṭān al-ḥarāfīsh* ("the sultan of the ruffians"), but for the sake of politeness, a more respectable term was chosen. The acting *naqīb al-ashrāf* did not simultaneously hold that post. Al-Muḥibbī wrote the biography of Sayyid Muḥammad b. Muḥammad Kamāl al-Dīn b. ʿAjlān (d. 1004/1596).[28] He was the father of a *naqīb al-ashrāf*, but he was not one. Unlike most of the *nuqabāʾ*, he was not an *ʿālim*, but made a living by silk weaving. He was a Sufi of the Rifāʿiyya *ṭarīqa*. He conducted the *dhikr* ritual in his *zāwiya*. As a manual worker himself, a *sharīf*, but definitely not an *ʿālim*, and a practicing Sufi with a reputation of saintliness, he was perfectly suited for the position of *shaykh mashāʾikh al-ḥiraf*. A learned and aristocratic *naqīb al-ashrāf* would have regarded the post as beneath his dignity.

A sharīf*'s career*

Naturally, the *ashrāf*'s career in Ottoman Damascus varied from one individual to another; nevertheless, a typical career strategy can be discerned.

First, the membership in a prestigious family of *ashrāf* whose *sharaf* credentials were without blemish was the basis. The Banū ʿAjlān and Banū Ḥamza were such a family, and they produced several outstanding *nuqabāʾ* throughout the Ottoman period. The family's support was of utmost value; naturally, power struggles for the post occurred within the family.

The channel for progress was *ʿilm*, religious learning. The usual long-term strategy was studying in Damascus, where aspirants could find locally several serious shaykhs who taught them the various religious disciplines. Several students went to Cairo to extend their studies and connections. The great city offered illustrious teachers who gave the ambitious students *ijāza*s, written personal permits to teach to students what they had taught him, or even to issue *fatwā*s. As usual in the Muslim scholarly tradition, these certificates were personal, and were not issued formally by a *madrasa*. The student returned to his native Damascus, to teach or to hold a certain post. After a while, he would go to study in Rūm, the Turkish central parts of the Ottoman Empire, almost always to the Ottoman capital. By then, he was already an accomplished *ʿālim*, and his mastery in Arabic was certain to impress his Turkish-speaking peers, and thus his success was assured.

The Arabic term for such training in the capital was "he took the path of the Turks" (*salaka ṭarīq al-mawālī* [the high-ranking Ottoman ʿulama] or *al-Arwām* [the Turks]), and similar expressions, expressing that it was "their" (non-Arabs') path that was taken. The Arabic sources report that many ʿulama from Syria took the scholarly training program of the *Arwām* in Istanbul or, less frequently, in another major city. Another common strategy was choosing a famous *ʿālim* in the Ottoman capital as their scholarly and religious mentor (the term is called *mulāzama*, namely, close adherence). The verb is "*lāzama min Shaykh Fulān*" (he became a close disciple of Shaykh x). In some cases, the mentor was no less than *Şeyhülislām*, the Grand Mufti, the highest-ranking man of religion in the Ottoman Empire. Also, the chief *naqīb al-ashrāf* of the Empire was a good option. Naturally, the disciples from Syria tried to establish good relations with their patrons and to flatter them.

Some Syrians stayed in Istanbul for a long period, but almost all of them had come with the intent of returning home. They used their stay in the capital in order to gain the favor of influential people there so that they would be able to return provided with appointments to desired positions, beginning with the office of *naqīb al-ashrāf* itself, and/or additional positions in the judicial and educational systems of their native town, as deputy qadis, or another office in that system, or as an administrator (*nāẓir*), or a professor of a *madrasa*.

The new appointee was often awarded an Ottoman educational degree, *dākhil* or *khārij*, which was routine in the Ottoman elaborate system of the time, but unknown in Arab Muslim education outside the Ottoman center. Some were given an honorary degree as judges in a certain town. This custom was spreading in Ottoman Syria under Ottoman influence during the seventeenth century.[29] This trend did not extend to Egypt, partly because of the Ottomans' policy of minimal interference in the independence of the Egyptian ʿulama.

Finally, it was natural that non-*sharīfi* Damascene ʿulama used the same tactics as the *ashrāf* in order to achieve their objectives. The *ashrāf* had the advantage of their status as descendants of the Prophet. Also, they were usually wealthier than most of the other ʿulama, and their transition to Istanbul was easier.

It is worth noting again that during the first two centuries of Ottoman rule, much of the above did not apply to Egypt, since the *nuqabāʾ al- ashrāf* in Egypt were not local *ashrāf*, but appointees from Istanbul.

Three examples

The *ashrāf* learned at an early stage how to take advantage of their connections in Istanbul. In the year 939/1533, Sayyid ʿAlī b. Muḥammad Kamāl al-Dīn b. Ḥamza returned from Rūm after being appointed as *naqīb* (*amīr*) *al-ashrāf* replacing Sayyid Tāj al-Dīn al-Ṣaltī, who had been the *naqīb* already in 922/1516. Ibn Ḥamza was also appointed as the administrator of the important Shāmmiyya Juwwāniyya Madrasa instead of the incumbent. His brother, who returned from Istanbul with him, was awarded the professorship of that *madrasa*, removing a Turkish teacher.[30]

Sayyid Muḥammad b. ʿAlī b. Ḥamza serves as an example of a talented *ʿālim* who was greedy and corrupt. After studying in Cairo, he returned to Damascus and was a successful teacher. Then he traveled to Istanbul and took the path of the *Arwām*. He became the *mülāzim* (close disciple) of *Şeyhülislām* Yaḥyā b. Zakariyyā, whom he praised in rhyme and flowery prose. He received a teaching position in Damascus, with the Ottoman scholarly rank of *dākhil*. He took away positions of other people. He was known to receive appointments for posts that he did not fulfill. Such behavior made people dislike him, and he died a lonely man (1082/1671).[31]

Sayyid Muḥammad b. Ḥasan, called Ibn ʿAjlān (d. 1096/1684), was appointed *naqīb al-ashrāf* and then dismissed, so he traveled to Istanbul. He received the Salīmiyya Madrasa (the one founded by Sultan Selim I after the conquest of Damascus). He returned, and when the previous *naqīb* died, he got the post. He was dismissed and reappointed several times, until he became firmly established. He also became a deputy qadi, and the qadi for matters of inheritances. He had the reputation of a man of learning and owned a large library. He was an expert in *tafsīr* (Qur'ān exegesis) which he taught at the Salīmiyya. He also taught hadith at home.[32] It is remarkable that these two subjects were the most popular, and also easier than *fiqh*, jurisprudence.

Foreign charismatic ashrāf

There were *ashrāf* in Damascus who were not a part of the local community, but by their charisma played a role in the religious life. Sayyid Muḥammad b. Sulaymān al-Maysūnī (d. 1062/1651) was born in Egypt and settled in Misrabā, one of the Ghawṭa villages near Damascus. He was a saintly Sufi, and people came to him, some barefoot, for blessing.[33]

ʿAlī b. Maymūn al-Fāsī was much more famous. He came to Syria toward the end of the Mamluk period. He was a highly charismatic Sufi shaykh, and his impact on Sufism in Syria was very strong. He arrived in Syria from his native Morocco after completing the hajj. Apart from a short stay in Anatolia, he spent his last years in Syria. He propagated his orthodox Shādhiliyya way, and created a network of Syrian disciples, some of whom were very impressive figures, who continued his heritage. In addition to ʿAlī b. Maymūn's personality and scholarship, his *sharīfi* status was always heralded and contributed to his fame.[34]

Kapı kulları *and some emirs against the* ashrāf

In the eighteenth century, with the strengthening of the military forces in Damascus, especially the *kapı kulları* (called locally *kabikul*) or the sultan's military slaves,[35] and the weakening of the central Ottoman government, public security deteriorated. Among the victims were the *ashrāf*, whom the soldiers envied for being more prosperous and more respected than them. The contemporary chronicles of Aḥmad al-Budayrī al-Ḥallāq and Ibn Kannān provide important information about violent and frequent clashes between the two groups.

Similarly to what often happened in Cairo, many confrontations started because soldiers murdered or insulted *ashrāf*. The Ottoman authorities in Damascus were afraid of the soldiers. If a soldier was punished for his crime, the *kabikul*'s reaction was violent. A fine that was imposed on them was not collected. Budayrī writes that an imperial edict was issued to drive them out of the city, but the governor thought that he could not do without them.[36]

The *ashrāf* of Damascus participated with others in violent demonstrations against taxes of all kinds, regular and irregular (*avarız*) in times of economic crises. Like their Egyptian counterparts, they too fought against armed militias and gangs that insulted or harassed them. The *ashrāf* suffered more casualties than those of Cairo. Their enemies were more violent, and they terrorized the local Ottoman authorities that did very little to help them. Al-Budayrī reports that after bloody attacks of the Janissaries against the *ashrāf*, the governor ordered an investigation, but people were afraid to testify. He reports about several clashes in which soldiers killed *ashrāf*, usually with impunity.[37] Public safety was worse in Damascus than it was in Cairo, not always a quiet place. The rulers of Cairo were more responsible and more capable of controlling soldiers' violence than the Ottoman representatives in Damascus.

In the year 1143/1730, a serious confrontation happened after an influential *sharīf* was killed by the soldiers for helping to bring to justice a leader of a town quarter who was executed by the court for robbery and extortion. The *kabikul*, who supported the condemned man, went on a rampage of killing and wounding *ashrāf*, and also looting in the town. They broke the *ashrāf*'s banner. When the *ashrāf* came to their *naqīb* to complain, he panicked and shouted that he was resigning. This reaction is a reminder of the lack of involvement of *nuqabāʾ al-ashrāf* of Cairo at the same time. The *ashrāf* turned to the chief qadi for justice, but again to no avail.[38]

The rulers showed no pity for *ashrāf* of low social status. In the poor and unruly quarters, several *zuʿar* (roughnecks), who assumed *sharīfi* descent were executed or severely punished by the governors. The harsh treatment of the rulers toward *ashrāf* of the poor neighborhoods is already reported in the late Mamluk period. In the year 903/1497, the Mamluk governor ordered a hand of the leader of the *zuʿar*, a *sharīf* named Quraysh (not an unusual name among the *zuʿar*) to be cut off, for a conspiracy with the local infantry. The same year, another *azʿar* was executed for murder. In 908/1502, a *sharīf azʿar* from the unruly al-Shāghūr quarter was beheaded.[39]

Ibn Kannān bemoans that in 1135/1723 the ruling pasha plundered obedient villages whose inhabitants were *ashrāf* with marks of their status.[40]

The rebellion of *naqīb al-ashrāf* of Jerusalem[41]

The Wafāʾī Ḥusaynī family of Jerusalem was an extremely successful clan of *ashrāf*. They held high positions, including the *niqābat al-ashrāf*, in Jerusalem and elsewhere during the two centuries since the Ottoman occupation of Syria in 1516. They were ʿulama and Sufis. They were in control of *awqāf* and private landed properties. They bolstered their position by marriage arrangements, economic activities, and involvement in politics. One member of the family even served as the *naqīb al-ashrāf* of Egypt in the early seventeenth century. Muḥammad b. Muṣṭafā al-Wafāʾī al-Ḥusaynī, the *naqīb al-ashrāf* at the beginning of the eighteenth century, was a very strong leader. In 1700, he successfully led the local ʿulama and notables against the Ottoman government's decision to allow a French consul to establish his presence in Jerusalem.

The city was going through hard times. A combination of serious drought, Bedouin attacks on hajj caravans, and the Ottoman policy of suppression and economic exploitation pushed the notables to rebel against the harsh policies and military actions that were hurting the interests of Jerusalem notables, such as the mufti. In May 1703, the *naqīb* was elected by the ʿulama and the notables as the head of the city, in charge over all the city quarters. The Ottoman representative was forced to leave with the troops that were not local. Jerusalem made preparations to resist military attacks and siege, and the city gates were closed. The mighty city wall and the sanctity of the *Ḥaram* deterred the Ottomans from using cannons.

The unity did not last. Many people, especially soldiers, could not do without the government salaries. The pilgrims were unable to get to the city, with subsequent loss of revenue. There developed a struggle between the supporters and the opponents of the rebellion. The qadi assumed power, and the Ottoman army occupied the city at the end of 1705. The *naqīb al-ashrāf* escaped, but was captured, sent to Istanbul, and put to death in 1707. The Wafāʾī family lost its property and its influence, and the Ghadiyya, another *sharīfi* family, attained the *niqābat al-ashrāf* and the position of the mufti. As is well known, the representatives of that family retained power in Jerusalem and parts of Palestine until the mid-twentieth century. In time, this family assumed the name of the fallen Ḥusaynīs, a matter that has caused confusion and arguments among modern historians.

The leadership of the rebellious *naqīb al-ashrāf* was based on his family's resources and his personality. Again, as in the case of ʿUmar Makram, his religious title was vital, but there is no evidence that Jerusalem's *ashrāf* played any special role in the events. As far as we know, he owed little to the *ashrāf* community.

Finally, the rebellion was a courageous move, but not a wise one. As often happened in the Ottoman Empire, Istanbul was preoccupied with a domestic crisis, so the desperate people of Jerusalem and their leader were under the illusion that the Ottoman government was too far away, too weak, or not determined to reassert its control of Jerusalem.

Ottoman Aleppo[42]

The special case of the ashrāf *of Aleppo*

The history of the *ashrāf* of Aleppo is unique among the Ottoman Arab cities. Nowhere else were the *ashrāf* so well organized, prosperous, and capable militarily. They were a few thousands strong. Many were not genuine *ashrāf*, but Aleppo's residents bought the titles for their considerable social and economic benefits. This was also observed in other cities, but not to such an extent. As elsewhere, it was the responsibility of the local *naqīb al-ashrāf* to check the genealogy of new applicants. Yet the *nuqabāʾ al-ashrāf* of Aleppo were successfully turning the *ashrāf* into a powerful economic, social, and military counterpart to the local Janissaries, and these considerations were the most important. So they built the *ashrāf* community as a strong militia with the purpose of exploiting the city's resources, in controlling land, houses, and taking part in the food and textile industry of Aleppo. This necessitated the creation of clienteles and powerful households.

The questionable lineage of many *ashrāf* notwithstanding, the respect owed to them by society was widespread. Bodman points out that *ashrāf* often used this to force members of the large and prosperous Christian community of Aleppo to pay fines (*avania*s) for real or assumed insults of the Prophet's descendents. Jealousy of the local minorities seems to have played into the hands of some *ashrāf*. Bodman notes that the records are full of incidents of *ashrāf* inciting the Muslim population against the minorities on the basis of disrespect toward a *sharīf*. While these records bring the minority point of view, the numbers and the manner in which they were reported leave an impression of *ashrāf* vindictiveness. In many, if not most cases there was an additional motive: the probability that an *avania* would be successfully exacted for the real or imagined injury.[43]

Another, more serious, cause of tension was the constant rivalry between the *ashrāf* and the large contingent of the Janissaries. Unlike Damascus, the city did not get *kapı kulları* troops from the Ottoman center, and the local Janissaries were less formidable. Nevertheless, they too were armed and organized, and bound together by common interests. They competed with the *ashrāf* for the same revenues, sometimes creating agreements with them (for example, against oppressive governors). More often, the two groups fought it out in pitched battles in the streets. In such clashes, the Janissaries finally had the upper hand.

***The struggles over the* niqābat al-ashrāf**

The struggles over the post of *naqīb al-ashrāf* in Aleppo were much fiercer than in Damascus or Cairo. The stakes were higher, and the various forces that were involved in the politics of the *ashrāf* and their *naqīb* were more determined to control the post, since the *ashrāf* of Aleppo were more militant than their counterparts in Damascus. Another important factor that protected the *nuqabā᾽ al-ashārf* of Damascus was the presence of the well-established and venerated *ashrāf* families there, who had a virtual monopoly on the *niqāba* throughout the Ottoman period.

In the late Mamluk period, in 904/1498, Ibn Jānbulāt, the governor of Aleppo at that period, was already humiliating the *naqīb al-ashrāf* of that town and ordering them to be beaten with whips. It was said that the *naqīb* died of this torture.[44]

The case of Sayyid Ḥusayn b. Muḥammad al-Bīmāristānī, who was murdered in 1013/1604–5 by order of the pasha, can serve as an example to the situation in Aleppo. Sayyid Ḥusayn was appointed to the *niqāba* of Aleppo after his father's death. He was challenged by another *sharīf* who had held the *niqāba* before Ḥusayn's father. However, Ḥusayn bribed the governor and got the post. He became rich by trade and money lending. He also drew an income from the budget of Aleppo. The biographer points out that unlike other *nuqabā'*, he did not take money from the *ashrāf* and did not confiscate their property. On the contrary, he gave them the revenues of villages that were under his jurisdiction, and helped them with their problems. Khudāverdi from the military force of Damascus controlled Aleppo and its countryside. Sayyid Ḥusayn tried to create an alliance with him by giving his daughter in marriage to Kudāverdi's son. Naṣūḥ Pasha, the new governor, wanted to settle accounts with the Damascene army. Ḥusayn flattered the new pasha too. Ḥusayn's brother hated him, and spread bad rumours about his brother, accusing him of drinking wine and wearing Christians' clothes. Even worse, he lied to Naṣūḥ Pasha that his brother rejoiced in the pasha's defeat in a battle against Emir Jānbulāt. Naṣūḥ Pasha heard the noise of a party and singing and music from Ḥusayn's house at night. He believed that *naqīb al-ashrāf* was celebrating his defeat. So he had Ḥusayn arrested, and secretly strangled. His body was thrown into a ditch and his property confiscated.[45]

Sayyid ʿAbdullāh al-Ḥijāzī Abū al-Fayḍ, also known as "Ibn Qaḍīb al-Bān," was a very gifted man. He was a Ḥanafī, a poet, and a man of letters. He could write official letters (*inshā'*) "in the three languages" (Arabic, Persian, and Turkish). He studied under the mufti of Aleppo and other local ʿulama. He taught in a *madrasa* in his town. Then he was appointed as *naqīb al-ashrāf*, and received the honorary rank of the qadi of Diyār Bakr. Grand Vizier Köprülü Fazıl Ahmet Pasha learned about his talents, invited him, and made him his boon companion. Because of palace intrigues, the vizier banished him to Diyār Bakr as a qadi. He was a poor administrator, and allowed a corrupt deputy to do the sentencing. He was dismissed, and lived in Istanbul in obscurity for five years. Afterwards, he approached the sultan and the grand vizier in Edirne and was pardoned. He returned to Aleppo and was given the task of inspection (*taftīsh*) of the *ashrāf* in Aleppo, activity that made him unpopular. His ambition was to carry out an investigation of *ashrāf*'s finances in all the Arab lands. He arrived in Egypt under the title of the qadi of Jerusalem, but was not permitted to fulfill this task, and had to escape. Upon going back to Aleppo, he returned to teaching and gained respect. Yet after a while he became involved in illegal activities, concerning manipulations of the price of wheat, which he and the qadi of Aleppo kept high. He was suspected of poisoning an official, and was lynched (1096/1685).[46]

The ashrāf *in the eighteenth century*

By the eighteenth century, the *ashrāf* of Aleppo had a very impressive and effective leadership, unlike the *nuqabā' al-ashrāf* in other Arab cities. The leading family was the Ṭahazādes, a Ḥanafī family of ʿulama who had dominated the posts of *naqīb al-ashrāf*, and sometimes the qadi, since the late seventeenth century. They were well connected in Istanbul and in their own city, and invested in food and textile production, as well as in urban and rural real estate. Their eponymous founder, Aḥmad Efendi Ṭahazāde, had served as *naqīb al-ashrāf* during the late 1730s and the early 1740s and was prosperous enough to found his own *madrasa*, the Aḥmadiyya. Aḥmad Efendi Ṭahazāde's son Muḥammad, known as Çelebizāde Efendi, served as the *naqīb al-ashrāf* for roughly twenty-five years, 1747–1767 and 1782–1786, becoming the "master of Aleppo" in the words of the French consul.

The next leader of the *ashrāf* (although not a *naqīb*; he was probably not a *sharīf* himself) was Ibrāhīm Qaṭar-Aghası (the leader of the hajj caravan of his town). When Bonaparte invaded Syria, the *ashrāf* of Aleppo came to the defense, separately from the Janissaries. As a reward, Ibrāhīm was appointed governor of the town. Later, he was appointed governor of Damascus, leaving his son in charge of Aleppo.

The struggles between the *ashrāf* and the Janissaries for the control of Aleppo's resources went on, however. It came to an end after the *ashrāf* were finally defeated by the Janissaries in 1805, and later, in 1813, when a determined Ottoman pasha massacred the leaders of the Janissaries and re-established direct Ottoman hold on the province.[47]

Concluding remarks

The assertiveness of the *ashrāf* under Ottoman rule was more intensive than it had been before or after that period. It is certain that the reason lies in the conditions created by Ottoman rule. As we have seen, the *ashrāf* defended themselves, or reacted to acts of injustice and aggression committed against them by Ottoman soldiers, Janissaries, or other units. There were *ashrāf* who belonged to the elite, and were men of means and culture. But many were common people, small traders, or villagers. Yet all shared the pride of being the Prophet's descendents, and were sensitive to their pedigree and status. The ethnic factor was important in creating tensions between the *ashrāf* and the soldiers. This was particularly true when the groups competed for the same sources of revenue, as proven in Aleppo.

A word of warning is in order. The ethnic tension was not political; nationalism appeared only centuries later. Even the rebellion of the *naqīb al-ashrāf* of Jerusalem was not an anti-Ottoman move. It was quite possible, even common, to be an Arabic-speaking Muslim in Egypt or Syria, loyal to the Ottoman sultan, and at the same time to hate the Janissaries, the Ottoman governor, or the qadi.

This kind of "sharīfism" was only one expression of the cultural identity of Arab Muslims against the Ottoman Turkish version of Islam. Another example is the strengthening of the Sufi *ṭarīqa*s, especially in Ottoman Egypt. While the Sufis were even less political than the *ashrāf*, they expressed their attitudes in their meek way, without open anti-Ottoman words or deeds. Their reservations about Turkish Sufism were shown by their rejection of the monistic doctrines of Ibn al-ʿArabī, whose ideas were officially adopted by the Ottoman highest religious authorities, and supported by Kanunī Sultan Süleyman himself. Also, the chief Turkish *ṭarīqa*s of the Bekṭāshiyya and the Mevleviyya did not attract Arab Sufis, since they seemed too heterodox. The Persian cultural component in Turkish Sufism was another factor for the Arab rejection of this kind of mysticism.

Notes

1 The following are samples of the listings of unnamed *sāda/ashrāf* found in the tax registers from early Ottoman Damascus: (1) *Waqf al-sāda al-ashrāf al-Ḥusayniyyīn* in Damascus. It includes 24 pieces of property in the villages of the Ghawṭa of Damascus. This *waqf* was founded in 573/1177–8, but was still active in early Ottoman Damascus. *Tapu Defteri*, no. 393:149 (early Ottoman Damascus; *Başbakanlık Arşivi*, Istanbul). Another *waqf* for *sāda/ashrāf*. Ibid., 149. A *waqf* founded by a family of *sāda/ashrāf* in 695/1295–6. Ibid., 160. (2) *Waqf* for *sāda/ashrāf*, including land, houses and water mills. *Tapu Tahrir Defterleri*, no. 127:116 (early Ottoman Damascus; *Başbakanlık Arşivi*, Istanbul). (3) Family *waqf*, founded in 903/1497–8, providing for Ḥusaynī *sādāt/ashrāf* "wherever they may be" after the family dies out. *Tapu Defteri*, no. 393:86 (*Başbakanlık Arşivi*, Istanbul). (4) *Milk* and *waqf* of *sāda/ashrāf*, plantations. *Maliyeden Müdevver*, no. 247:13 (early Ottoman Damascus; *Başbakanlık Arşivi*, Istanbul). (5) Register of tax payers in a Damascus city quarter. Lists of unnamed *sāda/ ashrāf*. *Tapu Defteri*, no. 263:51, 71 (early Ottoman Damascus; *Başbakanlık Arşivi*, Istanbul). Also, ibid., 71, 112, 119. A neighborhood of unnamed people employed in manual works. Some are listed as *ashrāf* and *sāda*. (6) All the revenues of ʿAlwāna, a small village in the Marj, are *waqf* for *sāda/ashrāf*. *Tapu Defteri*, no. 263:499 (early Ottoman Damascus; *Başbakanlık Arşivi*, Istanbul). (7) Family *awqāf* made by *ashrāf*, after the family dies out (*baʿd al-inqirāḍ*), the revenues will provide for poor *ashrāf*. One *waqf* specifies Ḥusaynī *ashrāf*. *Tapu Defteri*, no 393:160 (*Başbakanlık Arşivi*, Istanbul). The *waqf* was founded in 695/1296 and registered in the *sicill* (court register) in 864/1460–1. The *waqf* was active in early Ottoman Damascus. Another *waqf* founded by a family of *ashrāf* as a family *waqf* in 920/1514 stipulates that after the family dies out, the revenues were to go to poor *ashrāf*.

2 Some of the information in this section is taken from my book: Michael Winter, *Egyptian Society under Ottoman Rule, 1517–1798* (London and New York: Routledge, 1992), 185–198, and bibliographical notes, 281–286; as well as fromWinter, "The *Ashrāf* and *Niqābat al-ashrāf* in Egypt and Ottoman Times," *Asian and African Studies* 19 (1985): 17–41.

3 Also in Palestine, some villages were named after the root *sh-r-f*, such as Shurafā, Shurafāt, and the like. See, Taufik Canaan, *Mohammedan Saints and Sanctuaries in Palestine* (London: Luzac, 1927), 306–308.

4 Jalāl al-Dīn al-Suyūṭī, *al-Ḥāwī li-l-fatāwī*, 2 vols (Beirut: Dār al-Kutub al-ʿIlmiyya, 1402/1982), II:83.

5 C. van Arendonk [W. A. Graham], "Sharīf," in H. A. R. Gibb et al. eds, *The Encyclopaedia of Islam*, new ed., 13 vols (Leiden: Brill, 1960–2009; hereafter *EI2*), IX:329–337.

6 The *ashrāf*'s honor must be respected. Even when a *sharīf* is incarcerated, he must be kept in a separate prison. See, Herbert L. Bodman, Jr., *Political Factions in Aleppo, 1760–1826* (Chapel Hill, NC: University of North Carolina Press, 1963), 92ff., citing Mouradgea d'Ohsson, *Tableau général de l'empire othoman* (1788). That source follows Ibrāhīm al-Ḥalabī, who died in 956/1549 in Istanbul where he lived more than fifty years. Al-Ḥalabī is the author of *Multaqā al-abḥur*, the manual of Ḥanafī law of the Ottoman Empire.

7 In such a case, which took place in 1112/1700, the murderer who belonged to the ʿAzab regiment was sentenced to death by the pasha. The rabble of Cairo and several *ashrāf* lynched him. Ḥallāq, Muḥammad ibn Yūsuf, *Tarih-i Misir-i Kahire*, MS Istanbul University Library, T. Y. 628, 243b–244a.

8 Aḥmad Shalabī (Çelebi) ibn ʿAbd al-Ghanī, *Awḍaḥ al-ishārāt fī-man tawallā Miṣr wa-l-Qāhira min al-wuzarāʾ wa-l-bāshāt al-mulaqqab bi-taʾrīkh al-ʿAynī*, ed. by ʿAbd al-Raḥīm ʿAbd al-Raḥmān ʿAbd al-Raḥīm (Cairo: Maktabat al-Khānjī, 1978), 256–257.

9 ʿAbdülkerīm ibn ʿAbdurrahmān, *Tevārīh-i Misir-i Kahire*, MS the Süleymaniye Library, Istanbul, Hacci Maḥmut Efendi 4877, 112b–113a. This qadi, named Sayyid ʿAbdullāh al-Ḥijāzī Abū al-Fayḍ, was for a while the *naqīb al-ashrāf* of Aleppo. On his life and violent death, see below the section about the *ashrāf* of Aleppo.

10 ʿAlī Bāshā Mubārak, *al-Khiṭaṭ al-Tawfīqiyya al-jadīda*, 20 vols in 5 (Bulaq: al-Maṭbaʿa al-Kubrā al-Amīriyya, 1305–1306/1887–1889). See Gabriel Baer, "Appendix: ʿAlī Mubārak's *Khiṭaṭ* as a Source for the History of Modern Egypt," in idem, *Studies in the Social History of Modern Egypt* (Chicago and London: University of Chicago Press, 1969), 230–246.

11 Mubārak, *Khiṭaṭ*, IX:78.

12 Muḥammad ibn Aḥmad ibn Iyās, *Badāʾiʿ al-zuhūr fī waqāʾiʿ al-duhūr*, ed. by Muḥammad Muṣṭafā, 5 vols, 2nd ed. (Cairo: al-Hayʾa al-Miṣriyya al-ʿĀmma li-l-Kitāb, 1402–1404/1982–1984), V:302.

13 Evliyā Çelebi provides information about the Ottoman *naqīb al-ashrāf* of Egypt. See *Evliyâ Çelebi Seyahatnâmesi*, vol. 10, ed. by Seyit Ali Kahraman, Yücel Dağlı and Robert Dankoff (Istanbul: Yapı Kredi Yayınları, 2007), 92, 180, 281, 386, 398, 407.

14 Aḥmad Shalabī, *Awḍaḥ al-ishārāt*, 226–228.

15 It should be noted that in the sphere of Islamic scholarship, the office of *Shaykh al-Azhar*, sometimes translated as the rector of al-Azhar, was created no earlier than the late seventeenth century. This was another expression of independent Egyptian Islam at that time.

16 Muḥammad Amīn al-Muḥibbī, *Khulāṣat al-athar fī aʿyān al-qarn al-ḥādī ʿashar*, ed. by Muḥammad Ḥasan Ismāʿīl, 4 vols (Beirut: Dār al-Kutub al-ʿIlmiyya, 1427/2006), III:421.

17 For al-Muḥibbī's praise of Banū ʿAjlān, see ibid.

18 Al-Muḥibbī, *Khulāṣat al-athar*, II:104.

19 Ibn Kannān mentions that in 1140/1728 a certain Sayyid Ḥamza al-ʿAjlānī was the *naqīb* over the *ashrāf* of Damascus. Muḥammad ibn Kannān, *Yawmiyyāt Shāmiyya min 1111 h ḥattā 1153 h–1699 ḥattā 1740 m (Ṣafaḥāt nādira min taʾrīkh Dimashq fī al-ʿaṣr al-ʿUthmānī)*, ed. by Akram Ḥasan al-ʿUlabī (Damascus: Dār al-Ṭabbāʿ li-l-Ṭibāʿa wa-l-Nashr wa-l-Tawzīʿ, 1414/1994), 388.

20 See Muḥammad Khalīl al-Murādī, *Silk al-durar fī aʿyān al-qarn al-thānī ʿashar*, ed. by Muḥammad ʿAbd al-Qādir Shāhīn (Beirut: Dār al-Kutub al-ʿIlmiyya, 1418/1997), 199–201. I am planning to research further the subject of the two clans separately.

21 See the following for the *awqāf* for the *sādāt al-Mālikiyya* in the sixteenth century (some were established earlier). *Tapu Defteri*, no. 393:167; no. 127:56–57, 156–157; no. 263:137 (early Ottoman Damascus; *Başbakanlık Arşivi*, Istanbul). The properties of these *awqāf* were considerably rich, with land, houses, gardens, and water mills, consisting of up to fifty units each. Some of the orchards were known as belonging to Maghrebis. Most of the *awqāf* were located in the city of Damascus itself and in the nearby fertile Ghawṭa villages.

22 Ibn Kannān, *Yawmiyyāt*, 305, 389, 396, 427.

23 Najm al-Dīn al-Ghazzī, *Luṭf al-samar wa-qaṭf al-thamar min tarājim aʿyān al-ṭabaqa al-ūlā min al-qarn al-ḥādī ʿashar*, ed. by Maḥmūd al-Shaykh, 2 vols (Damascus: Wizārat al-Thaqāfa wa-l-Irshād al-Qawmī, 1981–1982), I:129–130.
24 Al-Muḥibbī, *Khulāṣat al-athar*, I:221.
25 Evliyâ Çelebi, *Evliyâ Çelebi Seyahatnâmesi*, 132, 157, 161, 180, 386, 395, 398.
26 Shams al-Dīn ibn Ṭūlūn, *Ḥawādith Dimashq al-yawmiyya ghadāt al-ghazw al-ʿUthmānī li-l-Shām, 925–951*, ed. by Aḥmad Ibīsh (Damscus: Dār al-Awāʾil, 2002), 180, 232–233.
27 A. Raymond, "Shadd," in *EI2*, IX:166–169.
28 Al-Muḥibbī, *Khulāṣat al-athar*, IV:146. For another biography, see al-Ghazzī, *Luṭf al-samar*, I:69–70.
29 "The rank of *dākhil* that has become common in Damascus, following the people of Rūm." Al-Muḥibbī, *Khulāṣat al-athar*, I:362–363. *Khārij*, literally "outside," is the seventh grade of Ottoman *medrese* professors; *Dākhil*, literally "inside, interior," a high degree of *medrese* professors.
30 Ibn Ṭūlūn, *Ḥawādith Dimashq*, 261.
31 Al-Muḥibbī, *Khulāṣat al-athar*, I:60–63.
32 Ibid., III:421.
33 Ibid., III:458.
34 M. Winter, "ʿAlī ibn Maymūn and Syrian Sufism in the Sixteenth Century," *Israel Oriental Studies* 7 (1977): 281–308.
35 Literally, the servants of the gate (the central Ottoman government).
36 Aḥmad al-Budayrī al-Ḥallāq, *Ḥawādith Dimashq al-yawmiyya, 1154–1175 h/1741–1762 m*, ed. by Aḥmad ʿIzzat ʿAbd al-Karīm (Cairo: Maṭbūʿāt Lajnat al-Bayān al-ʿArabī, 1959), 111.
37 Al-Budayrī, *Ḥawādith Dimashq al-yawmiyya*, 50, 108–111.
38 Ibn Kannān, *Yawmiyyāt Shāmiyya*, 410–411.
39 See Ibn Ṭūlūn, Shams al-Dīn Muḥammad, *Mufākahat al-khillān fī al-zamān: Taʾrikh Miṣr wa-l-Shām*, ed. by Muḥammad Muṣṭafā, 2 vols (Cairo: al-Muʾassasa al-Miṣriyya al-ʿĀmma li-l-Taʾlīf wa-l-Tarjama wa-l-Ṭibāʿa wa-l-Nashr, 1381–1384/1962–1964), I:196, 262.
40 Ibn Kannān, *Yawmiyyāt Shāmiyya*, 354.
41 The following description of the revolt is based on the research of Adel Manna: ʿĀdil Mannāʿ, *Taʾrikh Filasṭīn fī awākhir al-ʿahd al-ʿUthmānī, 1700–1918, qirāʾa jadīda* (Beirut: Muʾassasat al-Dirāsāt al-Filasṭīniyya, 1999), 21–46; Manna, "The Revolt of *Naqīb al-Ashrāf* in Jerusalem, 1703–1705" (in Hebrew), *Katedra* 53 (Jerusalem, 1989): 49–74.
42 The subject has been treated in three studies: Bodman, *Political Factions in Aleppo, 1760–1826*; Abraham Marcus, *The Middle East on the Eve of Modernity: Aleppo in the Eighteenth Century* (New York: Columbia University Press, 1989); Jane Hathaway, with contributions by Karl K. Barbir, *The Arab Countries under Ottoman Rule, 1516–1800* (Harlow, England: Pearson and Longman, 2008), 90–94.
43 Bodman, *Political Factions in Aleppo*, 98.
44 Ibn Ṭūlūn, *Mufākahat al-khillān*, I:197.
45 Al-Muḥibbī, *Khulāṣat al-athar*, II:107–108.
46 Ibid., III:68–78.
47 Jane Hathaway makes the following observation:

> Yet while the *ashrāf* and their *naqīb* became quite wealthy and influential in other Arab capitals, notably in Cairo and Damascus, Aleppo's powerful, militarized *ashrāf* have no parallel in any other provincial city. On the other hand, the striking similarity they bear in their counterparts in Ayntab and Marash leads one to suspect that northern Syria and south-eastern Anatolia during the Ottoman period should properly be analyzed as a discrete region.
> (Hathaway, *The Arab Countries*, 94)

Part III

Sayyids and *sharīfs* beyond the Middle East

8 *Shurafā* in the last years of al-Andalus and in the Morisco period

Laylat al-mawlid and genealogies of the Prophet Muḥammad

Mercedes García-Arenal

It is difficult to know much about the religious life of the last century of the Nasrid sultanate of Granada. Surviving Arabic sources are generally scarce for the whole period, and for information on the history of Granada it therefore becomes necessary to turn to contemporary Christian chroniclers. However, such Castilian historical chroniclers were mainly interested in military and political affairs, and, in particular, in the dynastic squabbles that allowed Castilian monarchs to make alliances with one or other of the various factions within the Nasrid dynasty that rivalled for the throne. On the one hand, Castilian records reveal an overriding interest in data concerning Nasrid power and in the opportunities that arose for Castilians to make interventions in Islamic territory. On the other hand, the few Arabic records that have come down to us tend to be those that make reference to questions of property rights, inheritance, or land and water distribution; that is, the kinds of records that the Christian conquerors had an interest in preserving after the start of their own period in power, because such records were needed to complete the processes of occupation and sharing-out of land among the new settlers. Huge areas of life during the last Muslim century in the Iberian Peninsula, especially cultural and religious, remain in the dark.

Nevertheless, a considerable amount of information has come down to us concerning the Moriscos, namely, those Muslims who continued to live in Iberia and were forced to convert to Christianity (in 1502 in the lands of the Castilian crown and in 1526 in Aragon). We know, for example, about their religiosity and about the beliefs and practices of those who continued to be secret Muslims, but most of what we know comes from Inquisition trial proceedings against such individuals, who were persecuted as heretics and apostates when they continued to use Islamic rites after undergoing obligatory Christian baptism.[1] It is also possible to glean some information, especially regarding the issue I now intend to explore, from the Moriscos' own writings. During the one hundred years in which they lived as "new converts" in Spain, the Moriscos produced a so-called "*aljamiado*" literature – written in the Spanish vernacular, but using Arabic script – and once they had been expelled from the Iberian Peninsula in 1609, they also wrote books in Spanish in Latin script (not in *aljamiado*) from their exile in Tunisia and other places. The Moriscos had *aljamiado* as well as Arabic books and both the Inquisition confiscated.[2] Those books are very significant for studying the "local religion" of the Moriscos.

In general terms, however, there can be no doubt that any attempt to find out about the *sharīf* (pl. *shurafā*) in the final years of Iberian Islam will always turn out to be a difficult undertaking. With these difficulties in mind, in this essay I will try to answer the question of whether a number of phenomena so well represented and so well documented in Morocco had their equivalents on the other side of the Strait of Gibraltar; that is, to explore whether al-Andalus saw the beginning of developments that in Morocco were to lead to government by two dynasties of *shurafā*, that of the Saʿdids after the 1540s, and that of the Alawids a century later. In the work I have carried out into the role of the *shurafā* in sixteenth- and seventeenth-century Morocco, I have argued that the rise of sharifism, namely, the process by which the condition of being *sharīf* eventually led to the formation of a blood aristocracy, generated a paradigm according to which *sharīf* origin was an essential requirement for any individual wanting to exercise political and religious power. I have proposed elsewhere that these processes taken together were in turn related to the phenomena of messianism and led to the creation of a link between the proclamation or vindication of the title of caliph and a claim to be the long-awaited *mahdī*.[3] The prestige of families claiming to be descendants of the Prophet had been increasing in Morocco for almost two hundred years, and was bolstered by a growing cult of the figure of the Prophet associated with the Sufis. However, the most outstanding feature of sharifism in the sixteenth century was the gradual consolidation of the idea that descent from the family of the Prophet (being *sharīf*) was both a necessary and sufficient requisite for the execution of religious and political power. In this way, a blood aristocracy was formed that implicitly – and sometimes explicitly – carried with it the notion that some of the gifts of the Prophet (and even prophecy itself, a most heterodox belief) were hereditary. As the sixteenth century wore on, the shaykhs of all mystical brotherhoods began to claim a line of descent going back to the family of the Prophet. The post of shaykh of a brotherhood also started to become hereditary: a shaykh would tend to be the son of the previous shaykh rather than the man generally recognized as the most saintly or most brilliant disciple. Dynasties of holy men thus created holy lineages that were identified with sharifism. The *shurafā* became human sources of divine power.

The Islamic kingdom of Granada ended with the Christian conquest of 897/1492, well before the political power of the *shurafā* had become firmly established in the Maghreb. Among the Moriscos who continued to live in Iberia after that date, sharifism is a phenomenon that is hard to trace, given that the Morisco community no longer had the capacity to exercise political power and its religious manifestations were necessarily clandestine. However, the existence of the paradigm is supported by evidence of other phenomena and another series of signs whose trail it is possible to follow. These related mainly to the practice of Sufism, and in particular to the proliferation of *zāwiya*s or Sufi lodges. In addition, and still within the Sufi sphere, there was the cult of the figure of the Prophet Muḥammad as manifested in the celebration of the feast of the *mawlid*, namely, the festival that commemorated Muḥammad's birth. These are the aspects I intend to illustrate in this study, despite the general lack of sources, for the final period of the Islamic kingdom of Granada and for the Morisco period thereafter. I will argue that we have evidence of the presence of the strong prestige, even of the cult, of the prophetic descent, during the period of "late Spanish Islam,"[4] and that this prestige is linked to strong messianic and apocalyptic trends among the last Muslims of Iberia and maybe to Shiʿite strata of belief in the local or popular form of Islam that they adhered to.

Sufism in Granada

By comparison with Morocco, very little is known about the Sufi brotherhoods of the kingdom of Granada, although there are many references in the records to *zāwiya*s, *ribāṭ*s, *fuqarā* etc., some of which I will mention below. In fact, the kingdom of Granada had social and demographic characteristics that were different from those of Morocco. Not only was it, clearly, a much smaller territory, it was also much more densely populated as a result of having had to accommodate large numbers of people under the pressure of the great Christian territorial advances from the thirteenth century onwards. It was also a strongly urbanized region with a tribal structure that was more greatly diluted than that of Morocco. Throughout the entire history of al-Andalus, the Islamic territory of the Iberian Peninsula, the *ʿulamā* were strong, numerous and well-organized and they played a relevant role in society. The *ʿulamā* guaranteed, in fact, the kind of strict Māliki Sunnism of which the religious and political elite of al-Andalus were always deeply proud.

Those are among the reasons why we do not find in al-Andalus a process equivalent to the one in Morocco in which the shaykhs of the *zāwiya*s formed true dynasties of necessarily *sharīfī* origin, and where posts were handed down to their heirs. Apart from the fact that there was greater and denser urbanization, and that the bodies of *ʿulamā* were stronger and more corporatized, it may simply have been that there was no time for such developments. The kingdom of Granada came to an abrupt end in 897/1492 and it was not until the sixteenth century that such events played out in Morocco. However, there was always constant contact between al-Andalus and the Maghreb, and the period did see the initial implantation of the most powerful brotherhoods, the Shādhiliyya and the Qādiriyya, a process in which the *ʿulamā* also played their part.[5]

The Sufism of which we know anything at all during the last two centuries of Iberian Islam seems to have been deeply rooted in asceticism, in notions of individual action and withdrawal from the world.[6] Such was the case of two famous jurists belonging to the family of the Ibn al-Maḥrūq who had abandoned worldly honors and power to retire to the *rābiṭa* known as Ibn al-Maḥrūq. The abundance of Sufi lodges and individuals devoted to mysticism seem to have been striking features of life in the region, even to contemporary Muslim observers and travellers who used these lodges as accommodation. Ibn Baṭṭūṭa (d. 770/1368–9 or 779/1377) wrote of the large number of *zāwiya*s in Granada, the *rābiṭa* of al-ʿUkāb, the *zāwiya* al-Lijām, the Ibn al-Maḥrūq, and the Banū Sid-Bono. According to Ibn Baṭṭūṭa, there was such a large number of Sufis and *fuqarā* in the city that

> [O]ne finds in Granada numerous *fuqarā* who are from Muslim countries of non-Arabic languages (*al-ʿajam*), who have settled there because of the similarities between the region and their own countries. I will cite from among them the *ḥājj* Abū ʿAbd Allāh of Samarqand, the *ḥājj* Aḥmad of Tabriz, the *ḥājj* Ibrāhīm of Konya, the *ḥājj* Ibrāhīm of Khurasan, and two *ḥājj*s from India, ʿAlī and Rashīd.[7]

From this it appears that there may have been a small colony of mystics who had made their way from Iran and India, probably as pilgrims, and then moved on to Islam's extreme western frontier.

Ibn Baṭṭūṭa also visited the *zāwiya* of Abū Aḥmad Jaʿfar, whose novices gathered at the *zāwiya* every night. In their exercises, the recitation of passages from the Qur'ān was followed by the litany (*dhikr*) of the *ṭarīqa* and by the intoning of the poems of al-Ḥallāj until a state of mystical ecstasy had been attained:

> A sort of collective holy fury took control of those who were present and, stripping themselves of their rough and patched-up clothing until they were almost completely naked, they performed a kind of rhythmless dance until they fell exhausted to the floor.[8]

By contrast, Ibn al-Khaṭīb (d. 776/1375) writes in his *Iḥāṭa* of the Sufis and *fuqarā* who had come to Granada from the recently conquered Sharq al-Andalus. For instance, the Banū Sid-Bono were originally from Denia and went to Granada to found their own *zāwiya*. According to Ibn al-Khaṭīb, they had a house and founded a *zāwiya* and a *madrasa* in the Albaicin. Indeed, Ibn al-Khaṭīb himself founded and sponsored a complex that included a *zāwiya*, a *madrasa* and a mausoleum for his own dead body.[9]

The *mawlid*

In sixteenth-century Morocco, the *sharīfī* argument was forcefully invoked in the exercise of power and its legitimation. In acts of investiture, in the homilies that accompanied Friday prayers and in the rituals that marked the Muslim year, the presence of the *shurafā* provided an indispensable consecration.

During the *bayʿa*, the oath of allegiance to the sovereign, the *shurafā* were the first witnesses to be named because of the grace stemming from their genealogy. Nothing could be done without them. The *ʿulamā* were the custodians of the Prophet's teachings and tradition. The *shurafā* derived their primacy from the fact that their presence was a tangible manifestation of the Prophet's "mystical body."

The *shurafā* participated alongside the sultan in all great rituals. But it was during the annual celebration of the Prophet's birth that their ascendancy was at its most spectacular.

The importance of the celebration of the *mawlid al-nabī* as a form of political legitimation since its establishment by the Fatimids, as well as its relation with the political role of the descendants of the Prophet, has been well described and interpreted by many scholars, and in particular by N. J. G. Kaptein.[10] In the Maghreb, the celebration was introduced by Abū al-Qāsim al-ʿAzafī, lord of Ceuta, in the thirteenth century. It included features such as processions and lighted candles which were considered by some as *bidaʿ* or pernicious innovation because of their resemblance to Christian practices. Abū al-Qāsim also carried out a widespread propaganda campaign in an effort to consolidate the establishment of the *mawlid* and urged the last Almohads and the first Marinids to follow his example in celebrating it. According to Ibn ʿIdhārī, it was due to Abū al-Qāsim's insistence that the Almohad caliph al-Murtaḍā (r. 645–664/1248–1266) celebrated the *mawlid* in great splendor with all his dignitaries, marking the event by distributing gifts among his subjects.[11] Kaptein has argued that Abū al-Qāsim's efforts to popularize the *mawlid* derived from a conscious desire to promote unity among Muslims and to contribute to a process of moral rearmament in the face of the Christian threat.[12]

At all events, use of the *mawlid* by those in power must be related to the emergence of an increasingly visible and powerful group, the *shurafā*, who were especially influential in Ceuta. As had occurred under the Fatimids, the sacralization and glorification of Muḥammad became a way of glorifying the Prophet's Family. It was no coincidence that it had been in Ceuta where Qāḍī ʿIyāḍ (d. 544/1149) had written his *Kitāb al-shifā'*, a text identifying love of the Prophet with love of his family and descendants. It is also worth mentioning that the Marinid sultan Abū Yūsuf Yaʿqūb (r. 656–685/1258–1286) named his son Abū Yaʿqūb Yūsuf (r. 685–706/1286–1307) heir to the throne on a night of the *mawlid*. In doing so, Abū Yusūf Yaʿqūb deliberately highlighted the fact that his son was the son of a *sharīfa*, and therefore the aptest and most legitimate candidate to assume power. Abu Yūsuf Yaʿqūb also chose this day, envisaging his planned conquest of Ceuta, since both *mawlid* and *shurafā* were known to be particularly important in that city.[13]

During this period, Ceuta became a land of refuge for Andalusi immigrants. The Andalusi Sufi Abū Marwān al-Yuḥānisī emigrated to Ceuta and spent the last years of his life there, dying in 667/1268 and being buried in the city. Al-Bādisī recorded a description of how the saint Abu Marwān had celebrated in Ceuta the *laylat al-mawlid*, preparing a banquet with honey and cakes for the *fuqarā* and the *muḥibbūn* or novices. An ecstatic dance (*shaṭḥ*) took place by the light of glass lanterns.[14] It becomes clear from al-Bādisī's text, then, that the *mawlid* was also celebrated in mystical circles. In the circumstances, such celebrations of the *mawlid*, the birth of the Prophet in the past, were tinged with messianism, the hope of a birth in the future. Al-Yuḥānisī also seems to have celebrated the *mawlid* in al-Andalus, as early as 647/1250.[15]

Al-Qashtālī, who wrote a book dedicated to the life and teachings of al-Yuḥānisī, recorded a meeting that al-Yuḥānisī held on another occasion.[16] The saint was traveling toward Córdoba, which was under siege, with the aim of making *ribāṭ* there, that is, of collaborating with the efforts of holy war to assist in its liberation. Finding it impossible to reach the city, he headed instead for Seville, where he asked for news of any man who was well known among the people for his piety and virtue. He was told of a young man (*fatā*) by the name of Ibn Manẓūr who was famous for his chastity and purity (*ṣawn*, *ṭahāra*) and for having persevered in the personal struggle (*ijtihād*), although he had no formal master. God had given him powers that even he did not understand, causing him great personal anxiety and leaving him in a highly confused mental state.

The young man seems to have resolved these confusions by declaring himself *ṣāḥib al-waqt*, or Master of the Hour. He was convinced that he had been entrusted with the task of saving the people of al-Andalus, and that the salvation of the community, *ṣalāḥ hādhihi al-umma*, lay in his hands. When al-Yuḥānisī met him he was surrounded by a group of young men, followers of Ibn Manẓūr, and on hearing Ibn Manẓūr's claim to be responsible for saving the Umma, al-Yuḥānisī replied that that task corresponded to a member of the Banū Hāshim, namely, a *sharīf*. Ibn Manẓūr's answer was that he was a *sharīf*, at which al-Yuḥānisī "made a gesture with his arm," "one of those which bring bad luck to the Jews," that is, he ridiculed the young man by not only refusing to believe that he was the savior of the Umma, or even a *sharīf*, but by branding him a Jew. Ibn Manẓūr eventually met the usual fate of all such prophets and was crucified at the Bāb al-Mu'adhdhin of the city wall.

Ties between Ceuta and the kingdom of Granada were close. From Ceuta came the family of *shurafā* called al-Sharīf al-Gharnāṭī, who arrived in Granada during the reign of Muḥammad II (r. 671–701/1273–1302). According to Emilio García Gómez, the celebration of the *mawlid* in Granada was not only influenced by the example of Ceuta but also by that of Tlemcen, which is known to us from the description of it by Yaḥyā Ibn Khaldūn included in his *Bugyat al-ruwwād*.[17] However, the official inauguration by a ruler of the festival of the *mawlid* in Granada itself is attributed to Muḥammad V (r. 754–760/1354–1359, 763–793/1362–1391). This is a well-documented event because it was the subject of a detailed description by Ibn al-Khaṭīb in a famous text included by the Granadan polymath in his work *Nufāḍat al-jirāb*.

Emilio García Gómez was the first scholar to produce an extensive discussion and translation of Ibn al-Khaṭīb (on the basis of two manuscripts, one in Rabat and the other in Leiden), included in a wonderful and insightful book, *Foco de Antigua luz sobre la Alhambra*,[18] in which he establishes a connection between the building of the new rooms of the Alhambra under Muḥammad V and the inauguration of a whole new political symbolism that found its stage setting in the new salons. Ibn al-Khaṭīb situates the court ceremony dedicated to the *mawlid al-nabī* within the context of Nasrid dynastic history and contemporary politics. The *mawlid* presented an opportunity to celebrate the recovery of the Nasrid throne by a namesake of the Prophet, Muḥammad ibn ʿAbd Allāh, who had returned to Granada after three years of exile in the Marinid court of Fez. Muḥammad V triumphed over his dynastic rivals in Jumādā II 763/March–April 1362 and in the nine months before the celebration of the *mawlid* on 12 Rabīʿ I 764/30 December 1362, he had given monumental expression to his victory in architectural works that were inaugurated on the occasion of the *mawlid*.

The Nasrids never claimed a *sharīfī* genealogy but, as Ibn al-Khaṭīb himself explains in his biography of Muḥammad I (r. 629–671/1232–1273),[19] traced their ancestry back to the Anṣār, namely, the first companions to assist the Prophet Muḥammad in Medina. They descended from Saʿd b. ʿUbāda, of the tribe of Khazraj, who was elected caliph by the other Anṣār after the death of the Prophet. Although that bid to become caliph did not prosper, Saʿd continued to consider himself the head of the Muslim community until his death.[20] This is what allowed the Nasrids to claim the title of caliph, an attitude that was especially prevalent under Muḥammad V, who on proclaiming his caliphate announced that his residence was to be known as *Dār al-Khilāfa*. Muḥammad V is mentioned as a caliph in the inscriptions on the extension to the Alhambra known as the Palace of Lions (e.g., in the inscription on the fountain in its patio) and mention is made of the *kursī al-khilāfa*, that is, the seat of the caliphate, in an inscription in the *mirador* of Lindaraja, another part of Muḥammad V's extension.[21]

In 768/1367 Muḥammad V adopted the title of *al-Ghanī bi-Allāh*, thereby following the same path taken by the Umayyad caliph of Córdoba ʿAbd al-Raḥmān III (r. 299–349/912–961) on adopting the title of caliph: legitimacy of the Anṣār was invoked in order to assume the caliphate, followed by direct inheritance of that legitimacy by the Nasrids, and a defence of Islam. The extension of the Alhambra as *Dār al-Khilāfa* and the celebration of the *mawlid* were thus an integral part of Muḥammad's effort to legitimize his position as caliph. The extension of the Alhambra palaces was also an emulation of the famous palace of ʿAbd al-Raḥmān, Madīnat al-Zahrāʾ. The detailed description given by Ibn al-Khaṭīb of the first celebration of the *mawlid* established by Muḥammad V also confirms this hypothesis. Ibn al-Khaṭīb describes the pomp and the hierarchical ranking of those who attended the ceremony, and portrays the *shurafā* as playing a leading role in it. According to Ibn al-Khaṭīb,[22] the order observed by those who attended the *mawlid* was as follows:

1. The *shuyūkh al-qabāʾil* or tribal chiefs.
2. The *shurafā*, described in the text as "*al-ashrāf Banū al-Fawāṭim*."

3. Relatives of the monarchs and members of the several branches of the Nasrids.
4. The *ʿulamā*.
5. *Fuqarā* and Sufis.
6. Representatives of foreign mystical brotherhoods (*arbāb al-khiraq al-musāfirīn*).
7. Christians who came/were invited to the feast (*al-ʿajam al-wāridīn*).
8. Tradesmen.
9. Other social classes (*sāʾir al-ṭabaqāt*) and local notables (*ʿuyūn al-raʿiyya*).

Strikingly absent from this list are the military officials, unless they were included in the group of the tribal chieftains, and this is an absence that it is hard to explain in the light of Muḥammad's self-representation as a champion of the armed struggle to defend Islam. The mention in this list of *shurafā* descending from "*al-ashrāf Banū al-Fawāṭim*" connects with a tradition to ennumerate *al-Fawāṭim* and *al-ʿAwātik* as important members of the Prophet's kin.[23] García Gómez concludes: "Apart from growing Islamic veneration for the Prophet, other factors were involved in the gestation of the festival of the *mawlid*, such as Shiʿite religious and political influences, Sufi and *marabout* currents, and an emulation of Christianity."[24] I will return to this point later.

There is not much difference between the terms used in the celebration inaugurated by Muḥammad V, or the hierarchal terms established in his *khāṣṣa*, and those used a couple of centuries later during the reign of the sultan of Morocco Mūley Aḥmad al-Manṣūr al-Dhahabī (r. 986–1012/1578–1603). Aḥmad al-Manṣūr also built his famous palace in Marrakech, known as the Badīʿ, as a stage for his great ceremonies and, in particular, to celebrate the *mawlid*.[25] Aḥmad al-Manṣūr constructed a palace of his own, or rather, a palatial complex of buildings, known as the *Dār al-Makhzen*, with the intention of showing that his own *sharīfī* dynasty was superior to any that had ruled Morocco before it.

Moroccan Arabic sources state that it was more magnificent than anything that had ever existed in Baghdad or Damascus, and also that it surpassed the palace of Madīnat al-Zahrāʾ built by the Umayyads outside Córdoba. The walls had tiles with intertwined floral and vegetable motifs and others that simulated the rich embroideries of silk coats. In the upper part of these tiles there were stucco caligraphical inscriptions in which specially commissioned works by court poets exalted the beauty of the site and the merits of its patron, as in the Alhambra palace of Granada. These Arabic sources lay particular stress on the construction and characteristics of the palace of al-Badīʿ (the "Incomparable," one of the names of God) and the various celebrations that took place within it, especially the celebrations of the *mawlid* on the birthday of the Prophet Muḥammad. There also existed a clear link between court ceremonial and architecture: the sources dwell on the ceremonies and lavishness of the celebrations, but also on the pomp and pageantry with which the sultan traveled and received visitors in audience.

Descriptions of al-Badīʿ are accompanied by accounts of the fabulous celebrations with which al-Manṣūr marked the feast of the *mawlid*. These were elaborate and solemn celebrations clearly intended to exalt the figure of the caliph rather than that of his forebear the Prophet Muḥammad, but at all events they sought to emphasize the direct link between the former and the latter. The magnificence of the *mawlid* celebrations at al-Badīʿ, in which all the classes and hierarchies of the realm participated in order of social importance, were obviously a thing of wonder to participants and spectators alike, and this included even the most influential groupings of them all, such as the *shurafā*, qadis, holy men and vizirs.

Sufis and the *mawlid*

The *mawlid* was not only observed at the Nasrid court, but also continued to be celebrated in the Sufi lodges. Ibn al-Khaṭīb provides us with the information that the inhabitants of Granada visited these places on the two canonical festivals, and especially at the time of the *mawlid*. Ibn al-Khaṭīb gives no details of these celebrations, but the famous *muftī* al-Wansharīsī (d. 914/1508) includes in his *Miʿyār* various *fatwā*s by Andalusian scholars who severely condemn the *mawlid* celebrations of the *fuqarā*. The oldest of these *fatwā*s were made by two near-contemporary *muftī*s, Muḥammad al-Ḥaffār (d. 811/1408) and Abū Isḥāq al-Shāṭibī (d. 790/1388). Both made pronouncements on the legality of properties left as *ḥabs*/*waqf*s or pious foundations to finance the *laylat al-mawlid*. The two men described the celebration as *bidaʿ*, that is, innovation or error, and ruled that any *waqf* aimed to be used to finance such a practice should be revoked. Al-Ḥaffār took the opportunity to describe with great repugnance how the celebration was carried out by the *fuqarā*, who included chants (*al-ginā*ʾ) and trances (*al-shaṭḥ*) in the ceremony. According to al-Ḥaffār, the *fuqarā* were in the habit of telling common Muslims that this was the best way to reach God and that it turned them into the "brotherhood of God's saints" (*ṭarīqat awliyā*ʾ *Allāh*). In fact, wrote al-Ḥaffār, it turned them into followers of Satan and led other Muslims into perdition.[26] Another *fatwā* survives from the second half of the ninth/fifteenth century, in which the qadi of Granada Abū ʿAmr ibn Manẓūr severely condemns the imam of a town who had abandoned his duties for several days in order to go to a nearby *zāwiya* and celebrate the *mawlid*.[27] The severity of the *ʿulamā*'s reaction to observance of the *mawlid* in mystical circles is proof of the tension between the *ʿulamā* and the *awliyā*ʾ *Allāh*, to which I have made reference above.

The *mawlid* and the Moriscos: their books on the Prophet Muḥammad

It was of course very difficult for the Moriscos to stage communal or public celebrations of any kind. They were under constant surveillance, and forced to engage in an exclusively individual and secret form of religious practice, carried out within the bosom of the family and behind closed doors. Nevertheless, we do know of the survival of a *marabout* tradition among the Moriscos. I will mention a few examples. First, there is the case of the well-known figure of the holy woman known as "*la Mora de Úbeda*," who lived in the outskirts of the Puerta de Elvira in Granada. This woman was visited by Moriscos who sought her guidance and advice. El Mancebo de Arévalo described her in the following terms:

> She was 93 years old and her body and limbs were so large that they were frightening. I have never seen her like, and neither have I heard from anyone who has seen such a woman, and I shall say nothing of her strangeness save that her little finger was greater than my ring-finger. She wore rough cloth and esparto grass sandals.[28]

Such quasi-monstrous physical features, indicative of supernatural powers in certain individuals, are found in a great number of hagiographical texts of Maghrebi origin.

Inquisition trials also throw some light on the cult of tombs of certain *awliyāʾ*, or at least suggest that the memory of such practices was still alive: such was the case of the trial of a Morisco from Guadix who had been working with a group of Old Christians in a field where there was a pile of stones. The Christians said that at night an *ignis fatuus* could be seen coming out of the pile which they attributed to Saint Torquatus. The Morisco imprudently said to them: "Here where these stones are, a holy Moor died and the fires that you say appear there are not on account of Saint Torquatus but because of this holy Moor who died here."[29]

In any case we know that Moriscos were in contact with North Africa and seeked from the Maghreb works that included the most diffused and widely read works on Sufism. As an example we have the Valencian *faqīh* Gaspar Rahech who was tried in 1608, because he had a mosque at his house and taught Muslim Law and Qurʾān to many Moriscos and held meetings with other *fuqahāʾ*. In one of those meetings they decided there was a book they were very much in need of, and sent someone to get it in Algiers.[30] It is remakable that this book that the Valencia Moriscos needed so much was not other than *Ḥizb al-bāhir* of al-Shādhilī (d. 656/1258), precisely the founder of one of the most important *ṭuruq* in the Maghreb.

We have attested proof of the celebration of the *mawlid* by Muslim minorities in Christian Iberia until the years prior to the forced conversion to Catholicism. An example: in 1517 fray Maestro de Figuerola (author of a *Tratado contra el Alcorán*) wanted to engage in religious disputation different *fuqahāʾ* of the Muslim communities in Aragon (where the forced conversion took place in 1526). He chose to go to Zaragoza and present himself at night in the mosque during the celebration of the *laylat al-mawlid* (*celebración de la Natividad de Mahomat*) knowing that he would find there gathered together the Muslims from Zaragoza itself and all the smaller places in the vicinity where Muslims lived. The imam of the mosque begged him not to disturb such a solemn and important occasion and asked him to come back the next day to his own house, where he would be expecting Figuerola with the leading *fuqahā'* of the region.[31] Juan Andrés, a converted Muslim and polemicist, former *alfaquí* of Xátiva in Valencia, wrote in his *Confutación de la secta mahomética y del Alcorán* (1515) that the Muslims of his old native village celebrated the *mawlid* with special lavishness.[32]

There are also isolated references in the inquisitorial records to continued Morisco celebration of the *mawlid*, or at least, given that Inquisition files never actually use the term *mawlid*, to celebrations in which Moriscos gathered together all night by the light of candles and read out stories about the Prophet Muḥammad.[33] The *aljamiado* literature which has reached us includes a great number of poems of the genre called *mawlūdiyyāt*, panegyrics of Muḥammad.[34] Some of those poems contain legendary stories of the Prophet which were recited during the night of the *mawlid*. On such occasions, the Moriscos also put on short theatrical performances about the Prophet's life. There are a number of references to theatre performances among the Moriscos, which may have resembled the *ta'ziya* of the Shi'ites. They are mentioned in records of Inquisition trial proceedings and in other documents, such as a commentary on religious poetry by the Aragonese Morisco Ibrāhīm de Bolfad, who reports the performance of a comedy based on the miracles of Muḥammad:

> This is one of the miracles recorded in many writings, both in Arabic and Castilian, from where the Spanish poet took before our expulsion the comedy of the *Milagros de nuestro Sancto Profeta*[35] which was played at court one day, showing in it his truth and representing him in his green clothing strewn with stars, and how the moon parted and he entered into it and each half came out of his sleeve . . . When they were playing it again another day to the great interest and amusement of the audience, the Inquisition sent for the comedians and the poet; the former were banned from doing it again, and the latter they wished to punish.[36]

The Moriscos, as I explained briefly at the start of this article, kept and copied books in Arabic as well as translating and writing many others in "*aljamía*," that is, Spanish in Arabic script. The Inquisition confiscated and destroyed these books whenever it found them, but a number of batches of books that were hidden in bricked-up rooms, attics or cellars have subsequently come to light. The items recovered from such findings only add up to about two hundred texts in all: religious and legal compendia, works of anti-Christian polemic, Qur'āns, *qiṣaṣ al-anbiyā'* (stories of prophets) and, above all, stories of the Prophet Muḥammad.[37] The stories of the prophets, of Muḥammad and his kin were meant to inspire courage and religious conviction. But even if we only have about two hundred *aljamiado* books in the nine hundred trials of Moriscos that are extant from the Inquisition of Zaragoza (the region of Spain where most *aljamiado* literature was produced) between 1568 and 1609, 409 individuals were accused of possessing books written in Arabic script, which were usually destroyed by the Holy Office.[38]

From the collections confiscated on those occasions we see that the *Kitāb al-shifāʾ* of Qāḍī ʿIyāḍ continued to be very popular among Moriscos,[39] just as it was in the neighboring Maghreb and had earlier been in the kingdom of Granada. This was a work, as I have said, that seems to have been linked to the cult of the figures of the Prophet and his descendants. For, the *Kitāb al-shifāʾ* was an apologetic work and draws on many of the terms that were dearest to Morisco anti-Christian polemic, such as the ideas that Muḥammad is the seal of the prophets, that his coming was announced in Jewish and Christian writings, and that his attributes and his numerous miracles prove how exceptional and illustrious a figure he was. The *Shifāʾ* is the most-cited book in Morisco polemics: whenever the miracles of Christ were evoked, the Moriscos invariably compared them with those performed by the Prophet exactly as they had been described by Qāḍī ʿIyāḍ in this text.[40]

More extraordinary was the success of the *Kitāb al-anwār* by al-Bakrī, a Middle Eastern author of the thirteenth century. This book was extremely popular among the Moriscos, as can be seen from the various *aljamiado* versions that have come down to us from findings in Ricla, Uclés and Urrea de Jalón, all places in Aragón.[41] We know of another "*Libro de las luces*" pertaining to a collection of Morisco books found in Muel, in Aragón. The catalogue of this collection, which was established by Miguel Casiri, the Maronite who was cataloguing the collection of Arabic books at El Escorial, says its author was "Abulhassan Alansari," from Seville.[42] The fact that four *aljamiado* copies of this work, plus another in Arabic, have survived is a good indication of its popularity if we remember that there are only two hundred extant Morisco *aljamiado* manuscripts. The text was even re-written in verse by an Aragonese Morisco, Mohamad Rabadán, whose work was entitled *Discurso de la Luz* and consisted of 1,700 verses.[43] The book must have been circulating in Iberia since the Middle Ages: a recent publication proves that the *Kitāb al-anwār* or one of its versions was translated to Latin by Herman de Carinti in the mid-twelfth century with the title *Liber de generatione Mahumet.*[44] One of its versions or maybe another, similar book is the *Kitāb nasab Rasūl Allāh.* Of this book, also to be bound up with the doctrine of Prophetic Light (*Nūr Muḥammadī*) and the abundant literature on the *mawlid*, at least two copies have been preserved in Morisco hoards.[45] This book, as the *Kitāb al-anwār*, deals with the light emanating from Adam to Muḥammad and into the family of ʿAlī, a notion which found fertile ground among the Shiʿites. It seems to have been circulating in Iberia since Medieval times and was used by Peter the Venerable – who travelled to Spain in 1142 – in his *Liber generationis Mahumet.*[46] The preservation and use by the Moriscos of *Kitāb al-anwār* and *Kitāb nasab Rasūl Allāh*, with both books circulating since Medieval times, bestow upon them an added significance.

The original work by al-Bakrī was a very detailed study of the Prophet Muḥammad's genealogy. It listed his entire ancestry and continued with accounts of the glorious deeds of the Prophet and all his descendants. The book was written in a legendary tone, and gave ʿAlī a highly prominent role. For the Moriscos such a text would have provided exaltation not only of Muḥammad's lineage but of that of all Muslims. This was seen as a holy lineage that brought Muslims closer to their Creator than any other people, and was reflected in a series of glorious deeds that told of a triumphal past. Inquisition trials also provide proof of the popularity of this "Book of Lights" or *Libro de las Luces* – above all, it seems, because of the stories it contained of past Muslim victories ("our glorious past deeds").[47] Morisco celebrations on the night of the *mawlid* probably included readings of extracts from the "Book of Lights,"[48] as is shown by several Inquisition trials from places close to Pastrana, where the Inquisition confiscated a copy of the book in Arabic. This was a thirteenth-century manuscript copied in Denia[49] which is probably the copy currently held in the Vatican Library.[50] Among the other books found in Pastrana there were also works by Qāḍī ʿIyāḍ.

In the *Libro de las Luces*, the themes that were so dear to the Moriscos such as their holy ancestry, their glorious lineages and the deeds performed in a portentous past, were laid out with particular stress and exaggeration. It was a highly entertaining book and suitable for reading aloud, given that it was full of epic tales of a moving and edifying nature. Mentions of ʿAlī and of his sons are very frequent, remarkably frequent in fact, in the Inquisition trials of Moriscos.[51] The book's extraordinary success in Iberia and among the Moriscos is worth emphasizing, for it certainly did not enjoy the same sort of reception in the rest of the Arabic-speaking world, where al-Bakrī's work had come under vehement attack from the medieval Sunnite *ʿulamā*.

Al-Bakrī wrote widely on the subject of the primordial existence of the Prophet Muḥammad and on the theme of the Light, or *Nūr Muḥammadī*. The scholars of *aljamiado* literature have pointed to the presence of this element in the characterization of the Prophet Muḥammad in the Morisco literature.[52] The theme of the *Nūr Muḥammadī* was greatly to the taste of the Sufis but ran the risk of shading into what came to be defined as Shiʿite heterodoxy. The *Nūr Muḥammadī*, which had its origin in pre-eternal times and was a luminous mass of primordial adoration in the form of a transparent column that made Muḥammad God's first creation, was a major leitmotiv in the *Kitāb al-anwār*.[53] In the Middle East, the book was mainly popular among Shiʿites. In his study dedicated to the work, B. Shoshan points out that al-Majlisī, the well-known seventeenth-century Shiʿite author, included the complete text of the *Anwār* in his famous opus *Biḥār*, where he praised its reliability and presented it to Shiʿite *ʿulamā* as suitable reading material in *mawlid* sessions. Shoshan also points to interesting similarities between passages of the *Anwār* and *Ithbāt al-waṣiyya li-l-imām ʿAlī b. Abī Ṭālib*, a work usually attributed to al-Masʿūdī (d. 345/956), "but undoubtedly a Shiite tract, regardless of whether its attribution to al-Masʿūdī is correct and whether al-Masʿūdī was indeed a Shiite."[54] Similarities in content and phrasing between the two works are easy to detect, though the passages that are similar in the two works do not appear to be of any special Shiʿite significance.[55] However, it seems clear that al-Bakrī's book was influenced by Shiʿite ideas or more precisely Ismaʿilite, a fact that alarmed a good number of Middle Eastern Sunnite *ʿulamā*.

The wide diffusion that this book had among the Moriscos is no doubt remarkable; it is still more remarkable that this book never appears in the repertoires and bibliographical dictionaries that we have from al-Andalus as attested by the data base, directed by Maribel Fierro, *Historia de los Autores y Transmisores Andalusíes*.[56] Probably it is a work that was also frowned upon by Andalusi *ʿulamā* because of its challenge to the Sunnite and Māliki orthodoxy of the Andalusian establishement, but was popular at other levels, mainly in Sufi circles. In this way, Morisco culture allows us to have a glimpse of the survival of popular or local religion in a way rarely allowed by the works produced by the intellectual and religious elite of al-Andalus.

Of more interest when it comes to demonstrating the widespread diffusion and influence of al-Bakrī's work is the Arabic text that was fabricated by Moriscos in the late sixteenth century and is known as the Lead Books of Sacromonte. These forged texts pretended to constitute a new gospel transmitted by the Virgin Mary to a group of Paleochristian Arab martyrs who had traveled to Spain with the Apostle Saint James and had been converted and given religious instruction by him before meeting their deaths in Granada. The texts presented a version of Christianity as close to or syncretic with Islam. According to the Lead Books, the first Christian settlers in Granada had been Arabs and the Virgin Mary had spoken in Arabic to her faithful followers.

This fascinating forgery sought to pass itself off as a Christian text (and was considered such until its official anathematization by the Vatican in 1682), but it clearly derived from Arabic sources. In the course of the long, intense debate that the Lead Books provoked over several decades and that only came to an end when they were officially anathematized by the Vatican, this Islamic derivation was pointed out by several contemporary theologians. For example, Marcos Dobelio, the Maronite scholar from La Sapienza in Rome, traveled to Spain to translate the Lead Books and showed that the miracles attributed in the texts to Jesus Christ had in fact been lifted from the tale of the *Shifāʾ* by Qāḍī ʿIyāḍ and from al-Bakrī's *Kitāb al-anwār*. The Lead Books thus provide further important proof of the popularity and importance of both texts among the Moriscos of Granada.[57]

Al-Anwār al-nabawiyya by Muḥammad ibn ʿAbd al-Rafīʿ

Another "Book of Lights" has also survived from this period, in this case one that came out of the Morisco milieu after their expulsion from Spain. This was a work written in exile, in Tunisia, and even more interestingly as far as the theme of this study is concerned, it documents the continued existence among the Moriscos of families of *shurafā*. In fact this book proves it in a definite way, while for the Morisco families in the Peninsula we have only brief hints such as the following: Pedro Guerra de Lorca, who dedicated most of his life to the evangelization of the Moriscos of Granada, declares himself shocked by the fact that the said Moriscos have a Christian name for public life in

Christian society, and a Muslim name to use among themselves. He says then, that "Hamete" is a very common name, which is the same as "Mohamed," but that they only use this form, Muḥammad, for the persons who descend from the Prophet.[58] The royal decree issued by Philip II (r. 1556–1598) that in 1567 banned the use of the Arabic language also prohibited the use of Arabic names and surnames. Lineages were from then on, clandestine.[59] This explains the relevance of the book we are considering as well as the fact that it was written outside Spain.

The full title of the book is *Kitab al-anwār al-nabawiyya fī ābā' khayr al-bariyya*, by Muḥammad al-Sharīf al-Ḥusaynī al-Ja'farī al-Mursī al-Andalusī (d. 1051/1642). Like al-Bakrī's "Book of Lights," this work covers the genealogy of the lineage of the Prophet from the beginnings of time.[60] However, the book is above all a vindication of the Morisco families of *sharīfī* origin, listing all the *sharīfī* lineages of al-Andalus and placing emphasis on those families that over the centuries had come and gone between Tunisia and al-Andalus, or that had had members or branches of the family on one side or another of the Mediterranean. The author of the text explains that he wrote it at the request of the Sharīf 'Alī al-Nawālī al-Sarrāj, who wanted to establish his family tree and prove descent from the *Ahl al-Bayt*. Al-Nawālī was the *naqīb* of the *shurafā* of Andalusian origin in Tunisia and the book is written in defence of the lines of *shurafā* who had moved to that country from al-Andalus. These lines of descent were contested by the *shurafā* already living in Tunisia, who, as the following quotation makes clear, denied the newcomers the privileges that they felt were due to them as descendants of the *Ahl al-Bayt*.

> We, the group of Andalusians who descend from the Prophet, have suffered greatly from this challenge by our brothers in religion in Tunisia. They said, "Where does their nobility come from which they say comes from the Prophet, when the fact is that they were living in the land of the infidel – may God destroy it – where they have lived for hundreds of years in such and such a manner? There does not remain among them any one who can remember the Islamic period, and they have mixed with the infidel . . ." and other reflections of this nature.[61]

Here, it seems, is proof of the fact that after the conquest of Granada, families of *shurafā* remained in the region and then had difficulty being recognized as such when they were expelled from Spain.

It is worth pointing out that the leading *sharīfī* families of al-Andalus, according to Ibn 'Abd al-Rafī', included the descendants of Sa'd b. 'Ubāda, the ancestor of the Nasrids, who are described as if they belonged to the family of the Prophet by connection and proximity rather than through true blood ties.[62] The work also provides information that allows us to assume that the *shurafā* had a leadership role within their community. Ibn 'Abd al-Rafī' tells us that, some time after 1604,

> some of us secretly began to leave [Spain], some for the Maghreb, some for the Mashriq, pretending to profess the religion of the Unbelievers (*muẓhiran dīn al-kuffār*) . . . Some of our beloved brothers, such as the honored *faqīh* and teacher (*mudarris*) Abū al-ʿAbbās Aḥmad al-Ḥanafī, known as ʿAbd al-ʿAzīz al-Qurashī, a *sharīf*. . . went to the city of Belgrad in the province of the great Constantinople, and had a meeting with the minister Murād Bāshā, one of the *wazīr*s at the court of the great regretted sultan Aḥmad Khān.[63]

The aim of this meeting was to ask for assistance from the Ottoman authorities in admitting Moriscos as recognized subjects. Ibn ʿAbd al-Rafīʿ, of course of a *sharīfī* family himself, also points to the fact that the two first *shaykh al-Andalus*, the heads of the Morisco community as designated by the Ottoman authorities of Tunis, Luis Zapata and Mustafá de Cardenas, also claimed *sharīfī* ancestry. Both of them were in frequent contact with the Andalusian *sharīf* of Testur, Muḥammad ibn Maḥfūẓ and with Muḥammad al-Nawālī, founders of the *Madrasat al-Andalusiyyīn*.[64]

Both this work and the popularity of that of al-Bakrī reveal the Morisco need – or at least the need of noble Moriscos – to be recognized as part of a genealogical line going all the way back to the Prophet, and their desire to claim the rights and privileges that derived from their condition of double nobility, that is, nobility of blood and of prophetic descent. Both texts are therefore extremely interesting sources.

However, and bearing in mind the scarceness of information on which we can draw, we must not forget that the notion of deriving legitimacy for the exercise of power from the lineage of the *Ahl al-Bayt* during the final period of al-Andalus was always opposed by the traditional idea of Andalusian caliphal legitimacy *par excellence*, which was that of the Umayyad lineage. This is clearly illustrated by the case of Don Hernando de Córdoba y Valor, the Morisco nobleman elected as king by the rebels of the Alpujarra in 1568–1570 during their war against the Christians. Luis del Mármol, the Castilian chronicler of the War of the Alpujarras, wrote of this election:

> Don Hernando de Córdoba y Valor was a Morisco, a man esteemed among those of his nation because he could trace his origins back to the caliph Marwān; and his forebears, according to what was said, as inhabitants of the city of Damascus [called] Shām, had been involved in the death of the caliph Ḥusayn, son of ʿAlī the nephew of Muḥammad, and had fled to Africa and then Spain and through their own courage had occupied the kingdom of Córdoba and held it for a long time under the name of ʿAbd al-Raḥmān, since the first of them was called ʿAbd al-Raḥmān; but his proper surname was Ibn Umayya.[65]

To this information we can balance the fact that the Moriscos of Aragon and of Castile shortly before the expulsion were still expecting a hidden king that they called "el Moro Alfatimi," which I am going to mention in relation to the next work to be examined, the *Crónica y relación de la esclarecida descendencia xarifa.*

Crónica y relación de la esclarecida descendencia xarifa

During their lives in Spain, the Moriscos wrote most of their works in *aljamía*, but after the expulsion and once they had settled in Tunisia or Morocco, they wrote mainly in Spanish and used Latin rather than Arabic script in doing so. To this latter group of Morisco works in Spanish belongs a miscellaneous manuscript kept at the University Library of Bologna (MS D 565), which contains a series of translations ordered and paid for by Muḥammad Rubio, a Morisco originally from Villafeliche in Aragon who became a merchant in Tunis and financed the stocking of his own library there.[66] From this set of miscellaneous works, which includes translations of Qāḍī ʿIyāḍ, I would like to highlight here the work entitled *Crónica y relación de la esclarecida descendencia xarifa.*

The translator of this work was very probably a well-known Morisco writer, Ibrāhīm Taybili. Taybili was the author of a long poem in Spanish defending the Islamic faith and contradicting that of Christians, written in Tunis in the mid-seventeenth century.[67] This poem was dedicated to the same man, the *naqīb* or *mizwār* of the *shurafā* of al-Andalus, al-Nawālī, who had asked Ibn ʿAbd al-Rafīʿ to compose the work discussed in the previous section.[68] At the end of the poem Taybili placed a colophon, also directed to his patron and protector whom he calls "señor Sarife Ali Alniguali," in which he said that he planned to write further works, saying that, among them

> I have also translated from Arabic to Castilian all in verse, in octaves like the present verses, the death of Haçan, the son of Çaydi Hali Ybnu Abi Talib, *radia Alahu hanhu* [*sic*], one of the best and most heartfelt that I have ever read . . .[69]

It is this colophon that allows us to deduce that the *Crónica y relación de la esclarecida descendencia xarifa* may have been translated by Taybili. The book is, once again, a genealogical work on the Prophet Muḥammad and his descendants, the twelve Imams, receivers of the *Nūr Muḥammadī.* It is, in other words, a work of a markedly Shiʿite character, to such an extent indeed that its editor, J. F. Cutillas, considers it may have been a *maqtal* for the day of the ʿĀshūrāʾ, especially because of the coverage it provides of the death of al-Ḥusayn in Karbala and because of the inclusion in the work of references and hadiths that are only to be seen in Shiʿite works.[70] The text certainly focuses on the death of Imam al-Ḥusayn and states: "and thus any who may read it on the day of the ʿĀshūrāʾ will be given by *Allah taʿālā* a prize such as he who died *shahīd.*"[71] What the *Crónica* has to say about al-Ḥasan al-ʿAskarī (Abū Muḥammad al-Ḥasan ibn ʿAlī) is also highly significant:

> [D]ue to his condition they called him Elhaliz [*sic*], which is to say the pure one [*al-khāliṣ*], the one who is clean and without any blemish, and they called him the honored one of his God, He who ordered in His eternity to come out of his loins the Imam Muḥammad Elmehdi El Fatimi [*sic*], whose coming is awaited by the people, called Elfatimi [*sic*], of whom the wise make mention. Allah did this on his account [Elmehdi] and so that from him should come to this world so much good, being the *ṭahāra* of his *nachaça* [*nasab*].[72]

Why would a Tunisian Morisco translate a Shiʿite work? It is clear that neither the translator nor Muḥammad Rubio, who financed the translation and the entire collection of works gathered in the miscellaneous volume, saw anything suspicious or reprehensible in it. There is nothing Shiʿite about the rest of Ibrāhīm Taybili's known work. So what does it mean when the two most important works on the genealogy of the Prophet and his family found among the Moriscos have such a markedly Shiʿite character? It is obvious that in order to answer these questions adequately we would need sources and records that are completely lacking. However, part of it must surely have had to do with the Morisco need to emphasize their prophetic lineage, the figure of Muḥammad and his own holy descendants. This need was largely driven by the fact that they had lived in polemical circumstances, that is, in a situation of permanent defence and apology within a hostile Christian environment. In the words of one Morisco polemicist who wrote a defence of Muḥammad against the Christians, the latter "not content with denying his prophecy, raise up against him so many lies and testimonies, denying the books which record his miracles," that is, just those books that were most revered by the Moriscos.[73]

In the *Libro de las Luces*, the themes that were so dear to the Moriscos concerning their holy ancestry, their glorious lineages, the deeds performed in a portentous past that allowed them to cleanse the humiliations of the present and look forward to a triumphal future, were given particular emphasis and this provided an answer, among other things, to Christian allegations about the bastard origins of the descendants of Ismael, the children of the slave-woman Hagar. The exaltation of the martyrdom of the Prophet's descendants must have been especially moving to the members of a harassed and persecuted minority. Inquisition trial records provide ample proof that the Moriscos praised as martyrs all those who were condemned by the Holy Office. There was, for example, the trial of Gabriel de Carmona, a Morisco from Almagro, who was accused, among other things, of having shown joy when speaking of a Morisco who had recently been burned to death by the Holy Office and until the final moment "had wished to die in his law."[74] Carmona had said that "the said Morisco had been a brave martyr for Muḥammad."[75]

Martyrdom was, in other words, a familiar issue for the Moriscos and one with which they found it easy to identify. This was also linked to the messianic beliefs that were so widespread among the Moriscos and according to which, as in the quotation from the *Crónica* above, they awaited the arrival of the *mahdī* called "el-Fatimi" who would bring them salvation. For the Moriscos of Aragon, el-Fatimi was a "sleeping" and "hidden" (in *gayba*?) emperor who would reappear riding a green horse to save the Moriscos and defeat the Christians.[76] The figure was thus a sort of mirror image of Santiago or St James, the patron saint of the Spaniards who, it was believed, had miraculously appeared on a white horse to defeat the Muslims. The belief of a hidden "*encubierto*" saviour of the Moriscos appears in *aljamiado* texts.[77] That this belief was also shared by the Moriscos of Granada is supported by evidence in Mármol, the chronicler of the revolt of the Alpujarras, who recorded the following:

> At that time God will send a king of great stature, hidden, higher than the mountains, whose hand will reach the sea and will rend it and from it will come a bridge . . . and they will enter Fez and they will find the hidden one in the mosque with the sword of Idrīs in his hand and dressed as a Moor; having seen which, all the Christians will become Moors.[78]

The sword of Idrīs was that of Idrīs b. ʿAbd Allāh b. al-Ḥasan b. al-Ḥasan b. ʿAlī (d. 175/791), the brother of Muḥammad al-Nafs al-Zakiyya, the founder of Fez and of the first dynasty of *shurafā* of the Maghreb, the first ruler in the Maghreb to call himself *mahdī*.[79]

Another part of the answer to this question might relate to the influence of Sufism and the characteristic interpretation of it that took place in the Muslim West, where there were so many Shiʿite influences. As Morimoto Kazuo has said about the kind of materials we have been analysing, "These materials were transmitted beyond the boundaries separating Sunnites and Shiʿites, and their logic and teachings were shared by the pro-*sayyid/sharīf* elements within both sects."[80] But we can also think in terms of the general features of Maghrebi Islam. In my opinion, and as I have suggested in a recent work, the Islamization of the Islamic West was largely carried out under Shiʿite terms, or perhaps it would be more accurate to say, during the period before Shiʿism as such had been defined, fenced off and set apart from orthodoxy. If this were the case, it might be more accurate to see the period of "late Spanish Islam" as defined by something like the survival of a local Islam as it had been practised by the rural populations of al-Andalus and the Maghreb along the "Middle Ages."[81]

This was a kind of Islam that was deeply imbued with respect for the supernatural, the magical, and for the holy lineage of the Prophet, which palliated or impeded an absolute separation between God and his creatures; where people looked up to the prophets as their principal guides in their quest for the afterworld as well as their guides for the unknown in this world and guides for human behavior and actions; a talismanic religion no different from what is found in the same period in other regions of Islam under Shiʿite influence, as shown for example by the so-called "Books of Omens" so abundant in sixteenth century Ottoman and Safavid lands.[82]

Another important bulk of Morisco production and of works very frequently diffused among the Moriscos, which we can also say "were transmitted beyond the boundary separating the Sunnites and the Shiʿites," are the books on magic and divination, of interpretations of dreams, of astrology or a synthesis of knowledge on astrology and magic.[83] They were books that were often attributed to Solomon,[84] to the prophet Daniel or Imam ʿAlī and most frequently to Imam Jaʿfar al-Ṣādiq, the sixth Imam who is associated with the texts on magic, alchemy and divination titled *jafr*.[85] In Spain the works of Abū Maʿshar al-Balkhī (d. 272/886), which had been translated to Latin and to Spanish, were widely read and consulted. Under the Spanished name of Abulmasar, his theory of astral conjunctions as signals of the end of a cycle or dynasty helped the Morisco belief in the coming of a prophet.[86] Magic and divination was an important part of local, Morisco Islam and it included the lives and deeds of Prophet Muḥammad and its progeny, especially ʿAlī, including his miraculous deeds and attributes. This magical literature must have contributed, in the minds of the Moriscos, to the prestige of the descendants of Muḥammad as sources of guide and of divine power.

Notes

1 On the difficulties and limitations of inquisitorial material, see M. García-Arenal, "Religious Dissent and Minorities: The Morisco Age," *Journal of Modern History* 81 (2009): 888–920.
2 M. García-Arenal, "La Inquisición y los libros de los moriscos," in *Memoria de los moriscos: Escritos y relatos de una diáspora cultural. Catálogo de la exposición* (Madrid: Biblioteca Nacional de España, 2010), 57–72.
3 This is the main argument of M. García-Arenal, *Messianism and Puritanical Reform: Mahdis of the Muslim West* (Leiden: Brill, 2006). Also, M. García-Arenal, *Ahmad al-Mansur: The Beginnings of Modern Morocco* (London: Oneworld, 2009).
4 To use the term coined by B. Vincent, "Las múltiples facetas del Islam tardío español," in A. Stoll ed., *Averroes dialogado y otros momentos literarios y sociales de la interacción cristiano-musulmana en España e Italia* (Kassel: Edition Reichenberger, 1998), 213–227.
5 For the implantation of Sufism in al-Andalus, the work of Miguel Asín Palacios is still the unavoidable reference, especially his articles collected in *Obras escogidas* (Madrid: Consejo Superior de Investigaciones Científicas, 1946).
6 M. Marín, "*Zuhhad* de al-Andalus (390/912–420/1029)," *Al-Qanṭara* 12 (1991): 439–469.
7 E. Lévi-Provençal, "La visite d'Ibn Battuta à Grenade," *Mélanges offerts à William Marçais par l'Institut d'Études Islamiques de l'Université de Paris* (Paris: G. P. Maisonneuve, 1950), 216.
8 Ibid., 218.
9 E. García Gómez, *Foco de antigua luz sobre la Alhambra* (Madrid: Instituto Egipcio de Estudios Islamicos en Madrid, 1988), 38.
10 N. J. G. Kaptein, *Muḥammad's Birthday Festival: Early History in the Central Muslim Lands and Development in the Muslim West until the 10th/16th Century* (Leiden: Brill, 1993).
11 Ibid., 93.
12 Ibid., 96.

13 H. Beck, *L'image d'Idrīs II, ses descendants de Fās et la politique sharifienne des sultans marīnides (656–869/1258–1465)* (Leiden: Brill, 1989), 100ff.
14 ʿAbd el-Haqq El-Bâdisî, *El-Maqsad (Vies des saints du Rîf)*, trans. by G. S. Colin, Archives marocaines 26 (Paris: H. Champion, 1926), 90–91.
15 Al-Qashtālī, *Tuḥfat al-mugtarib bi-bilād al-Maghrib fī karāmāt al-shaykh Abī Marwān (Milagros de Abu Marwān al-Yuḥānisī)*, ed. by F. de la Granja (Madrid: Instituto Egipcio de Estudios Islámicos, 1974), 68. Now translated into Spanish by Bárbara Boloix Gallardo, *Prodigios del maestro sufí Abū Marwān al-Yuḥānisī de Almería: Estudio crítico y traducción de la* Tuḥfat al-mugtarib *de Aḥmad al-Qaštālī* (Madrid: Mandala ediciones, 2010).
16 Ibid., 174–175.
17 Trans. by A. Bel, Algiers, 1903, apud E. García Gómez, *Foco de antigua luz*, 45.
18 See n. 9 above.
19 M. Jesús Rubiera, "El califato nazarí," *Al-Qanṭara* 29/2 (2008): 297.
20 M. Fierro, "The Ansaris: Nasir al-din and the Nasrids in al-Andalus," *Jerusalem Studies in Arabic and Islam* 31 (2006): 232–247.
21 Rubiera, "El califato nazarí," 303.
22 García Gómez, *Foco de antigua luz*, 53.
23 M. Fierro, "On al-Fāṭimī and al-Fāṭimiyyūn," *Jerusalem Studies in Arabic and Islam* 20 (1996): 139–140.
24 García Gómez, *Foco de antigua luz*, 42.
25 I follow here the arguments developed in M. García-Arenal, "Pouvoir sacré et mahdisme: Ahmad al-Mansur al-Dhahabi," *Al-Qanṭara* 17 (1996): 453–471, and more recently in M. García-Arenal, *Ahmad al-Mansur*.
26 Kaptein, *Muḥammad's Birthday Festival*, 135–137.
27 For references to other *fatwā*s against the celebration of the *mawlid* by the mystics, see Kaptein, *Muḥammad's Birthday Festival*, 139 and n. 48.
28 L. López-Baralt, *La literatura secreta de los moriscos* (Madrid: Trotta, 2009), 88.
29 R. Martín Soto, *Magia e Inquisición en el antiguo Reino de Granada* (Málaga: Editorial Arguval, 2000), 329.
30

> de ordinario traya consigo el libro del Alcorán para leer la secta de Mahoma; y tenía en su casa mezquita para enseñarla, y allí acudían muchos moriscos y moriscas a aprender; y que habiéndose juntado doce alfaquines acordaron que les faltaba un libro llamado Hizbalbac, que era un libro grande el qual contenía muy por extenso toda la secta de Mahoma y que no le avía en estos reynos sino en Argel, y determinaron que fuesse por él uno de los mayores alfaquines . . .

From C. Barceló and A. Labarta, *Archivos moriscos: Textos árabes de la minoría islámica valenciana, 1401–1608* (Valencia: Universidad de Valencia, 2009), 63.
31 MS Real Academia de la Historia (Madrid), MSS. Gayangos, 1922/36, 246.
32 "*[A]lmilid* por toda parte del mundo fazen gran fiesta aquella mesma noche los moros y fazen mucho gasto y ballen y tañen mayormente en la morería de Xátiva." Juan Andrés, *Confusión o confutación de la secta mahomética y del Alcorán*, ed. by Elisa Ruiz García (Mérida: Editorial regional de Extremadura, 2003), 213.
33 L. P. Harvey, "The Terminology of Two Hitherto Unpublished Morisco Calendar Texts," in A. Temimi ed., *Les actes de la première table ronde du CIEM* (Tunis: Centre d'Etudes sur les Morisques, 1986), 70–77; P. Dressendörfer, *Islam unter der Inquisition: Die Morisco-Prozesse in Toledo (1575–1610)* (Wiesbaden: Franz Steiner Verlag, 1971), 84.
34 C. López Morillas, *Textos aljamiados sobre la vida de Mahoma: El Profeta de los moriscos* (Madrid: Consejo Superior de Investigaciones Científicas, 1994); T. Fuente Cornejo, *Poesía religiosa aljamiado-morisca: Poemas en alabanza de Mahoma, de Alá y de la religión islámica* (Madrid: Fundación Ramón Menéndez

Pidal, 2000), 26, 39–99; A. Salmi, "Le genre des poèmes de nativité (Mauludiyyat) dans le royaume de Grenade et au Maroc du XIII au XVIIème siècle," *Hespéris* 43 (1956): 387; V. Barletta, *Covert Gestures: Crypto-Islamic Literature as Cultural Practice in Early Modern Spain* (Minneapolis: University of Minesota Press, 2005), 79–103.

35 MS Biblioteca Nacional de España, Madrid (henceforth BNE), 9653.

36 M. Fernández y González, *Estado social y político de los mudéjares de Castilla* (Madrid: Fomento, 1866, repr., Madrid: Hiperion, 1985), 237, n. 1. For more on Morisco theatrical representations, see J. Fournel-Guerin, "Le livre et la civilisation écrite dans la communauté morisque aragonaise (1540–1620)," *Mélanges de la Casa de Velázquez* 15 (1979): 254.

37 López Morillas, *Textos aljamiados sobre la vida de Mahoma.*

38 Fournel-Guerin, "Le livre et la civilisation écrite."

39 L. Bernabé Pons, "El qadi Iyad en la literatura aljamiado-morisca," *Sharq al-Andalus: Estudios Mudéjares y Moriscos* 14–15 (1997–1998): 201–218.

40 L. Cardaillac, *Morisques et Chrétiens: Un affrontement polémique* (Paris: Klinsieck, 1977), 215.

41 M. L. Lugo de Acevedo ed., *El Libro de las luces: Leyenda aljamiada sobre la genealogía de Mahoma: Edición crítica* (Madrid: Sial, 2008).

42 BNE, A. Caja 1/4. I am grateful to Fernando Rodríguez Mediano for this reference.

43 J. A. Lasarte, *Poemas de Mohamad Rabadán: Canto de las lunas. Día del juicio. Discurso de la luz. Los nombres de Dios* (Zaragoza: Diputación General de Aragón, 1991), 73–270; F. Corriente, *Relatos píos y profanos del manuscrito aljamiado de Urrea de Jalón*, intro. by M. Jesús Viguera (Zaragoza: Institución Fernando el Católico, 1990); A. Vespertino, "El Discurso de la Luz de Mohamed Rabadan y la literatura aljamiada de los últimos moriscos de España," in A. Temimi ed., *Actes du IV Symposium International d'Etudes Morisques* (Zaghouan: CEROMDI, 1990), 279–291.

44 O. de la Cruz Palma, "Notas a la lectura del *Liber generatione Mahumet* (traducción de Hermán de Carintia, 1142–1143)," forthcoming in the *Actas del V Congreso Internacional de Latín Medieval Hispánico, septiembre, 2009.*

45 Julián Ribera-Miguel Asín, *Manuscritos árabes y aljamiados de la Biblioteca de la Junta* (Madrid: Junta de Ampliación de Estudios, 1912), 44, 50.

46 James Kritzeck, *Peter the Venerable and Islam* (Princeton: Princeton University Press, 1964), 84.

47 This may have been the case of Francisco de Espinosa from El Provencio (Cuenca), who "read out of a book things about Muḥammad . . . and in particular how he had won and ruled over many lands." The Moriscos were said to have "been greatly pleased" with such readings. M. García-Arenal, *Inquisición y moriscos, los procesos del Tribunal de Cuenca* (Madrid: SigloXXI, 1978), 87. The same occurred in Aragon, where many trial records specify that the accused had read from the "*Libro de las luces.*" Fournel-Guerin, "Le livre et la civilisation écrite," 251.

48 For the celebration of the *mawlid*, as well as the taste in Sufi circles for the reading of the *Kitāb al-anwār*, see B. Shoshan, "Al-Bakri's Biography of Muḥammad," in B. Shoshan, *Popular Culture in Medieval Cairo* (London: Cambridge University Press, 2002), 37ff. See also N. J. Kaptein, *Muḥammad's Birthday Festival*, 129ff.

49 The report on the finding of 1622 can be found in Archivo Histórico Nacional, Madrid (henceforth AHN), Inquisición, Leg. 3096. The Inquisitor of Toledo, Gaspar de Peralta, collected the books on 30 July 1622.

50 This manustript was taken to Rome in 1627 by Camillo Massimo, the Papal nuncio in Madrid. The same nuncio took a total of twenty-one Arabic manuscripts from Spain to the Vatican Library. M. L. Lugo, "Introducción" to the edition of *El libro de las luces*, 41. P. S. Van Koningsveld has shown that most of the Arabic

manuscripts taken from Spain to the Vatican Library were provided by the Inquisition, "Andalusian-Arabic Manuscripts from Christian Spain: A Comparative Intercultural Approach," *Israel Oriental Studies* 12 (1992): 75–110.

51 See, for example, the case of Brianda Suarez (AHN, Inquisición, Toledo, Leg. 197, 17) who had a book in which she read stories of "the ancient prophets of the Muslims" or of Agustín de Ribera (AHN, Inquisición, Toledo, Leg. 197, 16) who said in his declaration in front of the Tribunal that "ʿAli es tenido entre los Moros por hombre santo y gran guerrero y que era capitán de Mahoma," i.e., "ʿAlī is considered by the Moors as a saint and a great warrior, captain of Muḥammad." Mercedes García-Arenal, "A Catholic Muslim Prophet: Agustín de Ribera, 'the boy who saw angels'," *Common Knowledge* 18/2 (2012): 267–291.

52 López Morillas, *Textos aljamiados sobre la vida de Mahoma.*

53 U. Rubin, "Pre-existence and Light: Aspects of the Concept of *Nur Muhammad*," *Israel Oriental Studies* 5 (1975): 62–119.

54 Shoshan, "Al-Bakri's Biography of Muḥammad," 38.

55 Shoshan, "Al-Bakri's Biography of Muḥammad," 34–35.

56 M. Fierro, "Manuscritos de al-Andalus: El proyecto H.A.T.A. (Historia de los Autores y Transmisores Andalusíes)," *Al-Qanṭara* 19 (1998): 173–502.

57 Mercedes García-Arenal and Fernando R. Mediano, *Un Oriente español: Los moriscos y el Sacromonte en tiempos de Contrarreforma* (Madrid: Marcial Pons, 2010), chapter 10.

58 P. Guerra de Lorca, *Catecheses mystagogicae pro advenis ex secta Mahometana* (Madrid: Petrum Madrigal, 1586), 101.

59 J. Caro Baroja, *Los moriscos del Reino de Granada* (Madrid, 1957, 2nd ed., Madrid: Itsmo, 1976), 82.

60 Muḥammad al-Sharīf al-Ḥusaynī al-Jaʿfarī al-Mursī al-Andalusī, *Kitāb al-anwār*, MS Bibliothèque Générale, Rabat, K1238. Partial French translation by A. Turki, "Documents sur le dernier exode des andalous vers la Tunisie," in M. Epalza and R. Petit eds, *Études sur les morisques andalous en Tunisie* (Madrid: Instituto Hispano-Arabe de Cultura, 1973), 114–134.

61 Ibid., 116.

62 Ibid., 117.

63 Ibid., 119. See also G. A. Wiegers, "European Converts to Islam in the Maghrib," in M. García-Arenal ed., *Conversions islamiques: Identités religieuses en Islam méditerranéen* (Paris: Maisonneuve et Larose, 2001), 231.

64 Turki, "Documents," 120.

65 L. del Mármol, *Historia de la rebelión y castigo de los moriscos del Reino de Granada*, facsimile ed. of the ed. of 1600, with intro. by A. Galán (Málaga: Arguval, 2004), libro IV, chapter 7 (entitled "Que trata de don Hernando de Córdoba y de Válor, y cómo los rebeldes le alzaron por rey" [Chapter about Hernando de Córdova y de Válor and how the rebels proclaimed him as king]), 122.

66 A summary of the characteristics and content of this manuscript can be found in J. Penella, "Littérature morisque en espagnol en Tunisie," in de Epalza and Petit eds, *Études sur les morisques espagnols en Tunisie*, 187–198.

67 L. F. Bernabé Pons, *El cántico islámico del morisco hispanotunecino Taybili* (Zaragoza: Institución Fernando el católico, 1988).

68 Ibid., 139–140. This is how al-Nawālī's name is presented here: "Al señor Sarife Ali Alniguali Abençeraje, Cahia del Ylustrisimo y excelentísimo señor Yuçuf Day."

69 Bernabé Pons, *El cántico islámico*, 266.

70 J.-F. Cutillas Ferrer ed., *Crónica y relación de la esclarecida descendencia xarifa (Un maqtal chií en castellano escrito por un morisco exiliado del siglo XVII)* (Alicante: Servicio de Publicaciones de la Universidad de Alicante, 1998).

71 Ibid., 23.

72 *Crónica y relación de la esclarecida descendencia xarifa*, 99. "*Nachaça*" at the end stands obviously for "*nash'a*," and not for "*nasab*" as Cutillas Ferrer proposes.
73 Cardaillac, *Morisques et Chrétiens*, 216.
74 Those who were sentenced to death by burning could instead be strangled or put to death more quickly and then burned after their deaths if they showed repentance.
75 AHN, Inquisición, Leg. 2106, 17.
76 P. Aznar Cardona, *Expulsión justificada de los moriscos españoles y suma de las excelencias de nuestro rey don Felipe el Católico tercero deste nombre*, 3 vols (Huesca: Pedro Cabarte, 1612), II:11. The same in M. de Guadalajara, *Prodición y destierro de los Moriscos de Castilla* (Pamplona: Nicolás de Assiayn, 1614), 25, apud M. García-Arenal, "'Un reconfort pour ceux qui sont dans l'attente': Prophétie et millénarisme dans la péninsule ibérique et au Maghreb (XVI–XVII siècles)," *Revue de l'histoire des religions* 220/4 (2003): 445–486.
77 M. Sánchez Álvarez, *El manuscrito misceláneo de la Biblioteca Nacional de París (leyendas, itinerarios de viajes, profecías sobre la destrucción de España y otros relatos moriscos)* (Madrid: Gredos, CLEAM, 1982), 246ff.
78 Mármol, *Historia de la rebelión*, libro IV, chapter 3.
79 M. García-Arenal, *Messianism and Puritanical Reform*, 44.
80 See Morimoto's contribution to this volume.
81 M. García-Arenal, *Messianism and Puritanical Reform*, chapter 1.
82 I refer to the essays contained in the excellent volume, M. Farhad and S. Bagci eds, *Falnama: The Book of Omens* (London: Thames & Hudson, 2009).
83 See, e.g., L. López-Baralt, *La literatura secreta de los últimos musulmanes de España* (Madrid: Trotta, D. L., 2009).
84 See, e.g., the following *aljamiado* books: *Medicina, farmacopea y magia en el 'Miscelánea de Salomón' (Texto árabe, traducción, glosas aljamiadas, estudio y glosario)*, ed. by J. Albarracín Navarro and J. Martínez Ruiz (Granada: Universidad de Granada, 1987); Libro *de* dichos maravillosos*: misceláneo morisco de magia y adivinación*, ed. by Ana Labarta (Madrid: CSIC-ICMA, 1993).
85 AHN, Inquisición, Leg. 197, 16. Juan de Sosa, Morisco of Toledo, had "un libro de moros que se decía el Jafari," i.e., he had a Muslim book of *jafr* (?). In that book he had read miraculous deeds of "Ali Enabitali" such as covering enormous distances in an hour because the land folded under his horse. Agustín de Ribera had read in one such book that apocalyptic events were to be expected in 1540 heralded by catastrophic signs in the sky and a big deluge as well as wars between Muslims: "en el año cuarenta (1540) había de haber muchas señales en el cielo e muy espantosas e que en el mismo año de cuarenta había de haber muchas guerras entre moros e cristianos e que había de haber un gran diluvio . . ."
86 J. Vernet, "Cuestiones catalográficas referentes a autores orientales: Problemas bibliográficos en torno a Albumasar," *Biblioteconomía* 9 (1952): 12–17, reprinted in *Estudios sobre la historia de la ciencia medieval* (Barcelona: Bellaterra, 1979), 278–282. Don Martín García, who before being appointed bishop of Barcelona by Ferdinand the Catholic had spent time preaching to the Muslims of Aragon, maintained that "the wise men of the Moors" used to read the "Libro de las Conjunciones" of Abulmasar and use it to predict what would happen to "their sect." S. Cirac Estopañán, *Los sermones de Don Martín García, obispo de Barcelona, sobre los Reyes Católicos* (Zaragoza: La Academia, 1955), 20.

9 The role of the *masharifu* on the Swahili coast in the nineteenth and twentieth centuries

Valerie J. Hoffman

Who are the Swalihi?

Questions of cultural identity and of the social role of a particular group within society are rarely uncontested, but perhaps nowhere in the world is there a society where questions of cultural origins and identity are as contested as on the Swahili coast. For decades there was much discussion among scholars and among the Swahili themselves concerning the "African" or "Asiatic" origin of Swahili culture and the nature of Swahili identity. The name "Swahili" means "coastal," and until recently Swahili was a designation for Sunni Muslims living along the East African coast who spoke a Bantu language with a vocabulary that is approximately 30 percent Arabic in origin. A major sub-group of Swahili speakers call themselves "Shirazi," based on putative descent from Arab princes who came from the city of Shiraz in southern Iran and settled in East Africa in the tenth century. For many centuries Islam in East Africa remained a largely coastal and urban phenomenon closely linked to trade. A series of Muslim principalities arose along long-distance trade routes on the southern Somali coast, including Mogadishu, Merca and Brava, which all became sultanates in the twelfth century, and as Swahili civilization extended southward along the coast from the fourteenth through sixteenth centuries, Lamu, Pate, Mombasa and Kilwa all became virtual city-states, usually ruled by a family claiming Arab descent.

Vasco da Gama visited Kilwa in 1498, and within a few years the Portuguese had captured and destroyed both Kilwa and Mombasa, the two greatest Shirazi cities. Portugal was the strongest naval power in the region throughout the sixteenth century, and directly contributed to the decline of Shirazi civilization, which was also hastened by attacks by African groups. In the mid-seventeenth century, a new dynasty in Oman challenged Portuguese supremacy in the Indian Ocean, capturing Mombasa, Pemba and Kilwa. The period from 1650 to 1730 was one of ongoing struggle between the two maritime powers. By the nineteenth century, the Omani empire included the Swahili coast, and indeed in 1832 the sultan of Oman transferred his capital from Muscat in Oman to Zanzibar in East Africa. From 1832 to 1856, Zanzibar was the capital of a vast empire that included Oman and the Swahili coast from Mogadishu in southern Somalia to some distance south of the Rovuma River in northern Mozambique. In 1856, the British brokered a division of the Omani empire between competing princes of the Bū Saʿīdī dynasty.[1]

Arabs on the Swahili coast

Most Omani settlers in East Africa belonged to the Ibāḍī sect of Islam, but they seem to have made little or no effort to proselytize. According to Trimingham, Omanis regarded Ibāḍism as a "tribal religion" that marked their separateness from and superiority to the indigenous population.[2] Although Omanis took African concubines, and the offspring of such unions were social equals to the offspring born to their Omani wives, the Omanis remained socially distinct. The overwhelming majority of the indigenous population of the Swahili coast follows the Shāfiʿī school of Sunni Islam. The Arabs who exercised the greatest religious influence in East Africa, by far, were Ḥaḍramīs, descended from immigrants who came from the Ḥaḍramawt region of southeast Yemen[3] and settled in the Lamu archipelago and the Comoros islands.[4] The tremendous social and spiritual influence in the Ḥaḍramawt of descendants of the Prophet, known as *sayyid*s or *sharīf*s, is well-known,[5] and the impact *sayyid* families from the Ḥaḍramawt made on Swahili society is also considerable. The Ḥaḍramīs are famous for their maritime adventures and missionary activities throughout the Indian Ocean; the nineteenth-century explorer Richard Burton wrote of them:

> They are the Swiss of the East, a people equally brave and hardy, frugal and faithful, as long as pay is regular . . . Natives of a poor and rugged region, they wander far and wide, preferring every country to their own; and it is generally said that the sun rises not upon a land that does not contain a man from Hazramaut.[6]

The Ḥaḍramīs claim credit for introducing Islam to both East Africa and Southeast Asia, and this claim is not far-fetched to anyone acquainted with these societies. Not only does Shāfiʿī Islam preponderate in both, as it does in the Ḥaḍramawt, but the frequency of distinctly Ḥaḍramī family names, the propagation of Islamic literature that was also favored in the Ḥaḍramawt, and the derivation of the content of Swahili narrative and didactic poems, coupled with the fact that Ḥaḍramīs are some of the most zealous Muslims on earth, make their claim quite believable. Ḥaḍramīs intermarried with the local population and became integrated into Swahili society, and many of them lost their fluency in Arabic. More than three-quarters of the *ʿulamāʾ* before the mid-twentieth century were of Ḥaḍramī background, many from *sayyid* families, although Ḥaḍramīs constituted probably no more than 2 percent of the Sunni population of East Africa.[7] *Sayyid* families from the Ḥaḍramawt settled on the Swahili coast as early as the fourteenth century, and new *sayyid* families came during the sixteenth and seventeenth centuries to fight the Portuguese, and subsequently established themselves as rulers of city-states as well as resident scholars. Bā ʿAlawī sultanates were secured in the Comoros, Kilwa, Zanzibar, Timbatu, and at Vumba Kuu.[8]

During the nineteenth century Swahili society consisted of Omani overlords who were Ibāḍī, Baluchi soldiers who were Ḥanafī Sunnis, Indian merchants who were Ismāʿīlī, Bohorā[9] and Hindu, Ḥaḍramī scholars and traders who were Shāfiʿī, and African subjects and slaves who were Shāfiʿī or followed indigenous religions. Until the development of African nationalisms in the late 1950s and early 1960s, Arabs often enjoyed political power and religious and cultural prestige in East Africa, and special respect was given to the *shurafā'* – or, as they are called in Swahili, *masharifu*.[10]

Veneration for the Prophet and his descendants on the Swahili coast

Western scholars and observers of religious life on the Swahili coast have rarely been scholars of Islam, and have therefore tended to see aspects of Swahili religious life as unique to that region, even if in fact these phenomena can be found throughout the Muslim world.[11] One feature that struck Western scholars as peculiarly Swahili is the central role of veneration of the Prophet in Muslim devotional life. Pouwels, for example, marveled that the Prophet is seen by the Swahili as sinless, a worker of miracles, intercessor, guarantor of salvation, and possessor of a portion of the divine light, although such beliefs are absolutely mainstream throughout both Sunni and Shīʿite Islam, except among certain reformist circles. Pouwels saw the centrality of the Prophet's role in Islamic life on the Swahili coast as an African-type "personality cult."[12]

In Qur'ān schools on the Swahili coast, children memorize not only the Qur'ān but also a lengthy poem that praises the Prophet Muḥammad – the famous *mawlid* (*maulidi* in Swahili) of a sharīfian scholar originally from northern Iraq, Jaʿfar b. Ḥasan al-Barzanjī (1690–1765). A second *maulidi*, that of al-Ḥabshī, was introduced into Lamu in the early twentieth century by Ṣāliḥ b. ʿAlawī Jamal al-Layl (1844–1935), a *sharīf* popularly known as Habib Saleh, who founded the Riyadha mosque and *madrasa*, patterned after the al-Riyāḍ mosque *madrasa* founded in the Ḥaḍramī city of Say'ūn in 1878 by Sayyid ʿAlī b. Muḥammad al-Ḥabshī (d. 1914), the leading scholar of his day in the Ḥaḍramawt. Habib Saleh challenged the exclusiveness of Islamic education within established patrician families, offering it to underprivileged and previously excluded groups. Both *maulidi*s relate that the first thing God created was the Muḥammadan Light, made from a handful of God's own light, and from this all other things were made. Hence, the cosmos is permeated by the light of the Prophet Muḥammad, for whom indeed it was made. The *maulidi*s trace the transmission of this light from person to person until the conception of the Prophet, whose gestation was marked by miraculous occurrences.[13] In Swahili towns the Prophet's birthday is celebrated with open-air communal recitation of these *maulidi*s and, in the case of the Lamu *maulidi*, with processions and small hand-held drums and tambourines.[14] Groups of children also recite it on other important occasions, such as weddings.

The *sayyid* clans, embodying the blessing of the Prophet by virtue of their descent from him, were thought to have special intercessory powers and superior claims to pronouncements on matters of law. Their presence was seen as assuring the holiness and well-being of the towns in which they settled.[15] Their "immanent holiness" allowed them to integrate into the privileged ranks of society and drew the respect of the upper classes and the veneration of the lower classes. They enjoyed special gifts and tax exemptions.[16] To use Purpura's phrase, they "brought home the *baraka*" (spiritual power) of their remote ancestor and their remote homeland.[17]

The Ḥaḍramawt's reputation as the source of both scholarship and sanctity drew pilgrims from the Swahili coast, some of whom wrote accounts of their journeys. This is expressed perhaps most poetically in the title of a travelogue written by ʿAbdallāh Bā Kathīr (1860–1925), *Riḥlat al-ashwāq al-qawiyya ilā mawāṭin al-sāda al-ʿalawiyya* [The Journey of Strong Desires for the Homeland of the ʿAlawī *Sayyids*].[18] Bā Kathīr undertook this journey with the permission of his teacher and colleague, Sayyid Aḥmad b. Sumayṭ (1861–1925), one of the most famous scholars of the Swahili coast,[19] in order to come into first-hand contact with the wellsprings of *baraka* that had so blessed his revered master. Aḥmad b. Sumayṭ's Ḥaḍramī father had settled in the Comoro Islands, like so many other *sayyid* families, but Ibn Sumayṭ returned to the Ḥaḍramawt for study and made his career in Zanzibar. Bā Kathīr, who was raised in Lamu but also made his career mainly in Zanzibar, was of Ḥaḍramī but non-sharīfian origin, and his reverence for Ibn Sumayṭ (who was, after all, a year younger than he) was such that he refused to serve as a judge as long as Ibn Sumayṭ was alive.[20]

Debates over the meaning of *sharaf* (nobility)

It is well known that in Islamic law descent is reckoned according to the paternal lineage. This, and the necessity of male authority over women, led to the articulation of the legal principle of *kafāʾa* in the Ḥanafī, Shāfiʿī and Ḥanbalī schools, according to which a Muslim woman cannot marry a man whose lineage is less prestigious than her own.[21] Therefore, a *sharīfa* can only marry a *sharīf*. Only the woman's guardian (*walī*) can override this prohibition.

By the late nineteenth century, however, there were some who argued that nobility (*sharaf*) can be derived from knowledge as well as from lineage, resulting in a major controversy in 1898 when ʿAbdallah Wazir Msujini (d. 1904), a scholar in Zanzibar of Ḥaḍramī background but non-sharīfian descent, married two *sharīfa*s without the presence of a guardian, claiming that the *sharaf* derived from his scholarship sanctioned these marriages, and that in any case he could have sharīfian descent, but simply did not know for sure.

A *sayyid* of Zanzibar, Ḥasan b. Muḥammad b. Ḥasan Jamal al-Layl (d. 1904), wrote a scathing denunciation.[22] He marshalled scholarly evidence against ʿAbdallah Wazir's position, but he also attacked the latter personally, arguing that ʿAbdallah Wazir was not qualified to do *ijtihād* (independent interpretation of the sources) but should only practice *taqlīd* (follow the rulings of his predecessors), and had no right to try to build legal arguments by citing the Qur'ān and Sunna. He pointed out that scholars in the Ḥaḍramawt kept meticulous genealogical records, so if he were of sharīfian descent this would be documented; there could be no uncertainty. He also accused Shaykh ʿAbdallah of lying when he claimed never to have discussed this issue with him, as apparently Sayyid Ḥasan had taken Shaykh ʿAbdallah to the chief Shāfiʿī *qāḍī* of Zanzibar[23] for adjudication of the matter.[24] Although the incompleteness of the existing copy of Sayyid Ḥasan's manuscript precludes verification of the judge's decision, the tenor of the writing implies that he agreed with Sayyid Ḥasan. Sayyid Ḥasan marvels that anyone would try to raise himself to the status of the *Ahl al-Bayt*. He cites a sharīfian scholar of the Ḥaḍramawt, ʿAlī b. Ḥasan al-ʿAṭṭās (1709–1758), who wrote:

> I have seen people in our time whom God has afflicted with hatred and enmity for the *Ahl al-Bayt*, . . . placing obstacles in the way of the love for them that is required, out of envy for them and injustice against them, especially those who are said to be scholars and who are known for their teaching. How can anyone exalt his humble self over the *Ahl al-Bayt*?[25]

Indeed, wrote Sayyid Ḥasan, no matter how much knowledge a scholar has he can never equal the nobility that a *sharīf* possesses by virtue of his lineage, because the *sharaf* of descent from the Prophet is an attribute of essence (*dhātī*), whereas the *sharaf* of scholarship is acquired, and is therefore "accidental" (in the philosophical sense – *ʿaraḍī*) and is subject to change. This was why the sixteenth-century Egyptian scholar and Sufi, ʿAbd al-Wahhāb al-Shaʿrānī, wrote that Sufi shaykhs should never take *sharīfs* as disciples, because however much a shaykh has risen (*taraqqā*) in spiritual station and however much the veils over the unseen realm have been removed for him and he has seen by the lights of his inner vision the secrets of existence, he can never attain the station of the one whom God has made a *sharīf* without any effort.[26]

Islamic reformism

It was the introduction of modern reinterpretations of Islam, of both the modernist and fundamentalist varieties, that undermined the status of the *masharifu* on the Swahili coast. *Al-Manār*, the journal issued in Egypt by Muḥammad ʿAbduh and Rashīd Riḍā, made a controversial first appearance in Zanzibar in the early twentieth century, but Islamic reformism first made a real impact on the Swahili coast through the efforts of Shaykh al-Amīn b. ʿAlī al-Mazrūʿī (Mazrui) of Mombasa (1890–1947). Though a student of the most famous ʿAlawī shaykhs in Zanzibar, Shaykh al-Amīn adopted a more anti-Sufi point of view in the 1930s and became the major inspiration of Islamic reform in East Africa. He founded several reformist journals, taught many subsequent reformist scholars, and became Grand Kadhi (Qāḍī) of Kenya.[27] He was the first to introduce a distinct anti-*bidʿa*[28] discourse in East Africa that was directed against Sufi practices. He also stressed the importance of modern (not only Islamic) education and female education, and wrote texts in Swahili rather than Arabic. His most influential student, Abdallah Salih Farsy, wrote that Mazrui "created a tremendous uproar by publishing newspapers and books vilifying forbidden matters and pagan practices."[29] Under Mazrui's tutelage, Farsy, a Zanzibari who had studied with the great ʿAlawī shaykhs on the island,

> turned ideologically against his intellectual ancestors and spearheaded a reformist movement which became increasingly dominated by Wahhabi doctrine. Farsy, who served as Chief Kadhi from 1968–1980, was often at odds with local *ʿulamāʾ* who resented him as a "foreigner" or even denounced him as an "unbeliever."[30]

In recent decades young men from the Swahili coast have taken advantage of educational scholarships to study abroad in countries such as Saudi Arabia, Egypt, Pakistan and Kuwait, and have returned with reformist points of view that are decidedly hostile to many aspects of popular Islam on the Swahili coast. Kresse writes that some Swahili elders came to view the Islam of those who studied abroad as a "new religion," a "religion of money."[31] Local critics call the reformists "Wahhabis," while the reformists call themselves the "Ahlul Sunnah" movement or *watu wa sunna* (people of the Sunna).

Reformist criticism of the *maulidi* made many question its legitimacy. Although once an unquestioned part of social life and an instrument of communal solidarity, reformist criticism has led people "to feel insecure about its status from an Islamic perspective."[32] Even some of its defenders now describe it as a local custom rather than an Islamic practice.[33]

Even more directly relevant to the topic of this paper are the criticisms of the *masharifu* made in a booklet on the life of ʿAlī b. Abī Ṭālib published in 1965 by Shaykh Muhammad Kasim Mazrui (1912–1982; he served as Chief Kadhi of Kenya from 1963–1968), a student of Shaykh al-Amin bin Ali Mazrui. Muhammad Kasim had written very popular booklets in Swahili on the lives of the first three caliphs, but his booklet on the life of ʿAlī, the fourth caliph, proved controversial because of his extensive criticisms of what he saw as excessive veneration of the *masharifu*, including belief in the *baraka* of their presence, the medicinal qualities of their saliva, and the value of their intercession. He was especially critical of the belief that the *masharifu* are not to be criticized if they violate the precepts of the *Sharīʿa*. Muhammad Kasim recounts a story he had heard:

> One day a *sharīf* was caught sleeping with someone else's wife on her bed in her house. Since he was a *sharīf*, the man of the house did not dare

> do anything but say a few words [in anger]. The *sharīf* became angry, got off the bed, dressed, and left in a fury. As if that wasn't enough, he went and told the people, "So-and-so appeared at my house with his wife and insulted me!" All the people of the village rose up against the man whose house had been violated and told him, "Don't you see that it is a great honor for you that a *sharīf* slept on your bed?! Don't you know that he can rescue a woman from hellfire?!" The poor man got no peace until he apologized to the *sharīf*.[34]

In another story, a person visiting a village in Uganda decided to pretend to be a *sharīf*, certain that these Ugandans would not know the difference. In order to take full advantage of the privileges of his pretended nobility, he requested that his host provide him with one of his wives for the night, assuring him that this was perfectly legal as long as they bathed in the morning.[35] This story serves as a warning not only against believing that the *masharifu* are above the law, but also that one should not believe every claim to descent from the Prophet.

El Zein wrote that the *masharifu* interpreted Muhammad Kasim Mazrui's failing eyesight as divine retribution for criticizing the *masharifu*,[36] although Mazrui points out in the foreword to the second printing of his booklet that his poor eyesight was a hereditary condition from which he had suffered since childhood. In any case, the controversy surrounding Mazrui's attacks on the *masharifu* is probably a factor in the rarity of copies of this particular biography, in contrast to the ubiquity of his biographies of the first three caliphs.[37]

The impact of African nationalism

The social status of the *masharifu* was further undermined by the rise of African nationalism on the Swahili coast, entailing rejection of the formerly dominant "foreign" classes. In Kenya, Muslims are a largely disempowered minority, their desire for independence of the coast from the mainland abruptly thwarted when Kenya was granted independence in 1963. Zanzibar, which was overwhelmingly Muslim, was granted independence in December 1963 as a constitutional monarchy under Sultan Jamshīd b. ʿAbdallāh al-Bū Saʿīdī, but in January 1964 the government was overthrown in a violent coup led by a Ugandan Christian named John Okello, who styled himself "Field Marshall," and in April 1964 Zanzibar joined with Tanganyika to form the Republic of Tanzania. The Zanzibar revolution was a revolt led by African mainlanders against Arab and Indian political and economic dominance; although slavery had ended more than a half-century earlier, the Arabs remained a privileged class. Arabs sometimes continued to address blacks as "slave" and held a strong sense of racial superiority. Swahilis who identified themselves as Shirazis also regarded the mainlanders as savages (*washenzi*).[38] Indians did not have the same political power or social prestige as Arabs or Shirazis, but they had become the wealthiest segment of society, owning most of the land and businesses. The black African majority was clearly disadvantaged in every way.

The leaders of the revolution encouraged black Africans to attack non-blacks; a horrific massacre ensued, in which some ten thousand unarmed civilians were murdered. Thousands of Arabs and Indians fled Zanzibar at this time, but many were unable to leave. Those who remained "lived in the shadow, seeking more to make themselves forgotten than to recapture lost advantages," often accused of anti-revolutionary plots.[39] The revolutionaries specifically targeted Zanzibar's Islamic heritage; most of the Arabic manuscripts in the Zanzibar National Archives have been vandalized. Eyewitnesses say that Qurʾāns and other Islamic books were burned in the streets, although 98 percent of Zanzibar's population was Muslim.[40] Homes were invaded and people of lighter skin were selected for extermination, often in hideous fashion, so that no body could remain for burial. Okello allegedly bragged that he personally killed more than eight thousand people. In the new socialist order, plantations were nationalized and redistributed, while stone houses in town were confiscated and became government property.[41]

There is no room for social privilege based on Arab blood or descent from the Prophet in the new society, a fact painfully and shockingly brought home by the forced marriage of four girls "of Persian origin" to senior government officials, including two members of the Revolutionary Council, in September 1970; the government claimed that such marriages were the only way to ensure racial equality and harmony.[42] Of the "Arabs" who survived the massacre of the revolution, many escaped to Oman or other countries.[43] Consequently, "individuals who are still distinguished by descent identities rendered in Islamic religious terms are considered with some ambivalence in Zanzibar."[44]

Interestingly, one of the stories Muhammad Kasim Mazrui tells in order to illustrate the abuses of the *masharifu* concerns an upcountry convert to Islam who became a disciple of a Sufi shaykh in a town on the coast. One day during a conversation with a friend and the friend's sharīfian wife, the call to prayer sounded. The young man suggested they go to pray, but the *sharīfa* rained curses on him for interrupting the conversation. The young man related the shocking incident to his shaykh, who cautioned him against criticizing the *masharifu*. Incredulous that God would discriminate between people based on their lineage, the young man abandoned the shaykh and his Sufi teachings and turned to Islamic reformism.[45]

This story can serve as a metaphor for the decline of the *masharifu* in the new Africa, an Africa in which neither Arab nor Prophetic descent carries any privileges. As more and more African Muslims hail from the mainland and interior, an Islam that privileges an obsolete patrician class holds little attraction. By the mid-twentieth century, the Ḥaḍramawt no longer played the role of religious homeland it had enjoyed only decades earlier. Scholars of Egypt and Saudi Arabia became the new authorities at a time that saw the rise of both socialist and Islamic reformist ideologies in the Arab world as well as in Africa. Reformist attacks on popular religion increased in intensity, and the rise of anti-Arab African nationalism led to the decline of Arab power and prestige, most brutally in the bloodbath of Zanzibar's revolution. The Ḥaḍramawt itself was taken over in 1969 by radical Marxists who conducted a brutal purge of the *sayyid* class and destroyed books and manuscripts that carried the legacy of the Ḥaḍramawt's intensely Sufi and sharīfian Islamic life. Despite the intense religiosity that continues to characterize Ḥaḍramī society, many young people are entirely unaware of this heritage or of the Ḥaḍramawt's role in the Islamic life of the Indian Ocean region.[46]

But is that the end of the story? Not necessarily. Economic incentives led the government of Tanzania since 1986 to retreat from its socialist policies and to encourage the return of Arab and Indian entrepreneurs, and many politically and culturally prominent individuals on the Swahili coast (and in south Yemen) carry the names of well-known sharīfian families, though no effort is made to draw attention to their status as descendants of the Prophet. There is, however, one phenomenon that is worth noting: the impact of the Iranian revolution on politicized Muslims of Kenya, leading to a number of conversions to Shīʿite Islam. The rival Islamist governments of Saudi Arabia and Iran have tried to influence Islamic trends in East Africa, particularly in Kenya. While the Saudi government and al-Qāʿida are both anti-Shīʿite, Iran promotes Sunni–Shīʿite rapprochement and its own brand of Islamic activism in East Africa. Many young Kenyan Muslims admire Iran for promoting a politically relevant and modern form of Islam. There have been a number of conversions of Sunni Muslims to Shīʿism in Kenya, and this trend continues.[47] Until recently, Twelver Shīʿite identity was closely linked with Persian or Indian ethnicity, and a Swahili by definition was a Sunni Muslim. That is no longer the case, as is demonstrated by the example of Shaykh Abdilahi Nassir (born 1932), a well-known scholar who converted to Twelver Shīʿism in the 1980s.[48] Some defenders of *maulidi* have tried to demonstrate Muslim unity through common Sunni–Shīʿa *maulidi* celebrations in Mombasa.[49] Given the very strong connection of Shīʿism to veneration for the *Ahl al-Bayt*, does the new relevance of Twelver Shīʿism in Kenya signal the possibility that veneration of the Prophet and of his descendants could once again come into vogue among the vanguard of Swahili Muslim society? At this point, there is no evidence that converts to Shīʿism are motivated in any way by nostalgia for the previous social order; on the contrary, Shaykh Abdilahi Nassir has been outspoken against local ethnic and racial discrimination.[50] He says that he was drawn to Shīʿism because of its emphasis on taking responsibility for oneself, in contrast to the predestinarian theology that predominates in Sunni Islam. Shīʿism, he felt, at least in its Iranian incarnation, combines intellectual and political activity with a Sufi-oriented spirituality motivated by pure love for God.[51] Nonetheless, in 1967, well before his conversion to Shīʿism, he wrote a stinging rebuttal of Muhammad Kasim Mazrui's attack on the *masharifu*, and he still feels that the hostility between the *watu wa sunna* and the *masharifu* represents an even greater threat to Muslim unity than the Sunni–Shīʿite divide.[52]

Conclusion

In conclusion, although individual descendants of the Prophet may be found in the intellectual and spiritual elite of Swahili society, the *masharifu*, as a class, are no longer dominant. Their influence has been systematically and effectively undermined both by the political events that overthrew the old order and by Islamic reformist ideologies that denounce traditional veneration of the Prophet and his descendants as heresy. This veneration is not entirely a thing of the past, but the sun has clearly set on the heyday of the *masharifu* on the Swahili coast.

Notes

1 For a general introduction to Swahili society and history, see R. L. Pouwels, *Horn and Crescent: Cultural Change and Traditional Islam on the East African Coast, 800–1900*, African Studies Series, 53 (Cambridge and New York: Cambridge University Press, 1987) or M. Horton and J. Middleton, *The Swahili: The Social Landscape of a Mercantile Society* (Oxford, UK and Malden, Massachusetts: Blackwell Publishers, 2000) or, for a briefer introduction, L. W. Hollingsworth, *A Short History of the East Coast of Africa* (London: Macmillan & Co., 1961).

2 J. S. Trimingham, *Islam in East Africa* (Oxford: Clarendon Press, 1964), 73.

3 Wādī Ḥaḍramawt is a vast 160-km-long dried riverbed, with innumerable smaller *wādī*s as tributaries. In ancient Roman times it was a vast forest in the middle of the desert and was considered a great wonder. Today it still has underground aquifers that supply fresh water, and there are palm groves and agricultural plots on the vast dried riverbed, but the forest is gone and the desert has taken over.

4 F. Le Guennec-Coppens, "Social and Cultural Integration: A Case Study of the East African Hadramis," *Africa* 59/2 (1989): 185–195.

5 R. B. Serjeant, *The Saiyids of Ḥaḍramawt* (London: School of Oriental and African Studies, University of London, 1957). A *sharīf* (*sharīfa* if female) is a descendant of the Prophet; the plural is *shurafāʾ* or *ashrāf*, although the latter can also mean the notable men of society, regardless of descent. In the Ḥaḍramawt and on the Swahili coast, men who are descended from the Prophet receive the title of *sayyid*, meaning "master." The terms *sayyid*s and *sharīf*s are, therefore, interchangeable. Concerning the role of *sharīf*s in the Ḥaḍramawt, Mostafa al-Badawi writes in the introduction to his translation of *Key to the Garden*, a Sufi text by a Ḥaḍramī *sayyid*:

> Among the most illustrious of *Ahl al-Bayt* are the ʿAlawi *sayyid*s of Hadramawt. Their ancestor, Imam Ahmad ibn ʿIsa known as the "Emigrant," abandoned the land of Iraq, troubled by sedition and civil unrest, for Hadramawt. Of his descendants only those of one of his grandsons, Imam ʿAlawi, survive to this day and are still called after him. Their presence in Hadramawt transformed it from a land ruled by the heretic *Khawarij* to one ruled by the orthodox *sunni* school of Imam Ashʿari as concerns beliefs and that of Imam Shafiʿi in legal matters. They soon produced countless scholarly saints who strove to spread the Book of God and maintain the purity of the prophetic Sunna through the vicissitudes of changing times. They traveled East as far as the Philippines, being the main teachers of Islam in Malaya and Indonesia, and West to East Africa where their influence is still very much in evidence. Leading ʿAlawis were originally given the title "Imam," this was later changed into "shaykh,"

then, by the time of Imam ʿAbdallah al-Haddad in the 11th century H., into "*Habib*," which is one of the attributes of their ancestor, the Prophet, the literal meaning of which is "beloved."

From A. M. Haddad, *Key to the Garden*, trans. by M. al-Badawi (London: The Quilliam Press, 1990, repr. Beirut: Dar al-Hawi, 1997), viii–ix.

I first became aware of this book when I found it used as a textbook at a private *madrasa* in Zanzibar.

6 R. F. Burton, *First Footsteps in East Africa*, ed. by Gordon Waterfield (London: Routledge & Kegan Paul, 1966), 58.

7 A. H. Nimtz, Jr., *Islam and Politics in East Africa: The Sufi Order in Tanzania* (Minneapolis: University of Minnesota Press, 1980), 20.

8 Pouwels, *Horn and Crescent*, 42.

9 Technically Bohorās are also Ismāʿīlīs, of the Dāʾūdī branch of the sect that acknowledged al-Mustaʿlī (r. 1094–1101) rather than his brother Nizār to succeed his father al-Mustanṣir in the Fāṭimid Caliphate of Egypt. But on the Swahili coast "Ismāʿīlī" refers only to the followers of the Aga Khan, and Bohorās do not recognize themselves as Ismāʿīlī at all. The name *bohorā* is not originally a religious term; it means "trader," from the Gujarati *vohōrvū*, "to trade." Some who belong to the Bohorā community in western India are not Dāʾūdī Ismāʿīlī at all, but are Sunnis, and some are even Hindus. But on the Swahili coast, *bohorā* refers to the followers of Dāʾūdī Ismāʿīlism.

10 The singular of *masharifu* is *sharif*.

11 Indeed, Western specialists in sub-Saharan Africa tend to speak of "African Islam" as something distinct from "Arab Islam," although I would contend that there is no single "Arab Islam," and that the very features that strike Western observers as uniquely African are to be found in the Arab world as well.

12 Pouwels, *Horn and Crescent*, 70–71.

13 J. Knappert, *Swahili Islamic Poetry*, vol. 1. (Leiden: Brill, 1971), 30–60.

14 A. W. Boyd, "To Praise the Prophet: A Processual Symbolic Analysis of 'Maulidi', a Muslim Ritual in Lamu, Kenya," unpublished Ph.D. dissertation, Indiana University, 1980.

15 A. Purpura, "Knowledge and Agency: The Social Relations of Islamic Expertise in Zanzibar Town," unpublished Ph.D. dissertation, City University of New York, 1997, 69–74.

16 Le Guennec-Coppens, "Social and Cultural Integration," 186–188.

17 Purpura, "Knowledge and Agency," 81.

18 Ed. by ʿA. al-Saqqāf (Zanzibar: Maṭbaʿat al-ʿUlūm, 1358/1939).

19 A. K. Bang, *Sufis and Scholars of the Sea: Family Networks in East Africa, 1860–1925* (London: RoutledgeCurzon, 2003), 104–112.

20 Aḥmad b. Sumayṭ's son ʿUmar also made a study tour/pilgrimage to the Ḥaḍramawt and wrote about it. When he returned to Zanzibar in 1954, he became principal of the Muslim Academy. In 1969 he moved to the Grand Comoro.

21 *Kafāʾa* is usually translated as "equality," leading some Muslim scholars to make disingenuous statements that husband and wife must be equal. But that is not true: a man may marry a woman beneath his status – even far beneath his status. There is only a problem if a woman marries beneath her status. This is why a Muslim man may marry a Jewish or Christian woman but a Muslim woman may only marry a Muslim man, because such a situation "would result in an unacceptable incongruity between the superiority which the wife should enjoy by virtue of being Muslim, and her unavoidable wifely subjection to her infidel husband" (Y. Friedmann, *Tolerance and Coercion in Islam: Interfaith Relations in the Muslim Tradition* [Cambridge: Cambridge University Press, 2003], 161). Likewise, the marriage of a *sharīfa* to a non-*sharīf* would present the anomaly of a man

of lower status having authority over a woman of higher status. For this reason, I would translate *kafāʾa* as "sufficiency" rather than "equality."

22 Farsy says that this was a book entitled *al-Ajwiba al-shāmila* [Complete Answers], and that he sent this book to the Grand Mufti of Mecca, Muḥammad Saʿīd Bābsayl, who provided a written testimony of the accuracy of the book's contents, with an inscription dated 31 May 1898 (A. S. Farsy, *The Shafiʿi Ulama of East Africa, ca. 1830–1970*, trans. by R. L. Pouwels [Madison: University of Wisconsin African Studies Program, 1989], 82). Only a fragment of this manuscript remains in the Zanzibar National Archives, no. ZA 8/58.

23 Shaykh Burhān al-Dīn b. ʿAbd al-ʿAzīz al-Amawī (1861–1935). Shaykh Burhān was of Qurashī (Umayyad) but not sharīfian descent, and was known for his deep respect for and generous gifts to the *masharifu*. Farsy, *The Shafiʿi Ulama*, 48.

24 Farsy tells us that Burhān al-Dīn b. ʿAbd al-ʿAzīz served as Chief Qāḍī in Zanzibar from 1891–1932, a period of 42 years. Ibid.

25 Sayyid ʿAlī b. Ḥasan al-ʿAṭṭās, *al-Riyāḍa al-muʾniqa fī al-alfāẓ al-mutafarriqa*, cited in Ḥasan b. Muḥammad b. Ḥasan Jamal al-Layl, *al-Ajwiba al-shāmila*, ZA 8/58. Al-ʿAṭṭās's complaint dates back to the first half of the eighteenth century. On the life and writings of Sayyid ʿAlī b. Ḥasan al-ʿAṭṭās, see ʿA. al-Saqqāf, *Taʾrīkh al-shuʿarāʾ al-ḥaḍramiyyīn*, 5 vols in 1, 3rd printing (Taʾif: Maktabat al-Maʿārif, 1418/1997), I:158–168.

26 ʿAbdallah Salih Farsy (1912–1982), a shaykh of Salafī/Wahhābī orientation, scoffed at the prohibition of marriage between a non-*sharīf* and a *sharīfa*, pointing out that many prominent non-sharīfian scholars had married *sharīfa*s (Farsy, *The Shafiʿi Ulama*, 70). Presumably, however, they did so with the consent of the women's guardians.

27 R. L. Pouwels, "Sh. Al-Amin b. Ali Mazrui and Islamic Modernism in East Africa, 1875–1947," *International Journal of Middle East Studies* 13/3 (1981): 329–345; idem, *Horn and Crescent*, 201–202.

28 *Bidʿa* is commonly translated as "innovation," but the latter has a positive connotation in English, whereas *bidʿa* is something that is inauthentic or heretical. According to conventional wisdom, one should follow the example of the Prophet and avoid introducing new practices. Classical scholarship nonetheless distinguished between good and bad *bidʿa*; for example, although it was universally admitted that the birthday of the Prophet was not celebrated in early Islam, its later celebration was seen as a good innovation. In the modern period, however, it has become customary to condemn all of Sufism as *bidʿa* and therefore inauthentic and not part of "true" Islam.

29 Farsy, *The Shafiʿi Ulama*, 122.

30 K. Kresse, *Philosophising in Mombasa: Knowledge, Islam and Intellectual Practice on the Swahili Coast* (Edinburgh: Edinburgh University Press, 2007), 89–91, citing M. Bakari, "The New ʿUlama in Kenya," in M. Bakari and S. S. Yahya eds, *Islam in Kenya: Proceedings of the National Seminar on Contemporary Islam in Kenya* (Nairobi: Mewa Publications, 1995), 181 and A. Yassin, "Conflict and Conflict Resolution among the Swahili of Kenya," unpublished Ph.D. dissertation, University of London, 2004, 212–214.

31 Kresse, *Philosophising in Mombasa*, 92–95.

32 Ibid., 256, n. 17.

33 Ibid., 84. This is true not only in Kenya, the subject of Kresse's study, but in Zanzibar as well. See S. Ngalapi, "Feature about Maulidi ya Homu (Maulidi ya Salama)." www.arterialnetwork.org/sidenav-fr/projets/projets-mis-en-place/arts-journalism-workshop/articles-written-by-the-arts-journalists/saphia-ngalapi/document.2008-11-27.4852235790/view?set_language=fr (accessed 15 September 2009). Today *maulidi* is often performed for tourists or in artistic venues rather than serving as a truly communal event.

34 M. K. Mazrui, *Maisha ya al-Imam Aly khalifa wanne*, 2nd printing (Mombasa: H. O. Adam & Sons, 1973; originally published 1965), 13.
35 Ibid., 13–14.
36 A. M. El Zein, *The Sacred Meadows: A Structural Analysis of Religious Symbolism in an East African Town* (Evanston, IL: Northwestern University Press, 1974), 149.
37 K. Kresse, "'Swahili Enlightenment'? East African Reformist Discourse at the Turning Point: The Example of Sheikh Muhammad Kasim Mazrui," *Journal of Religion in Africa* 33/3 (2003): 283–284 [279–309].
38 It is interesting to note that the first president after the revolution, Abeid Amani Karume, a mainlander, presented himself as the son of a Shirazi mother, in order to cast himself as an authentic Zanzibari, despite his recent immigration to the island. A. Crozon, "Les Arabes à Zanzibar: Haine et fascination," in F. Le Guennec-Coppens and P. Caplan eds, *Les Swahili entre Afrique et Arabie* (Paris: Credu-Karthala, 1991), 184.
39 Ibid., 184–185.
40 Religious scholars were known for their ability to manipulate Qur'ānic verses, letters and numbers for talismanic purposes. Purpura says that the president of Zanzibar ordered a purge of books on witchcraft, but since the revolutionaries could not read Arabic, all sorts of books were taken and burned ("Knowledge and Agency," 139–141). It was not until the early 1970s, with the presidency of Aboud Jumbe, that Islamic learning would again gain some official recognition as an important but neglected part of Zanzibari culture and identity. The government has encouraged mainland migration to Zanzibar, where it is said that the population is now only 90 percent Muslim.
41 A. Clayton, *The Zanzibar Revolution and Its Aftermath* (London: C. Hurst & Co., 1981), 137, 145.
42 G. W. Triplett, "Zanzibar: The Politics of Revolutionary Inequality," *The Journal of Modern African Studies* 9/4 (1971): 616–617 [612–617].
43 Indeed, it was the revolution that forced Farsy to relocate to Kenya. Toward the end of his life he moved to his ancestral home in Oman.
44 Purpura, "Knowledge and Agency," 127.
45 Mazrui, *Maisha ya al-Imam Aly khalifa wanne*, 13.
46 On the South Yemen under Marxist rule, see T. Y. Ismael and J. S. Ismael, *The People's Democratic Republic of Yemen: Politics, Economics and Society: the Politics of Socialist Ttransformation* (London: F. Pinter, 1986). My comments on local memory of the past in the Ḥaḍramawt are based on my own research there in February–March 2001.
47 Conversions to Shīʿism are discussed at A. Oded, *Islam and Politics in Kenya* (Boulder and London: Lynne Rienner Publishers, 2000), 118. My comment on the continuation of the trend is based on personal communication from Shaykh Hammad Kassim Mazrui, Shaykh Ahmad Msallam, and Kadara Harith Swaleh during a conference in Berlin, May 2007.
48 Kresse, *Philosophising in Mombasa*, 81–82, 256, n. 13.
49 Ibid., 96.
50 Kresse comments that in the 1960s,

> Sheikh Abdilahi was resented by members of his own community for befriending the Mijikenda and upcountry Africans who, at that time, were often still called *washenzi* (savages) and regarded as little other than servants and former slaves by the Swahili and Arab communities.
>
> (Ibid., 185)

51 Ibid., 197.
52 Ibid., 190–191.

10 *Dihqān*s and sacred families in Central Asia

Ashirbek Muminov

Introduction

Noble families in contemporary Central Asia, those claiming sacred status through Islam, are marked by the utmost diversity. They differ not only by their appellations (*ovlat/awlād, khwāja, sayyid, khwān, mīr, makhdūm-zāda, shāh, īshān, miyān*) but also by their origins. They ascribe their origins to many well-known figures of the early period of Islam, namely, Qurashīs, such as the four Rightly-Guided Caliphs (Abū Bakr, ʿUmar, ʿUthmān, ʿAlī) and certain prominent Companions of the Prophet (e.g., Khālid ibn al-Walīd, Saʿd ibn Abī Waqqāṣ). In scholarship, these groups have been discussed in terms of such categories as "sacred families" or "descendants of saints" (*awlād-i awliyā*ʾ). Descendants of ʿAlī ibn Abī Ṭālib through Fāṭima, the daughter of the Prophet Muḥammad – that is, *sayyid-zāda*s, *sayyid*s or *sharīf*s – unlike their counterparts in many other societies in the Muslim world, do not occupy a position distinct from the general mass of sacred families. In some societies of Central Asia, their status is equal to that of other sacred families (*saḥāba-zāda, khwāja*); in some cases they are even less esteemed than other families (for example, in Turkmen and Kazakh Muslim societies).[1] The study of the various categories of sacred families in Central Asia, on the basis of reliable sources – with epitaphs prominent among them – may thus shed light upon the historical processes of the formation and development of these families' status and of their functions in the life of their societies.

Written sources from pre- and post-Mongol Mawaraannahr (Transoxiana, i.e., the region between the Amu Darya and the Sir Darya) reveal a distinct discrepancy between the two periods with regard to the honorific titles used to signify membership in those sacred families. One such honorific title that apparently was in wide circulation in the pre-Mongol period was "*dihqān*." This study will focus on this title and elucidate who those *dihqān*s were. As can be expected, this exercise will involve a reconsideration of the prevailing understanding that the term "*dihqān*" had come to denote ordinary peasants by the eleventh century. Our chief sources are epitaphs from the medieval cemetery of Chākar-dīza in Samarqand.

"Arab" scholars in the pre-Mongol period

As is widely known, no evidence pertaining to the Samanid (261–389/875–999) and Qarakhanid periods (389–609/999–1212) indicates that Shīʿī groups, who recognized members of the Prophet's family (*Ahl al-Bayt*) as their spiritual leaders (*imāms*), could perform their activities lawfully and openly in those periods; likewise, there is no indication of any loyalty toward members of the Prophet's family on the part of official authorities. After the attempted *coup d'état* by the Qarmaṭīs in the capital city, Bukhara, and in other cities of Mawaraannahr in 331/943, Qarmaṭīs and Ismāʿīlīs (the most active currents of Shīʿī Islam at that time) were declared to be illegal, and their leaders were officially persecuted.[2]

In the same periods, among the huge masses of local *ʿulamāʾ* (religious scholars), we encounter descendants of eminent figures of the early period of Islamic history (the Prophet Muḥammad, his Companions from among the *Muhājirūn* and *Anṣār*, heroes of early Islam, and members of various Arab tribes). Those ancestors included many clients (*mawālī*) who adopted the names of their Arab patrons as their own *nisbas*. The "Qurashī" origins of these scholars, as well as the origins of others claiming descent from other northern- and southern-Arab tribes, were most likely recorded as a means of confirming the reliability (*thiqa*) of texts and traditions of a sacred character (hadiths, *riwāyas*) that they transmitted (*naql*). For example, the ʿAlid family of Abū Shujāʿ al-ʿAlawī (d. 466/1073–4), the fame of which lasted for three generations, was quite well known in Samarqand; Shams al-A'imma ʿAbd al-ʿAzīz ibn Aḥmad al-Ḥalwāʾī al-Bukhārī (d. 448/1056–7), a descendant of Jaʿfar ibn Muḥammad ibn al-Ḥanafiyya, was prominent in Bukhara.[3] It goes without saying that all these *ʿulamāʾ* were strict followers of Sunnī Islam.

It is paradoxical that our sources do not provide evidence regarding direct descendants or continuators of these lines of "Arab" scholars later on, in the post-Mongol period.[4] It may be suggested that the accumulation of an enormous stock of knowledge, as facilitated by these talented scholars, was in all likelihood a phenomenon of several generations at the most, and that the Arabs were probably regarded, in that milieu, merely as natural bearers and transmitters of the sacred language of Islam and of Islamic sciences and traditions. Claiming Arab descent was meaningful in this context. Those brilliant experts of religious knowledge, however, could not put down deep roots in local societies and thereby turn themselves into hereditary spiritual authorities for the local population.

The *dihqāns*

Whom, then, did the local population respect as representatives of "noble families": the newly arrived Arabs, or "old aristocrats"? Such a question was first posed by Oleg G. Bol'shakov, a St Petersburg specialist in Arabic and Islamic studies, who published an article that focused for the first time on the use of the title "*dihqān*" in texts from pre-Mongol Mawaraannahr. Analyzing the Arabic epitaph on a *qayrāq* (gravestone) from Samarqand, dated 541/1146, that mentioned this title,[5] Bol'shakov concluded that, as a result of a profound transformation in socio-economic relations following the rule of the Samanids, the word "*dihqān*," which originally signified an "aristocrat," was already used to denote an ordinary peasant in the Qarakhanid period.[6] However, the concrete historical situation confirms the opposite of this thesis: a large group of religious scholars of Mawaraannahr from among the urban population (from Bukhara, Samarqand, Kāsān, etc.) bore the honorific title "*dihqān*," denoting a person of aristocratic and sacred origin. This is seen in epitaphs from the tenth to the fourteenth century found at the Chākar-dīza Cemetery, an elite burial place for the *ʿulamāʾ* in Samarqand.

The Chākar-dīza Cemetery was an elite graveyard of Samarqand during the middle ages. Religious scholars, jurists (*fuqahāʾ*), and other religious figures were buried there, as is evident not only from literary sources but also from epigraphic materials. One of the great and well-known scholars buried there was Abū Manṣūr al-Māturīdī (d. 333/944–5), founder of the Māturīdī school of theology, whose tomb was located at the center of the cemetery. The appellation of the cemetery, and of the city quarter known by the same name, was derived apparently from the Chākar-dīza Canal, which, already in the early middle ages, flowed toward the *shahristān* of Samarqand. On the eastern bank of the canal stood a fortress (*dīza*), in which, as is suggested by the name itself, a military unit (*chākar*) was probably stationed.[7] In the early middle ages – that is, in the pre-Islamic period – a Zoroastrian necropolis, in which ossuary burials were practiced, was situated near one section of the Chākar-dīza Canal.[8]

The inscriptions discovered so far on *qayrāq*s from the Chākar-dīza Cemetery have been studied by a group of researchers including Bakhtiyar M. Babadzhanov, Lola N. Dodkhudoeva, Ulrich Rudolph and the author of these lines.[9] Here we would like to focus on several texts found on these *qayrāq*s. All the epitaphs examined here are written in Arabic.

Qayrāq *I*[10]

The text on this *qayrāq* reads:

ll. 1–3: This is the tomb of the powerless slave [of God], the one who hopes for the prayers of Muslims [for his sake],
ll. 4–7: the honorable *dihqān* of pure origin (*al-dihqān al-jalīl al-aṣīl*), Maḥmūd ibn Muḥammad ibn Aḥmad ibn Abī Ṣāliḥ al-Farābī. May God fill his tomb with light!
ll. 8–10: May God moisten his resting place! May God grant him peace and excellence! [He died] in the year five hundred fifty-three (1158–9).

Figure 10.1 *Qayrāq* I (Q-050), dated 553/1158–9

Two features of the text of this inscription are noteworthy for our purposes. First, the inscription emphasizes the remarkable and noble origin of the deceased. Second, it names his place of origin (Farāb). On this basis, we can infer that the use of the title "*dihqān*" as an honorific title for a member of a sacred family was not a local phenomenon specific to Samarqand, but was spread widely across the region of Mawaraannahr.

Qayrāq *II*[11]

The text on this *qayrāq* reads:

l. 1:	This is the tomb
l. 2:	of the shaykh, the one who performed the *ḥajj* more than once,
l. 3:	the felicitous, the martyr (*al-shahīd*),
l. 4:	the pride of the *dihqāns* (*fakhr al-dahāqīn*),
l. 5:	the ornament of the pilgrims and the two Holy Places (i.e., Mecca and Medina),
l. 6:	ʿAlī ibn Abī Bakr ibn ʿAlī
l. 7:	the *muʾadhdhin* and/of the . . .

Figure 10.2 *Qayrāq* II (Q-067), dated 560/1165

l. 8: May God forgive him!
l. 9: [He died] on the eighth of Dhū al-Ḥijja
l. 10: in the year five hundred sixty (15 October 1165).

The inscription presents the deceased as a devout and eminent Muslim. He is identified as a shaykh, pilgrim (*ḥajjāj*) and martyr; his service to the religion as a *muʾadhdhin* is also mentioned. It is, however, the deceased's quality as the "pride of the *dihqāns*" that stands out among such creditable features of a good Muslim.

Qayrāq *III*[12]

The text on this *qayrāq* reads:

l. 1: This is the tomb of
l. 2: the dearest son (*walad al-ʿazīz*), the *dihqān*,
l. 3: ʿAlī, the martyr, ibn Muḥammad ibn

Figure 10.3 *Qayrāq* III (Q-126), dated 607/1210

l. 4: ʿAlī, the coppersmith *(al-ṣaffār)*. He
l. 5: died as a martyr in the middle of
ll. 6–7: Jumādā I in the year six hundred seven (the beginning of November 1210).

There is no question that the title "*dihqān*" in this inscription indicates the origin, not the trade, of the person. The fact that the deceased worked as a coppersmith contradicts Bol'shakov's view that the term "*dihqān*" had come to denote an ordinary peasant by the period in question.[13] Rather, the title "*dihqān*" functioned in this period as an indicator of the sacred origin of its bearer. The fact that he is buried at the Chākar-dīza Cemetery indicates his status as a religious scholar.

It is clear that the composers of these written monuments, by adding the title "*dihqān*" to the list of exalted religious titles (shaykh, imam, *zāhid*, *qārī*ʾ, *ḥāfiẓ*, *shahīd*, etc.), sought to emphasize the "noble" origin of the deceased. Epitaphs of the elite *ʿulamā*ʾ from the Chākar-dīza Cemetery in Samarqand show that the title "*dihqān*" was used at that time to distinguish members of noble families. The *qayrāqs* also suggest that these *dihqāns*, in addition to being Islamic religious scholars, were somehow connected to the elites of the pre-Islamic period.

The Persophone *ʿulamāʾ*

Recent studies have shown that some groups of the *ʿulamāʾ* who emphasized local cultural traditions alongside Islamic ones were influential in Mawaraannahr, and especially in the urban communities of Bukhara and Samarqand, in the eighth–twelfth centuries. For example, the aspiration to give the Persian language a status equal to that of Arabic was a widespread phenomenon among such scholars.[14] Unique information concerning scholars of this type in Bukhara and Samarqand is given by an unpublished Arabic ethical work, entitled *Rawḍat al-ʿulamāʾ*, by Abū al-Ḥasan ʿAlī ibn Yaḥyā al-Zandawīsatī al-Bukhārī (d. ca. 400/1009–10).[15] According to this source, these *ʿulamāʾ* frequently gave sermons to ordinary townspeople (*ʿāmma*), and they spoke in Persian (*Fārsī*) on those occasions. Subjects of the sermons included the interpretation of the Qurʾān (*tafsīr*), the ethical-moral norms of Islam (*akhlāq*), and the connection of such norms with the acts of ritual worship (*ʿibādāt*); the sermons included citations, in Persian translation, from works by authors of non-Arab origin such as Kaʿb al-Aḥbār (d. 32/651–2), Wahb ibn Munabbih (d. 110/728 or 114/732), Muqātil ibn Sulaymān al-Balkhī (d. 150/767) and Sahl ibn ʿAbdallāh al-Tustarī (d. ca. 283/896). The scholars quoted hadiths not only in Arabic but also in Persian translation. One of the hadiths that circulated among them said: "The languages of the people of paradise are Arabic and Persian" (*Lisān ahl al-janna al-ʿArabiyya wa-l-Fārisiyya al-Dariyya*).[16] This implies that in their interpretation, the Persian language had turned into a sacred language of Islam.

These scholars, moreover, considered it permissible to recite the Persian translation of Qurʾānic verses during the prescribed prayers (*ṣalāt*); in this they relied upon the authoritative statement of Abū Ḥanīfa (d. 150/767), taken from his "*Kitāb al-ṣalāt*."[17] Also regarded as permissible was the pronunciation of *takbīrs* in Persian or in any other language at the beginning of the prayer.[18] Among these *ʿulamāʾ* were found many who bore the title "*dihqān*," such as Abū al-Faḍl Aḥmad ibn Muḥammad al-Dihqān al-Barmaghdīzī.[19] These Persophone scholars whom al-Zandawīsatī presents in his *Rawḍat al-ʿulamāʾ* included ascetics, Karrāmīs and Ḥanafīs.[20] Subsequently, representatives of these groups of scholars came to be found among Ḥanafīs, Ismāʿīlīs and Sufis.[21]

Among these Persophone *ʿulamāʾ*, reference to an Arab origin was not an important argument for the eminence, sacred power, or spiritual capabilities of a given scholar. It was indeed none other than these Persophone *ʿulamāʾ* who sacralized Abū Ḥanīfa, the highest religious authority in the region, by ascribing a non-Arab origin to him. As the Ḥanafī school gradually became the dominant school of jurisprudence in the region, its eponym came to be regarded as a lineal descendant of the legendary *shāh*s of ancient Iran.[22] This claim can be found in the works of such local authors as Abū ʿAbdallāh Muḥammad ibn Abī Ḥafṣ al-Kabīr al-Bukhārī (d. 274/878), Abū al-Faḍl Bakr ibn Muḥammad ibn ʿAlī al-Zaranjarī (d. 512/1118–9), Abū al-Muʾayyad al-Muwaffaq ibn Aḥmad ibn Isḥāq al-Makkī al-Khwārazmī (d. 568/1172) and Ẓahīr al-Dīn al-Marghīnānī (d. ca. 600/1203).[23]

As the local population gained more and more influence in the politics of the region, the influence of these Persophone *ʿulamāʾ* became increasingly significant. This shift was reflected in the strategies of legitimization adopted by the Samanids and the Qarakhanids, as they appealed to the ancient Iranian heritage: the former pretended to be the descendants of Bahrām Chūbīn, a legendary military leader of the Sasanids, while the latter claimed ties with Afrāsiyāb, the legendary hero of Tūrān.[24] In such a milieu, where local patriotic sentiments prevailed among most of the Central Asian population, the traditional culture of the region had substantial significance and relevance. The *ʿulamā*'s desire to elevate their social status through appeals to their roots in ancient culture must be understood in light of this environment. The advancement of the *ʿulamā*'s social status through engagement in the sacred religious sciences of Islam was boosted by their putative descent from ancient local aristocrats, the *dihqān*s.

The Post-Mongol transformation

The situation discussed in the preceding section began to change fundamentally with the establishment of Mongol rule after the conquests of Chinggis Khan (r. 1206–1227). The most important transformation in the spiritual sphere was the transfer of initiative from the representatives of the traditional Islamic sciences (*ʿulamāʾ*, *fuqahāʾ*, *ahl al-ḥadīth*) to the representatives of the ascetic-mystical dimension of Islam (Sufism). The formation of Sufi brotherhoods (the Khwājagān and others) was accelerated and the influence of their leaders on the population was intensified.

These new spiritual leaders consisted generally of the members of sacred families, which had by this time come to claim Arab descent. Many families of Sufi shaykhs emerged and extended their influence. In the case of Bukhara, one may count the family of Khwāja Muḥammad Pārsā (d. 823/1420) – who claimed descent from the prominent Ḥanafī scholar Ḥāfiẓ al-Dīn al-Bukhārī (d. 693/1294), of the line of *Ṣadr*s (actual rulers of Bukhara in the period 495–629/1102–1232), as well as the Jūybārī Khwājas – putative descendants of the ascetic Abū Bakr ibn Saʿd (d. 359/970) – among such families.[25] The ancestors of both families were presented, in pre-Mongol sources, as Muslims of ordinary origin, and as typical experts in the religious sciences; nothing was known of their *sayyid* status. However, in post-Mongol sources, their descendants began to be considered as people of noble origin and as the founders of several great sacred families among the Bukharan *ʿulamāʾ*.

In this new milieu, to be a family of Islamic scholars meant to be a family of noble origin. The same transformation of origins took place also with the two families of the *Shaykh al-Islāms* in Samarqand: the descendants of Abū al-Layth al-Samarqandī (d. 370/981) and those of Burhān al-Dīn al-Marghīnānī (d. 593/1197). The two families duly began to trace their origins to the caliphs Abū Bakr al-Ṣiddīq and ʿUthmān ibn ʿAffān, respectively. All these point to a fundamental transformation in the conception of the families of "sacred origin" that took place in Mawaraannahr in the post-Mongol period.

Dihqāns in peripheral regions

Of great importance for the purposes of this study are the epitaphs of Kūhistān, from the eleventh to nineteenth century, published by Ahrar Mukhtarov.[26] These inscriptions originate from the upper Zarafshān valley, far upstream from the oasis area where the capital cities of Samarqand and Bukhara are situated. The fact that many epitaphs published by Mukhtarov contain the title "*dihqān*" demonstrates that the use of this title was a widespread phenomenon. Like those from Samarqand, the *qayrāq*s from Kūhistān also indicate that the bearers of the title "*dihqān*" were holders of religious offices (imam, *mu'adhdhin*, etc.) and specialists in Islamic sciences (*faqīh*, *muftī*, shaykh, *muḥaddith*, etc.). Mukhtarov's publication is also important for showing that such titles as "*dihqān*," "*sayyid*," "*khwāja*" and "*khāwand-zāda*" were sometimes used together in one text.[27] This indicates that *dihqān* families established links with other noble families through marriage. Mukhtarov's observation that the title "*dihqān*" began to drop out of use during the fourteenth century is useful for further studies, as well.

Conclusion

The primary factor in the transformation of spiritual life that differentiates pre- and post-Mongol Mawaraannahr was the tribes that arrived in the region from Turkestan (all Muslim regions located to the east of the Sir Darya) together with the Mongol conquerors. For this reason, studying the formative processes of sacred families in the urban centers of Turkestan, where nomadic tribes dominated, holds distinct scholarly value for elucidating the evolution of sacred families and the formation of Sufi brotherhoods.

The newly arrived members of sacred families established marital relations with members of local aristocratic clans and came to form influential families of the descendants of the Prophet, such as the Khwāja-Aḥrārīs, Makhdūm-i Aʿẓamīs, and the descendants of Luṭfallāh Chustī. As epitaphs of later centuries from Kūhistān have shown, some *dihqān* families also took part in the formation of these new sacred families. Other *dihqān* families were pushed away into peripheral areas of Central Asia. Since that time onward, most probably, the term "*dihqān*" began to denote a simple and ordinary peasant.

Acknowledgment

The author would like to thank Professor Devin DeWeese, Professor Ablet Kamalov, Mr Kimura Satoru and Professor Morimoto Kazuo for their assistance in the translation of this contribution from Russian into English.

Notes

1 S. M. Demidov, *Turkmenskie ovliady* [Turkmen Ovlads] (Ashkhabad: Ylym, 1976); A. K. Muminov, in cooperation with A. Sh. Nurmanova and S. Sattarov, *Genealogicheskoe drevo Mukhtara Auezova* [Genealogical Tree of Mukhtar Auezov] (Almaty: Zhibek Zholy, 2011), 28–48.

2 V. V. Bartol'd, "Turkestan v èpokhu mongol'skogo nashestviia" [Turkestan at the Time of Mongol Invasion], in V. V. Bartol'd, *Sochineniia*, vol. 1 (Moscow: Izdatel'stvo vostochnoi literatury, 1963), 302–306.

3 For the family of Abū Shujāʿ al-ʿAlawī and al-Ḥalwāʾī al-Bukhārī, see al-Qurashī, *al-Jawāhir al-muḍiyya fī ṭabaqāt al-Ḥanafiyya*, ed. by ʿAbd al-Fattāḥ Muḥammad al-Ḥulw, 5 vols, 2nd ed. (Giza: Hajr li-l-Ṭibāʿa wa-l-Nashr wa-l-Tawzīʿ wa-l-Iʿlān, 1413/1993), II:429–430, III:28, 317–318, IV:53.

4 Here, perhaps, the well-known family of the *Sayyid*s of Tirmidh marks an exception. According to the late family chronicles of the *Sayyid*s of Tirmidh, their ancestor Abū Muḥammad al-Ḥasan wrote a letter of recommendation to the Caliph al-Muntaṣir (r. 247–248/861–862) and petitioned him to show favor to Arqūq, the "ancestor" of the Samanids who claimed descent from the Persian commander Bahrām Chūbīn. The request was granted and Arqūq was appointed to the governorship of Balkh. In gratitude for this service, Arqūq placed Tirmidh under the control of al-Ḥasan. The friendly relationship between these two families was consolidated by marriage: a daughter of Ismāʿīl I (r. 279–295/892–907), Māh-i Sīm, was given in marriage to Sayyid Abū Muḥammad ʿAbdallāh, and the children from this marriage and their lineal descendants came to attach the ancient Iranian title *khudāywand-zāda/khudāwand-zāda/khāwand-zāda/khwān-zāda* to their names. The next historical episode in which one of the *Sayyid*s of Tirmidh was involved in a political event was connected with the conflict between Khwarazm-shah Muḥammad (r. 596–617/1200–1220) and the ʿAbbasid Caliph al-Nāṣir (r. 575–622/1180–1225). The Khwarazm-shah denounced the ʿAbbasids as usurpers of the caliphate, and ordered that *khuṭba*s in his territories be read in the name of the "legitimate" caliph from among the *Sayyid*s of Tirmidh: *Khudāywand-zāda* ʿAlāʾ al-Mulk I. The *Sayyid*s of Tirmidh were active participants in the political life of the Chaghatay khanate (1227–1363) and the Timurid dynasty (771–913/1370–1507). Their attempts were for the most part unsuccessful, and entailed some severe consequences for themselves. Eventually, they were expelled from their home territory of Tirmidh to Shahr-i Sabz. During the reign of the Timurid sovereign Ulugh Beg (811–853/1409–1449), the mausoleum known as the Gunbadh-i Sayyidān (the Tomb of *Sayyid*s) or Dār al-Siyāda (the Shelter of *Sayyid*s) was erected over their burials in Shahr-i Sabz. The branch of the family that had stayed in Tirmidh came to be known by the name "Ṣalavāt Khwājas" (after the name of a settlement near Tirmidh, Ṣāliḥ-ābād/Ṣalavāt), and until recently they were the keepers of the family mausoleum called "Sulṭān-Sādāt." See A. A. Semenov, "Proiskhozhdenie termezskikh seiidov i drevniaia usypal'nitsa "Sultan-Sadat" [The Origin of the *Sayyid*s of Tirmidh and the Ancient Mausoleum "Sultan-Sadat"], *Protokoly zasedanii i soobshcheniia chlenov Turkestanskogo kruzhka liubitelei arkheologii* (Tashkent) 17 (1914): 3–20; B. M. Babadzhanov,

"Sadat-i Tirmiz," in S. M. Prozorov ed., *Islam na territorii byvshei Rossiiskoi imperii: Entsiklopedicheskii slovar'*, vol. 1 (Moscow: Izdatel'skaia firma "Vostochnaia literatura" RAN, 2006), 338–341; B. M. Babadzhanov and A. K. Muminov, "al-Aʿradzh," in Prozorov ed., *Islam na territorii byvshei Rossiiskoi imperii*, 36–40.

5 This *qayrāq* is currently kept at the Samarqand Museum of History and Art of the Uzbek People under the accession number A-69–96.

6

> Any craftsman possessing a small plot of ground outside the city could proudly call himself a *dihqān* . . . There is no doubt that at this time the word "*dihqān*" begins to obtain its current meaning, i.e., to designate a peasant. It is true that sources do not offer explicit references in this respect, but in some cases the word "*dihqān*" could also mean a peasant.

From O. G. Bol'shakov, "Nadgrobie 541/1146 g. iz Samarkanda" (A Tombstone of 541/1146 from Samarqand), *Èpigrafika Vostoka* 14 (1961): 9–11.

7 Bartol'd, "Turkestan v èpokhu mongol'skogo nashestviia," 238.

8 A. Berdimuradov, "Archeological Report on the Excavation of Chākar-dīza," in B. M. Babadzhanov, L. N. Dodkhudoeva, A. K. Muminov, U. Rudolph, *Funeral Epigraphic Inscriptions of Samarqand (Samanids, Qarakhanids, and Chaghataids)* (Samarqand, Tashkent, Almaty, Dushanbe, Zurich, forthcoming).

9 Babadzhanov et al., *Funeral Epigraphic Inscriptions of Samarqand*. Some inscriptions on gravestones have been published in L. N. Dodkhudoeva, *Èpigraficheskie pamiatniki Samarkanda XI–XIV vv.* [Epigraphic Monuments of Samarqand, Eleventh–Fourteenth Centuries], vol. 1 (Dushanbe: "Donish", 1992), 154–155.

10 Accession number Q-050, The Samarqand Museum of History and Art of the Uzbek People. The dimensions of the extant portion of the *qayrāq*: 70×18×12.5 cm. The calligraphic style: *naskhī*, with irregular diacritical marks. The text of the epitaph is inscribed within a frame with a scalloped arch above, topped by a trefoil decoration. No damage was done to the text by the loss at the bottom of the *qayrāq*. Some U-shaped decorations are placed over lines of the text. There are losses, errors and ambiguous places in the text.

11 Accession number Q-067, The Samarqand Museum of History and Art of the Uzbek People. The *qayrāq* was delivered to the museum by P. P. Arkhangel'skii and I. A. Sukharev from the *mazār* of Shaykh Abū Manṣūr al-Māturīdī on 24 December 1927. Dimensions: 46×11×4.3 cm. Calligraphic style: *naskhī*, without diacritical marks. The top of the *qayrāq* is lost (without damage to the inscription). The text is framed within borders with a scalloped arch above. Spaces between some lines are filled with floral ornaments. Some words in the text are damaged; it was not possible to read the *nisba* of the deceased or the name of the mosque where he served as *muʾadhdhin*.

12 Accession number Q-126, The Samarqand Museum of History and Art of the Uzbek People. Dimensions: 33×11×6 cm. Calligraphic style: cursive, not professional, without diacritical marks. The text is placed within a frame with scalloped arches above and below and a trefoil decoration at the top; multi-petaled semicircular decorations appear on the frame's right and left edges. The inscription was obviously executed by an apprentice with a poor knowledge of Arabic. The text is marred by particular mistakes that make adequate reading and translation difficult.

13 In an inscription dated 541/1146, the deceased, assigned the title "*dihqān*," was a tailor (*khayyāṭ*) by trade. Dodkhudoeva, *Èpigraficheskie pamiatniki Samarkanda*, 132.

14 A. K. Muminov, "Srednevekovye diskussii o vozmozhnosti perevoda Korana na natsional'nye iazyki Tsentral'noi Azii" [Medieval Discussions on the Permissibility of Translating the Qurʾān into the Local Languages of Central Asia], in *III*

mezhdunarodnyi kongress tiurkologii. Aktual'nye problemy i perspektivy sovremennoi tiurkologii (obshchii iazyk, istoriia i alfavit) (Turkestan: Mezhdunarodnyi kazakhsko-turetskii universitet im. A. Iasavi, 2009), 422–424.

15 ʿAlī ibn Yaḥyā al-Zandawīsatī, *Rawḍat al-ʿulamāʾ*, MS Institute of Oriental Studies named after Abu Rayhan al-Biruni, Academy of Sciences of the Republic of Uzbekistan, fond IVRU-1, no. 2972.

16 Burhān al-Dīn al-Kabīr al-Bukhārī, *al-Muḥīṭ*, MS Institute of Oriental Studies named after Abu Rayhan al-Biruni, Academy of Sciences of the Republic of Uzbekistan, fond IVRU-1, no. 5982, 70b.

17 Al-Zandawīsatī, *Rawḍat al-ʿulamāʾ*, 2b, 127b.

18 Ibid., 127b.

19 Ibid., 16a, 162b.

20 Ibid., 409a.

21 Ibid., 8b, 307b.

22 A. K. Muminov, "Evoliutsiia obraza Abu Khanify v srednevekovoi istoriko-biograficheskoi literature Tsentral'noi Azii" [The Evolution of the Image of Abu Hanifa in the Medieval Historical-Biographical Literature of Central Asia], in A. Radzhabov, R. Mukimov, M. Karim-zada eds, *Èpokha Imama Aʿzama i ee znachenie v istorii kul'tury narodov Tsentral'noi Azii i Blizhnego Vostoka* (Dushanbe: Akademiia nauk Respubliki Tadzhikistan, 2009), 165–178.

23 Ibid., 168–172.

24 For the Samanid case, see C. E. Bosworth, "The Heritage of Rulership in Early Islamic Iran and the Search for Dynastic Connections with the Past," *Iran* 11 (1973): 51–62. For the Qarakhanid claim, see Muḥammad ibn ʿAlī al-Samarqandī al-Kātib (twelfth century), *Aghrāḍ al-siyāsa fī aʿrāḍ al-riyāsa*, ed. by Jaʿfar Shiʿār (Tehran: Dānishgāh-i Tihrān, 1349 AHS/1970–1), 37–43.

25 A. Muminov and Iu. Paul', "Mukhammad Parsa," in Prozorov ed., *Islam na territorii byvshei Rossiiskoi imperii*, 293–296; B. M. Babadzhanov, "Iz istorii odnogo 'sviatogo semeistva' srednevekovoi Bukhary (rodoslovnaia i rodstvennye sviazi Dzhuibaridov)" [From the History of a "Sacred Family" in Medieval Bukhara (The Family Tree and Kinship Relations of the Jūybārīs)], in *Uzbekistan v srednie veka: istoriia i kul'tura (doklady mezhdunarodnoi konferentsii)* (Tashkent: Institut istorii AN RUz, 2003), 86–99.

26 A. Mukhtarov, *Èpigraficheskie pamiatniki Kukhistana (XI–XIX vv.)* [Epigraphic Monuments of Kuhistan (Eleventh–Nineteenth centuries)], 2 vols (Dushanbe: "Donish", 1978–1979).

27 Ibid., I:80, 98, 101, 107, 156, 234, II:92–113.

11 Sacred descent and Sufi legitimation in a genealogical text from eighteenth-century Central Asia

The Sharaf Atāʾī tradition in Khwārazm

Devin DeWeese

Introduction

During the eighteenth century, as Central Asia was shaken by profound political, economic, and religious changes, the region saw a proliferation of literary works focused on the genealogical connections of prominent families, yielding a series of texts that widen considerably the range of descent groups for which we have a substantial and relatively early record of their genealogical traditions, beyond the lineages tied to Khwāja Aḥrār or Makhdūm-i Aʿẓam or the Jūybārī shaykhs that were prominent in the sixteenth and seventeenth centuries.[1] These eighteenth-century works include (1) the wide-ranging compendium of genealogical lore by Khwāja ʿAbd al-Raḥīm Ḥiṣārī, the *Tuḥfat al-ansāb-i ʿalavī* (1149/1736), focused on a lineage traced to the seventeenth-century Yasavī saint ʿĀlim Shaykh of ʿAlīyābād; (2) a compendium of genealogical and Sufi lore linked with the Yasavī saint Sayyid Ata, compiled by Raḥmatullāh b. Sayyid ʿAbd al-Raḥīm Hāshimī Atāʾī Valī-i Bukhārī, entitled *Favāʾid-i muntakhab-i shajara va ansāb va manāqib dar shaʾn-i ḥażarāt-i āl-i banī Fāṭima va ʿAlī b. Abī Ṭālib* (1192/1778); (3) an untitled work by Amīr Sayyid Shaykh Aḥmad Nāṣir al-Dīn b. Amīr Sayyid ʿUmar al-Marghīnānī tracing his descent from the Prophet and each of the four Caliphs, as well as his multiple Sufi affiliations (*ca.* 1790); (4) a "family history" by Muḥammad Ṣadr b. Khwāja Muḥammad Amān, entitled *Risāla-yi nuzdahum* [*sic*], focused on a lineage from Khwārazm connected with the Yasavī saint Ḥakīm Ata (*ca.* 1780); and (5) the earliest among these works, a brief untitled genealogical account focused on descendants of Sharaf Ata, a figure also linked with the Yasavī tradition (1122/1710).

The latter text will be the focus of this study; space will not allow a fuller discussion of the other works, but it is worth noting that three of them overlap in significant ways with the Sharaf Atāʾī tradition explored here. That tradition is linked closely with Khwārazm, where both Sayyid Ata[2] and Ḥakīm Ata[3] are said to be buried, and where descent groups linked to both may have competed with families linked to Sharaf Ata for prestige and patronage; as we will see, such competition may be echoed in traditions about the saintly rivalry between Sayyid Ata and Sharaf Ata, and the work focused on Ḥakīm Ata is of further interest for suggesting the overlap, continuity, and redefinition of lines of natural and spiritual descent, paralleling the situation in the Sharaf Atāʾī text. In the case of the third work noted above, meanwhile, known from a single manuscript preserved in Tashkent, its author, Sayyid Aḥmad Nāṣir al-Dīn Marghīnānī, is clearly to be identified with the compiler of a valuable, but now seemingly lost, work on the Yasavī tradition discussed long ago by Zeki Velidi Togan, and assigned by him the "title" *Tārīkh-i mashāʾikh al-turk*; excerpts from this work published by Togan include the most extensive narrative material we have about the figure of Sharaf Ata.[4]

The genealogical and historical material included in the short Sharaf Atāʾī text discussed here illustrates several important trends in the way sacred descent was understood and marked in early modern Central Asia. First, it centers on traditions of descent linked to a saint, Sharaf Ata, with a recognizable, if relatively sparse, hagiographical profile (preserved both in literary works and in oral tradition). Second, it links to this saint a host of religiously prominent figures – above all Sufi shaykhs and *qāżī*s – from what was, at the time of the text's compilation, recent history, suggesting that their social prominence may have enhanced their reputation for (or need for?) sacred descent, rather than "following" from established patterns of genealogically based respect and privilege. Third, it offers some hints that by the early eighteenth century, already, claims of descent from either of the first three Caliphs had come to be regarded as virtually equivalent, in terms of social prestige, to claims of descent from the Prophet through ʿAlī. This development (which is more clearly visible in Central Asia during the latter nineteenth and early twentieth century) may be signaled already in the simple affirmation that the ancestral saint himself, Sharaf Ata, was of Bakrid descent on his father's side, and of Ḥusaynī *sayyid* descent on his mother's side; but a specific figure evoked, somewhat obliquely, in the Sharaf Atāʾī text suggests a broader pattern of the "transfer" of genealogically based sanctity, with descent from a prominent jurist and *sayyid* "feeding into" claims of descent and initiatic transmission from a Sufi saint, and both giving way to generic claims of multiple descent lines supporting a level of social prestige not qualitatively different from that entailed by the status of *sayyid.*

Sharaf Ata in hagiographical tradition and folkore

The eighteenth-century Sharaf Atāʾī text of interest here, written, in Persian, by a certain Qāżī Khwāja Khān b. Khwāja Muḥammad Fāżil, evidently in 1122/1710, survives in a single manuscript preserved in Tashkent[5]; it traces various branches of a Khwārazmian family claiming descent from Sharaf Ata. Before discussing the text itself, a few words are in order about this figure, who occupies a somewhat unusual place in the Yasavī Sufi tradition. Unlike the case with Ḥakīm Ata and Sayyid Ata, who are the subjects of stories linking them with the Yasavī tradition that were in circulation by the end of the fifteenth century, Sharaf Ata is scarcely mentioned in written sources until relatively late.[6] Not until the *Ḥujjat al-ẕākirīn*, written by Mawlānā Muḥammad Sharīf around 1080/1670, is "Shaykh Sharaf Ata" mentioned as a disciple, and indeed as the first *khalīfa* (Sufi successor) of Ḥakīm Ata (typically cast as the major disciple of Aḥmad Yasavī), who is said to have loved Sharaf Ata as a son.[7] Such a characterization at once suggests possible genealogical ramifications of the relationship between Sharaf Ata and Ḥakīm Ata, but also implicitly gives Sharaf Ata precedence over Zangī Ata, the more famous figure typically cast as a disciple of Ḥakīm Ata (again, in sources from the late fifteenth century), and the one through whom such figures as Sayyid Ata and Ṣadr Ata (with their companions Badr Ata and Uzun Ḥasan Ata) were linked to the Yasavī *silsila* (lineage of spiritual transmission). The entire Yasavī *silsila* as known in Central Asia from the sixteenth century through the eighteenth, we may note, is traced through Ṣadr Ata, but the natural and spiritual descendants of Sayyid Ata were also prominent throughout this period; the hagiographical and genealogical "footprint" of Sharaf Ata is considerably smaller.

Another brief account, preserved in a nineteenth-century work, cites Qāsim Shaykh (d. 989/1578) ascribing a Turkic saying to "the holy Sharaf Ata, who was among the foremost successors of Sulṭān Khwāja Aḥmad Yasavī and was the *sulṭān* of his time in this *silsila*."[8] It is perhaps suggestive of the relative obscurity of Sharaf Ata that these two accounts assign him different positions within the Yasavī *silsila*, one making him a disciple of Ḥakīm Ata, and the other implying, at least, that he might have been a direct disciple of Aḥmad Yasavī. A third position is assigned to him in what is, so far as I have been able to trace, the only other account to explicitly place Sharaf Ata in the Yasavī *silsila*, namely the so-called *Tārīkh-i mashā'ikh al-turk*, the work of Marghīnānī cited extensively by Togan. This account portrays Sharaf Ata as a disciple of Zangī Ata, along with his other four well-known disciples, including Sayyid Ata, but affirms that Sharaf Ata had "seen" Ḥakīm Ata (typically cast as Zangī Ata's master), and had been "looked upon as a son" by Ḥakīm Ata (thus echoing part of the account in the *Ḥujjat al-ẕākirīn*). This special favor in itself suggests one foundation, common in many hagiographical traditions, for jealousy toward Sharaf Ata on the part of Zangī Ata's other disciples, but the work in fact includes a specific narrative accounting for an intense animosity between Sharaf Ata and Sayyid Ata.[9]

The story is interesting in itself, but here it will suffice to note that it links both Sharaf Ata and Sayyid Ata with a "wealthy Türkmen" named Bābā Érsārī, whom we may recognize at once as the legendary eponym of the Ersarï tribe of the Türkmens.[10] This link is of further interest in connection with an account, found in the *Shajara-yi tarākima* (a compendium of genealogical and historical lore about the Türkmens compiled in the middle of the seventeenth century by Abū al-Ghāzī Khān, of the Chinggisid dynasty that ruled in Khwārazm from the sixteenth century to the eighteenth), which affirms that a "Shaykh Sharaf Khwāja" of Urgench translated a religious book into Turkic at the behest of a Türkmen patron named "Ārsārī Bāy."[11] According to Abū al-Ghāzī, the work was the *Muʿīn al-murīd*, while oral tradition recorded in the early twentieth century preserves a similar account noting the work's title as *Rawnaq al-islām*.[12] The specific connection between either of these titles[13] and "Shaykh Sharaf" is less important, for present purposes, than the association of his name with written works, and the status this undoubtedly reflects for him, as a representative of Islamic piety and sanctity. This status is in fact quite widely attested for "Shaykh Sharaf" (a name more common, in fact, than the appellation "Sharaf Ata") in popular religious lore from Khwārazm and among the Türkmens. A prominent shrine in Khwārazm is known popularly as that of Shaykh Sharaf, who is the subject of a substantial body of legendary narratives; among them are stories affirming his ancestry of particular descent groups, including some in Khwārazm and others in southern Turkmenistan (where another shrine ascribed to Shaykh Sharaf is found).[14]

These traditions, taken together, reflect a quite familiar pattern in hagiographical lore from the nineteenth and twentieth centuries: they show a saint associated with one or more shrines, linked, if loosely, with the Yasavī Sufi tradition, ascribed various important deeds with overtones of Islamization and communal formation, identified as an ancestor by particular social groups among the settled population, and further connected with another figure (in this case, the Ersarï eponym) who is linked even more directly with the ancestry of particular tribal groups among the nomads. More specifically, the traditions surrounding Shaykh Sharaf's reputation as a saint linked with the Yasavī tradition, his shrine, and his status as a communal ancestor suggest that the stories preserved about him reflect a developmental trajectory for the hagiographical and genealogical lore about Sharaf Ata running parallel to the material preserved in the text explored here, from the early eighteenth century; the eighteenth-century account preserves, in effect, a redaction of these traditions that is for the most part earlier, more learned, and more specifically attuned to genealogical details.

The Sharaf Atāʾī genealogy, I: Sufis and *qāżī*s of Khwārazm and Bukhārā (seventeenth century)

Let us return, then, to the Sharaf Atāʾī genealogical text itself. The brief "work" of Qāżī Khwāja Khān is actually two texts, with the first part (197a–198b) tracing Sharaf Ata's ancestry and various lineages descended from him, and the second part (199b–201a) recounting the author's lineage back to Sharaf Ata, and following various collateral and maternal lines, with considerable overlap between the two texts. In the second text (199b), the author identifies himself (mentioning also his two brothers, Muḥammad Ṣāliḥ Khwāja and

Muḥammad Sharaf Khwāja), and says that his father, Khwāja Muḥammad Fāżil,

> was *qāżī* in the *qubbat al-islām* of Khwārazm, known at present as Urgench, in the time of Abū al-Ghāzī Bahādur Khan, toward the end of his reign, and in the beginning of the rule of his son Abū al-Ghāzī Sayyid Anūsha Muḥammad Bahādur Khan.

These chronological indications suggest that the author's father was active early in the second half of the seventeenth century (Abū al-Ghāzī Khān ruled from ca. 1053/1643 until his death in 1074/1663, and was succeeded by his son Anūsha). The author's mother, meanwhile, named ʿĀʾisha Bégim, was the daughter of "Yūsuf Khwāja b. Pādshāh Khwāja b. Bābā Khwāja Sharafī" (the *nisba* implies that he too was a descendant of Sharaf Ata, as is indeed made clear from a subsequent genealogical account, at f. 197b); her mother, in turn, is identified as Ḥalīma Sulṭānïm, the daughter of Tūghān (or Ṭūghān) Khwāja Qara-bāghī Sayyid Atāʾī, thus linking the Sharaf Atāʾī lineage with the better-known Sayyid Atāʾī tradition (but just one generation before the author).

The author's father, Muḥammad Fāżil, had died, according to the account (199b), while performing the *ḥajj* (via India), and was buried in "*bandar Maskat*" in the Ḥaḍramawt in Yaman [*sic*]. Muḥammad Fāżil's father, in turn, was a learned scholar and teacher "in the capital (*dār al-khilāfa*), that is, Khīvaq, during the time of Naẕr Muḥammad Khān [who ruled in Bukhārā from 1051/1642 to 1055/1645] and the beginning of the [reign of] Abū al-Ghāzī Khān" (i.e., 1053–1074/1643–1663), and is said to have been *qāżī* in the city of Kāt during the time of Abū al-Ghāzī; his name is in fact not mentioned here, but is given later in this text (200a) and in the previous text (197b–198a) as Muḥammad Sharaf Khwāja Ākhūnd. His grave, the author adds, is in Kāt, near the shrine of Shāh ʿAbbās Valī, a well-known landmark near the site of Kāt.[15] He left two sons, Muḥammad Fāżil and Khwāja Muḥammad Jalāl (the latter of whom was buried in Bukhārā outside the gate of the shrine of Bahāʾ al-Dīn Naqshband), as well as a daughter named Bībī-jān.

Muḥammad Sharaf Khwāja's father, in turn – the author's great-grandfather – was ʿAzīzān Muḥammad Ṣāliḥ Khwāja, identified as a Sufi master (*murshid-i rāh-i yaqīn, ṣāḥib al-karāmāt va-l-maqāmāt*) and the chief of wayfarers "in the *ṭarīq al-khafiyya va-l-yasaviyya*," that is, in the Naqshbandī and Yasavī "orders"; his shrine, we are told, is in Bukhārā, in the *tūmān* of Khiṭfar [*sic*][16] (known also as Zandanī), in the village of Awdānī, in the locality (*mawżiʿ*) of Qurghān, and near his grave was a *khānqāh*, built on his behalf by the *amīr al-umarā* Muḥammad Yār Bīy Atalïq,[17] at the beginning of the reign of ʿAbd al-ʿAzīz Khān (r. 1055–1092/1645–1681). These particulars make it clear that the "ʿAzīzān Muḥammad Ṣāliḥ Khwāja" mentioned here as the author's great-grandfather, and shown elsewhere as a ninth-generation descendant of Sharaf Ata (see below), is the "Ṣāliḥ Khwāja Urganjī" mentioned in various sources as a successor of the Yasavī master ʿĀlim Shaykh ʿAlīyābādī (author of the *Lamaḥāt*), and as a teacher of Mawlānā Muḥammad Sharīf, author of the *Ḥujjat al-ẓākirīn*.[18] This is further suggested by the marital ties noted in this text, for the author mentions that one of Muḥammad Ṣāliḥ Khwāja's daughters (by a different wife, that is, not the mother of the author's ancestor[19]) was Khān-zāda Bégim, who was married to "Ākhūnd Mullā Muḥammad Sharīf al-Ḥusaynī al-Bukhārī, who was originally from Shahr-i Sabz" (known as the birthplace of the famous Yasavī shaykh Muḥammad Sharīf); she was the mother of his son Khwāja Nūr al-Dīn Muḥammad Laṭīf, known as ʿAbdullāh Khwāja (b. 1092/1681, one of his father's important Sufi successors), and of his daughter, Shāh-zāda Bégim, who married the learned scholar of Bukhārā, Khwāja Muḥammad Salīm Ṣiddīqī Karmīnagī. These relationships suggest the complex pattern of interconnections, in this era, between initiatic and hereditary lineages linked with the Yasavī tradition; they also suggest the degree to which such familial ties cut across the "political" boundaries of Central Asia as defined, in the seventeenth century, by the rule of distinct and rival Chinggisid lineages (as signaled also by the author's chronological references, given as often in terms of the reigns of Ashtarkhānid rulers in Bukhārā as in terms of the reigns of rulers in Khwārazm). In any case, Muḥammad Ṣāliḥ Khwāja's ancestry is traced back, as noted, through eight intermediaries to Sharaf Ata; his mother and father were first-cousins, and he was thus a "Sharaf Atāʾī *khwāja*" on both sides (concern for such double-lineages, and indeed for tracing connections to saintly ancestors through multiple lines, is also a common feature of the genealogical texts of this era).

The first text, alone, gives the author's full genealogy back to Sharaf Ata; it also gives a version of Sharaf Ata's descent from Abū Bakr, but more complete accounts of his father's Bakrid lineage, and of his mother's ʿAlid lineage, appear in the second text, and it is only there, too, that we find collateral lines traced from Sharaf Ata (i.e., descendants of his three daughters, supplementing the lineage traced from his son leading to the author). The account portrays "Shaykh Sharaf al-Dīn Aḥmad, known as Sharaf Ata," as a descendant of the Caliph Abū Bakr through his father (the two versions differ regarding his genealogical "distance" from Abū Bakr, one showing fifteen generations between him and Sharaf Ata, the other showing only eight[20]); the Sharaf Atāʾī lineage's ʿAlid status comes through the founding saint's mother, Amīna, who is shown as a sixteenth-generation descendant of ʿAlī.[21] Otherwise these texts offer little information about the "founder" of the Sharaf Atāʾī lineage; in particular, it is worth noting that these texts, with their primarily genealogical focus, pay no attention at all to the identity of Sharaf Ata's master in Sufism, and make no reference to either Ḥakīm Ata or Zangī Ata. Nevertheless, Sharaf Ata's status as a Sufi shaykh is clearly affirmed: the account tells us that Sharaf Ata's successor in his Sufi *silsila* was Sayyid Jalāl Kurlānī (his *nisba*, written *k.r.lānī*, refers to Gürlen, a town of Khwārazm), who married one of Sharaf Ata's daughters (the account also follows Sayyid Jalāl's ancestry back to Ḥusayn b. ʿAlī, and traces the descendants of Sayyid Jalāl and Sharaf Ata's daughter, as we will see). We will return shortly to the identity of this Sayyid Jalāl, and its implications for the Sharaf Atāʾī lineage.

Sharaf Ata himself (his wife is never identified) is ascribed a son and three daughters; the two texts' genealogical elaboration of the descendants of Sharaf Ata follows chiefly the lineage of the son and that of just one of the daughters. The son of Sharaf Ata, Muḥammad Khwāja, is shown as the ancestor of the lineage leading to the author (the direct lineage may be reconstructed thus: Sharaf Ata > Muḥammad Khwāja > ʿAṭā Khwāja > Ibrāhīm Khwāja > Yaʿqūb Khwāja > Ibrāhīm Khwāja > ʿAṭā Khwāja > Khwājagī Maḥmūd > Muḥammad Futūḥ Khwāja, known as Ulugh Khwāja > ʿAzīzān Muḥammad Ṣāliḥ Khwāja > Muḥammad Sharaf Khwāja > Khwāja Muḥammad Fāżil > Qāżī Khwāja Khān, the author). The repetition of names in the early part of the lineage may reflect actual familial naming patterns, but more likely suggests that these appellations are little more than generational place-holders. Of more significance is the attention given to the "branching" of the lineage after five more generations, namely, after the second ʿAṭā Khwāja, in the sixth-generation after Sharaf Ata: this ʿAṭā Khwāja is ascribed two sons, called here Khwājagī Aḥmad and Khwājagī Maḥmūd. The latter son, Khwājagī Maḥmūd, was the author's ancestor, through his son Khwāja Muḥammad Futūḥ, said to be known as Ulugh Khwāja; but considerable attention is given to the other son's lineage, which was evidently regarded as senior, and in any case the two lineages were closely interconnected through multiple intermarriages. These marital ties are followed in both texts, but the presentations differ somewhat in detail and complexity.

The other branch, evidently senior, begins with ʿAṭā Khwāja's son Khwājagī Aḥmad, who had a son, Bābā Khwāja, and three daughters. One of the daughters, ʿĀbida Bégim, married Khwāja Muḥammad Futūḥ (Ulugh Khwāja), and became the mother of Muḥammad Ṣāliḥ Khwāja (the author's great-grandfather); this marriage of first cousins, noted above, was why Muḥammad Ṣāliḥ Khwāja was identified as a Sharaf Atāʾī through his paternal and maternal lines. Another daughter of Khwājagī Aḥmad, whose name is not given, married a certain Ḥusām al-Dīn Khwāja, and bore him two sons, Rukn al-Dīn Khwāja and ʿAlāʾ al-Dīn Khwāja; she died while still nursing the latter, who was then cared for by his aunt, ʿĀbida Bégim, the mother of Muḥammad Ṣāliḥ Khwāja, and we are told that this ʿAlāʾ al-Dīn and Muḥammad Ṣāliḥ were *khāla-bachcha*s ("aunt's children") of one another (200a, 198a). Rukn al-Dīn Khwāja is further identified as having served as *qāżī* during the time of "ʿArab Khān" (that is, ʿArab-Muḥammad Khān of the Khwārazmian dynasty, Abū al-Ghāzī's father, r. 1011–1030/1603–1621; the text identified the town where he was *qāżī*, but this information is lost because the page is torn). The first text alone also mentions another son of Ḥusām al-Dīn Khwāja, by another mother, named Muḥammad Zāhid Khwāja, of whom nothing more is said. The third daughter of Khwājagī Aḥmad, finally, is also not named, but is said to have been married to "Khwāja Mullā Khwāja," who is identified as "the *qāżī* of Isfandiyār Khān" (i.e., the son of ʿArab-Muḥammad Khān who, with his brother Abū al-Ghāzī, opposed the two rival sons, Īlbars and Ḥabash, who had blinded, deposed, and killed their father, finally defeating them and establishing himself as *khān* in 1032/1623; he reigned until his death in 1051/1641); the second text alone mentions a son, ʿAvaż Khwāja, born to Khwāja Mullā and the third daughter of Khwājagī Aḥmad.

The son of Khwājagī Aḥmad, meanwhile, Bābā Khwāja, appears to have been the most prominent member of the extended family; his sisters and daughters married into the lineage of his uncle (i.e., the other son of ʿAṭā Khwāja, Khwājagī Maḥmūd), and Bābā Khwāja is shown making decisions, for instance, about the many intermarriages that linked the descendants of Khwājagī Aḥmad and Khwājagī Maḥmūd. Bābā Khwāja's own marital connections are not specified, but both texts pay close attention to his sons and daughter. The daughter, called Ṣiddīqa Bégim, was married to the author's grandfather, Muḥammad Sharaf Khwāja, and was the mother of his two sons, Muḥammad Fāżil (the author's father) and Muḥammad Jalāl (the second text alone mentions also a daughter born to them, called Bībī-jān *shahīda*, indicating an untimely but otherwise unexplained death). This relationship thus united again the two Sharaf Atāʾī lineages stemming from Khwājagī Aḥmad and Khwājagī Maḥmūd (Ṣiddīqa Bégim's husband, Muḥammad Sharaf Khwāja, was already, through his father, descended from both Aḥmad and Maḥmūd); and the same pattern was maintained with the two sons of Bābā Khwāja, each of whom was married to a Sharaf Atāʾī daughter from the lineage descended (paternally) from Khwājagī Maḥmūd. As the text explains, first, "Bābā Khwāja gave Gadāy Bégim, the daughter of his sister, who was the sister of Muḥammad Ṣāliḥ Khwāja, to his son, Pādshāh Khwāja." In other words, Gadāy Bégim was the sister of Muḥammad Ṣāliḥ Khwāja, and their mother, ʿĀbida Bégim, was Bābā Khwāja's sister; Gadāy Bégim was given in marriage to Bābā Khwāja's son, Pādshāh Khwāja, and bore him two sons (Muḥammad Yūsuf Khwāja, Khwāja Yādgār) and two daughters (Māh Bégim, Jamāl Bégim). One of the sons of Pādshāh Khwāja and Gadāy Bégim, Muḥammad Yūsuf Khwāja, as noted earlier, married a descendant of Sayyid Ata, who bore him a daughter named ʿĀ'isha Bégim; here again the two Sharaf Atāʾī lineages were united, inasmuch as ʿĀ'isha Bégim married Muḥammad Fāżil (the son of Muḥammad Sharaf Khwāja b. Muḥammad Ṣāliḥ Khwāja and Ṣiddīqa Bégim bt. Bābā Khwāja), and bore him three sons (including the author) and two daughters. The other son of Bābā Khwāja, finally, was named Sharaf Khwāja, and married Sayyida Bégim, the daughter of Muḥammad Ṣāliḥ Khwāja, again linking the (already linked) Sharaf Atāʾī lines. Sharaf Khwāja and Sayyida Bégim had two sons and four daughters; only the sons are named (in the second text alone). One was Yaʿqūb Khwāja, who had a son, Bālta Khwāja, and a daughter, Māhrūy Bégim; the other was Kūchuk Khwāja, who is said to have had two sons and nine daughters (none of them is named).

The close attention given to these branches, and to their interrelationships, suggests not only the author's interest in his recent family history, but the broader pattern of intermarriage intended to keep and "concentrate" sacred descent within close limits; we have narrative accounts of the reluctance of some *sayyid* groups to give their daughters in marriage to "commoners,"[22] but here we seem to see this principle in action, and with a group that seems to have defined itself primarily in terms of Bakrid descent (as discussed shortly). Another point worth noting with regard to the later generations, and the multiple branchings of the Sharaf Atāʾī lineage, reflected in these brief texts is the relatively rich information provided on figures who appear to have been of some religious and social prominence in seventeenth-century Khwārazmian society; we find here, that is, names of figures identified as *qāżī*s under particular rulers and in particular places. It is unfortunately impossible to identify any of the individuals named in the account from these later generations and thereby corroborate the Sharaf Atāʾī text; but it must be kept in mind that the historiography of Khwārazm is quite sparse for this period, amounting to just one major source from the mid-seventeenth century (the work of Abū al-Ghāzī), and the much later work of Muʾnis and Āgahī, from the early nineteenth century, the *Firdaws al-iqbāl*.

It is also of interest, finally, that the author pays attention to demonstrating some documentary attestation for the relationships he describes. At the end of the first text, he first notes that his accounts are based on "*maktūbāt-i akābir*," namely, texts written by "eminent figures," and upon what he had heard from reliable sources; he then cites other kinds of evidence that in fact suggest the absence of more detailed genealogical texts. First, he mentions the seal of Khwāja Mullā, which he says identifies him as "Khwāja Mullā b. Khwāja Ulugh [?] Sharafī"; this would seem to refer to Muḥammad Ṣāliḥ Khwāja, identified as the son of "Ulugh Khwāja" (as Muḥammad Futūḥ was known). Next, he refers to another seal, or signet ring (*tawqīʿ*), of Khwāja Rukn al-Dīn, whom we know as the son of a certain Ḥusām al-Dīn Khwāja and a daughter of Khwājagī Aḥmad; the inscription there, the author writes, refers to the owner as "Rukn al-Dīn b. Ḥusām al-Dīn al-Ṣiddīqī." Finally, he refers to the *quṭb al-mashāʾikh* ʿAlāʾ al-Dīn Khwāja (i.e., the brother of Rukn al-Dīn), noting that this figure had written "in several of his books" that on such and such a date, they had been completed by "ʿAlāʾ al-Dīn b. Ḥusām al-Dīn al-Ṣiddīqī"; the author notes that he was thus honoring his maternal lineage. In addition to the indication here that ʿAlāʾ al-Dīn Khwāja (whose close relationship with Muḥammad Ṣāliḥ Khwāja is stressed in both texts) was a Sufi shaykh and the author of written works, these passages are of interest for confirming that the prestige of the Sharaf Atāʾī lineage was based on its Bakrid descent in the paternal line of Sharaf Ata, rather than the ʿAlid descent of Sharaf Ata's mother.

The Sharaf Atāʾī genealogy, II: ʿAlid "input" into the female lines and the role of Sayyid Jalāl Kurlānī

We may turn now to the three daughters of Sharaf Ata. One of them, called Mihr-nigār Bégim, is said to have become the wife of "Shaykh Mukhtār," who is not further identified or again mentioned in this work, but must surely be linked in some way, or identified outright, with the famous Mukhtār Valī whose shrine is a famous landmark in Khwārazm.[23] The third daughter, Ṣiddīqa Bégim, is said to have married a certain Khwāja ʿAbd al-Ghaffār, whose ancestry is shown (with evident abbreviation), making him a Bakrid on his father's side,[24] and an ʿAlid on his mother's side (her genealogy is not given, but she is said to have been a descendant of Imam Zayn al-ʿĀbidīn). For reasons that are not clear (i.e., in terms of the prominence of the figures named), the account notes that Khwāja ʿAbd al-Ghaffār and Ṣiddīqa Bégim bt. Sharaf Ata had a son and two daughters, naming none of them, but affirming that one of the daughters married a "Khwāja Ḥusām al-Dīn Tahāmī" [?], whose lineage is traced, again in clearly truncated fashion, back to ʿAlī through only six generations[25]; presumably the descendants of this Khwāja Ḥusām al-Dīn were known as a prominent family of ʿAlid descent, and the account was intended to link their ancestor with the Sharaf Atāʾī tradition (as was done in the case of Shaykh Mukhtār), but I have not traced other references to Ḥusām al-Dīn or to the *nisba* assigned to him.

It is the second daughter of Sharaf Ata, called in one instance simply Sayyida Bégim and elsewhere Salīma Bégim, who is of greatest importance, for she is said to have married her father's chief *khalīfa*, Sayyid Jalāl Kurlānī.[26] The account then follows their offspring, but only as far as the sixteenth century; this in itself suggests that the compiler of this text had access to older traditions about familial groups that defined themselves in terms of descent from Sayyid Jalāl, but adapted them as part of a project to highlight a specifically Sharaf Atāʾī identity for his own lineage. One of the sons of Sayyid Jalāl Kurlānī and Salīma Bégim was Sayyid ʿAlāʾ al-Dīn Khwāja, who is not explicitly identified (though his descendants are traced through two more generations), but who may have been understood as the figure whose shrine is still a prominent landmark in Khiva[27]; the second text alone follows two more generations after ʿAlāʾ al-Dīn, affirming that he had three sons, ʿUmar Khwāja, ʿIṣmatullāh Khwāja, and ʿAbdullāh Khwāja, and that the latter also had three sons, called Muṭahhar Khwāja, Muṣaghghar Khwāja [?], and Mukarram Khwāja. No further details are offered here, but the mention of Sayyid ʿAlāʾ al-Dīn is of interest insofar as it matches part of an account of the descendants of "Shaykh Sharaf" recorded in the early twentieth century.[28]

Our eighteenth-century manuscript pays much more attention to the lineage of the other son of Sayyid Jalāl Kurlānī and Salīma Bégim, who is identified as "Sayyid Shihāb al-Dīn Manzil-khānī," and is in turn ascribed a son called "Jalāl al-Dīn Khwāja." These names, and especially the *nisba* of Sayyid

Shihāb al-Dīn, are again of special interest, insofar as they evoke the name of a Khwārazmian locality associated with "Khwāja Jalāl al-Dīn of Manzil-khāna"[29] who is mentioned in a collection of Turkic stories focused on Ḥakīm Ata, compiled perhaps as early as the seventeenth century. In one of these stories, Khwāja Jalāl al-Dīn of Manzil-khāna is implicitly portrayed as a descendant of Ḥakīm Ata who discovered his saintly ancestor's gravesite after it had been inundated and forgotten for forty years; this Jalāl al-Dīn, according to the account, then served as caretaker (*mujāvir*) at the shrine of Ḥakīm Ata, until he was displaced by Sayyid Ata, because of the Prophet's promise to Ḥakīm Ata (on the night of the *mi'rāj*) that a *sayyid* would serve as *mujāvir* at his shrine.[30] This story thus ignores, or implicitly rejects, the *sayyid*-status ascribed to Jalāl al-Dīn Khwāja in the family tradition of Sharaf Ata's descendants (although the account by no means dishonors Jalāl al-Dīn, who is shown receiving a sign, before relinquishing Ḥakīm Ata's shrine to Sayyid Ata, that he should become the caretaker of another Khwārazmian shrine, which pilgrims would visit before going to that of Ḥakīm Ata). The story makes no mention, of course, of Jalāl al-Dīn's descent from Sharaf Ata or Sayyid Jalāl al-Dīn Kurlānī, but these traditions may nevertheless signal another aspect of the rivalry between descent-lines linked to Sayyid Ata and Sharaf Ata that are hinted at also in the story from the *Tārīkh-i mashā'ikh al-turk*.

Only the second text gives the further lineage from Sayyid Jalāl Kurlānī (200a–200b, here reversing the order): Sharaf Ata > Sayyida [or Salīma] Bégim and Sayyid Jalāl Kurlānī > Sayyid Shihāb al-Dīn Manzil-khānī > Jalāl al-Dīn Khwāja > Niẓām al-Dīn Khwāja > Ḥusām [al-Dīn Khwāja] > Abū al-Fażl Khwāja > Abū al-Futūḥ Khwāja > Sayyid Mu'īn al-Dīn Muḥsin Khwāja Kubravī [!] Naqīb. Of this last figure, the eighth-generation descendant of Sharaf Ata, we are told that in 944/1537–8, Ilbārs Khān gave him a document bearing a seal (*nishān bā muhr*) testifying to his *sayyid*-status. Either the *khān*'s identity or the date must be incorrect here, insofar as Ilbārs Khān, the effective "founder" of the Khwārazmian Uzbek dynasty, ruled roughly from 916/1511 until 923/1518.[31] The date corresponds, however, with the time in which the son and grandson of Ilbārs Khān, Sulṭān Ghāzī and 'Umar Ghāzī, respectively, were effectively in rebellion against Avanish Khān (the rebellion resulted in the *khān*'s execution of Sulṭān Ghāzī, but the grandson, spared, soon instigated the attack on Khwārazm by 'Ubaydullāh Khān, of the rival Chinggisid dynasty ruling in Bukhārā, that ended the rule, and life, of Avanish Khān), and we might suppose that a document issued by a would-be ruler identifying himself as the son or grandson of Ilbārs Khān might have been imperfectly preserved, so as to conceal the name, or might simply have been misunderstood. In any case, the account then mentions three sons of Sayyid Mu'īn al-Dīn: Sayyid Jalāl al-Dīn Maḥmūd Khwāja, Sayyid Ḥusām al-Dīn Yūsuf Khwāja, and "Muḥammad Fażl Khwāja, known as Fāżil Khwāja" [*sic*], "who in the year 900/1494–5" – or 940/1533–4 (the "40" is crossed out) – "was made chief *ṣadr* (*ṣadr al-ṣudūr*) by Īv.n.sh Khān." In this case, accepting the reading "940" would bring the account into correspondence with what is known of the chronology of Avanish Khān (whose name seems to be the one masked by the form given in the text); his rule began *ca.* 935/1529–30, and lasted until the Bukharan invasion sent by ʿUbaydullāh Khān in 946/1539.

The identity of Sayyid Jalāl Kurlānī, who is thus integrated into the natural and spiritual succession from Sharaf Ata, is of considerable interest with regard to trends in the understanding of familial sanctity and charisma. His name clearly reflects that of a prominent fourteenth-century Ḥanafī jurist active in Khwārazm, "Sayyid Jalāl al-Dīn al-Kurlānī al-Khwārazmī," who is mentioned as the author of a commentary on the famous *Hidāya* of Burhān al-Dīn al-Marghīnānī (d. 593/1196–7),[32] and is linked with many of the leading Ḥanafī jurists of Central Asia during the late thirteenth and early fourteenth centuries (including his teacher, ʿAlāʾ al-Dīn ʿAbd al-ʿAzīz al-Bukhārī [d. 730/1329], and his pupil, Ṭāhir b. Islām al-Khwārazmī, author of the *Jawāhir al-fiqh* [771/1369–70]); more intriguingly, another of Kurlānī's works is cited by the Yasavī master ʿĀlim Shaykh in defending the legitimacy of the vocal *ẕikr*,[33] suggesting that Kurlānī's reputation might indeed have been linked with at least some aspects of the Yasavī Sufi tradition represented by Sharaf Ata, as our genealogical text claims. That text also gives a *sayyid* lineage for Sayyid Jalāl Kurlānī that overlaps, to some degree, with a lineage attested already in the early thirteenth century,[34] suggesting that this part of the genealogical material reflected in our Sharaf Atāʾī text may be corroborated, in a traditionally authoritative way, unlike most of the material from the same text more directly linked to Sharaf Ata.

We know, moreover, that this prominent Ḥanafī jurist was already implicated in genealogical traditions, involving the transmission of a sacred legacy, by the sixteenth century. This is clear from the poetic *taẕkira* of Sayyid Ḥasan "Nis̱ārī" Bukhārī, the *Muẕakkir-i aḥbāb,* completed around 1565, which gives an extended account of the author's own genealogy. The account traces Nis̱ārī's lineage on his father's side down from Zangī Ata, but also notes that Nis̱ārī's paternal uncle, Shaykh ʿAlī Khwāja, was a descendant, through his mother, of "Sayyid Mīr Jalāl Kurlānī"[35]; and it was through her descent from Kurlānī, the account affirms, that Shaykh ʿAlī Khwāja had inherited a Sufi cloak (*khirqa*) that had belonged to the Prophet himself. Nis̱ārī further affirms that, on his father's side, Shaykh ʿAlī Khwāja enjoyed the devotion of most of the tribes of "the *ulūs* of Ṣāʾin Khān," referring to nomadic groups dwelling, in the sixteenth century, in what is now southwestern Turkmenistan[36]; these tribes, we are told, had "hereditary discipleship" (*irādat-i mawrūs̱ī*) to Shaykh ʿAlī Khwāja, but it was specifically on account of the *khirqa* inherited from his maternal ancestor, Sayyid Jalāl Kurlānī, Nis̱ārī writes, that he received frequent visits from the Chinggisid elite, as "*sulṭān*s and *khāqān*s used to come as pilgrims to pay homage to that *khirqa*." Nis̱ārī adds that when Shaykh ʿAlī Khwāja died, at age 63 (the age at which the Prophet died), the brother of the deceased, Nis̱ārī's father, received a letter from "the *naqīb*, Sayyid Jaʿfar

Khwāja"; the latter figure is known from other sources as a descendant of Sayyid Ata, and the contents of the message he sent appear to be cited as confirmation, in effect, of Shaykh ʿAlī Khwāja's *sayyid* status (which, again, was inherited through his mother). The Sayyid Atāʾī *naqīb*'s letter referred to a miracle witnessed at Shaykh ʿAlī Khwāja's funeral, explaining:

> When they placed Shaykh ʿAlī Khwāja in his grave and the people dispersed, two riders appeared, on white horses and wearing white shirts, reciting the *ẕikr*; they heard the sound of the *ẕikr* coming from the shaykh's grave, and they said, "We are his forefathers."[37]

We have no firm indication that descent from Kurlānī was understood to have come to Niṣārī's uncle through the daughter of Sharaf Ata mentioned in our eighteenth-century source, but this in itself may suggest an interesting trajectory for the source of prestige and charisma claimed by a particular descent group as it developed through several centuries. We may suggest, that is, that we find an early glimpse of this group in Niṣārī's work, where it is defined in terms of descent from a famous Ḥanafī jurist; later on, in our eighteenth-century text, the jurist is noted, and indeed sanctioned, as part of a wider genealogical framework defined in terms of descent from the "Sufi" saint Sharaf Ata. At the same time, however, other references to some of the more prominent figures belonging to this group (above all ʿAzīzān Muḥammad Ṣāliḥ Khwāja) suggest that by the latter seventeenth century, the group was also known in terms of, and was in some circles perhaps more prominent because of, its descent from Abū Bakr, as indicated by the use of the *nisba* "Ṣiddīqī"; by the nineteenth century, such basic designations signaling descent traced from the first four Caliphs would predominate (as is the case already, for example, in the work of Marghīnānī discussed above), and would often overshadow group identities based on descent from a medieval saint such as Sharaf Ata.[38]

In any case, the trajectory of familial sanctity suggested here might also have had multiple branchings, as the reputation of that medieval saint, in this case Sharaf Ata, became "public property." The saint, that is, though leaving few traces in hagiographical accounts produced in Sufi circles, was celebrated in popular hagiographical memory in his native region, as "Shaykh Sharaf," in connection with his shrine and with still wider genealogical frameworks in which he was made, in effect, a tribal ancestor, complete with a role in communal legends of origin; but his status as a familial ancestor was preserved as well, in connection with traditions, recorded as late as a century ago (by Samoilovich, as noted above), that make clear the equivalence of "Shaykh Sharaf" and "Sharaf Ata," and are of particular value for emphasizing a lineage different from the one followed in our eighteenth-century manuscript. We may add, finally, that these genealogical and folkloric traditions are not mere abstractions, but refer to concrete social groups: despite the relative obscurity of the family represented in the Sharaf Atāʾī text explored here, or of other Sharaf Atāʾī families, in written sources, the prominence of the "Sharaf Atāʾī *khwājas*" in Khwārazm as a recognized social group is clear from documentary sources.[39]

Conclusion

The various echoes of the Sharaf Atāʾī tradition, including our eighteenth-century text and the more tangential accounts from the *Ḥakīm Ata kitābï* or the *Tārīkh-i mashāʾikh al-turk* studied by Togan, suggest also another feature of local genealogical traditions of sacred descent, common in other Central Asian contexts as well: they suggest that the Sharaf Atāʾī genealogical lore developed in contact with – sometimes in competition with or even antagonism toward, sometimes simply in awareness of – the genealogical lore being developed by other groups, in this case the Sayyid Atāʾī tradition being most important, but including also the group, signaled by the *Risāla-yi nuzdahum*, linked with the legacy of Ḥakīm Ata. To be sure, we need not overstep our sources and insist that accounts making Jalāl al-Dīn of Manzil-khāna a descendant of Ḥakīm Ata, and other accounts linking this Jalāl al-Dīn with Kurlānī, and other accounts declaring Sharaf Ata a virtual "son" of Ḥakīm Ata, and still other accounts highlighting "saintly jealousy" between Sharaf Ata and Sayyid Ata all reflect a systematic opposition between the Sayyid Atāʾī tradition and a Sufi/familial complex of sorts linking Ḥakīm Ata, Jalāl Kurlānī, and Sharaf Ata; after all, our eighteenth-century Sharaf Atāʾī text records intermarriage with a Sayyid Atāʾī family, and Nis̱ārī shows a Sayyid Atāʾī leader treating a Kurlānī descendant with respect and kindness. But there are definite indications of tensions between prominent family groups linked with the legacies of Sharaf Ata and Sayyid Ata, indications that are framed in terms of rivalries between Sufi disciples, and in terms of competition for the prestige and "resources" that accompany the custody of important shrines.

More broadly, the Sharaf Atāʾī text (together with the other eighteenth-century genealogical works mentioned at the outset) suggests the increased currency of traditions about sacred descent highlighted as foundations of religious, social, political, and economic prestige; it suggests a "leveling" of descent groups, with genealogical ties to the first four Caliphs, or even to prominent shaykhs or jurists of medieval times, regarded as essentially equivalent to genealogical links with the Prophet himself; and it suggests the close intertwining of traditions about sacred descent with other kinds of connections to the Prophet and other sacred personages of Islamic tradition, including above all Sufi *silsilas*. These eighteenth-century materials are of further interest as links between genealogical works from the sixteenth and seventeenth centuries, focused on the major families noted at the outset, and the wider range of genealogical texts from the nineteenth and twentieth centuries (often still in private hands) that construct the history, and assert the

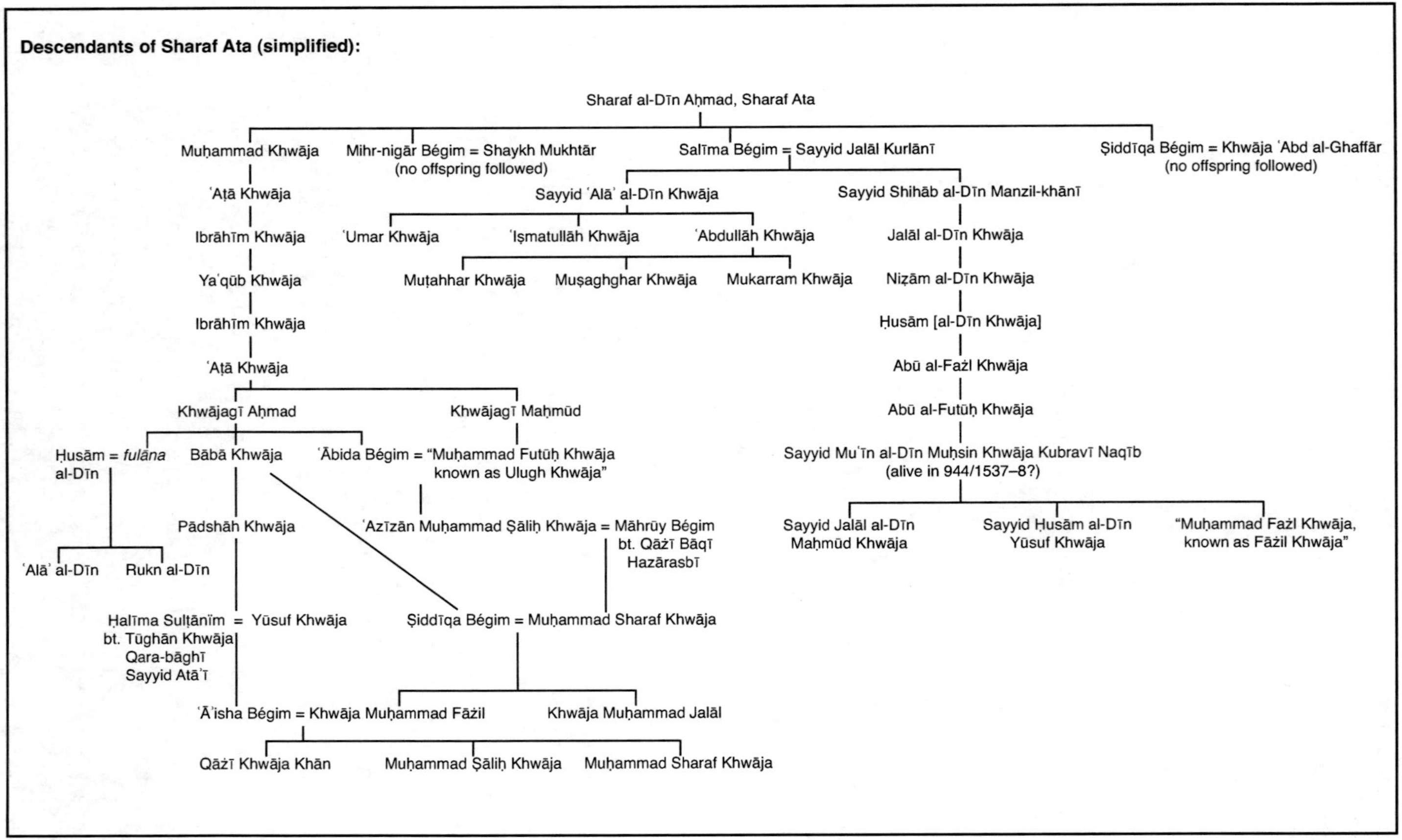

Figure 11.1 Descendants of Sharaf Ata (simplified)

prerogatives, of descent groups ascribed sacred status as well as religious and social prerogatives on the basis of genealogical ties, often in regions beyond the traditional urban centers of Central Asia.[40]

Notes

1 See the discussion of dynastic families in Central Asia, in connection with shrine traditions, in R. D. McChesney, *Central Asia: Foundations of Change* (Princeton, NJ: Darwin Press, 1996), 71–115.

2 On traditions about Sayyid Ata's role in the conversion of Özbek Khān, see my discussion in *Islamization and Native Religion in the Golden Horde: Baba Tükles and Conversion to Islam in Historical and Epic Tradition* (University Park: Pennsylvania State University Press, 1994), 101–106, 133–135, 226–229, 483–490, as well as my "Atāʾīya Order," in Ehsan Yarshater ed., *Encyclopaedia Iranica* (London and Boston: Routledge and Kegan Paul, 1982–; hereafter *EIr*), II:904–905 (the reference to this group as an "order" in the heading to this entry was unfortunate). On the Sufi lineage traced to Sayyid Ata, see my "A Neglected Source on Central Asian History: The 17th-Century Yasavī Hagiography *Manāqib al-akhyār*," in Denis Sinor and Bakhtiyar A. Nazarov eds, *Essays on Uzbek History, Culture, and Language* (Bloomington: Research Institute for Inner Asian Studies, 1993), 38–50. The descent groups linked with Sayyid Ata are discussed in my "The Descendants of Sayyid Ata and the Rank of *Naqīb* in Central Asia," *Journal of the American Oriental Society* 115 (1995): 612–634, and my "The Sayyid Atāʾī Presence in Khwārazm during the 16th and Early 17th Centuries," in Devin DeWeese ed., *Studies on Central Asian History in Honor of Yuri Bregel* (Bloomington: Research Institute for Inner Asian Studies, 2001), 245–281.

3 On this figure, see my brief "Ḥakīm Ata," in *EIr*, XI:573–574, and my translation of "Three Tales from the Central Asian 'Book of Hakīm Ata'," for John Renard ed., *Tales of God's Friends: Islamic Hagiography in Translation* (Berkeley: University of California Press, 2009), 121–135.

4 Togan discussed this work in his "Hwārazmde yazïlmïş eski türkçe a̱sarlar" (in Ottoman script), *Türkiyyat majmūʿasī* 2 (1928): 323–324 [315–345], and in his "Yesevîliğe dair bazı yeni malûmat," in *[60 doğum yılı münasebetiyle] Fuad Köprülü Armağanı* (Istanbul: Osman Yalçın Matbaası, 1953), 523–525 [523–529].

5 MS Tashkent, Institute of Oriental Studies of the Academy of Sciences of the Republic of Uzbekistan (hereafter IVRUz), inv. no. 8707, 197a–201a; the catalogue description, in A. A. Semenov et al. eds, *Sobranie vostochnykh rukopisei Akademii nauk Uzbekskoi SSR*, vol. 6 (Tashkent: Fan, 1963), 59–60, no. 4202, assigns the work the title "*Nasab-nāma-yi Qāżī Khwāja Khān maʿa barādarānish*," and says that the work occupies only ff. 199b–200b; the notes on ff. 197a–198b are clearly part of the same work, however, and no special heading is given in the work itself. The text is often unpointed and is occasionally difficult to read; parts of some of the folios have been damaged as well. The date is found in another section of the manuscript, which appears to have been copied by the same hand.

6 There is no trace of him in the key early sources on the personalia of the Yasavī tradition such as the *Nasāʾim al-maḥabba* of Navāʾī (d. 906/1501) or the *Rashaḥāt-i ʿayn al-ḥayāt*; the works of the sixteenth-century Yasavī writer Ḥazīnī make no mention of him, while the most important Central Asian source on the Yasavī tradition, the *Lamaḥāt min nafaḥāt al-quds* of ʿĀlim Shaykh, from the first half of the seventeenth century, once mentions verse ascribed to Sharaf Ata, but never identifies him further or even affirms his place in a Yasavī *silsila* (MS St Petersburg, Institute of Oriental Manuscripts of the Russian Academy of Sciences [hereafter

SPIVR], no. C1602, 121a; see the description of the manuscript in N. D. Miklukho-Maklai ed., *Opisanie tadzhikskikh i persidskikh rukopisei Instituta narodov Azii*, vyp. 2, *Biograficheskie sochineniia* [Moscow: Izdatel'stvo Vostochnoi Literatury, 1961], 133–135, no. 187).

7 Mawlānā Muḥammad Sharīf, *Ḥujjat al-ẕākirīn*, MS SPIVR, B3787, 152b; the manuscript is noted in O. F. Akimushkin et al., *Persidskie i tadzhikskie rukopisi Instituta narodov Azii AN SSSR (Kratkii alfavitnyi katalog)*, vol. 1 (Moscow: Nauka, 1964), 152, cat. no. 1027. The same brief notice on Sharaf Ata is repeated in the untitled nineteenth-century hagiographical compendium of Mīr Musayyab Bukhārī, MS St Petersburg University, no. 854, 465a); see the description of the manuscript in A. T. Tagirdzhanov, *Opisanie tadzhikskikh i persidskikh rukopisei Vostochnogo otdela Biblioteki LGU*, t. I, *Istoriia, biografii, geografiia* (Leningrad: Izd-vo Leningradskogo Universiteta, 1962), 362–368, no. 150.

8 The passage appears in the work of Mīr Musayyab Bukhārī (MS St Petersburg University, no. 854, 522b), but may have been taken from a now-lost hagiography compiled by one of Qāsim Shaykh's disciples in the late sixteeth century.

9 Togan, "Hwārazmde yazïlmïş eski türkçe aṣarlar," 323–324. It may be noted that the masters and contemporaries ascribed to Sharaf Ata suggest that he must have lived in the latter thirteenth and early fourteenth centuries.

10 On Ersarï Baba in Türkmen genealogical lore, see A. Dzhikiev, "Materialy po ètnografii mangyshlakskikh turkmen," *Trudy Instituta istorii, arkheologii i ètnografii Akademii nauk Turkmenskoi SSR*, t. 7, Seriia ètnograficheskaia (Ashkhabad: Izdatel'stvo Akademii nauk Turkmenskoi SSR, 1963), 192–202; Kh. Iusupov, *Priuzboiskie turkmenskie plemena XIV–XV vv.* (Ashkhabad: Ylym, 1975), 57–62, 78–84, 95–98; and Amantagan Begjanov, *Ärsarï-baba ve ärsarïlar* (Ashgabat: Rukh, 1993).

11 A. N. Kononov ed. and trans., *Rodoslovnaia turkmen: sochinenie Abu-l-gazi khana khivinskogo* (Moscow and Leningrad: Izdatel'stvo Akademii nauk SSSR, 1958), 75 (trans.), 73 (Chaghatay text); cf. Ebulgazi Bahadır Han, *Şecere-i Terākime (Türkmenlerin Soykütüğü)*, ed. by Zuhal Kargı Ölmez (Ankara: Simurg, 1996), 220 (text), 269 (trans.).

12 A. Samoilovich, "Po povodu izdaniia N. P. Ostroumova 'Svetoch Islama'," *Zapiski Vostochnago otdeleniia Imperatorskago Russkago arkheologicheskago obshchestva* 18 (1908): 0158–0166.

13 Turkic works bearing these titles have survived. The *Rawnaq al-islām*, which includes an introduction affirming its composition in 869/1464–5, is nowadays customarily ascribed in Türkmen scholarship to a certain "Vafā'ī." The authorship of the *Mu'īn al-murīd*, which survives in a single copy affirming its completion in 713/1313 (see the published text, *Mu'înü 'l-Mürîd*, ed. by Recep Toparlı [Erzurum: Atatürk Üniversitesi Fen-Edebiyat Fakültesi Yayınları, 1988]), has occasioned considerable discussion, which cannot be addressed here.

14 The prominent structure in Köne Urgench identified by historians of architecture as the mausoleum of the Khwārazmshāh Tekish is linked in popular tradition, rather, with "Shaykh Sharaf" or "Shaykh Sharap Baba"; see the discussions in Nazar Khalimov, *Pamiatniki Urgencha (sooruzheniia, nadpisi i legendy)* (Ashkhabad: Turkmenistan, 1991), 26–30, and Kh. Iusupov, "O dvukh pamiatnikakh Kunia-Urgencha," *Izvestiia Akademii nauk Turkmenskoi SSR*, 1991/1:47–52. Another shrine of "Shikh-Sherep" is found in the village of Nokhur, in southern Turkmenistan; see G. P. Vasil'eva, "Turkmeny-Nokhurli," *Sredneaziatskii ètnograficheskii sbornik*, vol. 1, Trudy Instituta ètnografii im. N. N. Miklukho-Maklaia, Novaia seriia, t. 21 (Moscow and Leningrad: Izd-vo AN SSSR, 1954), 211 [82–215], noting that "Shikh-Sherep" is regarded as the ancestor of some of the *khoja*s of Nokhur, an issue discussed further in Samoilovich, "Po povodu izdaniia N. P. Ostroumova," 0159–0161, and in S. M. Demidov, *Turkmenskie*

ovliady (Ashkhabad: Ylym, 1976), 71–73. On Shikh Sheref/Shaykh Sharaf in general, see S. M. Demidov, *Sufizm v Turkmenii* (Ashkhabad: Ylym, 1978), 46–48, 68–70; for oral tradition about "Shikh Sherep" as the ancestor of Khivan *khoja*s, see V. N. Basilov, *Kul't sviatykh v Islame* (Moscow: Mysl', 1970), 112–113.

15 The shrine of Shaykh, or Shāh, ʿAbbās Valī (contracted to "Shabbas") was located near the site of the old Khwārazmian town of Kāt; see, for further references, Shir Muhammad Mirab Munis and Muhammad Riza Mirab Agahi, *Firdaws al-iqbāl: History of Khorezm*, trans. by Yuri Bregel (Leiden: Brill, 1999), 553–554, n. 164, and 627, n. 769.

16 On the Bukharan district of Khitfar (usually spelled thus), see W. Barthold, *Turkestan Down to the Mongol Invasion*, trans. by V. and T. Minorsky, ed. by C. E. Bosworth, 4th ed. (London: Luzac & Co., 1977), 114.

17 I have been unable to find other references to this *khānqāh*. A mosque of Muḥammad Yār Bīy Atalïq, in a district of Bukhārā that also bears his name, is mentioned already in a document dated 1668–9; see O. A. Sukhareva, *Kvartal'naia obshchina pozdnefeodal'nogo goroda Bukhary (v sviazi s istoriei kvartalov)* (Moscow: Nauka, 1976), 180.

18 Muḥammad Sharīf himself refers, in his *Ḥujjat al-ẕākirīn* (182b), to "ʿAzīzān Ṣāliḥ Khwāja Ṣiddīqī" (alluding to his Bakrid descent, but not indicating that it was through Sharaf Ata), and notes that he became the master of ʿĀlim Shaykh's son, Muḥammad ʿĀbid (ancestor of the Niẓāms of Hyderabad).

19 The mother of the author's ancestor was Māhrūy Bégim, daughter of Qāżī Bāqī Hazārasbī, whose father was of ʿAlid descent (Qāżī Bāqī is identified as the brother of Qāżī Afżal b. Mawdūd b. Shaykh Muḥammad Amīn ʿAlavī), and whose mother was a descendant of Abū Bakr through Imam Zāhid (199b; cf. 198a); Māhrūy Bégim also bore, in addition to Muḥammad Sharaf Khwāja, another son of Muḥammad Ṣāliḥ Khwāja, named Khwāja Muḥammad Bāqī, said to have been buried near the shrine of Khwāja ʿAbd al-Khāliq Ghijduvānī, as well as a daughter called simply "Sayyida Bégim" (she was given in marriage to Sharaf Khwāja, a son of Bābā Khwāja, another Sharaf Atāʾī descendant from a collateral line noted below). The mother of Khān-zāda Bégim, by contrast, was a *sayyida* of Bukhārā whose lineage went back to Sayyid ʿAlī Hamadānī (200a). By the same *sayyida* who bore Khān-zāda Bégim, Muḥammad Ṣāliḥ Khwāja had another son, Khwāja Muḥammad Futūḥ, who is identified in the text as a Sufi (a practitioner of *awrād* and *aẕkār*), as a *ḥājjī*, and as an intimate of the "*qātil al-kuffār*, Shāh Awrangzīb" (i.e., the Moghul emperor Awrangzīb, r. 1068–1118/1658–1707). Unfortunately, the details of this Khwāja Muḥammad Futūḥ's relationship with Awrangzīb are not indicated here, but another source (the nineteenth-century work of Mīr Musayyab, 544b–545a) says that Ṣāliḥ Khwāja, when he neared death, consigned his own son, Khwāja Muḥammad Futūḥ, to the training of Muḥammad ʿĀbid (ʿĀlim Shaykh's son, and a disciple of Ṣāliḥ Khwāja), who then granted Muḥammad Futūḥ license to guide disciples in his own right; this relationship suggests that Muḥammad Futūḥ might indeed have established himself in India, as so many "*Tūrānī*" notables were doing in this era, although it is possible that he was simply received at court while traveling to perform the *ḥajj*. In any case, the Sharaf Atāʾī text does tell us of three sons of Muḥammad Futūḥ (Khwāja Qiyām al-Dīn, Khwāja Kamāl al-Dīn, and Khwāja Qamar al-Dīn) and two daughters (Bulāqī Bégim, who married a certain "Khwāja Yādgār b. Pādshāh Rāziq Dahbīdī," thus signaling ties with yet another prominent family, and another, called simply "Sayyida Bégim").

20 [Text I]: Aḥmad, known as Sharaf Ata < Mu'ayyad < Muvaffaq < Aḥmad < Abū Saʿīd < Muḥammad < Isḥāq < ʿAbd al-Sallām < Muslim < Nāfiʿ < Musʿad [?] < Ṭufayl < ʿUtba < Ṭalḥ [*sic*] < Qāsim < Muḥammad < Abū Bakr. [Text II]: Sharaf

Ata < Mu'ayyad or (*yā*) Muvaffaq < Musʿad [or Saʿd?] < Mu'ayyad < Ṭufayl < ʿUtba < Ṭalḥa < Qāsim < Muḥammad < Abū Bakr (with each name except Sharaf Ata and Abū Bakr followed by the title *khwāja*).

21 Sharaf Ata < Amīna < Sayyid Yūsuf Khwāja < Sayyid Sirāj al-Dīn Uzgandī < Sayyid ʿĀrif < Sayyid Muḥammad < Sayyid Ibrāhīm < Sayyid Isḥāq < Sayyid Jaʿfar < Sayyid Imām ʿAlī Naqī < Sayyid Imām Muḥammad Taqī < Imām ʿAlī Rižā < Imām Mūsā Kāẓim < Imām Jaʿfar Ṣādiq < Imām Zayn al-ʿĀbidīn < Imām Ḥusayn < Imām ʿAlī.

22 The reluctance of *sayyid*s to give their daughters in marriage to commoners extended to royal suitors as well, and there were conflicts between Sayyid Atā'ī groups and rulers of the Qonghrat dynasty of Khwārazm over this issue; see, for example, *Firdaws*, trans. by Bregel, 635, n. 887, with further references.

23 See *Firdaws*, trans. by Bregel, 633, n. 852.

24 Khwāja ʿAbd al-Ghaffār b. Badr al-Dīn b. ʿUbayd al-Dīn [*sic*, perhaps to be read "ʿAmīd al-Dīn"?] b. Ṣafī al-Dīn b. Niẓām al-Dīn b. Imām Zāhid.

25 Khwāja Ḥusām al-Dīn b. Shaykh Shihāb al-Dīn Ṣadr b. Shaykh Rukn al-Dīn Vāykhāqī [?, apparently to be read thus], with the latter said to be linked to ʿAlī through four intermediaries.

26 That is, the text affirms that the learned Sayyid Jalāl Kurlānī "was the best among the *khulafā* of Shaykh Sharaf Ata, and was also his son-in-law" (200b); later it adds that Sharaf Ata "conferred his *silsila* upon the holy Sayyid Jalāl" (*silsila-rā ba-ḥażrat-i sayyid jalāl tafvīż karda-and*).

27 See *Firdaws*, trans. by Bregel, 593, n. 414.

28 A genealogical account recorded by Samoilovich ("Po povodu izdaniia," 0163), from a manuscript belonging to the same figure who provided the oral account of Shaykh Sharaf paralleling the version in Abū al-Ghāzī's work, affirms that Shaykh Sharaf had one son named Khwāja Muḥammad, and three daughters – "Selimè-bikim, Mihr, and Dzhemal-bikim" – who were married, respectively, to "Dzhelial Kermanskii," "Sheikh Mukhtar the Great," and "Lukman-bai" (from the first daughter and "Jalāl Kirmānī" – whose name is undoubtedly a deformation of "Jalāl Kurlānī," as discussed below in connection with another, earlier account – was born, the account adds, "Ala-ud-din").

29 On the locality called "Manzil-khāna," typically understood as a popular deformation of the old name of Mizdahqān, see *Firdaws*, trans. by Bregel, 608, n. 593 (the popular pronunciation clearly precedes the nineteenth century, however).

30 See the translation of this account in my "Three Tales from the Central Asian 'Book of Hakīm Ata'," 129–130. It may be noted that the name assigned to Sharaf Ata's successor also recalls that of "Jalāl Ata," who is mentioned, in a story recorded in the sixteenth century, as a direct disciple of Aḥmad Yasavī.

31 See Yuri Bregel, "Ilbārs Khan," in *EIr*, XII:644.

32 Jalāl al-Dīn Kurlānī's commentary on the *Hidāya*, entitled *al-Kifāya*, was written before 748/1347, the date of a manuscript copy; see Carl Brockelmann, *Geschichte der arabischen Litteratur*, 2 vols (Weimar, 1898–1902, 2nd ed., Leiden: Brill, 1943–1949), I:377; 3 supplement vols (Leiden: Brill, 1937–1942), I:645.

33 ʿĀlim Shaykh, *Lamaḥāt min nafaḥāt al-quds*, MS SPIVR, C1602, 7b, 8a, 142a. The work cited is Kurlānī's commentary on the *Mishkāt al-maṣābīḥ* (itself based on al-Baghawī's *Maṣābīḥ al-sunna*), on which see Brockelmann, *Geschichte*, supplement vols, I:622.

34 Sayyid Jalāl's father is called Sayyid Shams al-Dīn Shīrāzī; he is said to have been the *naqīb* of Shīrāz, and to have come to Khwārazm. The lineage is then traced back through thirteen intermediaries to ʿAlī. Nothing is said about the first six names (Sayyid Shams al-Dīn < Sayyid Murtażā < Sayyid Sulaymān [or Salmān?] < Sayyid Ḥamza < Sayyid ʿAbd al-Ẓāhir < Sayyid Muḥsin < Sayyid ʿAlī), but the father of

Sayyid Jalāl's seventh ancestor (Sayyid ʿAlī) is called Sayyid ʿUbaydullāh, and is identified as having been the *naqīb* of Baghdād; his father, in turn, is called Sayyid Aḥmad, and is said to have been a poet whose verse is famous in the lands of the Arabs. Sayyid Aḥmad's father is called Sayyid ʿAlī ʿUrayżī, whose *nisba* is explained as referring to a village of Madīna; and this figure, we are told, was the son of Imam Jaʿfar-i Ṣādiq, whose lineage is traced back as usual (Imām Jaʿfar < Imām Muḥammad Bāqir < Imām Zayn al-ʿĀbidīn < Imām Ḥusayn < Imām ʿAlī [200b]). This lineage is of interest for providing more detail about the most recent *and* the earliest "non-traditional" links (i.e., Sayyid Jalāl's father, and the first three descendants of Imam Jaʿfar-i Ṣādiq); it contrasts with the Bakrid lineage given for Sharaf Ata, which provides nothing but names for any of his ancestors (and, as noted, gives two different versions of these), and also with the ʿAlid lineage given for Sharaf Ata's mother, which offers at least the suggestive "Uzgandī" *nisba* for her grandfather, but nothing more for any of the earlier links. It is unclear what sources the compiler of the Sharaf Atāʾī text might have used, but an early thirteenth-century work on ʿAlid lineages gives a genealogy for a group of hereditary *naqībs* (in Yazd, not Shīrāz or Baghdād) that partly overlaps with the lineage given here: ʿAlī < ʿUbaydullāh < "Aḥmad al-Shaʿrānī" < ʿAlī al-ʿUrayḍī (the first ʿAlī is further shown as the father of a Muḥammad, he of another ʿAlī, and he of "al-Muḥsin, the *raʾīs* in Yazd"); see Ismāʿīl b. al-Ḥusayn al-Marwazī al-Azwarqānī, *al-Fakhrī fī ansāb al-ṭālibiyyīn*, ed. by Mahdī al-Rajāʾī (Qum: Maktabat Āyatullāh al-Marʿashī, 1409/1988), 31–32 (I am indebted to Morimoto Kazuo for this reference).

35 Khwāja Bahā al-Dīn Ḥasan Nithārī Bukhārī, *Mudhakkir-i-Aḥbāb ("Remembrancer of Friends")*, ed. by Syed Muḥammad Fazlullah (New Delhi: Ministry of Education and Hyderabad: Daʾiratu'l-Maʿarif Press, 1969), 503; the text adopted by the editor reads "Kirmānī," but two manuscripts (including the oldest) give instead "K.r.lānī," and there can be little doubt that this is the intended form. Cf. Sayyid Ḥasan Khwāja Naqīb al-Ashrāf Bukhārī "Niṡārī," *Muẕakkir-i aḥbāb*, ed. by Najīb Māyil Haravī (Tehran: Nashr-i Markaz, 1377 AHS/1999), 304, reading "Kirmānī," without comment, again signaling simply the greater familiarity of the town of Kirmān.

36 "The *ulūs* of Ṣāʾin Khān" no longer meant the *ulus* of Jochi in general (as I had suggested in *Islamization*, 376–377); it undoubtedly included elements with hereditary ties to the Jochid *ulus*, which by this time, however, were integrated into the nomadic communities that would become known in later times as the "Yaqa" Türkmens.

37 Niṡārī, *Muẕakkir*, ed. by Fazlullah, 505; ed. by Māyil Haravī, 304.

38 I have suggested such a shift in my "The Politics of Sacred Lineages in 19th-Century Central Asia: Descent Groups linked to Khwaja Ahmad Yasavi in Shrine Documents and Genealogical Charters," *International Journal of Middle East Studies* 31/4 (1999): 507–530 (esp. 520–522). Such a shift is also evident, I believe, in one of the genealogical texts mentioned at the outset, namely the untitled work of Amīr Sayyid Shaykh Aḥmad Nāṣir al-Dīn b. Amīr Sayyid ʿUmar al-Marghīnānī, preserved in a single copy in Tashkent (MS IVRUz, 11290, described in Bakhtiiar Babadzhanov, Ul'rike Berndt, Ashirbek Muminov, and Iurgen Paul' eds, *Katalog sufiiskikh proizvedenii XVII–XX vv. iz sobranii Instituta Vostokovedeniia im. Abu Raikhana al-Biruni Akademii Nauk Respubliki Uzbekistan*, Verzeichnis der orientalischen Handschriften in Deutschland, Supplementband 37 (Stuttgart: Franz Steiner Verlag, 2002), 108–110, no. 49 [by Shovosil Ziyadov]; the work stresses the author's genealogical ties in lineages that, though nominally originating with the Prophet and the four Caliphs, pass through prominent Sufi shaykhs of the medieval era.

39 See Iu. È. Bregel', "K izucheniiu zemel'nykh otnoshenii v khivinskom khanstve (Istochniki i ikh ispol'zovanie)," *Pis'mennye pamiatniki Vostoka* 1969:52 and

n. 115 [28–103], referring to five "*yarlïgh-dārs*" (i.e., holders of tax-exempting *yarlïqs* from the *khān*) among the "*Sharaf Atāī khwāja-lar*," in a Khivan document.

40 These include the many *nasab-nāmas*, genealogical texts and "sacred histories" of particular descent groups (*khojas*), that have begun to be rediscovered during the past two decades, in the wake of the end of Soviet-style antireligious pressures. See, for further references, my "The Politics of Sacred Lineages," and the recent publication of genealogical texts related to "holy families" of what is now southern Kazakhstan, Ashirbek Muminov, Anke von Kügelgen, Devin DeWeese, Michael Kemper eds, *Islamizatsiia i sakral'nye rodoslovnye v Tsentral'noi Azii: Nasledie Iskhak Baba v narrativnoi i genealogicheskoi traditsiiakh*, Tom 2: *Genealogicheskie gramoty i sakral'nye semeistva XIX–XXI vekov: nasab-nama i gruppy khodzhei, sviazannykh s sakral'nym skazaniem ob Iskhak Babe / Islamization and Sacred Lineages in Central Asia: The Legacy of Ishaq Bab in Narrative and Genealogical Traditions*, Vol. 2: *Genealogical Charters and Sacred Families: Nasab-namas and Khoja Groups Linked to the Ishaq Bab Narrative, 19th–21st Centuries* (Almaty: Daik-Pre Press, 2008).

12 Trends of ashrāfization in India

Arthur F. Buehler

> Last year I was a Julaha or weaver; this year I am a Shaikh; next year if prices rise, I shall be a Sayyid.

Introduction

Let us start with geography. The demographic center of the contemporary Islamic world runs right through the South Asian subcontinent (near Karachi) with almost one-third of the world's Muslim population. Indo-Islamic culture is distinctive because of the confluence of 1) the Islamic religious inheritance from the Arabic tradition, 2) the government, law, dress, and food from the Turkic origin of many of the rulers and aristocracy, 3) the pervasive influence of Persian literature, fine arts, mysticism, and philosophy, and 4) the indigenous Indian environment in which Islamic culture thrived.

In other majority Muslim countries, Sayyids as putative lineal descendants of the Prophet typically had a distinctive socio-religious status. This included special opportunities in government employment, subsidies, and landgrants in addition to marriage prerogatives. With its indigenous Hindu caste system and overwhelmingly majority non-Muslim population, Muslim immigrants coming to India developed a more nuanced array of social distinctions than those that had existed in their native regions. Although Sayyids remained at the top of Indo-Muslim social structure, there were three other high-status social groups of roughly equal status: Shaykhs, putative descendants of the Companions, Mughals, putative descendants of Turkic origin, and Pathāns, putative descendants of Afghans.[1] *In toto* these four social strata, with Sayyids having the highest status, were named *ashrāf*, the Indian Muslim social stratum of nobles who claim to be foreign-born or descendants of non-South Asian Muslims. In the available Indo-Muslim literature, *ashrāf* are discussed as a conglomerate instead of individually as one of the four *ashrāfī* subgroups. Occasionally authors discuss Sayyids in special contexts. The aim of this article is to learn more about the Sayyids in Indian Muslim society through the (usually) only available lens of the *ashrāf*, who became socially distinct from Indian converts, "the commoners" (*ajlāf*), as early as the thirteenth century (at least from the texts we have available).

Even though the *ashrāf* highlight their non-Indian identities, there has been a deep-rooted and all-pervading influence of indigenous culture on South Asian Islam. Indeed, the largely non-Muslim environment molded the contours of what is now Indo-Muslim culture. The vast majority of the Muslims in India were from native Indian families, so the customs, culture, and mentalities of Indian society infused the increasingly growing Indo-Muslim society like any other confluence of a world religion and a new culture. The strident Islamic revivals of later centuries and recent nationalist tendencies have tended to obscure this indigenous element (or exaggerated it under the guise of Hindu customs). Without the contributions of Indian civilizations and cultures, the creative synthesis that became Indo-Muslim culture could have never arisen. Indo-Muslim culture is the dynamic result of a tension between identifying with a non-Indian genealogy and Indian *ashrāfī* values in the larger context of indigenous South Asian Muslim cultures. Seeking to outline the history of Sayyids in India, this article analyzes the category of *ashrāf* in the context of Muslim social stratification where Sayyids remained the highest status group. Although there were Mughal governmental controls to prevent false claims to Sayyid-ship, many common Muslims attempted to join the ranks of Shaykhs, Turks, and Pathāns in a bid to "bask in the shadows of Sayyid-ship," a process of ashrāfization where Muslims attempted to modify their Muslim identities.

Social stratification among Muslims

Based on ritual pollution, India's caste system has had one of the most rigid social stratification systems in the world. Foreign Muslims coming to India had their Islamic version of social stratification also, even though the Qur'ān says that there is no superiority among people except in piety or righteousness (*taqwā*): "For God, the most honored among you is the one who is the most righteous" [Qur'ān, XLIX:13]. God is one thing, however, and fellow human beings are another. It did not take long for the nascent seventh-century Muslim community to revert to tribal affiliations. Nor is it any coincidence that the subsequent leaders of the Muslim community were from the aristocratic Quraysh tribe. Muḥammad's attempts to erase pride in one's genealogy – for example, "There are no genealogies in Islam" and "The sole title to nobility in Islam is piety and fear of God" – apparently did not have much effect.[2] According to his cousin and son-in-law, ʿAlī b. Abī Ṭālib, "Nobility (*sharaf*) is derived only from knowledge (*ʿilm*) and beautiful behavior (*adab*), not from inherited merit (*ḥasab*) and lineage (*nasab*)."[3] This too was an ideal soon to be transformed. Upon his death the pinnacle of status and nobility was to be related to Muḥammad and the progeny of ʿAlī and Muḥammad's daughter Fāṭima.

The Prophet left one loophole for successive generations to develop an *Islamic* social stratification system. He declared that marriage should be contracted between equals, the principle of equality of status between two people commonly known in Islamic law as *kafā'a*. On this basis, Ḥanafī jurists developed the following status guidelines[4]: 1) Arabs are superior to non-Arabs; 2) among Arabs Qurayshīs have equal standing among themselves and all other Arabs are equal; 3) for non-Arabs a man is equal to an Arab at birth if both his father and grandfather had been Muslims and he is wealthy enough to pay the bride price (*mahr*); 4) a learned non-Arab is equal to an ignorant Arab even if that Arab is a Sayyid; 5) a Muslim judge or jurist ranks higher than a merchant and a merchant ranks higher than a tradesman.[5] Social stratification in medieval Islam cultures involved inherited nobility just like in pre-Islamic Persia or Arabia. In the Iranian case, those of inherited noble status were forbidden to associate with commoners. For Arabs, "knowledge of the common descent of certain groups [and] the glory of a tribe . . . stood at the center of Arab social consciousness."[6] Over time, certain groups dominated in Islamic societies as ethnicity and pride of birth became determining factors binding the community together.

Social stratification in Muslim South Asia

It is easy to see how birth as a principle of status was significant in early Indo-Muslim society. The rulers gave positions of status and authority to men of foreign origin, whether descended from the invading armies or prior immigrants. Baranī, a fourteenth-century chronicler, noted that Iltutmish (r. 607–633/1211–1236) dismissed thirty-three *ajlāf* from government service on account of their being native-born Indians.[7] In the same fashion, Balban (r. 664–686/1266–1287) removed low-born persons (*ajlāf*) from all important offices and sharply reprimanded the courtiers who had given Kamāl Mohiyyār, an Indian Muslim, a post as a tax collector (*mutaṣarrif*) of Amroha. Muḥammad Tughluq (r. 725–752/1325–1351) consciously initiated the policy of giving preference to foreign-born Muslims in administration and government, and systematically ignored the claims of Indian Muslims.[8] By the fifteenth century, the Bengali poet Vipra Das referred to the Muslim preachers and judges of Satgaon as Sayyids, Mughals, and Pathāns.[9]

Being among the *ashrāf* was an important consideration for Sufi authority, at least if one wanted to attract disciples and get government "donations." For many centuries the Chishtī lineage, which depended financially on voluntary donations, included such Sayyids as Muʿīn al-Dīn Chishtī (d. 633/1236 in Ajmer), Naṣīr al-Dīn Chirāgh (Delhi), Quṭb al-Dīn Bakhtiyār Kākī (d. 633/1235), Gēsūdarāz (d. 825/1422 Gulbarga), and Ashrāf Jahāngīr Simnānī (d. 808/1405 Jaunpur). Makhdūm-i Jahāniyān (d. 785/1384), from the Suhrawardiyya, a lineage that generally depended on government patronage, was also a Sayyid.[10] Bahā' al-Dīn Zakariyya (d. 661/1262) was a Qurayshī and Abū ʿAlī Qalandar of Panipat was a descendant of Abū Ḥanīfa (d. 150/767 Baghdad). Some have tried to claim Sayyid descent for Farīd al-Dīn Ganj-i Shakar (d. 664/1265) from Ḥusayn, a grandson of the Prophet.[11] An aspirant looking for a Sufi teacher would probably want a Sayyid if possible for his shaykh, and if not then an *ashrāfī* shaykh would suffice. In addition, Sayyid and other *ashrāfī* Sufis have greater status because they are perceived to be more *Sharīʿa*-minded (in the literature *bā sharīʿat*) and more pious in their formal Islamic practices, which are presumed to have taken the place of indigenous customs. Sufis who are perceived to be lax in behaving according to Islamic law (*bī sharīʿat*) tend to attract the lower classes (*ajlāf/ardhāl*).[12]

Sayyid Sufis were not shy about their genealogies. Sayyid Gēsūdarāz says, "There are few men who are at once a *faqīh* (jurist), a Sufi, a Sunni, and a Saiyid. All these four qualities are present in me."[13] Almost four centuries later there is a Naqshbandī-Mujaddidī of Delhi, Sayyid Mīr Dard (d. 1199/1785), whose family was closely related to the Mughal emperor Aurangzēb's household. However, it was descent from the Prophet rather than any royal lineage that Dard and his father ʿAndalīb emphasized. Mīr Dard mentions how his parents possessed special grace which God had bestowed on their ancestor Muḥammad and "again after 1100 and odd years this special grace became visible from the interior fountain of (my father), the true *sayyid* and most true leader, the world illuminating sun of the sphere of sayyid-ship . . ."[14] His greatest source of pride was that he was a Sayyid from both his mother and father. Normally Naqshbandī-Mujaddidīs highlight their spiritual lineage through Abū Bakr, but Mīr Dard and his father put more emphasis on their ʿAlid lineage rather than their spiritual lineage through Abū Bakr.[15] One cogent spiritual reason to emphasize the former Sayyid connection is Dard's implying that he and his father had received Prophetic knowledge through the Imāmī lineage via the mediation of their forefather, Ḥasan al-ʿAskarī (d. 260/874), the eleventh Imāmī Imam.[16]

South Asian Sufis have almost always avoided any identification with the trades or attaching professional attributions (*nisba*s) to their names because tradesmen were considered to be at the lower rungs of Muslim social strata. One apt "*ashrāfī*" translation of this lower strata, *ajlāf*, is "coarse rabble," which includes tradesmen such as weavers, cotton carders, oil-pressers, barbers, and tailors. In prominent hagiographical compendia of South Asia, almost all of the major hagiographic works make a point of mentioning the high pedigree of the leading shaykhs.[17] This situation contrasts sharply with Sufis coming from the Iraqi–Khurasan–Bukhara region where it has been common to mention the person's profession. Farīd al-Dīn ʿAṭṭār (d. 618/1221) or Manṣūr al-Ḥallāj (mart. 309/922) are famous Sufis who come to mind immediately as a druggist/perfumer and cotton carder respectively.[18] In South Asia there is a virtual non-existence of professional *nisba*s among prominent Sufis. As Riazul Islam notes, "In the Indian social scene a Sufi would only be inviting ridicule and insult if he attached *ḥajjām* [barber/circumcizer] to his name."[19]

In the Mughal context, there were controls in place for the *ashrāf* to guard their prerogatives, both social and governmental. In Bengal, for example, the *ashrāf* under Turk-Afghan and later Mughal rule (and today) consistently refused to engage in agriculture. There was actually an aversion to converting Bengali cultivators to Islam. Islām Khān, a major Mughal administrator during Jahāngīr's reign (1014–1037/1605–1627) and the Sayyid Salīm Chishtī's (d. 979/1572) grandson,[20] even opposed Islamization of local Bengalis. He even punished one of his officers for letting it happen once.[21] Islām Khān's chief naval officer, Ihtimām Khān, got very upset when the governor of Bengal and his son had treated him like native Bengalis (*ahl-i Hind*). Ihtimām Khān was an Indian-born Muslim from the Panjab who apparently had acquired *ashrāfī* attitudes while in Mughal service.[22]

During Mughal rule, there was an impetus to maintain a subculture to retain non-Indian customs, to bolster education in Persian and Arabic (and later Urdu), and most importantly, to keep the status quo of *ashrāfī* privileges. It was a semi-permeable border. Like Ihtimām Khān, one could acquire *ashrāfī* culture in the Mughal culture of the ruling elite. Language was part of this ashrāfization boundary mechanism. Early Bengali literary sources indicate an opposition to translating Persian and Arabic religious texts into Bengali, the rationale being that doing so would profane these holy texts.[23] The Mughals administratively accommodated the local and regional Indian cultures and people. In their personal lives they apparently lived in their separate Muslim *ashrāfī* subculture.

Since Sayyids had special governmental privileges such as stipends and landgrants, people resorted to making false genealogies, which not only defrauded the government but was considered morally corrupt. By the latter part of the sixteenth century, there was a special post of *niqābat* created and filled by a distinguished Sayyid who had the authority to look into the authenticity of Sayyid claims and who issued certificates of genealogy to those who were legitimate.[24] His function as the *naqīb al-sādāt* was to take care of Sayyids' welfare and to act as an expert genealogist. In a description of this office in Mughal archives, it explicitly states that false claims would be severely punished as a deterrent to others.[25] This is a political manifestation of the study of genealogy (*ʿilm al-nasab*) manifesting in an imperial fashion. Almost a thousand years before, such a genealogical enterprise had originally been formulated for political purposes among the Arabs to distinguish tribal Arabs from their clients after the Arab conquests. The formal study of genealogy then became the purview of scholars as it developed into a special discipline.

Official monitoring of genealogy, particularly along with supporting and rewarding Sayyids, is one way to legitimize an Islamic government and make an ideological statement. With increasing urbanization and literacy, it was even more important to legitimize one's ancestry in accordance with the genealogical principles used by the government genealogist. In addition, the social evolution of the Mughal seat of empire meant that urban life became more complicated in terms of legal procedures for dividing legacies. Families also created more and more pious endowments (*awqāf*).[26] Genealogy mattered.

Ashrāf–ajlāf as a disputed category

From the textual evidence, there seems to be no doubt that this *ashrāf–ajlāf* social stratification existed in medieval Indo-Muslim life, politically, socially, and even spiritually. But only the *ashrāf* are writing these texts. We do not have more than anecdotal accounts of what was actually happening in India. Contemporary sociologists and anthropologists researching in South Asia have found this simplistic black and white sociological schema problematic. Misra's work in Gujarat indicates that the distinction between the *ashrāf* and *ajlāf* does not exist in Gujarat.[27] Among rural Kashmiri Muslims in Kashmir the terms *ashrāf* and *ajlāf* are not categories that people use, since social stratification is based upon different criteria.[28] Imtiaz Ahmad asks whether the *ashrāf* and *ajlāf* categories constitute meaningful units of distinction for the study of social stratification among Indian Muslims since the *ashrāf–ajlāf* dichotomy has been carried over in sociological writings from the historical literature.[29] He concludes, and I agree, that the *ashrāf–ajlāf* dichotomy is a gross over-simplification of the existing reality, particularly in the last century. Each of these *ashrāfī* groups can be further subdivided into a number of smaller hereditary, endogamous groups that have their own unique matrix of interactions.[30] I imagine that the same held true for medieval India.[31]

It is important to recognize that Islamic social hierarchy, although apparently similar to the Hindu caste system's occupational hierarchy, is based upon an entirely different principle. Hindu "caste," a translation of *jāt* or *jātī*, is based on ritual purity, which has nothing to do with Islamic justifications for occupational hierarchy.[32] It is a conceptual error to equate Muslim social stratification with caste just because the outer form looks similar; for example, privileging religious knowledge over military prowess over tradesmen over manual labor. Without looking at Islamic precedents, one could conclude that South Asian Muslims have adopted the Hindu caste system because the hierarchy of professions in Indo-Muslim culture in many ways parallels that of the Hindus.

Professional status, however, had already been established in Islamic jurisprudence, with hadith precedents.[33] The upper literate classes despised manual occupations long before Muslims ruled India. One would expect there to be some parallels with Hindu occupational hierarchies since each particular hierarchy of occupations differs from region to region in the Islamic world and follows local custom.[34] Marc Gaborieau, extrapolating from this situation, asserts that the social strata of middle and lower classes should be called "castes."[35] His reasoning is that since local custom in India is the caste system and Muslims are following local custom, then Muslims are giving legitimacy to the caste system. There is no doubt that many aspects of the local Muslim social hierarchy outwardly parallel local notions of caste hierarchy, just like Muslim marriage customs conform to local Hindu customs. Both involve local notions of social parity, the underlying principles of which (e.g., ritual purity) may or may not be similar. It is easy to understand how Gaborieau, with his experience looking at a handful of small communities in South Asia, could validly come to the conclusion that "caste" significantly overlaps Hindu and Muslim communities. If castes are defined, à la Weber, as status groups who religiously believe that a lower caste will ritually pollute them, then Gaborieau needs much more data to establish this practice on the village level before even entertaining the possibility as a pan-Indian phenomenon. Until this evidence is forthcoming, the larger historical and religious context points to "caste" as an inappropriate term to use for South Asian Muslim social stratification outside of extremely limited local contexts.[36]

There have been many explanations of the *ashrāf–ajlāf* dichotomy, for example, Islamic and indigenous/native, text and practice, elite and folk, great tradition and little tradition, that simply transpose one dichotomy with another. K. A. Nizami (and others) have noted that there has been a tendency for some Muslims to resist assimilating to Indian culture, citing the previous Greek, Scythian, Mongolian, and Parthian conquerors who had become "Hinduized" in a few generations.[37] In a medieval context, *ashrāfī* culture could be interpreted as an immunization process against assimilation. This, however, is projecting modern politicized religious identities onto the medieval period. In the sources at my disposal, the *ashrāf* did not speak in these terms. Their concerns were *intra-Muslim*. Equally, it would be an oversimplification to propose an ajlāfization process, that is, a long-term cultural change that tends for greater assimilation and connection to indigenous Indian languages, literatures, and cultures.

A translation model gives us a more nuanced interpretation that transcends simple dualities.[38] South Asians found ways to appropriate, or as Tony Stewart says, translate, the ideas of other religious/cultural groups into the idiom/ritual practices of their own group. He cites periodic Muslim translation/interpretation of Hindu religion/religious texts beginning with al-Bīrūnī (d. 442/1051) and continuing at least until the end of the eighteenth century with Mīrzā Jān-i Jānān (mart. 1195/1781). However, this does not mean that the Muslim authors/translators became any more Hindu or "assimilated" to Indian culture as a result. They simply applied Islamic categories to what they saw or translated.

One example is the Arabic, Persian, and Ottoman Turkish translations of the *Amrita kunda* [The Nectar of Life], which have enabled Muslim readers to learn about the practices of the Nath Yogis. The text explains breath techniques, summoning deities, and meditation on chakras with accompanying Sanskrit mantras. Carl Ernst, who has studied this text in detail, notes that yogic technical terms such as *mantra*, *yantra*, and *chakra* are not mentioned in the translations.[39] Instead they are translated into Islamic categories and the corresponding Arabic terms: *dhikr*, *shakl*, *mawḍiʿ* (*laṭīfa* would also be a suitable translation). The term "yoga," originally meaning "yoking," is translated as *riyāḍa*, practices. Sufi hagiographic tales bring out the spiritual competition between Sufis and yogis where the yogis are respected but whose powers are trumped by God working through the Sufi. Muslims who read

Amrita kunda did not start incorporating Hindu practices into their daily worship, nor did their Muslim practices become "syncretized" with yogic practices. Likewise, the Hindus to whom Mīrzā Jān-i Jānān taught Naqshbandī practices did not become Muslims or "assimilated" to Muslim culture.[40] People remained in their religio-cultural spheres and practices or ideas that originated outside these spheres were translated into their own idiom to be assimilated as Islamic or Hindu. At the same time, within the Muslim community there have been those who conflate Arabic cultural practices with "authentic" Islamic practice. In India this perspective has not usually become popular outside certain circles of jurists. In short, this translation process changed *ashrāfī* culture over time without making it any more or less "Islamic."

In light of the simplified dichotomies mentioned above, this *ashrāfī* subculture surely involved the Islamicate heritage, text, elite, and great tradition, all of which was supported to some extent by the power of Mughal imperial authority. Medieval *ashrāf* culture overlapped considerably with Mughal government. This in turn involved the building of mosques, legitimizing the authority of jurisconsults, maintaining control over those who claimed to be Sayyids and fostering *ashrāfī* values among the Muslims. It created a high-status ideal, with Sayyids consistently with the highest status.

Ashrāfī culture had an explicit political dimension. The Bengali Mughal *ashrāf* had a special link with the pan-Indian Chishtīs, whose lineage through the fifteenth century was predominantly led by Sayyids. They maintained close ties with the Mughal aristocracy. For example, Islām Khān referred to Sufism as "our ancestral profession."[41] There was also a conceptual separation of religion and state. What this meant (in contrast to the Ottomans for example) was that non-Muslims were given full admission to the officer corps as non-Muslims. Instead of religion binding the troops, it was the ritual sharing of food and an intense loyalty of the higher-ranked officer to protect his lower-ranked people.[42] Mughal officials did not use Islam as a state religion. Muslims who violated Hindu sensibilities in Hindu districts were punished.[43] As noted above, there was a disinclination to convert Bengalis to Islam.[44] The above dichotomies are problematic because they ignore how many in the Mughal *ashrāfī* ruling class had *also* "become virtual Rajputs themselves" by the time they reached Bengal in the early seventeenth century.[45] Mughal *ashrāfī* culture was *much more* than a monolithic Muslim, textual, elite, great tradition. At the same time there were non-*ashrāfī* Muslims and Hindu converts who were able to join *ashrāfī* subculture in spite of the social and governmental measures to prevent social mobility. When the last vestiges of Mughal reign ended in 1858, the *ashrāf* were the ones who were hit the hardest. As we will see below, the ranks of the *ashrāf* increased exponentially in the next few generations when the social and political boundary mechanisms became defunct. This occurred within the context of British rule and what has been termed "Indo-Muslim revival."

Responses of *ashrāf* to British rule

Nineteenth-century Indo-Muslim Islamic revival was largely a response to foreign British political domination and the ensuing decimation of almost all indigenous, religious educational institutions.[46] The jurists among the *ashrāf* had the most to lose since the British mode of governance needed relatively few jurists. In addition, the British did not support an *ashrāf* qua *ashrāf* system in employing Indians. Knowledge of English was a prerequisite for lucrative government jobs, not ancestry. This did not mean that *ashrāfī* attitudes disappeared. Quite to the contrary, *ashrāfī* attitudes were reinforced as the *ashrāf* feared for their culture and status. This made religious learning a primary concern in the wake of British rule. Muḥammad Qāsim Nānawtawī (d. 1297/1880 and co-founder of Deoband Academy) said, "God entrusted religious learning to these four *qawm* [subgroups of *ashrāf*]."[47] The *ashrāf*, who tended to respect jurists more than the lower classes, responded to Nānawtawī's call. They contributed 80 percent of the donations that kept the Deoband school financially afloat during its first thirty years (1867–1897).[48] Later in 1933, the chief mufti of Deoband, M. Shafīʿ, condemned barbers, weavers, and dyers because their personal development and morals were affected by their occupations. The weavers of the Deoband area revolted against his *fatwā* and Shafīʿ had to resign from his post for a time.[49]

British who traveled around Sind in the early nineteenth century quickly observed how Sindis, from the rulers to the humblest peasant, gave great respect to Sufi *pīr*s (shaykhs) and Sayyids.[50] This respect was put to political uses in the Hyderabad, Sind Municipal Board election in 1913. "Sayyads [*sic*] and Pirs were called in from various parts of Sind for the purpose of influencing the Mohammadan [*sic*] voters."[51] By the time the independence movement was under way in November 1938, this political influence manifested in one-third of Sind's quota of delegates to the All-India Muslim League Council being *pīr*s and Sayyids.[52] The Muslim League received the support of *pīr*s and Sayyids not only because of their religious concerns, but also because the League promised to protect their economic and social interests. Political opponents resented one of the leaders, G. M. Syed, who was accused of constructing a "Saiyid League" (instead of a Muslim League).[53] Another Sindi political leader with close connections to the former ruling family of Sind, Hidāyatullāh, accused Syed of establishing a "Saiyid Raj." This had to do with the Sayyids as a group, not just G. M. Syed. Hidāyatullāh argued, "the party was not for *saiyid*s only, but for all Leaguers."[54] *Pīr*s and Sayyids came to be more appreciative of their Muslim League affiliation as the independence of Pakistan became imminent. For these *ashrāf* to retain their social status and economic influence, they needed to be reassured that the new Pakistani government would let them retain their ancestral privileges as landholders collecting taxes for the government, which it still has to a large extent in Sind.

In the early 1900s, Mawlawī A. Walī, a Bengali Muslim scholar from the *ashrāf*, said:

> The other classes [that is, the *ajlāf*] may become very prosperous, but such higher qualities as uprightness, independence, honesty, and implicit reliance on God (Islam) can hardly be expected from them and must be sought among the members of the genuine Arab families . . . [N]o Ashraf Muḥammad an [*sic*] of India cares what the majority of Muslims are called . . . Some of the writers go so far as to say that they are not truly Musalamans, but for political and other reasons it is well that they should be called Muslims.[55]

It is no wonder that the Bengali press of the nineteenth and twentieth centuries was concerned about "the sense of Brahmanism among high-born Muslims."[56]

The Bengali Muslim press in 1930 noted the cultural distance that the *ashrāf* felt from their native land:

> Though being raised in the lap of Bengal for many centuries and though they have heard Bengali from the lips of their mothers for ages the Bengali Muslims have not still learnt to love the Bengali language. The language and the country both still seem foreign to them.[57]

From the sixteenth century, there was a major schism between the *ashrāf* and the *ajlāf* (or as Roy calls them, the *aṭrāf*). The sociological divide was beyond rural and urban cultural differences. It involved the extreme cultural and social isolation of the *ashrāf* from others, to the point that Roy describes it as "linguistic apartheid."[58] Still in the 1960s an observer noticed that among Bengali Muslims: "Nobility was determined by immigration from the west in direct proportion to the nearness in point in time and distance in point of land of origin from Bengal to [*sic*] Arabia."[59] Thus, the elevated social status of the *ashrāf* apparently continues in Bengal. In other parts of India ashrāfization had began in earnest.

Ashrāfization

Paralleling Srinivas's term Sanskritization, Vreede de Steurs coined the term "ashrāfization" as a social process of aspiring *ajlāf* trying to become *ashrāf*.[60] There is modern evidence, after the office of *niqābat* had become vacant under British rule, and genealogical monitoring of Sayyids was no longer of governmental concern, that there was much to gain from adding an *ashrāfī nisba* to one's name. This resultant ashrāfization as a mass phenomenon did not involve people falsely claiming to be Sayyids. Instead they added "Shaykh" to their names. This process does not really begin until Mughal rule formally ends in 1858. In the United Provinces where 25 to 35 percent of Muslims at the end of the nineteenth century were reportedly *ashrāf*, we find in the 1970s that 75 percent of the Muslim population of Dehradun reports itself as "Shaykh."[61] In 1872 the total claimants for foreign origin for all of Bengal excluding Calcutta was 2 percent of the Muslim population; in 1901 over 91 percent were Shaykhs. As Sharif noted in the early twentieth century (also noted at the beginning of this essay), "Last year I was a Julaha or weaver, this year I am a Shaikh, next year if prices rise, I shall be a Sayyid."[62]

Ashrāfization, however, is more than just gaining social status and prestige. It is a means of moral and religious improvement that involves living a more devout Muslim life, for example, going to the mosque to pray, reading the Qur'ān daily, and sending one's children to be properly Islamically educated. Though it may involve social advancement, the long-term results are supposed to involve spiritual development and life in the Hereafter. This is because becoming a more practicing, pious, and educated Muslim brings one closer to God. On the economic level, a family aspiring for status in the modern context must keep women in seclusion, demonstrating that they earn enough money that the women do not have to work.

In the twentieth-century Panjab, there seems to be less sharing of customs across traditions as there apparently was in 1883. Ibbetson reported in the 1883 census that conversion to Islam did not affect one's social customs, marriage rituals, or inheritance rules. He also reported that Muslim revival movements in the Panjab had more and more Muslims adopting explicit Muslim customs and adhering more to the dictates of Islamic law.[63] On the village level, ashrāfization often involves Muslims abandoning what are interpreted to be so-called "Hindu customs," especially Hindu marriage practices where the woman's family is expected to provide a hefty dowry. Seeking to counter ashrāfization through simple name changes, Deobandis who supported Pakistan, for example, Ashraf ʿAlī T'hānawī (d. 1943) and Muftī Muḥammad Shafīʿ (d. 1976), supported a law forbidding low-status artisans to adopt Arab surnames.[64] In contemporary post-partition Indo-Pakistan, there are more and more Muslims who are differentiating themselves from their non-Muslim neighbors. The ashrāfization process discussed above involving low-status Muslims (*julāhā*s) changing their names to Anṣārīs is a way to consolidate the minority Muslim community and distance it from the Hindu majority.[65]

The importance of the *ashrāf–ajlāf* social dichotomy may be disappearing in contemporary South Asia. If one looks at contemporary South Asian Muslim marriage ads, education and profession apparently have become markers of social status and the two major criteria (after religion) of matching the status of bride and groom. On shaadi.com there are seventeen categories of "caste" for South Asian Muslims that do not indicate *ashrāf–ajlāf* status.[66] Being educated as a doctor or engineer apparently indicates a greater marriage status than *ashrāf–ajlāf* concerns. I suspect that the exponential increase of modernization and development that India is experiencing will diminish *ashrāf* status as the primary marker of Islamic social status.[67] Instead, money, permanent residence abroad, and education will determine social status more and more if marriage ads are any indication of current trends. But that is not to say *ashrāfī* status is going to be displaced any time soon as an important factor in selecting marriage partners. In a cursory survey of ads posted by parents for their children, a "good family" was almost always mentioned. I suspect that a person with *ashrāf* status will find it easier to satisfy this requirement than someone else.

Conclusion

Although Sayyids have not usually been explicitly mentioned in the textual treatments of *ashrāf*, Indo-Muslim social stratification patterns help us learn more about the correlation between Sayyids and the potential replication of indigenous Indian social structures. It is quite possible that the Muslims first coming to India adopted the same attitudes toward the lower Hindu castes as the Brahmins. When members of these castes subsequently converted to Islam, the attitudes persisted and the *ashrāf–ajlāf* social dichotomy developed.

Another rationale for Indo-Muslim social strata is centered around the notion of purity, paralleling the basis of the Hindu caste system that is based on ritual purity. According to the Qur'ān, purity is what differentiated prophets' families from other Muslims, also the case with Muḥammad and his family [Qur'ān, XXXIII:33]. This is why Muḥammad and his kin were not supposed to receive alms because of their purity since the intent of giving alms was to purify people of defilements.[68] The purity of Muḥammad's family prevented Sayyids from receiving alms and subsequently provided justification for subsequent governments, if they so decided, to give poor Sayyids monetary benefits. Continuing this reasoning, an expansion of Muḥammad's kin occurred. That is, the differentiation between Sayyids and common Muslims became a differentiation of the *ashrāf* from the *ajlāf* so that foreign-born Muslims became included in the elite of the "pure ones." Should subsequent research confirm this possibility, it will theoretically justify the use of caste, as a marker of purity, to be applied to both Indo-Muslims and Hindus. In the limited sources I have consulted, there are no references to purity in the context of the Sayyids or the *ashrāf*. It is possible that the extremely small number of Muslims in India relative to the Hindu majority engendered a response that resulted in an inclusion of foreign-born descendants of Companions, Turks, and Afghans into the ranks of what became known as the *ashrāf*. Perhaps this apparent "expansion of Muḥammad's family" from Sayyids to *ashrāf* was a replicative response to the dominant Hindu social system. In any case, the category of "pure ones" was expanded from Sayyids to a much larger group, a social phenomenon that apparently has only occurred in South Asia and that continues to leave its mark on South Asian Islam today.

Notes

1 Shaykh should only include those of pure Arab descent – so we have names of Ṣiddīqī from Abū Bakr al-Ṣiddīq the first successor to Muḥammad, Fārūqī from ʿUmar al-Fārūq the second successor, and ʿAbbāsī from ʿAbbās, Muḥammad's paternal uncle. By the early twentieth century Shaykh had become "little more than a title of courtesy" used by Hindu converts to Islam. Mughals are usually Persian

or Chaghatay descent and prefix Mīrzā or Amīrzāda to their names. Jaʿfar Sharif, *Islam in India: The Customs of the Muslamans of India*, trans. by G. A. Herklots, ed. by William Crooke (Delhi: Oriental Books Reprint Corporation, 1972), 10–11.

2 Ahmad Ashraf and Ali Banuazizi, "Class System: Classes in Medieval Islamic Persia" in Ehsan Yarshater ed., *Encyclopaedia Iranica* (London and Boston: Routledge and Kegan Paul, 1982–), available at www.iranica.com.

3 Ibid. Al-Bīrūnī (d. 442/1051) considered the rigid caste boundaries and strict barriers to social mobility in pre-Islamic Persia and India unnecessary and improper. *Alberuni's India*, trans. by Sachau, 75–79, cited in ibid.

4 The Ḥanafī school of jurisprudence is the predominant Sunni school in the Indo-Pakistani subcontinent.

5 Imtiaz Ahmad, *Caste and Social Stratification among the Muslims* (Delhi: Manohar, 1973), xxx.

6 Ashraf and Banuazizi, "Class System." The quote is taken from Ignaz Goldziher's observation.

7 For Baranī's personal contempt toward "low-born men," see H. M. Elliot trans., *Later Kings of Delhi, or Tarikh-i Firoz Shahi of Ziau-d Din Barni* [*sic*], ed. by John Dowson, The History of India as Told by Its Own Historians, vol. 14, 2nd ed. (Calcutta: Susil Gupta Ltd., 1953), 178.

8 Imtiaz Ahmad, "The Ashraf–Ajlaf Dichotomy in Muslim Social Structure in India," *Indian Economic and Social History Review* 3 (1966): 270 [268–278]. Indian in this context means people from families who did not trace their recent lineage to non-Indian Muslim regions.

9 Richard M. Eaton, *The Rise of Islam and the Bengal Frontier, 1204–1760* (Berkeley: University of California Press, 1993), 99–100. This was *ca.* 1495, and one can surmise that this differentiated *ashrāf* status had already been established at least a century before the Muslims began to enter Bengal in large numbers. This more recent scholarship corrects Barbara Metcalf's note in *Islamic Revival in British India: Deoband, 1860–1900* (Princeton: Princeton University Press, 1982), 239, n. 7, where Aziz Ahmad (with no reference) declared the *ashrāf* categorization to be a post seventeenth-century development in India.

10 Simon Digby, "The Sufi Shaykh as a Source of Authority," in Richard M. Eaton ed., *India's Islamic Traditions, 711–1750* (Delhi: Oxford University Press, 2003), 254 [234–262].

11 Riazul Islam, *Sufism in South Asia: Impact on Fourteenth Century Muslim Society* (Karachi: Oxford University Press, 2002), 199.

12 Marc Gaborieau, "India (Hind)," in G. Krämer et al. eds., *The Encyclopaedia of Islam*, 3rd ed. (Leiden and Boston: Brill, 2007–), 2007–1, 185–193.

13 Digby, "The Sufi Shaikh," 239. Note another comment by Gēsūdarāz:

> Khizr *Khayyat* (tailor) was an ordinary man, a *faqir* (darwesh), a *maula-zadah* (son of a slave or of a servant) of Amir Khusrau, the poet. He wanted me to instruct him . . . My elder brother was sitting with me. I said to myself: "If I instruct the man in his presence, he would say: 'Why are you doing this (spiritual) work on this contemptible fellow? You instruct such *rudhalgan* (base, vile fellows)'." I therefore sent away my brother on the pretext of getting *halwa* ready by the slave girl. Then clandestinely I instructed Khizr.
>
> (Riazul Islam, *Sufism in South Asia*, 203)

One wonders how many disciples from the lower social strata *ashrāfī* Sufis had.

14 Annemarie Schimmel, *Pain and Grace* (Leiden: Brill, 1976), 38. Annemarie Schimmel notes, "Even today Indian *sayyid* families may consider themselves as absolutely superior to any other human being and will tell the visitor how fortunate he is to touch the threshold of a descendant of the holy Prophet." Ibid.

15 Humayra Ziad, "Quest of the Nightingale: The Religious Thought of Khwajah Mir Dard (1721–1785)," unpublished Ph.D. dissertation, Yale University, 2008, 32–33.
16 Ibid., 325.
17 Riazul Islam, *Sufism in South Asia*, 204.
18 Riazul Islam mentions seventy to eighty Sufis with professional *nisba*s in ʿAbd al-Raḥmān Jāmī's *Nafaḥāt al-uns*. Ibid., 199.
19 Here he is making the comparison with Yāsīn al-Maghribī al-Ḥajjām of Marrakesh, the shaykh of the famous Imam Nawawī. Ibid., 202.
20 Salīm Chishtī was Akbar's spiritual guide.
21 Atis Dasgupta, "Islam in Bengal: Formative Period," in *Social Scientist* 32/3–4 (March–April 2004): 34 [30–41].
22 Richard M. Eaton, *The Rise of Islam and the Bengal Frontier, 1204–1760* (Berkeley: University of California Press, 1993), 170.
23 Asim Roy, *The Islamic Syncretistic Tradition in Bengal* (Princeton: Princeton University Press, 1983), 58.
24 Contrary to Theodore Wright's assertion that there was "no office of *naqīb* to police his fellow *Sadāt*" in "The Changing Role of Sadat in India and Pakistan," in Biancamaria Scarcia Amoretti and Laura Bottini eds, "The Role of the *Sâdât/Ašrâf* in Muslim History and Civilization," special issue, *Oriente Moderno* n.s. 18/2 (1999): 651 [649–659].
25 Ishtiyaq Ahmad Zilli ed., *The Mughal State and Culture, 1556–1598: Selected Letters and Documents from Munshaat-i-Namakin* (Delhi: Manohar, 2007), 47. There were some notable challenges to conventional approaches to establishing Sayyid-ship. See S. A. A. Rizvi, *A Socio-Intellectual History of Ithna Ashari Shia in India*, 2 vols (Canberra: Marifat Publishing, 1983), I:155, where he notes that Żiyāʾ al-Dīn Baranī (d. 758/1357) in his *Tārīkh-i Fīrūz Shāhī* mentions how the lineage authenticity of some Sayyids was based upon pious people seeing these living Sayyids in the form of the Prophet Muḥammad in a vision. In more recent times there is Sayyid Ḥusayn Aḥmad Madanī, one of the most celebrated Deobandis of the twentieth century who claimed to be a Sayyid because of two dreams, one, his own, where he as a baby swims to Fāṭima, the Prophet's daughter, who appeared to be his mother. The other was a dream of his shaykh seeing that he had a Sayyid ancestor. See Metcalf, *Islamic Revival*, 246.
26 Zoltan Szombathy, "Genealogy in Medieval Muslim Societies," *Studia Islamica* 95 (2002): 26–27 [5–35].
27 S. C. Misra, *Muslim Communities in Gujarat* (Bombay: Asia Publishing House, 1964), 138. Cited in Imtiaz Ahmad, "The Ashraf–Ajlaf Dichotomy in Muslim Social Structure in India" *Indian Economic and Social History Review* 3/3 (1966): 268 [268–278].
28 Ibid., 269.
29 Ibid., 271–272.
30 Ibid., 273.
31 On the same note, genealogy is still critical in Indian socio-political disputes. Note the disagreements between shrine custodians at Niẓām al-Dīn's (d. 725/1325) shrine over rivals who claim to be Sayyids. See Patricia Jeffery, "Creating a Scene: The Disruption of Ceremonial in a Sufi Shrine," in Imtiaz Ahmad ed., *Ritual and Religion among Muslims in India* (Columbia, MO: South Asia Books, 1981), 178 [162–194].
32 An Islamic justification for the extremely low status of cuppers or weavers in Ḥanafī jurisprudence has to do with the perception that menial tasks use the body and are considered intrinsically inferior to the use of the mind or spirit. See Louise Marlow, *Hierarchy and Egalitarianism in Islamic Thought* (Cambridge: Cambridge University Press, 2002), 162–163, 167.
33 Ibid., 25 and n. 59.

34 Ibid., 156. The discussion of the hierarchy of occupations continues to the end of the chapter (p. 173).
35 Gaborieau, "India (Hind)."
36 Cf. Rosalind O'Hanlon and Christopher Minkowski, "What Makes People Who They Are? Pandit Networks and the Problem of Livelihoods in Early Modern Western India," *The Indian Economic and Social History Review* 45/3 (2008): 395–398 [381–416] where Brahmins can lose their status by participating in occupations associated with lower castes. Munis D. Faruqui kindly suggested this article. There is another factor, that of being sensitive to descriptions of "the other." With the identity politics over the last century or so between Hindus and Muslims, most South Asian Muslims would not appreciate a totally Hindu term to describe them.
37 K. A. Nizami, *On Islamic History and Culture* (Delhi: Idarah-i-Adabiyat-i Delli, 1995), 15.
38 Proposed by Tony Stewart to conceptually go beyond the problematics of explaining Indo-Muslim cultures as "syncretic" and do justice to a plethora of under-appreciated Bengali-Muslim texts. See his "In Search for Equivalence: Conceiving Muslim–Hindu Encounter through Translation Theory," *History of Religions* 40/3 (2001): 260–287.
39 See his "Situating Sufism and Yoga," *Journal of the Royal Asiatic Society* 15/1 (2005): 15–43.
40 See Sher Ali Tareen, "Reifying Religion While Lost in Translation: Mirza Mazhar Jan-i-Janan (d. 1195/1781) on the Hindus," *Macalester Islam Journal* 1/2 (2006): Article #3.
41 Richard Eaton, "Who are the Bengal Muslims? Conversion and Islamization in Bengal," in Rafiuddin Ahmed ed., *Understanding the Bengal Muslims: Interpretive Essays* (New Delhi: Oxford University Press, 2001), 29 [26–51].
42 Ibid., 30.
43 The Mughal Emperor, Akbar (r. 963–1014/1556–1605), had Shaykh Aḥmad Sirhindī's (d. 1034/1624) father-in-law, Shaykh Sulṭān T'haneswārī executed in 1007/1598 after repeated complaints by Hindus.
44 Richard Eaton, *The Rise of Islam*, 174.
45 Richard Eaton, "Who are the Bengali Muslims?," 27.
46 See G. W. Leitner, *History of Indigenous Education in the Panjab since Annexation and in 1882* (Patiala: Languages Department, 1971).
47 Barbara Metcalf, *Islamic Revival*, 239.
48 Ibid., 248.
49 Gaborieau, "India (Hind)."
50 Sara Ansari, *Sufi Saints and State Power* (Cambridge: Cambridge University Press, 1992), 38.
51 Ibid., 103, second [*sic*] added.
52 Ibid., 118.
53 Ibid., 122–123.
54 Ibid., 124.
55 Asim Roy, *The Islamic Syncretistic Tradition*, 63–64.
56 Ibid., 64.
57 Ibid., 66.
58 Ibid., 70.
59 Ibid., 60.
60 M. N. Srinivas, *Social Change in Modern India* (Berkeley: University of California Press, 1966), and Cora Vreede de Steurs, *Parda: A Study of Muslim Women's Life in Northern India* (Assen, Netherlands: Von Gorkum, 1968).
61 Barbara Metcalf, *Islamic Revival*, 256.
62 Sharif, *Islam in India*, 10.

63 Akshayakumar Ramanlal Desai, *State and Society in India: Essays in Dissent* (Bombay: Popular Prakashan, 1975), 556–557.
64 Gaborieau, "India (Hind)."
65 Theodore Wright, "Changing Status of Former Elite Minorities," in Eric Kaufmann ed., *Rethinking Ethnicity* (New York: Routledge, 2004), 35 [31–39].
66 "Bengali, Dawoodi Bohra, Khoja, Memon, Muslim, Rajput, Shia, Shia Bohra, Shia Imami Ismaili, Shia Ithna Ashariyya, Shia Zaidi, Sunni, Sunni Ehle-Hadith, Sunni Hanafi, Sunni Hunbali, Sunni Maliki, Sunni Shafi" (spelling not corrected). www.shaadi.com/partner_search/matrimonial_search/index.php (accessed 26 February 2010).
67 Although anecdotal, Theodore Wright mentions that he got reports of *ashrāf–ajlāf* barriers breaking down in Mumbai in 1996. See his "The Changing Role of Sadat in India and Pakistan," 655, n. 34. In Hyderabad, Deccan, Syed Ali reports, "Increasingly Muslims seek status through education, profession, or income. Thus, most Muslims in Hyderabad experience caste membership, identity, and networks in a weakened or attenuated way." See Syed Ali, "Collective and Elective Ethnicity: Caste Among Urban Muslims," *Sociological Forum* 17/4 (December 2002): 593 [593–620].
68 Wilferd Madelung, *Succession to Muḥammad: A Study of the Early Caliphate* (Cambridge: Cambridge University Press, 1997), 14.

13 The *sayyids* as commodities

The Islamic periodical *alKisah* and the *sayyid* community in Indonesia

Arai Kazuhiro

Introduction

This study discusses the significance of being a *sayyid* in Indonesia today, with special attention paid to the Islamic magazine *alKisah*. As is the case with other regions in the Islamic world, Indonesia is a country that contains many descendants of the Prophet Muḥammad. *Sayyids* participate in a wide range of activities and have occupations such as entrepreneurs, politicians, government officials, professionals, artists and academics. However, it is in the religious sphere where being a *sayyid* matters the most. *ʿUlamāʾ* of *sayyid* descent have opened schools, built mosques, had disciples and conducted *daʿwa* (a call for Islam) in various parts of Southeast Asia. Some of them have come to be recognized as saints (*wali*) and a yearly visit to their tombs, called a *haul*, is a popular religious ceremony in the region, especially in Java. These activities in the religious sphere are by no means monopolized in Indonesia by the *sayyids*, who are indeed in the minority. However, their presence in the country with the largest Muslim population in the world is significant for their number.

The religious activities of the *sayyids* in Indonesia have recently entered a new phase. Many young *sayyids* are eager to receive religious education in Arabia, and leading religious figures have opened *majelis ta'lims* (Islamic study groups) or *pesantrens* (religious boarding schools) in Indonesia after returning home, bringing enormous passion to propagating their messages. These *sayyids* use the media to share information on their activities with others. Major *majelis ta'lims* and *pesantrens* have websites, announcing their activities and receiving reaction from students and supporters. Available at a fairly low cost, the internet is the most popular tool for small-scale organizations run by promising but not fully established religious figures. However, it is the print media that makes their activities known to the largest number of people. In this respect, the Islamic magazine *alKisah* seems to promote the religious activities of the *sayyids*. This leads us to the following questions: What is the purpose of this magazine? Does the operation of the magazine have something to do with the collective activities of the *sayyids*? How well is this magazine received?

In the present study, the outline of the *sayyid*s in Indonesia is presented. Following this, the contents of *alKisah* are discussed, focusing on the treatment of the *sayyids*. Finally, one of the significances of being a *sayyid* in contemporary Indonesia is suggested.

The *sayyids* in Indonesia

As already mentioned, the *sayyid*s can be found in many countries around the world, and their cultural, social and historical backgrounds vary from region to region. The *sayyid*s in Indonesia are no exception and have backgrounds that are different from their counterparts living in other regions such as Egypt, Morocco, Iran and India. The overwhelming majority of *sayyid*s in Indonesia are descendants of immigrants from the South Arabian region of Ḥaḍramawt (in today's Republic of Yemen). The large-scale migration of these *sayyid*s to Insular Southeast Asia, of which Indonesia occupies a considerable part, started in the nineteenth century and continued until the outbreak of World War II, which made further migration difficult. This means that almost all the *sayyid*s in Southeast Asia today are locally born, having the nationality of their respective countries of living. At the same time, many of them, including young people, have a strong attachment to Ḥaḍramawt. In addition to Indonesia, the *sayyid*s of Ḥaḍramī origin can be found in other Southeast Asian countries such as Malaysia, Singapore, Brunei and the Philippines. The *sayyid*s of non-Ḥaḍramī origin also live in Southeast Asia, but their ratio is small; more than 90 percent of Arab residents in Southeast Asia are said to be the descendants of Ḥaḍramī immigrants.[1] Although the small ratio of non-Ḥaḍramī *sayyid*s does not necessarily negate their importance, their importance is outside the scope of this study.

As not all *sayyid*s in Southeast Asia are of Ḥaḍramī origin, not all people of Ḥaḍramī origin are *sayyid*s. The *sayyid*s were actually minorities among the immigrants from Ḥaḍramawt. Although Ḥaḍramīs in Indonesia are collectively called *orang Arab* (Arabs) or *orang keturunan Arab* (people of Arab descent), one can occasionally observe a boundary or even tension between *sayyid*s and non-*sayyid*s. Aside from genealogy, what separates *sayyid*s from non-*sayyid*s is their marriage pattern. A *sayyid* often prevents his daughter (usually referred to as *sharīfa*) from marrying a non-*sayyid*. On the other hand, *sayyid* males are free to marry anybody with respect to genealogical and ethnic background. This unilateral restriction on marriage, though not as strict these days, has been a target of criticism against the *sayyid*s. At the same time, such a marriage pattern maintains the identity of the *sayyid*s. The first few decades of the twentieth century saw a conflict between the *sayyid*s and non-*sayyid*s. The latter criticized the former for their restrictions on a woman's marriage, exclusive use of the title "*sayyid*," and other practices deemed to be a *sayyid*'s prerogative.[2] This conflict is now a thing of the past, but a gap between the two groups in terms of their marriage pattern, personal relationship and organizational affiliation seems to remain.

Another characteristic of the Ḥaḍramī *sayyid*s in Indonesia is that they are still committed to the duty to record their genealogy. In terms of lineage, they are Ḥusaynīs and the descendants of one Aḥmad b. ʿĪsā al-Muhājir (the migrant), who left Basra in Iraq in 317/929 and, after living for a while in the Hijaz, settled in Ḥaḍramawt around 340/952.[3] Aḥmad b. ʿĪsā al-Muhājir's domed tomb in the eastern suburb of the town of Say'ūn is still maintained by the *sayyid*s. Over time, their numbers have increased and many families have branched out. Major families of the Ḥaḍramī *sayyid*s include al-Saqqāf, al-ʿAydarūs, al-ʿAṭṭās, al-Kāf, al-Ḥabshī, al-Shaykh Abū Bakr b. Sālim, Bin Shihāb, Bin Yaḥyā, al-Ḥaddād, Balfaqīh, Bin Sumayṭ and al-Miḥḍār. Almost all these families can be found in Southeast Asia. Each family has a distinct identity that is often connected to the eponymous ancestor and/or saints from that kin group. However, their identities as *sayyid*s transcend the boundaries of their families. One may occasionally observe rivalry between families for leadership of religious activities in a particular town. However, many notable saints serve as the source of identity for the whole *sayyid* clan no matter what families they belong to. Marriages between different families are common. Also, records of the *sayyid*s' genealogy are not kept separately by each family, but are kept together in the same place. At least two organizations in Jakarta, Rabithah Alawiyah[4] and Naqobatul Asyrof Al-Kubro,[5] respectively maintain and update the records of noble pedigree. Both organizations are trying to collect information on the genealogy of the whole Ḥaḍramī *sayyid*s. Also, both organizations issue identity documents to *sayyid*s, guaranteeing their genealogy. Considering these characteristics, it can be said that the *sayyid*s form a distinct social group in Indonesia.

The identity of the *sayyid*s is closely related to their religious activities. Most of them are Sunnīs and belong to the Shāfiʿī school of law as non-*sayyid* Ḥaḍramīs. They maintain that it was their ancestors who propagated the Shāfiʿī school in Ḥaḍramawt. In Southeast Asia, the *sayyid*s of Ḥaḍramī origin emphasize their contribution to the development of Islam in the region. Many *sayyid*s even believe that it was their distant ancestors who brought Islam to the archipelago. Whether this historical view is correct or not, the religious figures and philanthropists of *sayyid* descent have been active in the development of Islam in various parts of Indonesia. Their activities include building mosques, endowing the Muslim community with lands for gravesites, opening schools, conducting *daʿwa* and giving guidance to people as religious leaders. Biographical works of religious figures of *sayyid* descent in Southeast Asia as well as in Ḥaḍramawt have been written as manuscripts and published in Arabic and Indonesian/Malay. On the other hand, the life histories of other types of figures, such as politicians, entrepreneurs, rulers and academics are few, even though many of them are known to us.

The relationship between the *sayyid*s, and indeed all Arabs, and other residents of Indonesia is complicated. There are those who consider Arabs to be pious Muslims who originated from the Arabian Peninsula or the center of Islam, while others criticize them for their perceived arrogant attitude toward others and exploitative behavior in business. Whether viewed positively or negatively, Arabs, including the *sayyid*s, are still considered to be an ethnic group foreign to Indonesia, even though most of them were born in Indonesia and have Indonesian nationality. Still, Arabs are more assimilated to local society than other foreign groups such as the Chinese. Arabs have the same faith as most Indonesians, and almost all of them are of mixed blood with Javanese, Malay and other ethnic groups native to Indonesia.[6] Arabs tend to associate with each other in private life. In terms of social life, however, they are assimilated to Indonesian society, and their "Arabness" is usually not immediately obvious.

In any case, the *sayyid*s have shown a remarkable adaptability to changing social, cultural and political situations in and outside Ḥaḍramawt. Various historians and anthropologists have conducted research on Ḥaḍramawt and Ḥaḍramī migration in the Indian Ocean, especially since the 1990s. The results of the studies done by Ulrike Freitag, Engseng Ho and I show how the *sayyid*s secured or enhanced their position in society when facing a new situation.[7] Ismail Fajrie Alatas' study on the recent development of Bā ʿAlawī Ṭarīqa in Indonesia also emphasizes the successful adaptation of the *sayyid*s, especially young *sayyid*s, to a new political and cultural condition in the country.[8] The reasons for such adaptability can be found in the diversity of a clan's members in terms of professional, educational and even cultural background, and emphasis on education, whether "traditional" Islamic or modern.[9]

The growing commodification of Islam has been observed in various aspects in the religious life of Indonesian Muslims as discussed by Miichi Ken, Greg Fealy, Sally White and others.[10] Few, if any, however, have looked into the commodification of the *sayyid*s. The present study discusses how the *sayyid*s have adapted themselves to the new trend of Indonesian Islam in the context of the commodification of religion.

Islamic magazine, *alKisah*

While the *sayyid*s have become visible in Indonesian Islam in their own right, there are other factors that have contributed to their gaining popularity. One such factor is the publication of the Islamic magazine *alKisah*, which actively covers the *sayyid*s, especially the religious ones. *AlKisah* was first published in July 2003 as a biweekly magazine. The subtitles of the first issue were "Majalah Kisah and Hikmah" [Magazine of Story and Wisdom] and "Bacaan Keluarga Islam" [Reading for Muslim Family]. From the first edition in the magazine's fourth year (2–15 January 2006), the subtitle changed to "Majalah Kisah Islami" [Magazine of Islamic Stories]. The size of the magazine is 15.5cm × 21cm (approximately A5) and the same as other Islamic magazines such as *Sabili* and *Hidayah*. These two magazines and *alKisah* are often put side-by-side at bookstores, and it seems that all three are targeting the same readership. Each edition of *alKisah* contains around 150 pages, all of which are in color. The price of the first edition was 6,000 Indonesian rupiah (approximately US$ 0.70), but rose to 15,000 rupiah (US$ 1.60) in August 2010. The price of a special edition is slightly less than twice that of an ordinary edition. *AlKisah* is roughly twice as much as one meal from a street food stall and affordable for most Indonesians.

The founding editor of *alKisah* is Harun Musawa, an Arab Indonesian of *sayyid* descent who has been working full-time in the publishing business. Musawa's most notable position before *alKisah* was as editor of *Tempo*, an Indonesian magazine that was banned during the Soeharto era because it publicly criticized the government and was considered a threat to national stability. After resigning from *Tempo*, Musawa, together with his wife Nuniek, started several magazines that were in many cases for young people. *AlKisah* is the first Islamic magazine that Harun Musawa has published.[11] Musawa's family is in publishing and the family publishes five periodicals including *alKisah*, the most famous of which is *Aneka Yess!*, a magazine for adolescent females in Indonesia whose chief director (*directur utama*) is Harun's wife Nuniek H. Musawa.

It is difficult to determine the circulation of a magazine in Indonesia. According to the editorial office, the circulation of *alKisah* was around 60,000 in August 2009, and at the time of *maulid* (the Prophet Muḥammad's birthday), it rises by around 20 percent. At its peak, the circulation reached as many as 100,000 copies (120,000 at the time of *maulid*) but has been cut back due to the recent economic situation. Based on information given by distributors and industry participants, the editorial office says that the circulation of *alKisah* is higher than other Islamic periodicals such as *Hidayah* and *Sabili*.[12] These figures, however, need to be proved by other sources. Greg Fealy gives the number of readers and copies sold per edition of *Hidayah* and *Sabili* based on information given by ACNielsen in Jakarta. According to him, *Hidayah* is Indonesia's best-selling magazine and has about 2.1 million readers per edition.[13] *Sabili*, the other Islamic magazine, had its peak in 2002–2003 when it sold 140,000 copies (a readership of over 1 million) per edition. This figure has fallen, however, to 40,000.[14] The minimum circulation needed for a magazine to survive in Indonesia is said to be around 30,000 copies.[15] The fact that *alKisah* has survived for more than seven years indicates that it clears this hurdle. Whether or not its circulation exceeds other Islamic magazines, it can be said that *alKisah* succeeds in getting a stable number of readers. According to a study by Ismail Fajrie Alatas, the active readership of *alKisah* is characterized as mostly young people living in Java who are educated (or being educated) in high schools or universities with no background of *pesantren* (i.e., religious) education.[16]

An issue of *alKisah* consists of a variety of articles, but stories (*kisah*), from which the magazine takes its title, occupy the principal sections. Topics of these stories include the Qur'ān, life (*hayat*), faith (*iman*), defenders of the faith (*mujahid*), companions of the Prophet (*sahabat*), students of Islamic schools (*santri*), *'ulamā'*, Sufi, and saint (*wali*). Every edition has a lead story (*kisah utama*) that features matters related to Islam, such as marriage, testimony of the Prophet Muḥammad in the Old and New Testaments, importance of humbleness, the miracle of the Qur'ān, and so on. The section "Touching One's Heart" (*Sentuhan Kalbu*) tells stories about the ethical conduct of Muslims in which righteous people are rewarded and evil people are punished. Each story in this category comes with vivid illustrations. Among such articles, stories of saints and other great religious figures are popular topics. For example, there is a section called "*Manaqib*," which is a biography of a saint with special emphasis on his virtuous conduct and miracles. Another section related to saints is that of "*Haul*," a yearly ceremony commemorating a departed religious figure (often considered as a saint). The number of major *hauls* organized in Indonesia is limited, and therefore insufficient to be covered in every edition, but the editorial office seems to follow as many *hauls* as possible, especially those in Java. In addition to the religious figures of the past, *alKisah* also covers those in the present in sections including "Figure" (*Figur*), "Islamic Study Group" (*Majelis Ta'lim*), and "Islamic Boarding School" (*Pesantren*).

There are also sections in which readers can participate. In the "Reader's Letter" (*Surat Pembaca*) section, for example, reader's letters are published and the editorial office offers responses. The "Friends of *alKisah*" (*Sahabat alKisah*) section contains small portraits and profiles of readers who seek friends. Besides these, there are sections that offer religious (*agama*), dream (*mimpi*) and spirit (*spiritual*) consultation (*konsultasi*), in which readers send questions concerning these problems, and the consultant answers accordingly.

AlKisah is also conscious of female readers and previously had sections on Muslim women's fashion and Indonesian and other Muslim countries' cuisine. These sections have disappeared, but women's fashion has returned as a separate booklet called "*Gaya Muslimah*" [Muslim Woman's Style]. In addition to the sections whose primary targets are female readers, stories and articles on Muslim women are covered on a regular basis.

One of the characteristics of *alKisah* is that every issue comes with added extras. These are typically small prayer booklets (*wirid*, *doa* and *ratib*), small posters of religious figures and prayers, and stickers of prayers. Occasionally, a DVD/VCD is also added as an extra. The last edition of each year (in Common Era) comes with a calendar. Each year, these extras have become more luxurious. At first, a small booklet was the only extra that came with the magazine. However, a small poster of a religious figure was added as a perforated page within the magazine in issue 19, year two (13–26 September 2004). Issue 8 in year three (11–24 April 2005), a special edition for *maulid*, came with a CD of a prayer. The first appearance of small poster with prayers was in issue 15, year four (17–30 July 2006). The portrait became a separate item after issue 17, year four (14–27 August 2006). After issue 8, year two (12–25 April 2004), a VCD/DVD occasionally came with the magazine.[17] A sticker joined this already luxurious set of extras in issue 1, year seven (12–25 January 2009). After issue 25 in year seven (14–27 December 2009), the size of the portrait grew to 21 cm by 27.5 cm, far exceeding that of the magazine itself, and another booklet, this one dedicated to Muslim women's fashion, was added ("*Gaya Muslimah*"). The editorial office believes that people will buy *alKisah* partly because of these extras, and is therefore concentrating on them.[18]

On the whole, *alKisah* is intended to be light reading and targets a wide range of people, including those who are not well informed on religious matters. Most of the content is meant to provide readers with information rather than propagate a particular message with a sense of mission and passion. Fealy put *Hidayah* and *Sabili* in the lower end of the Islamic publication market which can be characterized as "sensationalist" and "mass-based."[19] *AlKisah* was a new addition to that market at its launch.

Sayyids and *alKisah*

Although *alKisah* is considered a new Islamic magazine that joins a burgeoning market, it is not an imitation of its predecessors. Rather, it has built up a new market by putting an emphasis on the religious figures of *sayyid* descent, who dominate the content of the magazine. This does not mean that the magazine excludes non-*sayyids*, and every issue comes with the biography, activities, and thoughts of the *ʿulamāʾ* native to Indonesia. In fact, the number of pages that cover the *sayyid*s does not far exceed, if at all, those that cover non-*sayyid* issues. The dominance of the *sayyid*s in the magazine can be observed in how they appear in the magazine rather than the amount of coverage they receive.

The special treatment of the *sayyid*s is visible in various parts of the magazine. The typical cover page of an edition of *alKisah* consists of two portraits, one large (around 15 cm × 10 cm), and the other small (around 3 cm × 4 cm) (see Figure 13.1). The large portraits are almost exclusively those of *sayyid*s and range from young and rising religious figures to old and established ones. On the other hand, the small portraits are usually non-*sayyid*s even though they are sometimes elders and have more experience of religious activities than the *sayyid*s on the same cover. The large portraits of non-*sayyid*s appear on the back cover, if at all.[20] Also, many of the saints covered in the magazine are *sayyid*s who are famous in their community, such as ʿAlawī b. Ṭāhir al-Ḥaddād (no. 24, year four), Muḥammad b. ʿAqīl Bin Yaḥyā (no. 20, year five) and Aḥmad b. Ḥasan al-ʿAṭṭās (no. 8, year eight). Many of the *haul*s covered are for Ḥaḍramī *sayyid*s, such as Aḥmad b. ʿAbd Allāh b. Ṭālib al-ʿAṭṭās (Pekalongan) and Muḥammad al-Ḥaddād (Tegal). In other sections, too, *sayyid*s enjoy special treatment. For example, they appear frequently in the "Figure" section, and many of the *majelis ta'lim*s covered are run by the *sayyid*s. Even if a *majelis ta'lim* is run by a non-*sayyid*, its connection to *sayyid* scholars is frequently mentioned. In the consultation sections on religious and spiritual matters, the consultant who provides answers or advice is Luṭfī Bin Yaḥyā, a member of the *sayyid* family of Bin Yaḥyā who lives in the Central Javanese town of Pekalongan and is the president of

Figure 13.1 Cover of *alKisah*, no. 2, year six (cover portrait is Ḥabīb ʿUmar).

an association of *ṭarīqa* (Sufi order, Jam'iyyah Ahlith Thoriqoh Al-Mu'tabarah An-Nahdliyyah) in Indonesia.

The *sayyid*s are also highly visible in the extras, and, as with the cover pages, most small posters are those of *sayyid*s, such as ʿUmar Bin Ḥafīẓ, Zayn Bin Sumayṭ, ʿAlī al-Ḥabshī, ʿAlī b. Ḥusayn al-ʿAṭṭās, and Munzir Almusawa, among others. The contents of the DVDs in 2009 were recitations of prayers and preaches by Shaykh b. ʿAbd al-Qādir al-Saqqāf, ʿAbd al-Raḥmān Bā Ṣurra, Jindān Bin Jindān, Muḥammad al-Bāqir al-ʿAṭṭās, Aḥmad b. ʿAbd Allāh al-Kāf and K. H. Saifuddin Amsir. All but the last of these are *sayyid*s. The only non-*sayyid* performer in 2009, K. H. Saifuddin Amsir, has a close relationship with the *sayyid*s and recites the *ratib* composed by ʿAbd Allāh b. ʿAlawī al-Ḥaddād (d. 1132/1720), one of the most famous Sufis in Ḥaḍramawt who was of *sayyid* origin. Also, the contents of the small booklets are often prayers composed by *sayyid*s such as the aforementioned ʿAbd Allāh b. ʿAlawī al-Ḥaddād, ʿAlī b. Muḥammad al-Ḥabshī and ʿUmar b. ʿAbd al-Raḥmān al-ʿAṭṭās. Those who appear in the calendars are all *sayyid*s.

The emphasis placed on *sayyid*s appears more conspicuous when compared to other Islamic magazines such as *Hidayah* and *Sabili*. Neither of these two magazines portrays *sayyid*s on their covers on a regular basis. Among the three Islamic magazines, *Sabili* is unique in that it frequently takes up matters related to Islamic radicalism, politics of Indonesia and other serious issues. Unlike *Sabili*, *alKisah* does not comment on the political issues of Indonesia or criticize the government.[21] What is more important for the present study is a comparison between *alKisah* and *Hidayah*. The contents of these two magazines are similar: both emphasize stories (*kisah*), use vivid illustrations and have a section of consultation on religious matters.[22] Most importantly, like *alKisah*, *Hidayah*, whose subtitle is "Sebuah Intisari Islam" [An Islamic Digest] is intended to be light reading. The difference between the two is that the *sayyid*s play an important role in *alKisah*. The consultants for religious matters in *Hidayah* are non-*sayyid*s (and non-Arabs). It is important to remember that *Hidayah* was started before *alKisah*, and it is reasonable to think that the latter adopted some features of the former. One may be tempted to see *alKisah* as a second *Hidayah* with a tinge of *sayyid*. In any case, comparison with other Islamic magazines makes the favorable treatment of the *sayyid*s in *alKisah* look quite obvious.

Although a variety of *sayyid*s appear in the magazine, some figures are covered more than others. The most notable of these figures are those related to Dār al-Muṣṭafā, a religious school in the town of Tarīm, Ḥaḍramawt. The school was founded in 1993 by ʿUmar Bin Ḥafīẓ (Ḥabīb ʿUmar), a famous religious figure of *sayyid* descent. Ḥabīb ʿUmar placed great emphasis on attracting students from Southeast Asia. These days, around thirty to forty students are sent from Indonesia to the school every year.[23] The school is not exclusively for the *sayyid*s, and non-*sayyid* Ḥaḍramīs or non-Arabs also study Islamic sciences there. Also, teachers of Dār al-Muṣṭafā consist of those from various ethnic and genealogical backgrounds. Nevertheless, the school can be considered as a *sayyid* institution for various reasons. First, two leading figures of the school, namely Ḥabīb ʿUmar and ʿAlī Zayn al-ʿĀbidīn al-Jufrī, ʿUmar's most notable disciple and financial supporter of the school, are *sayyids*. Second, many *sayyids* in and outside Ḥaḍramawt see the two figures as religious heroes from their own clan. Third, the school's educational policy, such as putting emphasis on the visit of graves, is in line with the *sayyids*' traditional education. The fact that *alKisah* likes to cover Dār al-Muṣṭafā can be understood in this context. Ḥabīb ʿUmar visits Southeast Asia every year and during these visits, he leads a *haul* commemorating al-Shaykh Abū Bakr b. Sālim,[24] which is held in the Cidodol district of Jakarta, and has meetings with Indonesian *ʿulamāʾ* in several places in Java, Kalimantan, Sumatra and the Malay Peninsula. Each year, *alKisah* offers a detailed report of the trip.[25] The graduates of Dār al-Muṣṭafā are active in religious activities in Indonesia and are often covered by *alKisah*. Some of them have founded their own school or other forms of organizations. An example of such figures is Munzir Almusawa, who runs Majelis Rasulullah, one of *majelis ta'lims* in Jakarta. Religious ceremonies organized by Munzir often attract thousands of participants, and he is considered to be one of the "new-generation" of *sayyids* who use the media and the internet for his religious activities. It could be argued that one of the reasons he has earned a good reputation is because of his coverage by *alKisah*.[26] On the other hand, it is also possible that *alKisah* is riding the wave of the emergence of young and religious-minded *sayyids*.

One can observe the magazine's attitude toward the *sayyids* by visiting the magazine's editorial office.[27] On the wall of the entrance hall hang portraits of more than twenty *sayyid* religious figures of the past and the present (see Figure 13.2). In the room adjoining the hall, books concerning Islam are sold, and most of them are on, or written by, the *sayyids*. Attached to the wall of the editorial office are sheets of paper that contain information on *sayyids* and *sayyid*-related religious activities. Even though "non-*sayyid* articles" occupy a considerable part of the magazine, the editorial office's point of focus is apparent.

The *sayyids* who appear in the magazine can be roughly classified into three groups. The first group consists of great religious figures of the past. The "*Manaqib*" section of the magazine is usually dedicated to their life stories. They are relatively well known among the Ḥaḍramī *sayyids*, but some of them, especially those who went through their lives in Arabia such as ʿAlī b. Muḥammad al-Ḥabshī (Sayʾūn) or Abū Bakr al-ʿAdanī al-ʿAydarūs (Aden), are probably unknown to most residents in Indonesia. The coverage of such figures familiarizes readers with the great ancestors of the *sayyids* in Indonesia. Also, the *hauls* covered by the magazine are for those in this group.

Those in the second group are figures currently involved in religious activities. In other words, they are a kind of "proven commodity" and have received religious education in or outside Indonesia and run their own educational institutions such as *pesantrens* and *majelis ta'lims*. People related to Dār al-Muṣṭafā, such as ʿUmar Bin Ḥafīẓ and Munzir Almusawa fall into

Figure 13.2 *Sayyid*s' portraits in the editorial office of *alKisah*.

this category. In addition to these "full-time" religious figures, *alKisah* publishes articles on people who are involved in religious activities but have other professions such as engineers, entrepreneurs, government officials and company employees. Abdurrahman bin Syech Alatas, an entrepreneur in Jakarta who runs a *pesantren* in the Javanese town of Sukabumi and a *majelis ta'lim* in Jakarta, and Ali Abubakar Shahab, the head of Daarul Aitam, an orphanage run by the *sayyid*s in Indonesia, are examples of such figures.

The third group consists of young *sayyids* who have not established themselves as religious figures or *ʿulamāʾ* yet but have a potential to earn such status in the future. In many cases, they are in their thirties, have experience of studying abroad and are eager to build their professional careers in teaching and *daʿwa*. For these people, appearing in the magazine has significant meaning. Once their introductions and/or interviews are published, the editorial office receives inquiries about the contact information of such figures, while some readers may ask them to attend religious functions. Thus, *alKisah* promotes those who are hidden in obscurity. Considering these points, it can be said that *alKisah* tries to cover the *sayyid* religious figures of the past, the present and the future. As a whole, *alKisah* will be remembered for its precious contemporary accounts of the *sayyid*s' activities in the early twenty-first century.

It is important to note that *alKisah* is not the first medium that put the images of the *sayyid*s on the market. The images of the *sayyid*s were sold before the publication of *alKisah*. For example, one can often see *sayyid* posters, some of which contain dozens of small portraits, at the shrines of saints or shops specializing in religious books and goods. Visitors to a *sayyid*'s house may also be able to see such posters on the wall. What is unique to *alKisah*, however, is that it uses the portraits of the *sayyid*s on an unprecedented scale. Regular readers of *alKisah* can get new portraits of the *sayyid*s on the cover or in the extras every two weeks, and because the magazine is distributed through news-stands in Jakarta and elsewhere in Indonesia, passersby will also regularly see these portraits. Another unique point is that *alKisah* makes use of the portraits of young *sayyids*. *Sayyid*s who appeared in posters before *alKisah* and whose reputations as religious figures had already been confirmed were either old or deceased. There was no place for young *sayyid*s in such posters. In *alKisah*, however, young, old and deceased *sayyid*s are given places in articles, cover pages and extras, and it could be argued that the mixing of *sayyid*s in different stages of education, experience and maturity in the same magazine has the effect of "equalizing" them in the eyes of the readers. The equal treatment of the *sayyid*s of all generations is clear in the calendar that comes with the last edition of each year. The calendar features a different *sayyid* for each month. The twelve *sayyid*s who appear in the calendar are a mixture of young, the old and those in the past. Being treated equally in the calendar, young *sayyid*s may appear in the eyes of the readers as religious figures who belong in the ranks of their great ancestors or at least on their way to becoming such figures in the future. The strategy of covering these kinds of *sayyid*s in the same place may contribute to the readers having a good image of the *sayyid*s as a whole. On the other hand, this could promote an unproven religious figure more than necessary, and this is one of the reasons why the magazine receives criticism as will be discussed later.

As an Islamic magazine run by a *sayyid*, *alKisah* occupies a unique place in the history of Arab periodicals in Southeast Asia. It is well-known that the Arabs have occupied a prominent place in the publishing industry in Indonesia, Malaysia and Singapore. Their strength is the publication of religious texts in Arabic or Jawi (Malay language in Arabic script) used in *pesantren*s. At the same time, they have, in the past, also engaged in the publication of periodicals. Such periodicals can be classified into two categories: 1) those that were for the public and, 2) those that were for the Arabs living in Southeast Asia. The periodicals of the first category were in local languages (e.g., Indonesian/Malay) and did not cover news of local Arab communities. Examples of such periodicals are *Warta Malaya* (Singapore, 1930–1941) and *Oetoesan Hindia* (Surabaya, 1914–1923). The periodicals of the second category were mainly for Arabs and contain information on local Arab (i.e., Ḥaḍramī) communities as well as Ḥaḍramawt. Many of them were in Arabic, sometimes in the Ḥaḍramī dialect, but some of them adopted local languages, too. The dispute between the *sayyid*s and non-*sayyid*s mentioned earlier took place in these periodicals, as many of them took sides with or were owned by either group. These periodicals were short-lived, but they appeared one after another and covered most of the period from 1914 to 1942 during which at least thirty-six "Arab periodicals" were published in the Netherlands East Indies and fifteen in the Strait Settlements and Peninsular Malay States.[28]

One can observe a significant decline in the publication of Arab periodicals after World War II. The dispute over the position of the *sayyid*s had become an issue of the past, and many of the Arabs came to accommodate themselves, whether voluntarily or not, to the new nation states. The number of Arabs in Southeast Asia whose mother tongues were Indonesian, Malay and other languages, rather than Arabic, increased. It is easy to see that the need for Arab periodicals was not as great as in the pre-war period. Against this background, *alKisah*, owned by a *sayyid* and giving information on local *sayyid*s, can be considered to be the first "Arab periodical" in Southeast Asia in more than half a century.[29] That said, there is one substantial difference between the Arab periodicals of the past and *alKisah*. The articles of the latter are written for non-*sayyid* Indonesians, as well as the *sayyid*s, even if the content is on the *sayyid*s. Targeting both *sayyid*s and non-*sayyid*s, *alKisah* occupies a unique position in the history of Arab periodicals.

A collective project of the *sayyid*s or a personal business?

Why does *alKisah* put a significant emphasis on the *sayyid*s, and what is the effect of the magazine on the *sayyid* community? Does the treatment of the *sayyid*s in the magazine reflect their desires and intentions? Considering the size of its circulation, *alKisah* is an ideal vehicle for the *sayyid*s to promote themselves. As mentioned earlier, religious figures of *sayyid* descent have been contributing to the development of Islam in Indonesia, and the non-*sayyid* Indonesians who live in the neighborhood of such figures are familiar with their activities. However, the number of *sayyid*s is limited, as is the number of religious figures. Although the *sayyid*s are known for the religious activities all over, their fame is more or less a local phenomenon. Distributed nationwide and covering *sayyid*s' activities in various places, *alKisah* makes people aware of the *sayyid* religious figures across the boundaries of regional communities, and because of this it has the potential to be a medium through which non-Arab Indonesians can familiarize themselves with the religious activities of the *sayyid*s.

Also, *alKisah* can be used for propagating the *sayyid*s' worldview. As already discussed, the *sayyid*s are proud of their contribution to the development of Islam in Indonesia. However, their view is not always shared by others. An example of the difference between the *sayyids* and others is their idea of how Islam came to Southeast Asia. The Islamization of Southeast Asia is a theme that is very difficult to discuss. Scholars have put forward theories that Islam came from the Arabian Peninsula, Iran, Iraq, Gujarat, Bengal, China and other parts of the world. Those who propagated the new religion among the Southeast Asian people are said to have been merchants engaged in long distance trade in the Indian Ocean and Sufis and *ʿulamāʾ* who came to the region specifically for *daʿwa*. The problem is that no conclusive evidence to confirm or reject any of these theories has been found. Scholars now seem to agree that it is pointless to specify a particular place from which Islam came, or a group of people through whom people were converted. Southeast Asia is a vast region and each place has ties with different places. It is more probable that each region in Southeast Asia has its own history and pattern of Islamization.[30]

Outside academic circles, however, the Islamization of Southeast Asia is still a hot topic. Various groups maintain the perception that those who brought Islam to the region were their ancestors or belonged to the same sect as theirs. For example, the Shīʿīs say that the region was Islamized by their predecessors. In a similar argument, the *sayyid*s insist that it was their ancestors who introduced and spread Islam in the region for the first time. According to them, the Wali Songo, the legendary nine saints in the fifteenth and sixteenth centuries who resided in the northern coastal towns of Java and spread Islam among the people, were their ancestors who migrated to Southeast Asia. Although this point seems to be shared by almost all *sayyid*s, it is accepted by others as just one of various theories. Apart from the Islamization issue, some *sayyid*s feel that their efforts in the development of host societies are not paid due respect. According to them, the achievements of the Arabs or *sayyid*s who are ethnically foreign to Indonesia are not mentioned enough in the national history of Indonesia.

Based on interviews with the *sayyid*s in the last ten years, I can say that they have a particularly strong desire to propagate their historical view. Meanwhile, *alKisah* has published articles that are in line with such desire. For example, "Mereka Mengislamkan Nusantara" [They Islamized the Indonesian Archipelago][31] introduces a theory that Indonesia was Islamized by *ʿulamāʾ* from Ḥaḍramawt. In that article, the author speculates that Muslims whose names appear in documents and on gravestones in the early stages of the Islamization of Southeast Asia were Ḥaḍramīs with no evidence. Also, "Meneguhkan Indonesia sebagai Tanah Air" [Confirming Indonesia to be the Homeland][32] gives an outline of the Indonesia Arab Party, a political party organized in the 1930s by the Arabs who considered Indonesia, rather than Ḥaḍramawt, to be their homeland and decided to fight for the country's independence. This article can be considered as a statement by the *sayyid*s that they should have a proper place in the national history of Indonesia. In light of these, it appears possible to speculate that, by presenting *sayyid*s' view in the form of light reading, *alKisah* is contributing to the (re)construction of the history of Indonesian Islam in their favor, without scholarly discussion or rigorous proof. The question here is whether the magazine is doing this by design and as part of a collective effort of the *sayyid*s.

The hypothesis that *alKisah* follows the *sayyid*s' agenda for propagating their historical view is immediately rejected by the fact that many religious-minded *sayyid*s criticize the magazine. In fact, most criticisms of the magazine come from *sayyid*s themselves, including those covered by the magazine more than once.[33] The criticism ranges from the unauthorized use of images and the misinterpretation of facts to excessive commercialism.

There are people who think that the *sayyid*s should not be promoted in the way that *alKisah* promotes them. One of the virtues of a *sayyid* is humbleness, and appearing in the media as a religious leader contradicts this. Even though some *sayyid*s of the younger generation become known nationwide through the magazine's coverage, this does not mean that his instant popularity helps him in a positive way in his career. In other words, such young people have a lot to work on before getting the attention of society. Recognition by the people as a religious figure, they insist, should be achieved by themselves without the help of any media, as was the case with their predecessors. This opinion is typical of the members of the older generation who know how hard their predecessors studied and worked without people knowing about it.

Another kind of criticism is that the magazine introduces just one of various aspects of the *sayyids*. What is presented in the magazine, according to some, is mostly based on the Sunnī-Shāfiʿī line of Islam, and others are bumped to the back. The magazine should encompass all variants of Islam (Shīʿa, Wahhābism and others) in Indonesia if it proclaims itself as an "Islamic magazine."[34] This opinion comes mainly from the *sayyid*s who converted to Shīʿa, those who have sympathy for the sect and those who do not stick to the traditional line (i.e., Sunnī-Shāfiʿī) the Ḥaḍramī *sayyid*s have been following.[35] Also, there are those who say that the scholarly and religious activities of the *sayyid*s are diverse, and they should not be understood in connection with saints and miracles only. These problems, however, are related to the active readership rather than the editors' thought and creed. Most Muslims in Southeast Asia are Sunnīs and belong to the Shāfiʿī school of law as Ḥaḍramīs, *sayyid*s or non-*sayyid*s. It is natural that an Islamic magazine that tries to attract as many readers as possible tailors its content to their religious orientation. Also, many readers are considered to be those without an educational background in religious institutions, and saints and miracles may be issues that can win their hearts and minds.

It is interesting that, although they express these kinds of criticisms, many acknowledge the benefit of publishing a magazine such as *alKisah*. Whether in a proper way or not, it spreads information on the thought and the religious activities of *sayyid*s. It can be said that the existence of criticism itself indicates the fact that *sayyid*s are aware of the influence of the magazine and try to improve the information and messages it conveys. Also, few people refuse to be covered by the magazine or break off relations with it completely. One of the virtues of the *sayyid* religious figures is generosity, and granting an interview to people who seek knowledge is their duty, no matter who the interviewers are. Another reason may be that the staff of *alKisah* and other *sayyid*s are from the same clan and related by marriage and it therefore does not make sense for them to separate because of the controversy over the issue of a commercial magazine.

If the publication of *alKisah* is not a project of the *sayyid* community in Indonesia, why does the magazine focus on the people of this holy lineage? A possible explanation is the genealogical background of Harun Musawa, the owner of *alKisah*. Being a *sayyid*, he may have a desire to promote his own clan through the publication of an Islamic magazine. Also, it may be easier for him to depend on his family ties than to contact other groups when looking for stories for the magazine. While these reasons seem plausible, we need to look for other possibilities. In this regard, the development of *alKisah* in its early stage gives us a clue to understanding the nature of the magazine.

As discussed above, the *sayyid*s are highly visible in each edition of *alKisah*. However, a close examination of the back issues reveals that this was not the case early on in the magazine's history. For example, the large portrait on the cover page of the first issue is not a *sayyid*, but Inul Daratista, an Indonesian female dangdut singer whose dancing style caused a controversy in Indonesia.[36] Having a female celebrity (or an artist) on the cover of the magazine continued to happen after the first edition. On the other hand, the typical subject of a small portrait during this period was already a religious figure. It is obvious that the focus of *alKisah* at this stage was female Muslims, although the focus of the articles was their religious life rather than their careers. A typical example that indicates the nature of the magazine in this period is the cover page of issue 7, year two (29 March–11 April 2004). The large portrait on the cover is Rieke Diah Pitaloka, a female writer, soap opera actress and political activist in Indonesia. The other portrait is ʿUmar Bin Ḥafīẓ, the above-mentioned founder of Dār al-Muṣṭafā in Ḥaḍramawt. ʿUmar was to become one of the most popular subjects of coverage by the magazine, but the size of his picture at this point was as small as that of non-*sayyid* figures on cover pages today. In fact, some *sayyid*s who regularly appear on the cover pages, such as Luṭfī Bin Yaḥyā and Anīs al-Ḥabshī, made their debut in this very early stage of the magazine. The difference is that they were playing a supporting role at this stage.

The turning point of *alKisah* was issue 19, year two (13–26 September 2004). Two figures, Habib Zain bin Smith (Zayn Bin Sumayṭ), a religious figure of Ḥaḍramī *sayyid* origin, and Dewi Yulia Razif, a casting director and promotion manager of a film company, make the cover of the issue. The lineup of the figures is more or less the same as those of previous editions. The difference is that the roles of the two are reversed. The picture of Habib Zain is treated as the main figure of the issue, whereas that of Dewi Yulia Razif is in the small box that had previously been reserved for male religious figures. As mentioned above, that issue came with a small poster of a *sayyid* as an extra for the first time. After this issue, the main figures of most of *alKisah*'s covers have been the *sayyid*s. After issue 10, year three (9–22 May 2005), veiled women disappeared from the cover, and their position was taken over by non-*sayyid* religious figures.

It is clear that *alKisah*, at its launch, was not designed to be a magazine that promoted the *sayyid*s. It is pertinent to think that Harun Musawa, having been working as a professional editor, chose an Islamic publication as his new enterprise as it was a burgeoning market at that time. Harun could clearly not decide the direction of the magazine for the first thirteen months, but his decision to use the picture of a *sayyid* in issue 19, year two, was well received by readers and distributors. At that time, the editorial office planned to use the portraits of not only the *sayyids* but also non-*sayyid* religious figures for cover pages and extras (small posters). It even planned to use the small posters of religious figures and those of female artists by rotation.[37] However, the demand from the market eventually resulted in only the *sayyids* at the center of the magazine.[38] While it is likely that Harun Musawa's genealogy, or family ties to be more exact, influences the content of *alKisah*, market power plays a bigger role in the development of the magazine.

It is now necessary to discuss the meaning of being a *sayyid* in Indonesia. We have already seen that the success of *alKisah* is closely related to the coverage of the *sayyids*, and the editorial policy of the magazine was decided more by the reaction from the market than the mission of particular people or editors. If the manner in which the *sayyids* are presented in the magazine reflects the readers' demands, the treatment of the *sayyids* in *alKisah* tells us at least one aspect of the *sayyids*' significance. Here, we should recall the fact that, although putting a special emphasis on the descendants of the Prophet, the content of *alKisah* is not necessarily all *sayyid* driven. In terms of quantity, articles on the *sayyids* do not far exceed those on other topics. The places the *sayyids* dominate are the cover pages, portraits and other kinds of added extras. They are the elements that represent the magazine and significantly influence its marketability. Therefore, I would argue that the visual images and religious activities of the *sayyids* have an appeal to the reader or the market. Also, by using the *sayyids*, *alKisah* has succeeded in differentiating itself from *Hidayah* and has found a place in the market. Harun Musawa probably did not originally notice the potential of using the *sayyids* as the "front men" of *alKisah*. The trial and error in the initial stages of the magazine was the process in which the editorial office of *alKisah* discovered the marketability of the *sayyids*.

Still, it is not clear what makes the *sayyids* marketable. Is it the prophetic descent itself or other attributes of the *sayyids*?

The readers of *alKisah* basically want knowledge on Islam. At the same time, they do not want, or understand, detailed discussions of Islamic sciences. What is suitable for such readers are light readings on Muslim ethical conduct, Sufis, saints, *'ulamā'*, miracles, Islamic law and history. In this regard, the *sayyids* as a group have many attributes that the readers evaluate highly. They have young and old figures active in the religious sphere. Some of their ancestors are saints who are known for their miracles as well as religious activities and some have composed prayers (*doa*) that are performed in Southeast Asia. Nowadays, they have a direct contact with Arabia (Ḥaḍramawt) based on religious education, and the graduates of religious schools such as Dār al-Muṣṭafā are making an impact on Indonesian Islam. Thus, the *sayyids* are likely to appear in the eyes of the readers as a group that has a complete package of upright Muslims' attributes. Also, their "Arab look" may play a role in gaining popularity among ordinary readers. It is not surprising that some people link these attributes to the genealogy that goes back to the Prophet Muḥammad, and the Ḥaḍramī *sayyids*' claim to the prophetic descent is backed by detailed records rather than legends. The prophetic descent in this case, is something that enriches the value of the religious figures who came to be known as such in their own right.

Conclusion

The discussion above indicates the fact that religious figures of *sayyid* descent can be popular commodities in Indonesia. The growing commodification of Islam has been observed in various aspects of Indonesian Muslims' religious life, and the *sayyids* succeed in following this trend, though not without criticism. The whole phenomenon is a good example of the *sayyids*' adaptability to new situations, and the fact that those responsible for this success do not come from the religious circle shows the diversity of the *sayyid* community in Indonesia. Whether it is correct or not, the popularity of the *sayyids* is growing through the publication of *alKisah*, and the publication may help them maintain their presence in Indonesian Islam. The commercial success of *alKisah* proves that there is a niche for the *sayyids* in the Islamic market in Indonesia.

Acknowledgments

This article is based on field research conducted in Jakarta, Indonesia, in August 2008 and August 2009. I would like to thank all of my informants whose comments and opinions were helpful in writing this article. Special thanks to Harun Musawa for providing me with precious information on *alKisah* as well as back issues of the magazine. I alone am responsible for any mistakes that may be found in this article. It should be mentioned that another article on *alKisah*, which shares some thoughts with this article, though with a different focus of discussion, has been published: Kazuhiro Arai, "The Media, Saints and Sayyids in Contemporary Indonesia," *Orient* 46 (2011): 51–71.

Notes

1 For the history of Ḥaḍramawt and Ḥaḍramī migration in the Indian Ocean, see Robert Bertram Serjeant, *The Saiyids of Ḥaḍramawt* (London: School of Oriental and African Studies, University of London, 1957); Ulrike Freitag, *Indian Ocean Migrants and State Formation in Hadhramaut: Reforming the Homeland* (Leiden: Brill, 2003) and Engseng Ho, *The Graves of Tarim: Genealogy and Mobility across the Indian Ocean* (Berkeley: University of California Press, 2006).

2 See Yamaguchi Motoki's article in this volume.

3 The complete genealogy of al-Muhājir is Aḥmad b. ʿĪsā b. Muḥammad b. ʿAlī al-ʿUrayḍī b. Jaʿfar al-Ṣādiq b. Muḥammad b. ʿAlī Zayn al-ʿĀbidīn b. Ḥusayn b. ʿAlī

b. Abī Ṭālib. For Aḥmad and the general outline of the Ḥaḍramī *sayyid*s, see Serjeant, *The Saiyids of Ḥaḍramawt*.

4 www.rabithah.net/in/index.php

5 http://freepages.genealogy.rootsweb.ancestry.com/~naqobatulasyrof/index.html

6 The first generation immigrants from Ḥaḍramawt were almost all male, and they married women from their respective host societies. After the first generation, however, the Ḥaḍramī Arabs tended to get married to each other.

7 Freitag, *Indian Ocean Migrants*; Ho, *The Graves of Tarim*; Kazuhiro Arai, "Arabs who Traversed the Indian Ocean: The History of the al-ʿAttas Family in Hadramawt and Southeast Asia, *c.*1650–*c.*1960," unpublished Ph.D. dissertation, University of Michigan, 2004. It should be noted that the mentioned studies by Freitag and Ho do not restrict their scope to the *sayyid*s. However, they put more emphasis on the *sayyid*s than others, partially because of the dearth of historical sources of non-*sayyid* Ḥaḍramīs.

8 Ismail Fajrie Alatas, "Securing Their Place: The Bā ʿAlawī, Prophetic Piety and Islamic Resurgence in Indonesia," unpublished MA thesis, Department of History, National University of Singapore, 2008.

9 Arai, "Arabs who Traversed the Indian Ocean," 365–373.

10 Miichi Ken, *Indoneshia: Isuramu Shugi no Yukue* [Indonesia: The Fate of Islamism] (Tokyo: Heibonsha, 2004); idem, "Penetration of 'Moderate' Islamism in Contemporary Indonesia," in Kisaichi Masatoshi ed., *Popular Movements and Democratization in the Islamic World* (London: Routledge, 2006), 126–142; and Greg Fealy and Sally White eds, *Expressing Islam: Religious Life and Politics in Indonesia* (Singapore: Institute of Southeast Asian Studies, 2008).

11 Personal communication, Harun Musawa, 18 August 2009, Jakarta.

12 Ibid.

13 Greg Fealy, "Consuming Islam: Commodified Religion and Aspirational Pietism in Contemporary Indonesia," in Fealy and White eds, *Expressing Islam*, 21–22 [15–39]. He does not give the figure of copies sold per edition.

14 Ibid. The readership of *Sabili* in 2007 was 324,000.

15 Syamsul Rijal, "Media and Islamism in Post-New Order Indonesia: The Case of Sabili," *Studia Islamika* 12/3 (2005): 444 [421–474].

16 Alatas, "Securing Their Place," 103–104 and 169–172. It should be noted that although the data used for the analysis is not complete and exhaustive, as the author of the thesis admits, I think that it nevertheless illustrates the characteristics of the active readership.

17 In "The Media, Saints and Sayyids," 59, I put the first appearance of VCD/DVD as issue 7, year five (26 March–8 April 2007). A further survey has revealed that the appearance of a VCD goes back to 2004. I apologize for this error.

18 Personal communication, Harun Musawa, 18 August 2009, Jakarta.

19 Fealy, "Consuming Islam," 21–22.

20 The motif of the back cover ranges from a religious figure's portrait to an illustration of a story and an advertisement.

21 The owner of *alKisah* told me that there would have been no problem had the magazine been published in the Soehart era. Personal communication, Harun Musawa, 18 August 2009, Jakarta.

22 The example of an illustration used in *Hidayah* can be found in Fealy and White eds, *Expressing Islam*, color plate 1.

23 Personal communication, Hasan Chalid, 20 August 2008. This number may sound small. But the school's curriculum lasts five years, and it means that around one hundred fifty to two hundred students are currently studying in that school. Considering the size of the school, this is quite impressive. For Dār al-Muṣṭafā and Ḥabīb ʿUmar, see Alexander Knysh, "The Tariqa on a Landcruiser: The Resurgence of Sufism in Yemen," *The Middle East Journal* 3 (Summer 2001):

399–414 and Knysh, “Contextualizing the Salafi–Sufi Conflict (from the Northern Caucasus to Ḥaḍramawt),” *Middle Eastern Studies* 43/4 (2008): 503–530.

24 A saint of *sayyid* descent in Ḥaḍramawt in the sixteenth century. Although he never visited Southeast Asia, his *haul* was launched recently in Jakarta.

25 For example, “Rihlah Habib Umar di Indonesia” [Trip of Habib Umar in Indonesia], *alKisah* 6/2 (14–27 January 2008): 38–42.

26 For Munzir Almusawa, see Alatas, “Securing Their Place,” especially the relationship between him and *alKisah* in pp. 102–105. For Mejelis Rasulullah, see http://majelisrasulullah.org/

27 The address of the office is Jl. Pramuka Raya No. 410, Jakarta 13120, Indonesia.

28 For Arab periodicals published in the Netherlands East Indies, see Natalie Mobini-Kesheh, “The Arab Periodicals of the Netherlands East Indies, 1914–1942,” *Bijdragen tot de Taal-, Land- en Volkenkunde* 152/2 (1996): 236–256 and for the Straits Settlements and Peninsular Malay States, William R. Roff, *Bibliography of Malay and Arabic Periodicals Published in the Straits Settlements and Peninsular Malay States 1876–1941* (London: Oxford University Press, 1972) and Ian Proudfoot, *Pre-war Malay Periodicals: Notes to Roff's Bibliography Drawn from Government Gazettes* (n.p., 19–).

29 The Ḥaḍramī Arabs covered in *alKisah* are in most cases *sayyids*, and one may consider it as a *sayyid* periodical rather than an Arab one. However, *sayyid*-owned Arab periodicals before the war also put emphasis on the *sayyids*. Because of this, I see no problem categorizing *alKisah* as an “Arab periodical.”

30 For an overview of discussions on the Islamization of Southeast Asia, see M. C. Ricklefs, *A History of Modern Indonesia since c. 1200*, 4th ed. (Stanford: Stanford University Press, 2008), 3–16.

31 *alKisah* 3/9 (25 April–8 May 2005): 31–33.

32 *alKisah* 4/16 (31 July–13 August 2006): 89–91.

33 Personal communication, Harun Musawa, 18 August 2009, Jakarta. I could not fully investigate the reaction from non-Arab Indonesians to the magazine, but it is unlikely that putting great emphasis on the *sayyids* is considered a problem. Rather, an Indonesian researcher of Islamic history pointed out that non-*sayyids* would be pleased with the stories of *sayyids*, saints and miracles presented in the magazine. Personal communication, Oman Fathurahman, 19 August 2009, Jakarta.

34 Personal communication, Quraish Shihab, 25 August 2009, Jakarta.

35 Personal communication, Umar bin Muḥammad Shahab, 17 August 2009, Jakarta. Personal communication, Umar Ibrahim Assaqaf, 17 August 2009, Jakarta.

36 *alKisah* 1/1 (July 2003).

37 *alKisah* 2/20 (27 September–10 October 2004): 3.

38 The information regarding the foundation of *alKisah* is based on personal communication with Harun Musawa, 18 August 2009, Jakarta, unless mentioned otherwise. Alatas, “Securing Their Place,” 102–103, tells a similar story based on the same source of information.

Index

Please note that page references in *italics* refer to Figures and Tables. Page numbers followed by the letter 'n' refer to notes.

ʿAbbās (Prophet's uncle) 41, 42, 89n, 242n
ʿAbbāsid Revolution 77, 83, 86
ʿAbbāsids 27, 77, 82, 88n, 89n, 125, 129; ʿAbbāsid–ʿAlid marriages 83–84, 90n
ʿAbdallah Wazir Msujini 188, 189
ʿAbduh, Muḥammad 50, 189
Abdülhamid II 11n
ʿAbdullāh b. al-Ḥasan b. al-Ḥasan (al-Maḥḍ) 82, 83
ʿAbdullāh Efendi (qadi of Jerusalem) 141
ʿAbdullāh al-Ḥijāzī, Sayyid Abū al-Fayḍ 153, 156n
ʿAbdullāh Khwāja (Khwāja Nūr al-Dīn Muḥammad Laṭīf) 215
Abū Aḥmad Jaʿfar (Andalusian Sufi) 164
Abū Bakr 29, 39, 41, 142, 198, 206, 215, 222, 234
Abū al-Ghāzī Khān 213, 214
Abū Ḥanīfa 41, 80, 204, 233
Abū al-Layth al-Samarqandī 41, 206
Abū al-Saʿūd Muḥammad b. Muḥammad, 44, 45
Abū Shujāʿ al-ʿAlawī 199
Abū Yaʿqūb Yūsuf (Marinids) 165
African nationalism, impact 191–193
Ahl al-Bayt 28, 59, 77, 92, 94, 129, 134, 136n, 175, 176, 189, 193, 194n, 199; *see also* House of the Apostle
"Ahlul Sunnah" movement 190
Ahmad, Imtiaz 236
Aḥmad b. ʿĪsā al-Muhājir 249, 264n
Aḥmad al-Manṣūr al-Dhahabī (Saʿdids) 168
ajlāf (Muslims of indigenous provenance in South Asia) 8; *see also ashrāf* (as foreign-born Muslims and their descendants in India); *ashrāf–ajlāf*, as disputed category
ʿAjlānīs *see* Banū ʿAjlān
Alatas, Abdurrahman bin Syech 257
Alatas, Ismail Fajrie 251
ʿAlawī b. ʿUbaydullāh 54, 68n
ʿAlawī–Irshādī dispute 49–71; Arabic periodicals, study based on 50; changes in issues 53–56; outset of 50–53; reconciliation attempts by two Islamic reformists 6, 56–62; subsidence of dispute 62–63
ʿAlawī Sayyid Congress (1934) 62
ʿAlawī Union 53, 57, 61, 66n, 69n, 70n
ʿAlawīs (Ḥaḍramī *sayyid/sharīfs*) 49–71; ʿAlawī–Irshādī dispute *see* ʿAlawī–Irshādī dispute; "kissing hands" practice 50, 52, 53, 64, 65n; pedigree 49, 54, 55, 59, 60, 63
Aleppo, Ottoman 7, 139; *ashrāf* of 151–154; *niqābat al-ashrāf*, struggles over 152–153
Alhambra 167
ʿAlī 17, 22, 77, 94, 190; *see also* ʿAlids (descendants of Prophet's paternal cousin ʿAlī b. Abī Ṭālib)
ʿAlī b. al-Ḥusayn, Zayn al-ʿĀbidīn 39, 42; mother of 90n, 100, 219
ʿAlī b. ʿĪsā (ʿAbbasid vizier) 26, 27–28
ʿAlī b. Maymūn al-Fāsī 149
ʿAlī b. Shaykh b. Shihāb, Sayyid 55
ʿAlids (descendants of Prophet's paternal cousin ʿAlī b. Abī Ṭālib) 2, 10, 28, 30n, 44, 77, 87n; "ʿAlidism" vs. Shīʿism 76; genealogy, marriage patterns and boundaries (eighth–twelfth centuries) 75–91; *kafāʾa* and descent 79–80; marriage patterns and social praxis 81–86; Sharaf Atāʾī tradition 219–223; Shiʿite view 80–81; terminology and sources 77–79; theoretical discussions 79–81; *see also* ʿAlī

ʿĀlim Shaykh ʿAlīyābādī 210, 215
Aljamiado literature (Spanish written in Arabic script) 7, 161, 162, 171
alKisah (Islamic magazine) 8, 247, 250–253, 253, *254*, 255–264; whether a collective project of the *sayyid*s or a personal business 259–264
All-India Muslim League *see* Muslim League
Almusawa, Munzir 256–257
Alpujarras, revolt of the 179
Anatolia 6, 123, 124, 149, 157n
Andrés, Juan 171
Antep 132
ʿArab (periodical) 50, 54–55, 63, 68n, 69n
Arab Association for Reform and Guidance 49
Arabs: "Arab" scholars in Mawaraannahr, pre-Mongol period 199; on Swahili coast 186–187
Aʿrajī, al-Sharīf 1
Arqūq ("ancestor" of the Samanids) 207n
Arslān, Shakīb 6, 50, 56, 59–62, 63, 64, 67n, 69n, 70n
asceticism 163
Ashʿarī, Aḥmad b. Isḥāq 28
ashrāf (as foreign-born Muslims and their descendants in India) 239–240; *see also ajlāf* (Muslims of indigenous provenance in South Asia); *ashrāf–ajlāf*, as disputed category
ashrāf–ajlāf, as disputed category 236–238; *see also ajlāf* (Muslims of indigenous provenance in South Asia); *ashrāf* (as foreign-born Muslims and their descendants in India)
ashrāfization, India 240–241
ʿĀşık Çelebi 124, 134
ʿaskerī class 133
ʿaskerī–reʿāyā division 135
ʿAṭṭār, Farīd al-Dīn 234
ʿAṭṭās, ʿAlī b. Ḥasan 189
ʿAṭṭās, ʿUmar 50–51, 52, 56, 64, 87, 91n
ʿAyyāshī, Muḥammad b. Masʿūd 40, 45, 46, 47n
ʿAzafī, Abū al-Qāsim 165
ʿAzīzān Muḥammad Ṣāliḥ Khwāja 214, 216, 222

Bā ʿAlawī *see* ʿAlawīs
Bā Juray, ʿAbdullāh b. ʿAqīl 53
Bā Kathīr, ʿAbdullāh 188
Bā Kathīr al-Makkī, Aḥmad b. al-Faḍl 22, 24
Babadzhanov, Bakhtiyar M. 200
al-Badawi, Mostafa 194–195n
Bādisī, ʿAbd al-Ḥaqq 166
Badr, battle of 43
Baghawī, Abū Muḥammad al-Ḥusayn 42, 45, 47n
Baghdad 94, 111, 124, 125
Bahrām Chūbīn 205, 207n
Baḥrī, Yūnus 53, 59
Bakrī (author of *Kitāb al-anwār*) 172, 173, 174, 176
Bakrī, Khalīl (*naqīb* of Egypt) 143
Bakrī, Muḥammad (*naqīb* of Egypt) 143
Balkḥi, Abū Maʿshar 180
Banū ʿAbbās *see* ʿAbbāsids
Banū ʿAjlān (Damascus) 145, 147
Banū Ḥamza (Damascus) 145, 147
Banū Hāshim 38, 39, 40, 41, 43, 44, 46, 77, 80, 89n, 136n, 166; *see also* Hāshimids
Banū Makhzūm, marriages with ʿAlids 82–83
Banū al-Muṭṭalib 38, 39, 43, 44, 89n
Banū Naḍīr 43
Banū Sid-Bono 164
Banū Thaqīf 86
Baranī, Żiyāʾ al-Dīn 233
Barzanjī, Jaʿfar b. Ḥasan 187
Basra 94, 249
bayʿa (oath of allegiance to the sovereign) 165
Bayḍāwī 41
Bayezid II (Yıldırım) 124
Bedouins 140–141
Bengali Mughal *ashrāf* 238
Bengali Muslim press 240
Biḥār al-anwar (al-Majlisī) 20, 21, 24, 40, 173
Bilād-i Shām (modern Greater Syria) 139
Bīmāristānī, Sayyid Ḥusayn b. Muḥammad 152–153
blood relationship 18
Bodman, Herbert L. 152
Bol'shakov, Oleg G. 199–200, 203
Bondowoso, skirmish in (1933) 67n
"Book of Lights" *see Libro de las Luces*
"Books of Omens" (*Fālnāma*) 179
Bregel, Y. 112
Bū Saʿīdī dynasty 186
Budayrī al-Ḥallāq, Aḥmad 149, 150
Buhari, Emir Sultan 124
Bujra, Abdalla S. 52, 65–66n
Bukhara, Sufis and *qāżī*s of (seventeenth century) 213–218
Bukhārī, Abū Naṣr 84; *Sirr al-silsila al-ʿAlawiyya* (genealogical text) 93, 100; Ḥasanids in *see* Bukhārī's text (*Sirr al-silsila*, tenth century), Ḥasanids in; Ismāʿīl

b. Jaʿfar *see* Bukhārī's text (*Sirr al-silsila*, tenth century), Ismāʿīl b. Jaʿfar al-Ṣādiq's descendants in
Bukhārī, Ḥāfiẓ al-Dīn 205
Bukhārī's text (*Sirr al-silsila*, tenth century), Ḥasanids in 94, *95–99*, 100; historical events involving Ḥasanids based on *95*, 113–114; locations of Ḥasanids' descendants based on *98*, 115–116; persecutions of Ḥasanids based on *96*, 114–115; possible birthplaces of Ḥasanids' concubines based on *99*, 116; presence of Ḥasanī individuals based on *97*, 115
Bukhārī's text (*Sirr al-silsila*, tenth century), Ismāʿīl b. Jaʿfar al-Ṣādiq's descendants in 100; locations of descendants *101*, 116
Bulliet, Richard 85
Burhāneddīn Efendi 142
Burton, Richard F. 186
Buṭḥānī family (Nishapur) 85
Buyid period 77, 80

Cairo 103, 140, 141, 142, 149, 150, 156n
Cardenas, Mustafá de 176
Carmona, Gabriel de 178
Çelebizāde Efendi, Muḥammad Ṭahazāde 154
Central Asia, noble families 198–209; "Arab" scholars, pre-Mongol period 199; *dihqān*s 199–204, 206; Persophone *ʿulamāʾ* 7, 204–205; post-Mongol transformation 205–206; *qayrāq* texts 200–204; sacred descent in 211
Chākar-dīza Canal 200
Chākar-dīza Cemetery 200, 203
charifisme 7
Chinggis Khan 205
Close-Up (Kiarostami) 1
Committee of Genealogies (Iraq) 1
Córdoba 166
cousin marriages, ʿAlids 81
Crónica y relación de la esclarecida descendencia xarifa (Taybili) 177–180
Cutillas, J. F. 177

Dār al-Makhzen 168
Damascus, Ottoman 7, 139, 144–151; *ashrāf's* career 147–148; examples, *ashrāf* 148–149; Mālikīs 145–146; social and economic conditions 146; whether two dynasties of *nuqabā al-ashrāf* in 144–145; *waqfs* 145
Dār al-Khilāfa 167
Dār al-Muṣṭafā (religious school) 255–256, 263
Dār al-salām fī mā yataʿallaqu bi-ruʾyā wa-l-manām (al-Nūrī al-Ṭabarsī) 21, 32n
Data Base Management System (DBMS) 112
daughters, as *sharīfa* 130
Day of Resurrection 16, 18
defterdār (officer responsible for finances) 146
Deoband Academy 239
Deobandis 241, 244n
devşirme 44
dihqān 7, 198, 199–204; in peripheral regions 206
Dimashqī, Abū al-Ghanāʾim 103
Dīwān (Ibn ʿUnayn) 33n
Dobelio, Marcos 174
Dodkhudoeva, Lola N. 200
Don Hernando de Córdoba y Valor 176
dream account 5; anatomy 17–19; Balkhi king 17–18, 27, 28; basic features 26–28; "incidents" 15–16, 20; morals of stories 26–29; sectarian differences 28–29; shared tradition 19–26; Shiʿite story collections 16, 17, 19–22, *23*, 28; Sunnite story collections 16, 23–26, 28; trans-sectarian tradition 15–36
Durr al-naẓīm fī manāqib al-aʾimma al-lahāhīm (al-Shāmī) 22

Eastern Union 53, 55, 57, 58, 67n, 68n
Egypt, Ottoman 7, 139, 140–144; *ashrāf* in nineteenth century 141; *naqīb al ashrāf* 142–143; origins of *ashrāf* in 140; status of *ashrāf* prior to nineteenth century 140–141
El Escorial 172
El Fatimi, Imam Muḥammad Elmehdi 178
El Zein, A. M. 191
emīr (as Prophet's kinsfolk) 3, 134
emir (Ottoman, in Damascus): against *ashrāf* 149–150
endogamy 84
Ernst, Carl 237
Evliyā Çelebi 142, 146
exogamous marriage 6, 82, 86, 87

Faḍāʾil al-ashrāf (Kammūna al-Ḥusaynī) 15, 20
Fakhrī fī ansāb al-Ṭālibiyyīn (al-Marwazī al-Azwarqānī) 103
Farsy, Abdallah Salih 190, 196n, 197n
Fatḥ (periodical) 50, 60, 61, 65n, 70n
Fāṭima 10, 19, 28, 41, 60, 77, 136n, 139, 198, 232, 244n
Fāṭima bt. al-Ḥusayn b. Zayd b. ʿAlī b. al-Ḥusayn 83

Fāṭima bt. Mūsā al-Kāẓim 94
Fatimids 75, 85, 100, 103, 165, 195
fay' 37, 40, 41, 42, 43
Fealy, Greg 250, 251, 253
female descent 90n, 129–131, 219–223
Fierro, Maribel 174
Figuerola, fray Maestro de 170, 171
Foco de Antigua luz sobre la Alhambra (García Gómez) 167
Freitag, Ulrike 250

Gaborieau, Marc 236–237
Gama, Vasco da 185
genealogy 60, 68n, 78, 79, 235–236, 244n
General Islamic Congress, Jerusalem 59, 60
Geographical Information System (GIS) 112
ghanīma 37, 39, 40, 41, 42, 45
Gharnāṭī, al-Sharīf (family) 166
Ghaznavids 85, 86
Gómez, Emilio García 166, 168
Granada: Nasrid dynasty 7, 161, 167, 169; Sufism in 163–169, 179, 180
Grand Kadhi (Kenya) 190
Grand Mufti 147
grandmothers 130
Guerra de Lorca, Pedro 174

Habib Saleh 187
Ḥabīb ʿUmar *see* ʿUmar Bin Ḥafīẓ
Ḥabshī, Sayyid ʿAlī b. Muḥammad 187, 255, 256
Ḥaddād, ʿAlawī b. Ṭāhir 53
hadith 18, 38, 39, 40, 41, 43, 45, 51, 149, 177, 199, 204, 236
Ḥaḍramawt (periodical) 50, 56, 58, 59, 60, 61, 69n, 70n
Ḥaḍramawt (region in Southern Arabia) 3, 49, 50, 52, 54, 61, 186, 188, 194n, 248, 249, 256, 265n
Ḥaḍramī, Abū Bakr al-ʿAlawī 24
Ḥaḍramī community, Southeast Asia 3, 6, 7, 8, 24, 49, 52, 87, 186, 266n
Ḥaffār, Muḥammad 169
hagiographical tradition, Sharaf Atā'ī 211–213
Ḥakīm Ata 210, 211
Hakīm Ata kitābi 223
Ḥallāj, Manṣūr 164, 234
Ḥalwā'ī al-Bukhārī, Shams al-A'imma 199
Ḥanafīs/Ḥanīfī school 38, 41, 42, 44, 45, 46, 80, 85, 89n, 188, 204–205, 243n
Ḥanbalites/Ḥanbalī school 21, 42, 188
Ḥarīfīsh, Shuʿayb b. Saʿd al-Miṣrī al-Makkī 26
Hārūn al-Rashīd 83, 84, 94
Ḥasan (grandchild of Prophet) 27, 28, 51, 60, 77, 129, 131, 134; *ashrāf* as descendants of 139
Ḥasan b. Zayd (Zaydī *dāʿī*) 104, 113, 114
Ḥasan b. Zayd b. al-Ḥasan b. ʿAli 85, 86
Ḥasan al-ʿAskarī 28, 33n, 177–178, 234
Ḥasan Efendi (*naqīb* in Egypt) 142
Ḥasanids 10, 77, 81, 82, 84, 85, 91n, 104; in al-Bukhārī's text *see* Ḥasanids in al-Bukhārī's text (*Sirr al-silsila*, tenth century); in Qum *see* Ḥasanids in Qum; women married to ʿAbbāsids 90n
Ḥasanids in al-Bukhārī's text (*Sirr al-silsila*, tenth century) 94, *95–99*, 100; historical events *95*, 113–114; locations of Ḥasanids' descendants *98*, 115–116; persecutions of Ḥasanids *96*, 114–115; possible birthplaces of Ḥasanids' concubines *99*, 116; presence of Ḥasanī individuals *97*, 115
Ḥasanids in Qum: locations of descendants (based on Qumī, *Tārīkh-i Qum*, tenth century) *107*, 118, 120; migrations from Qum (based on Qumī, *Tārīk-i Qum*, tenth century) *106*, *109*, 118, 119; migrations to Qum (based on Qumī, *Tārīk-i Qum*, tenth century) *105*, *108*, 118
Hāshim 39, 77
Hāshimids 10, 77; marriages 80, 91n; *see also* Banū Hāshim
Hassan, Ahmad (Persis) 52, 70n
Hathaway, Jane 157n
Haytamī, Ibn Ḥajar 24
Hidayah (periodical) 250, 251, 253, 255, 263
Ḥijāz 83, 86, 249
Ḥillī, al-ʿAllāma 19, 21, 22, 24, 25, 30
Hinds, Martin 83
Hindu caste system 231, 232, 236, 237, 241, 242
Hindu customs 232, 236, 241
Ḥiṣārī, Khwāja ʿAbd al-Raḥīm 210
Historia de los Autores y Transmisores Andalusíes (project) 174
Historical Atlas of Central Asia, An (Bregel) 112
Historical Atlas of the ʿAlids project 6, 92–122; data accompanying individual maps 113–120; diaspora 111; maps, notes on 111–112; methodology and criteria 111–112; sources 93–94; symbols and shadings used in maps *113*; *see also* ʿAlids (descendants of Prophet's paternal cousin ʿAlī b. Abī Ṭālib)
Ho, Engseng 65n, 91n, 250

honorific title ("*sayyid*"; "*sharīf*") 2, 3, 6, 7, 30, 50, 64, 125, 129, 130–131, 194n, 200, 201; disputes over the use of "*sayyid*" 54–62
House of the Apostle 44; *see also Ahl al-Bayt*
Hudā (periodical) 50, 54, 58, 60, 61, 62, 63, 68n, 70n
Ḥurra bt. al-Imām al-Muwaffaq Hibatullāh b. ʿUmar 85
Ḥusayn (grandchild of Prophet) 27, 28, 51, 60, 77, 91n, 129, 176, 177; *sāda* as descendants of 139
Ḥusaynī, ʿAlī b. Ismāʿīl b. Ḥamza (*naqīb* of Damascus) 145
Ḥusaynids 10, 30n, 77, 81, 83, 84, 91n, 104, 111, 139, 249; in Qum *see* Ḥusaynids in Qum
Ḥusaynids in Qum: locations of descendants (based on Qumī, *Tārīkh-i Qum*, tenth century) *110*, 120; migrations from Qum (based on Qumī, *Tārīkh-i Qum*, tenth century) *109*, 119; migrations to Qum (based on Qumī, *Tārīkh-i Qum*, tenth century) *108*, 118
Hussain, Saddam 1
Hussen, Nebil 87n
Huwwārī, Hūd b. Muḥakkam 39–40

Ibādism 39–40, 186
Iberian Islam, Sufism, Granada 163–169
Ibn ʿAbbās 39, 41, 43
Ibn ʿAbd al-Rafīʿ, Muḥammad 174–180
Ibn Abī Jumhūr al-Aḥsāʾī 19, 36n
Ibn Abī Ṭalḥa 43
Ibn ʿAjlān, Sayyid Muḥammad b. Ḥasan 148–149
Ibn ʿAjlan, Sayyid Muḥammad Kamāl al-Dīn 147
Ibn al-ʿArabī 44, 154–155
Ibn Bābūyah, Muntajab al-Dīn 21
Ibn Bābūyah, al-Shaykh al-Ṣadūq 2, 81
Ibn Baṭṭūṭa 164
Ibn Funduq al-Bayhaqī 84, 85
Ibn Ḥamza, Sayyid ʿAlī b. Muḥammad Kamāl al-Dīn 148
Ibn Ḥanbal 22, 43–44
Ibn ʿInaba 78
Ibn Iyās 142
Ibn Jānbulāt 152
Ibn al-Jawzī, Abū al-Faraj 25, 33n, 35n, 43, 47n
Ibn al-Kalbī, Hishām 78
Ibn Kannān 146, 149, 150, 156n
Ibn Kathīr 43, 45, 46
Ibn Khaldūn, Yaḥyā 166
Ibn al-Khaṭīb 164, 166, 167–168, 169
Ibn al-Maḥrūq 164
Ibn Manẓūr 166
Ibn al-Mubārak, ʿAbdullāh 15–16, 17, 18, 19, 22
Ibn Qaḍīb al-Bān *see* ʿAbdullāh al-Ḥijāzī, Sayyid Abū al-Fayḍ
Ibn Qudāma, Muwaffaq al-Dīn 33–34n
Ibn Shadqam, Ḍāmin 24, 32n
Ibn Sumayṭ, Sayyid Aḥmad 188
Ibn Taymiyya 2
Ibn ʿUnayn 22, 28, 33n
Ibrāhīm Qaṭar-Aghası 154
Idrīs b. ʿAbdullāh (Idrisids) 82; sword of 179
Ifrīqiyā 100, 103
Ihtimām Khān 235
ijtihād (independent interpretation of sources) 58, 189
ikhtilāf (difference) 45
ʿilm (religious learning) 147, 232
iltizām tax farms 141
Imamate 22
Imāmī Shīʿites 81, 103, 111
Imams 18, 22, 28, 29, 38, 40–45, 100, 104, 177
India 231–246; *ashrāf–ajlāf*, as disputed category 236–238; ashrāfization 240–241; Muslims, social stratification among 8, 232–233; responses of *ashrāf* to British rule 239–240
Indonesia: Arab Party 260; *sayyid* community in 8, 248–250
Inquisition 161, 162, 170, 171, 173, 178
Irshād (Jamʿiyyat al-Iṣlāḥ wa-l-Irshād al-ʿArabiyya) 49, 53, 54, 57, 60, 63
Irshādīs 54, 55, 56, 57, 60, 62, 64, 68n
Iṣfahānī, Abū al-Faraj 94
Iṣfahānī, Fatḥullāh b. Muḥammad al-Jawād 21
Islam, Riazul 234, 244n
Islām Khān 235, 238
Islamization of the Islamic West 179
Islamization of South East Asia 259, 260
Ismāʿīl b. Jaʿfar, locations of descendants 100; based on al-Bukhārī, *Sirr al-silsila* (tenth century) *101*, 116; based on al-ʿUmarī, *al-Majdī* (eleventh century) *102*, 116–117
Ismāʿīlī Shīʿites 103, 111, 173, 187, 195n, 199, 204
Istanbul 6, 128, 129, 142, 143, 147, 148, 151, 153

Jaʿfar al-Kadhdhāb 78
Jaʿfar al-Ṣādiq 46, 81, 83, 140, 180, 229
Jaʿfarids (in Buyid Qazwīn) 77

Jalāl al-Dīn of Manzil-khāna, Khwāja 220, 223
Jamal al-Layl, Ḥasan b. Muḥammad b. Ḥasan 188–189
Jamal al-Layl, Ṣāliḥ b. ʿAlawī 187
Jamharat al-nasab (Ibn al-Kalbī) 78
Jamʿiyyat Khayr (Association for Welfare) 51, 53, 66n
Jān-i Jānān, Mīrzā 237, 238
Jānbulāt, Emir 153
Janissaries 44, 150, 152, 154
Jawāhir al-ʿiqdayn (al-Samhūdī) 22, 24, 34n
Jerusalem 58, 59; rebellion of *naqīb al-ashrāf* 7, 150–151, 154
Jīlānī, ʿAbd al-Wāḥid 70n
Jufrī, ʿAlī Zayn al-ʿĀbidīn 256

kafāʾa (suitability of groom to the bride) 51, 66n, 79–80, 87, 89n, 188, 195n, 233
Kammūna al-Ḥusaynī al-Najafī, ʿAbd al-Razzāq 15–16, 17, 19, 30n
Kanunnāme-i Cedid 133
Kanūnnāme-i Sulṭānī li ʿAziz Efendi 128, 133
kapı kulları (military slaves) 149–150, 152
Kaptein, N. J. G. 165
Karume, Abeid Amani 197n
Kāshānī, ʿAbd al-Razzāq 44
Kāshānī, al-Fayḍ 44–45
Kashf wa-l-bayān (al-Thaʿlabī al-Nīsābūrī) 41
kazaskers 128, 134, 142
Khafājī, Aḥmad b. Muḥammad 24
Khaṭīb, ʿAbd al-Ḥamīd 59, 69n
Khaṭīb, Muḥibb al-Dīn 65n
Khudāverdi 153
khums, Qurʾānic commentary on verse 5, 37–48; early commentaries 38–42; interpretation dimensions 37–38; later commentators 44–45; middle period commentaries 42–44; Sufi commentators 44
Khurasan 42, 91n, 103, 104, 123, 164, 234
Khwājagī Aḥmad 216
Khwājagī Maḥmūd 216, 217
Khwarazm 111, 123, 210; Sufis and *qāżī*s of (seventeenth century) 8, 213–218
Kiarostami, Abbas 1
"kissing hands" practice, ʿAlawīs 50, 52, 53, 64, 65n
Kitab al-anwār (al-Bakrī) 172, 174–180; *see also Libro de las Luces*
Kitāb al-mudhish (Ibn al-Jawzī) 25, 33n
Kitāb al-murdifāt (al-Madāʾinī) 88n
"*Kitāb al-nikāḥ*" 79
Köprülü Fazıl Ahmet Pasha 153
Kresse, K. 190
Kufa 27, 111
Kūhistān 206
Kurlānī, Sayyid Jalāl 215–216, 219–223, 228n
Kuwayt wa-l-ʿIrāqī (periodical) 50, 53

laylat al-mawlid 165–166, 169, 170; *see also maulid, mawlid al-nabī*
Lead Books of Sacromonte 174
Leonardi, Sandra 111, 112
Libro de las Luces 172, 173, 174, 178; *see also Kitāb al-anwār* (al-Bakrī)
Lisān al-ʿArab (Ibn Manẓūr) 79
Lorca, Pedro Guerra de 174
Luṭfī Bin Yaḥyā 251

Madāʾinī 88n
Madīnat al-Zahrāʾ 167, 168
madrasa 145, 147, 148, 153, 154, 164, 187
Maghreb 60, 103, 111, 162, 163, 165, 170, 172, 176, 179; Idrisi royal dynasty of 142
Majdī fī ansāb al-Ṭālibiyyīn (al-ʿUmarī) 93, 100; *see also* ʿUmarī's text (*al-Majdī*, eleventh century)
majelis taʿlim (Islamic study group) 247, 252, 253, 256, 257
Majlisī, Muḥammad-Bāqir 20, 24, 32n, 173
Makhmalbaf, Mohsen 1
Makhzūmīs 82–83
maks (commercial tax) 28
Mālik b. Anas 42, 88–89n
Malik al-Ashraf Shaʿbān 140
Mālikīs/Mālikī school 42–43, 45, 80, 89n, 163, 174; Mālikīs of Ottoman Damascus 145–146
Malikshāh (Saljuqs) 86
Manār (periodical) 50, 51, 52, 57, 58, 66n, 87, 189
Manqūsh, ʿUmar b. Yūsuf 52
Manṣūr (ʿAbbāsids) 83, 84, 85, 90n, 94
Maqātil al-Ṭālibiyyīn (al-Iṣfahānī) 94
Maqrīzī 23–24, 27, 34n, 36n
Marghīnānī, Aḥmad Nāṣir al-Dīn 210, 211
Marghīnānī, Burhān al-Dīn 206
Maʿrifat mā yajibu li-Āl al-Bayt al-nabawī (al-Maqrīzī) 24
Mármol, Luis del 176, 179
marriage: ʿAbbāsid–ʿAlid marriages 83–84; with Banū Makhzūm clan 82–83; exogamous 6, 87; marriages in ninth century and afterwards 84–86; patterns and social praxis 81–86
martyrdom 178–179
Marwazī al-Azwarqānī, Ismāʿīl b. al-Ḥusayn 103

masharifu, role on Swahili coast in nineteenth and twentieth centuries 7, 185–193
Mashhūr, ʿAydarūs 56
maṣlaḥa (welfare) 52
Masʿūdī 23, 25, 35n, 173
Māturīdī, Abū Manṣūr 200
maulid (Prophet's birthday) 251, 252; *see also laylat al-mawlid*; *mawlid al-nabī*
maulidi 187, 190, 193, 196n
Mawaraannahr 198, 199, 200, 201, 204, 206; *see also* Transoxiana
Māwardī, ʿAlī b. Muḥammad 37, 38, 80, 84
mawlid al-nabī 7, 142, 163, 165, 166, 167, 168; and Moriscos 169–174; *see also laylat al-mawlid*; *maulid*
Maybudī 42, 46
Maysūnī, Sayyid Muḥammad b. Sulaymān 149
Mazrūʿī (Mazrui), al-Amīn b. ʿAlī 189–190
Mazrui, Muhammad Kasim 190–191, 192, 193
Mecca 28, 38, 51, 82, 94, 146, 196, 201
Medina 22, 24, 29, 83, 85, 94, 132, 167, 201, 229
Metcalf, Barbara 245n
Miichi Ken 250
Mirzā Mahdūm 125
Misra, S. C. 236
mizwār 177
Mobini-Kesheh, Natalie 65n
Mohiyyār, Kamāl 233
Morimoto Kazuo 75, 76, 77, 87n, 88n, 92, 103, 179
Moriscos 7, 161, 162, 180; and *mawlid* 169–174
Morocco 3, 7, 75, 162, 163, 164, 168
mothers, as *sayyida* 130
Mottahedeh, Roy Parviz 77
muʿāmalāt (interpersonal acts) 52
Mubārak, ʿAlī Bāshā 141
Mughīra branch, Banū Makhzūm 83
Muḥammad, Prophet 17, 18, 30n, 38, 42, 46, 123, 163, 169, 171, 173, 177; veneration for, on Swahili coast 187–188
Muḥammad b. al-Ḥanafiyya, 77, 129, 136n, 199
Muḥammad b. Ibrāhim (ʿAbbāsids) 83, 90n
Muḥammad b. ʿĪsā Aṭṭafayyish 40
Muḥammad b. Maḥfūẓ 176
Muḥammad I (Nasrids) 167
Muḥammad II (Nasrids) 166
Muḥammad V (Nasrids) 166, 167, 168
Muḥammad ʿAlī (Egypt) 141, 143, 144
Muḥammad-Ashraf al-Ḥusaynī 19, 20
Muḥammad al-Bāqir 40; mother of 89–90n
Muḥammad Pārsā, Khwāja 205
Muḥammad Ṣadr b. Khwāja Muḥammad Amān 210
Muḥammad Ṣāliḥ Khwāja 213
Muḥammad Sharaf Khwāja 214, 216, 217
Muḥammad Tughluq 233
Muḥammadan Light 187; *see also Nūr Muḥammadī*
Muḥibbī, Muḥammad Amīn 145, 147
Muhterem Efendi 124, 125, 129
Mukhtarov, Ahrar 206
mulāzama (close adherence) 147
Muqātil b. Sulaymān 38
Murad Pasha Foundation, Damascus 132
Murādī, Muḥammad Khalīl 145
Murtaḍā, al-Sharīf 9, 80, 81, 86–87
Murūj al-dhahab (al-Masʿūdī) 23, 25, 26
Mūsā al-Kāẓim 35n, 104
Musawa, Harun 251, 262–263
Muslim League 239
Mustadrak al-wasāʾil (al-Nūrī al-Ṭabarsī) 21
Muʾtamar al-Islāmī al-ʿĀmm *see* General Islamic Congress, Jerusalem
mutasayyid (false claimant to membership of Prophet's family) 124, 128, 129
Muṭṭalib b. ʿAbd Manāf 38, 77

Nabhānī, Yūsuf 24
Nafs al-Zakiyya, Muḥammad b. ʿAbdullāh 83, 84, 90n
Nānawtawī, Muḥammad Qāsim 239
naqīb al-ashrāf 1, 4, 6–7, 11n, 12n, 76, 104, 129, 140, 175, 235; duties 84, 128; of Jerusalem, rebellion of 7, 150–151; lack of leadership 143–144; in modern period 144; office of 142–143; in Ottoman Damascus 146, 147; in Ottoman Egypt 142–143, 144; Ottoman social structure 124, 125; prosopographical examination 6; register 124, 131; of the *shurafā* of Andalusian origin 175, 177; ʿUmar Makram as 143
*naqīb*s in Ottoman Empire 125, 128; listed *126–127*
Naqobatul Asyrof Al-Kubro 249
Naqshbandī-Mujaddidīs 234
nasab 51, 79, 80, 81, 89n, 100, 103, 232
Nasafī, ʿAbdullāh b. Aḥmad 44
Nasrid dynasty, Granada 7, 161, 167, 169, 175
Nassir, Shaykh Abdilahi 193
Naṣūḥ Pasha 153
Nattāʿī, Sayyid 124
Nawālī, Muḥammad 176, 177
Nawālī al-Sarrāj, Sharīf ʿAlī 175

Nazr Muḥammad Khān 214
Nicolay, Nicolas de 3
niqābat al-ashrāf 1, 7, 76, 85–86, 235, 240; Ottoman Aleppo 152–153; Ottoman Egypt 142, 143; *see also naqīb al-ashrāf*
Nishapur 85
Nizami, K. A. 237
Nūr Muḥammadī 172, 173
Nūrī al-Ṭabarsī, Ḥusayn b. Muḥammad-Taqī 20, 21, 32n

Oetoesan Hindia (periodical) 258
Okello, John 191, 192
Oman 185, 192
Omani settlers 186
Orthmann, Eva 89n
Ottoman social structure, reflection of Islamic tradition on 6–7, 123–137; institutionalization 124–125, 128–129; *naqīb*s in Ottoman Empire 125, *127*, 128; restrictions and privileges 131–132; status questions 133–134, 134; terminology 129–131

Palace of Lions (Alhambra) 167
Persatuan Islam (Persis) 52
pesantren (religious boarding school) 247, 251, 252, 256, 257, 258
Peters, Emrys 81–82
Philip II of Spain 175
Pitaloka, Rieke Diah 262
Pouwels, R. L. 187
pre-Mongol period 7; "Arab" scholars 199; transformation 205–206
Prophet *see* Muḥammad, Prophet
Prophetic Light doctrine 172
Purpura, A. 188, 197n

qadi 104, 125, 128, 132, 133, 141, 142, 146, 148, 149, 151, 153, 154, 169, 190, 211, 213–218
Qāḍī ʿIyāḍ 165, 172, 173, 174, 177
Qādir (ʿAbbāsids) 27
Qādiriyya 163
Qarakhanid period 199, 200
Qarakhanids 205
Qashtālī 166
qayrāq texts, *dihqān*s (Central Asia) 200–204
Qazwīn: in Buyid period 77
Qum 18, 28, 93, 104, 111; Ḥasanids in *see* Ḥasanids in Qum
Qumī, Ḥasan b. Muḥammad 36n, 93
Qummī, ʿAlī b. Ibrāhīm 40, 45
Qundūzī, Sulaymān 24
Qur'ān exegesis 5, 33n, 37–48, 149, 204
Qur'ānic commentary on *khums see khums*, Qur'ānic commentary on verse
Qurashī, ʿAbd al-ʿAzīz 176
Quraysh 2, 38, 39, 80, 82, 83, 232
Qurṭubī 22, 42, 45, 47n
Qushayrī, ʿAbd al-Karīm b. Hawāzin 44
Qushayrī, ʿAbd al-Wāḥid b. ʿAbd al-Karīm 21–22

Rabadán, Mohamad 172
Rābiṭa al-ʿAlawiyya *see* ʿAlawī Union; Rabithah Alawiyah
Rābiṭa al-Sharqiyya *see* Eastern Union
Rabithah Alawiyah 249; *see also* ʿAlawī Union
Rahech, Gaspar 170
Rashīd, ʿAbd al-ʿAzīz 53, 71n
Rawḍ al-fā'iq (al-Ḥarīfīsh) 26
Rāzī, Fakhr al-Dīn 78
reformism, Islamic 9, 49–71, 189–191
Rashīd Riḍā, Muḥammad 6, 49–50, 51, 52, 57–59, 63, 64, 65n, 66n, 67n, 87, 189; Shakīb Arslān compared 60; School for Propagation and Guidance 57
Rifāʿiyya 145, 147
Rightly-Guided Caliphs 8, 198
Risāla al-Qushayriyya (al-Qushayrī) 22
Riyadha mosque and *madrasa* 187
Riyāḥī, Abū ʿĀliya 38
Rome colloquium (Role of the *Sâdât/Ašrâf* in Muslim History and Civilization, 1998) 4, 11n, 92
Rudolph, Ulrich 200

Sabili (periodical) 250, 251, 253, 255, 265n
sāda, as descendants of Ḥusayn 139
ṣadaqa 39, 40, 41–42, 43, 46, 66n, 71n
Sādāt al-Wafā'iyya 66n, 142, 143, 144
Sakhāwī 24, 34n
Salām (journal) 63
Salīmiyya Madrasa 149
Saljuqs 85, 86
Ṣaltī, Sayyid Tāj al-Dīn 148
Samʿānī, Abū al-Muẓaffar 42
Samanid period 199
Samanids 200, 205, 207n
Samarqand 7, 36n, 40, 198, 199, 200, 203, 204, 206
Samhūdī, Nūr al-Dīn 22, 24, 34n
Ṣandalī (Nishapur) 85
Sanskritization 240
Saqqāf, Sayyid Ibrāhīm b. ʿUmar 53, 56, 57, 59, 63, 67n, 68n, 69n, 70n
Ṣawt Ḥaḍramawt (journal) 63
Say'ūn 187, 249, 256
Sayyid Ata 210, 211, 212, 220, 223, 225n

sayyida, mothers as 130
sayyido-sharifology 4, 9
Scarcia Amoretti, Biancamaria 4
Schacht, Joseph 41, 79
Schimmel, Annemarie 243n
Serjeant, R. B. 65n
Shādhiliyya 142, 149, 163
Shafīʿ, M. 239, 241
Shāfiʿī 37, 38, 41, 42, 43, 44, 80, 194n
Shāfiʿīs/Shāfiʿī school 37, 40, 41, 42, 45, 79, 80, 85, 89n, 186, 187, 188, 249, 261
Shahab, Ali Abubakar 257
Shajarī, ʿAbd al-Raḥmān 86
Shalabī (Çelebi), Aḥmad b. ʿAbd al-Ghanī 142
Shāmī, Yūsuf b. Ḥātim 22
shamma see "kissing hands" practice, ʿAlawīs
Shāmmiyya Juwwāniyya Madrasa 148
sharaf (nobility) 80, 89n, 139, 145, 147, 232; debates over meaning 188–189
Sharaf Ata 210–213, 215, 216, 221, 222, 225n, 226n; *see also* Sharaf Atāʾī
Sharaf Atāʾī: ʿAlid "input" into female lines 219–223; genealogy 213–223; in hagiographical tradition and folklore 211–213; Sufis and *qāżīs*, of Khwārazm and Bukhārā (seventeenth century) 8, 213–218; tradition 210–230
Sharaf al-Dawla (Buyid *amīr*) 27, 36n
sharaf dhātī (intrinsic nobility) 51, 189
Shaʿrānī, ʿAbd al-Wahhāb 189
Sharīʿa court register 130, 132, 155n
sharīfa 76, 130, 131, 188, 192, 195n; daughters and sisters as 130
sharīfa (title for female descendants among Ḥaḍramī *sayyids*) 50, 51, 248
sharīfazādes 131
shaṭḥ (ecstatic dance, trance) 166, 169
Shaykh al-Azhar, office of 156n
Shaykh al-Bakrī 143, 144
shaykh mashāʾikh al-ḥiraf wa-l-ṣanāʾiʿ 146
Shifāʾ (Qāḍī ʿIyāḍ) 165, 172, 174
Shiʿism 2, 9, 16, 28, 39, 40, 87n, 136, 173, 178–179, 193; as distinct from "ʿAlidism" 76; Imāmī Shiʿites 103, 111; *khums*, Qurʾānic commentary on verse 40, 43, 44, 48n; Shiʿite story collections 16, 17, 19–22, *23*, 28; stance on ʿAlids' marriage 80–81; *see also* Sunnism; Twelver Shiʿites
Shoshan, B. 173
shurafā: in al-Andalus and Morisco period 161–183
Sibṭ b. al-Jawzī 19, 21, 22, 23, 25–26, 35n
Ṣiddīqī Karmīnagī, Khwāja Muḥammad Salīm 215
Sirr al-silsila al-ʿAlawiyya (al-Bukhārī) 93, 100; *see also* Bukhārī, Abū Naṣr
sisters, as *sharīfa* 130
social class 133, 140
social stratification, Muslim South Asia 8, 232–235
Southeast Asia 49–71, 186, 247–266
Srinivas, M. N. 240
Steurs, Vreede de 240
Stewart, Tony 237, 245n
Sufism 133, 140, 154; commentary on verse of *khums* 44; in Granada 163–169, 179, 180n; *laylat al-mawlid* 165–166; *mawlid al-nabī* 7, 165, 169; and prophetic descent 4; Sufis, of Khwārazm and Bukhārā (seventeenth century) 8, 213–218; *see also* Naqshbandī-Mujaddidīs; Qādiriyya; Rifāʿiyya; Shādhiliyya; Wafāʾiyya; Yasavī Sufi tradition
Sufyān al-Thawrī 37
Sultan Süleyman Foundation, Damascus 132
Sunnism 87n, 136n, 174, 180, 186, 199, 249; *khums*, Qurʾānic commentary on verse 38, 39, 40, 42, 45, 46; and Ottoman state 127; stance on ʿAlids' marriage 80, 81; Sunnite story collections 16, 23–26, 28; *see also* Shiʿism
Sūrkatī al-Anṣārī, Aḥmad b. Muḥammad 51, 52, 53, 55, 61, 62, 63, 66n, 70n
Suyūṭī 77
Swahili coast: African nationalism, impact 191–193; Arabs on 186–187; identity of Swahili people 185–186; Islamic reformism 189–191; role of *masharifu* on, in nineteenth and twentieth centuries 7, 185–193; *sharaf* (nobility), debates over meaning 188–189; veneration for Prophet and his descendants on 187–188
Syed, G. M. 239

Ṭabarānī, Sulaymān b. Aḥmad 41
Ṭabarī 38–39
Ṭabaristān 85, 100, 104
Tabrisī, Faḍl b. al-Ḥasan 43, 46
Tadhkirat al-khawāṣṣ (Sibṭ b. al-Jawzī) 19, 21, 22, 23, 24
tafsīr see Qurʾān exegesis
tafsīr bi-l-maʾthūr (commentary explicated by tradition) 45
Tafsīr al-kabīr (al-Ṭabarānī) 41
Taftāzānī, Muḥammad al-Ghanīmī 59, 69n
Ṭahazāde, Aḥmad Efendi 154
Ṭahazādes 153
Ṭālibids 10, 15, 27, 76, 77; genealogies 79; works 78
Tanzania 191, 193

taqbīl see "kissing hands" practice, ʿAlawīs
Tārīkh-i mashā'ikh al-turk (Marghīnānī) 211, 212, 220, 223
Tārīkh-i Qum (Qumī) 33n, 36n, 93, 104, 111; ʿAlids' movements in 104, 105–110; Ḥasanids in Qum: locations of descendants *107*, 118, 120; migrations from Qum *106*, *109*, 118, 119; migrations to Qum *105*, *108*, 118
Tarīmī, Bā ʿAlawī 24
tax exemption 128, 132, 133, 139, 188
Thaʿlabī al-Nīsābūrī, Aḥmad b. Muḥammad 41
Tirmidh, *Sayyid*s of 207n
Togan, Zeki Velidi 211, 223
Transoxiana 42, 123, 198; *see also* Mawaraannahr
Trimingham, J. S. 186
Tuḥfat al-azhār (Ibn Shadqam) 24
Ṭūsī, Abū Jaʿfar 40, 45, 80
Twelver Shiʿites 2, 5, 6, 15, 40, 43, 45, 193; *see also* Shiʿism

ʿulamā' 128, 133, 139, 140, 141, 146, 147, 148, 150, 163, 165, 168, 169, 174, 199, 205, 247, 251; Persophone 204–205
Ulugh Beg 207n
Ulugh Khwāja (Muḥammad Futūḥ Khwāja) 216
ʿUmar Bin Ḥafīẓ 256, 262
ʿUmar Makram 143, 144, 151; as *naqīb al-ashrāf* 143
ʿUmarī, Najm al-Dīn Abū al-Ḥasan 103
ʿUmarī's text (*al-Majdī*, eleventh century), locations of Ismāʿīl b. Jaʿfar's descendants based on *102*, 116–117
ʿUmdat al-ṭālib (Ibn ʿInaba) 78
umm walad 82, 100
Umma (Muslim community) 2, 3, 58, 166
ʿUthmān b. ʿAffān, 38, 198, 206
Utusan Melayu (newspaper) 52

Virgin Mary 174

Wafā'ī al-Ḥusaynī, Muḥammad b. Muṣṭafā 150
Wafā'iyya 66n, 142, 143
Wahhābīs 190, 196n, 261
Wāḥidī al-Nīsābūrī, ʿAlī b. Aḥmad 41
Walī, Mawlawī A. 239–240
Wansharīsī 169
waqf 28, 61, 132, 139, 145, 155n, 169, 235
waqf al-sādāt al-Mālikiyya 145
Warta Malaya (periodical) 258
White, Sally 250
Wright, Theodore 244n, 246n

Yamani, Faisal 1–2
Yasavī Sufi tradition 211, 213, 215
Yemeni revolution (1962) 87
yoga 237
Yuḥānisī, Abū Marwān 165–166

Zain bin Smith, Habib 262
zakāt 43, 46, 71n
Zamakhsharī 41
Zandawīsatī al-Bukhārī, Abū al-Ḥasan ʿAlī 204
Zanjānī al-Mūsawī, Ibrāhīm 11n
Zanzibar 185–186, 191, 192, 193
Zanzibar revolution 191–192
Zapata, Luis 176
Ẓawāhirī, Muḥammad al-Aḥmadī 67n, 68n, 70n
zāwiya 145, 147, 163, 164, 169
Zaydī Imamate, abolition (1962) 87
Zayn Bin Sumayṭ *see* Zain bin Smith, Habib
Zaynab bt. ʿAbdullāh b. al-Ḥusayn, "*Zaynab laylatin*" 83, 84
Zaynab bt. Muḥammad al-Nafs al-Zakiyya 84
Zaynabīs 77
Zomeño, Amalia 80, 89n
Zubāra family (Nishapur) 85
Zubayrī, Muṣʿab b. ʿAbdullah 78
Zuhrī 41